SUSTAINABILITY AND EU MIGRATION LAW

Sustainable migration is the new objective of the EU migration policy. But what does this mean in terms of legal design? What instruments should be put in place to achieve it? And most importantly, what does it imply for migrants' rights? While sustainability has attracted scholarly attention in law and politics already since the 1990s, sustainable migration is an extremely understudied topic with no conclusive research carried out on the matter. The book covers a unique scholarly gap by being the first ever contribution that traces the history of sustainable migration in EU law, demonstrates its limitations and potentials, and puts forward concrete proposals on how EU migration law should develop in the future. This title is also available as open access on Cambridge Core.

ALEZINI LOXA holds a PhD in EU law from Lund University (LU), Sweden. Her PhD thesis was awarded the 2023 Oscar II Prize for best thesis in the LU Faculty of Law, the 2024 LU Agenda 2030 Honourable mention for interdisciplinary research on sustainable development by early career scholars, and the EGLP 2024 Thesis Prize for the best doctoral public law thesis characterized by its European dimension.

Cambridge Studies in European Law and Policy

The focus of this series is European law broadly understood. It aims to publish original monographs in all fields of European law, from work focusing on the institutions of the EU and the Council of Europe to books examining substantive fields of European law as well as examining the relationship between European law and domestic, regional and international legal orders. The series publishes works adopting a wide variety of methods: comparative, doctrinal, theoretical and inter-disciplinary approaches to European law are equally welcome, as are works looking at the historical and political facets of the development of European law and policy. The main criterion is excellence, i.e. the publication of innovative work, which will help to shape the legal, political and scholarly debate on the future of European law.

Books in the Series

Sustainability and EU Migration Law: Tracing the History of a Contemporary Concept
Alezini Loxa

Reimagining Prosperity: Toward a New Imaginary of Law and Political Economy in the EU
Marija Bartl

Open Strategic Autonomy in EU Trade Policy: Assessing the Turn to Stronger Enforcement and More Robust Interest Representation
Wolfgang Weiß and Cornelia Furculiţă

Trilogues: The Democratic Secret of European Legislation
Giacomo Rugge

The European Union, Emerging Global Business and Human Rights
Aleydis Nissen

The European Central Bank and the European Macroeconomic Constitution
Klaus Tuori

The Procedural and Organisational Law of the European Court of Justice: An Incomplete Transformation
Christoph Krenn

The New Economic Governance of the Eurozone: A Rule of Law Analysis
Paul Dermine

Digital Constitutionalism in Europe: Reframing Rights and Powers in the Algorithmic Society
Giovanni De Gregorio

Can the European Court of Human Rights Shape European Public Order?
Kanstantsin Dzehtsiarou

The Constitutional Boundaries of European Fiscal Federalism
Brady Gordon

Private Selves: Legal Personhood in European Privacy Protection
Susanna Lindroos-Hovinheimo

Fissures in EU Citizenship: The Deconstruction and Reconstruction of the Legal Evolution of EU Citizenship
Martin Steinfeld

The Boundaries of the EU Internal Market: Participation without Membership
Marja-Liisa Öberg

The Currency of Solidarity: Constitutional Transformation during the Euro Crisis
Vestert Borger

Empire of Law: Nazi Germany, Exile Scholars and the Battle for the Future of Europe
Kaius Tuori

In the Court We Trust: Cooperation, Coordination and Collaboration between the ECJ and Supreme Administrative Courts
Rob van Gestel and Jurgen de Poorter

Beyond Minimum Harmonisation: Gold-Plating and Green-Plating of European Environmental Law
Lorenzo Squintani

The Court of Justice of the European Union as an Institutional Actor: Judicial Lawmaking and its Limits
Thomas Horsley

The Politics of Justice in European Private Law: Social Justice, Access Justice, Societal Justice
Hans-W Micklitz

The Transformation of EU Treaty Making: The Rise of Parliaments, Referendums and Courts Since 1950
Dermot Hodson and Imelda Maher

Redefining European Economic Integration
Dariusz Adamski

Human Rights in the Council of Europe and the European Union: Achievements, Trends and Challenges
Steven Greer, Janneke Gerards and Rosie Slowe

Core Socio-Economic Rights and the European Court of Human Rights
Ingrid Leijten

Green Trade and Fair Trade in and with the EU: Process-based Measures within the EU Legal Order
Laurens Ankersmit

New Labour Laws in Old Member States: Trade Union Responses to European Enlargement
Rebecca Zahn

The Governance of EU Fundamental Rights
Mark Dawson

The International Responsibility of the European Union: From Competence to Normative Control
Andrés Delgado Casteleiro

Frontex and Non-Refoulement: The International Responsibility of the EU
Roberta Mungianu

Gendering European Working Time Regimes: The Working Time Directive and the Case of Poland
Ania Zbyszewska

EU Renewable Electricity Law and Policy: From National Targets to a Common Market
Tim Maxian Rusche

European Constitutionalism
Kaarlo Tuori

Brokering Europe: Euro-Lawyers and the Making of a Transnational Polity
Antoine Vauchez

Services Liberalization in the EU and the WTO: Concepts, Standards and Regulatory Approaches
Marcus Klamert

Referendums and the European Union: A Comparative Enquiry
Fernando Mendez, Mario Mendez and Vasiliki Triga

The Allocation of Regulatory Competence in the EU Emissions Trading Scheme
Josephine van Zeben

The Eurozone Crisis: A Constitutional Analysis
Kaarlo Tuori and Klaus Tuori

International Trade Disputes and EU Liability
Anne Thies

The Limits of Legal Reasoning and the European Court of Justice
Gerard Conway

New Governance and the Transformation of European Law: Coordinating EU Social Law and Policy
Mark Dawson

The Lisbon Treaty: A Legal and Political Analysis
Jean-Claude Piris

The European Union's Fight Against Corruption: The Evolving Policy Towards Member States and Candidate Countries
Patrycja Szarek-Mason

The Ethos of Europe: Values, Law and Justice in the EU
Andrew Williams

State and Market in European Union Law: The Public and Private Spheres of the Internal Market before the EU Courts
Wolf Sauter and Harm Schepel

The European Civil Code: The Way Forward
Hugh Collins

Ethical Dimensions of the Foreign Policy of the European Union: A Legal Appraisal
Urfan Khaliq

Implementing EU Pollution Control: Law and Integration
Bettina Lange

European Broadcasting Law and Policy
Jackie Harrison and Lorna Woods

The Transformation of Citizenship in the European Union: Electoral Rights and the Restructuring of Political Space
Jo Shaw

The Constitution for Europe: A Legal Analysis
Jean-Claude Piris

The European Convention on Human Rights: Achievements, Problems and Prospects
Steven Greer

Social Rights and Market Freedom in the European Constitution: A Labour Law Perspective
Stefano Giubboni

EU Enlargement and the Constitutions of Central and Eastern Europe
Anneli Albi

SUSTAINABILITY AND EU MIGRATION LAW

Tracing the History of a Contemporary Concept

ALEZINI LOXA
Lund University

CAMBRIDGE
UNIVERSITY PRESS

CAMBRIDGE
UNIVERSITY PRESS

Shaftesbury Road, Cambridge CB2 8EA, United Kingdom

One Liberty Plaza, 20th Floor, New York, NY 10006, USA

477 Williamstown Road, Port Melbourne, VIC 3207, Australia

314–321, 3rd Floor, Plot 3, Splendor Forum, Jasola District Centre, New Delhi – 110025, India

103 Penang Road, #05-06/07, Visioncrest Commercial, Singapore 238467

Cambridge University Press is part of Cambridge University Press & Assessment, a department of the University of Cambridge.

We share the University's mission to contribute to society through the pursuit of education, learning and research at the highest international levels of excellence.

www.cambridge.org
Information on this title: www.cambridge.org/9781009573146

DOI: 10.1017/9781009573122

First published 2025

A catalogue record for this publication is available from the British Library

A Cataloging-in-Publication data record for this book is available from the Library of Congress

ISBN 978-1-009-57314-6 Hardback

To the excluded, for market-related reasons or otherwise

ὑψοῦ γὰρ αἴρει θυμὸν Οἰδίπους ἄγαν λύπαισι παντοίαισιν· οὐδ᾽ ὁποῖ᾽ ἀνὴρ ἔννους τὰ καινὰ τοῖς πάλαι τεκμαίρεται, ἀλλ᾽ ἐστὶ τοῦ λέγοντος, ἢν φόβους λέγῃ.

—Σοφοκλής, *Οἰδίπους Τύραννος 914–197*

For Oedipus excites his soul overmuch with all manner of alarms, nor, like a man of sense, judges the new things by the old, but is at the will of the speaker, if he speak terrors.

—Translated by Richard C. Jebb (ed), *Sophocles: The Plays and Fragments, Volume 1: The Oedipus Tyrannus* (Cambridge University Press 2010)

CONTENTS

TABLES

ACKNOWLEDGEMENTS

This book marks an end and (hopefully) a beginning.

It is the ultimate end of a journey which began in 2019, when I started my PhD studies at Lund University. It would be impossible to thank all the individuals who have played a part in the development of the research(er) behind this work. My supervisors, Xavier Groussot and Vladislava Stoyanova, offered me the support and occasionally the distance necessary to develop and find my own place in EU law scholarship. Towards the end of the process, Moritz Jesse attentively reflected to me what this work really was about. John Harbord with his rigorous proofreading pushed me to take a final fresh look at my writing and added clarity to the outcome. Various colleagues in the Faculty of Law and the Agenda 2030 Graduate School at Lund University, but also in the academic communities of the European University Institute, the Europa Institute in Leiden University, the Centre for Migration Law in Radboud University, and the Centre for Fundamental Rights at the Hertie School, which hosted me over these past years, were crucial for the development of this project.

At the same time, I wish that this book marks the beginning of intellectual inquiries along two paths: sustainable migration and EU legal history. From 2019 to this day, people have always reacted enthusiastically upon hearing that my research dealt with sustainability and EU migration law. Sustainability is, after all, perceived as a self-evidently good cause at times when migration is fraught with contestation. The listeners assume intuitively that sustainable migration can offer a solution to what is framed as one of the major problems faced by the EU. The reality of what sustainable migration can achieve is a lot more complicated as the reader will discover. And that is – partly – because not all concepts raised in international and European governance come with specific purpose, clear-cut meaning, and legal implications. There is considerable value in interrogating the appearance of such concepts, examining their genesis, and looking at their interplay with legal norms before jumping on the bandwagon of institutional discourse and integrating new buzzwords into legal writing. At a time when sustainable migration is the professed objective of the EU, and new proposals are put on the table with the aim to achieve it, I hope that this work will spearhead scholarly dialogue grounded in what sustainable migration can and cannot deliver for migrants' rights in the present form of the EU legal system.

On the second path of EU legal history, little did I expect when I started engaging with this contemporary topic that I would turn to the past in search of answers. EU law scholars tend to be forward-looking, after all. And yet this work is not only an investigation into sustainable migration. It also offers a conclusive reconstruction of the history of EU migration law. The experience of collecting archival material, making information requests, not being able to locate the material that would answer all my questions, but rather finding tons of material, which, while far from my inquiry, significantly informed my intellectual perspective, was a unique pedagogical experience. Next to the personal function that legal historical research served for me, I am convinced that working on the history of EU law areas in times of fast-paced legal development provides a better scholarly ability to assess the function, continuity, and transformation of the EU legal system. At a time when EU legal history is beginning to take shape as an independent field of scholarly research, I hope this work can provide inspiration for similar paths less travelled.

In closing, I would like to thank Niamh Nic Shuibhne, Elise Muir, Sara Iglesias Sánchez, and Niklas Selberg for the enthusiasm with which they examined this work during my defence in October 2023, as well as Sharon MacCann for coordinating what was the most expeditious publication process I could ever imagine.

TABLE OF CASES

Judgment of 5 February 1963, *Van Gend & Loos v Administratie der Belastingen*, 26/62, ECLI:EU:C:1963:1

Judgment of 19 March 1964, *(Hoekstra) Unger v Bedrijfsvereniging voor Detailhandel en Ambachten*, 75/63, ECLI:EU:C:1964:19

Judgment of 9 June 1964, *Nonnenmacher v Sociale Verzekeringsbank*, 92/63, ECLI:EU:C:1964:40

Judgment of 15 July 1964, *Van der Veen v Sociale Verzekeringsbank*, 100/63, ECLI:EU:C:1964:65

Judgment of 2 December 1964, *Dingemans v Sociale Verzekeringsbank*, 24/64, ECLI:EU:C:1964:86

Judgment of 11 March 1965, *Betriebskrankenkasse der Heseper Torfwerke v Van Dijk*, 33/64, ECLI:EU:C:1965:19

Judgment of 11 March 1965, *Sociale Voorzorg v Bertholet*, 31/64, ECLI:EU:C:1965:18

Judgment of 1 December 1965, *Dekker v Bundesversicherungsanstalt für Angestellte*, 33/65, ECLI:EU:C:1965:118

Judgment of 9 December 1965, *Hessische Knappschaft v Singer et Fils*, 44/65, ECLI:EU:C:1965:122

Judgment of 30 June 1966, *Vaassen-Goebbels v Beambtenfonds voor het Mijnbedrijf*, 61/65, ECLI:EU:C:1966:39

Judgment of 13 July 1966, *Hagenbeek v Raad van Arbeid*, 4/66, ECLI:EU:C:1966:4

Judgment of 5 July 1967, *Ciechelsky v Caisse regionale de sécurité sociale du Centre*, 1/67, ECLI:EU:C:1967:27

Judgment of 5 July 1967, *Colditz v Caisse d'assurance vieillesse des travailleurs salariés*, 9/67, ECLI:EU:C:1967:30

Judgment of 5 July 1967, *De Moor v Caisse de pension des employés privés*, 2/67, ECLI:EU:C:1967:28

Judgment of 5 July 1967, *Guerra v INAMI*, 6/67, ECLI:EU:C:1967:29

Judgment of 30 November 1967, *Caisse regionale de sécurité sociale du Nord v Goffart*, 22/67, ECLI:EU:C:1967:47

Judgment of 30 November 1967, *Cossutta v Office national des pensions pour ouvriers*, 18/67, ECLI:EU:C:1967:46

Judgment of 5 December 1967, *Landesversicherungsanstalt Rheinland-Pfalz v Welchner*, 14/67, ECLI:EU:C:1967:48

Judgment of 5 December 1967, *Soziale Verzekeringsbank v Van Der Vecht*, 19/67, ECLI:EU:C:1967:49

Judgment of 12 December 1967, *Office national des pensions pour ouvriers v Couture*, 11/67, ECLI:EU:C:1967:52

Judgment of 19 December 1968, *De Cicco v Landesversicherungsanstalt Schwaben*, 19/68, ECLI:EU:C:1968:56

Judgment of 7 May 1969, *Caisse regionale de sécurité sociale du Nord v Torrekens*, 28/68, ECLI:EU:C:1969:17

Judgment of 15 October 1969, *Württembergische Milchverwertung Südmilch AG v Ugliola*, 15/69, ECLI:EU:C:1969:46

Judgment of 13 December 1972, *Marsman v Rosskamp*, 44/72, ECLI:EU:C:1972:120

Judgment of 11 April 1973, *Michel S. v Fonds national de reclassement social des handicapés*, 76/72, ECLI:EU:C:1973:46

Judgment of 3 July 1974, *Casagrande v Landeshauptstadt München*, 9/74, ECLI:EU:C:1974:74

Judgment of 29 January 1975, *Alaimo v Préfet du Rhône*, 68/74, ECLI:EU:C:1975:11

Judgment of 17 June 1975, *Mr and Mrs F. v Belgian State*, 7/75, ECLI:EU:C:1975:80

Judgment of 30 September 1975, *Cristini v S.N.C.F.*, 32/75, ECLI:EU:C:1975:120

Judgment of 23 November 1976, *Kermaschek v Bundesanstalt für Arbeit*, 40/76, ECLI:EU:C:1976:157.

Judgment of 16 December 1976, *Inzirillo v Caisse allocations familiales Lyon*, 63/76, ECLI:EU:C:1976:192

Judgment of 31 May 1979, *Ministère public v Even*, 207/78, ECLI:EU:C:1979:144

Judgment of 14 January 1982, *Reina v Landeskreditbank Baden-Württemberg*, 65/81, ECLI:EU:C:1982:6

Judgment of 9 February 1982, *Polydor and others / Harlequin and others*, 270/80, ECLI:EU:C:1982:43

Judgment of 26 October 1982, *Hauptzollamt Mainz / Kupferberg & Cie.*, 104/81, ECLI:EU:C:1982:362

Judgment of 23 March 1983, *Peskeloglou v Bundesanstalt Für Arbeit*, 77/82, ECLI:EU:C:1983:92

Judgment of 13 July 1983, *Forcheri v Belgian State*, 152/82, ECLI:EU:C:1983:205

Judgment of 12 July 1984, *Castelli v ONTPS*, 261/83, ECLI:EU:C:1984:280

Judgment of 13 February 1985, *Diatta v Land Berlin*, 267/83, ECLI:EU:C:1985:67

Judgment of 13 February 1985, *Gravier v Ville de Liège*, 293/83, ECLI:EU:C:1985:69

Judgment of 27 March 1985, *Hoeckx v Openbaar Centrum voor Maatschappelijk Welzijn Kalmthout*, 249/83, ECLI:EU:C:1985:139

Judgment of 6 June 1985, *Frascogna v Caisse des dépôts et consignations*, 157/84, ECLI:EU:C:1985:243

Judgment of 20 June 1985, *ONEM v Deak*, 94/84, ECLI:EU:C:1985:264

Judgment of 11 July 1985, *Ministère public v Mutsch*, 137/84, ECLI:EU:C:1985:335

Judgment of 17 April 1986, *Netherlands v Reed*, 59/85, ECLI:EU:C:1986:157

Judgment of 7 May 1986, *Gül v Regierungspräsident Düsseldorf*, 131/85, ECLI:EU:C:1986:200

Judgment of 18 June 1987, *CPAS de Courcelles v Lebon*, 316/85, ECLI:EU:C:1987:302

Judgment of the Court of 9 July 1987, *Federal Republic of Germany and others v Commission of the European Communities*, Joined cases 281, 283, 284, 285, and 287/85, ECLI:EU:C:1987:351

Judgment of 30 September 1987, *Demirel / Stadt Schwäbisch Gmünd*, 12/86, ECLI:EU:C:1987:400

Judgment of 2 February 1988, *Barra v Belgian State*, 309/85, ECLI:EU:C:1988:42

Judgment of 2 February 1988, *Blaizot v Université de Liège and others*, 24/86, ECLI:EU:C:1988:43

Judgment of 21 June 1988, *Brown / Secretary of State for Scotland*, 197/86, ECLI:EU:C:1988:323

Judgment of 21 June 1988, *Lair v Universität Hannover*, 39/86, ECLI:EU:C:1988:322

Judgment of 27 September 1988, *Belgian State v Humbel and Edel*, 263/86, ECLI:EU:C:1988:451

Judgment of 27 September 1988, *Matteucci v Communauté française de Belgique*, 235/87, ECLI:EU:C:1988:460

Judgment of 15 March 1989, *Echternach and others / Minister van Onderwijs en Wetenschappen*, 389/87 and 390/87, ECLI:EU:C:1989:130

Judgment of 31 May 1989, *Bettray v Staatssecretaris van Justitie*, 344/87, ECLI:EU:C:1989:226

Judgment of 27 September 1989, *Lopes da Veiga v Staatssecretaris van Justitie*, 9/88, ECLI:EU:C:1989:346

Judgment of 27 March 1990, *Rush Portuguesa v Office national d'immigration*, C-113/89, ECLI:EU:C:1990:142

Judgment of 20 September 1990, *Sevince / Staatssecretaris van Justitie*, C-192/89, ECLI:EU:C:1990:322

Judgment of 13 November 1990, *Di Leo v Land Berlin*, C-308/89, ECLI:EU:C:1990:400

Judgment of 31 January 1991, *Office national de l'emploi / Kziber*, C-18/90, ECLI:EU:C:1991:36

Judgment of 26 February 1992, *Raulin v Minister van Onderwijs en Wetenschappen*, C-357/89, ECLI:EU:C:1992:87

Judgment of 7 July 1992, *The Queen / Immigration Appeal Tribunal and Surinder Singh, ex parte Secretary of State for the Home Department*, C-370/90, ECLI:EU:C:1992:296

Judgment of the Court of 7 July 1992, *European Parliament v Council of the European Communities*, C-250/90, ECLI:EU:C:1992:294

Judgment of 8 July 1992, *Belgian State v Taghavi*, C-243/91, ECLI:EU:C:1992:306

Judgment of 16 December 1992, *Kus / Landeshauptstadt Wiesbaden*, C-237/91, ECLI:EU:C:1992:527

Judgment of 26 May 1993, *Tsiotras / Landeshauptstadt Stuttgart*, C-171/91, ECLI:EU:C:1993:215

Judgment of 20 April 1994, *Yousfi / Belgian State*, C-58/93, ECLI:EU:C:1994:160

Judgment of 5 October 1994, *Eroglu/Land Baden-Württemberg*, C-355/93, ECLI:EU:C:1994:369

Judgment of 5 April 1995, *Krid / Caisse nationale d'assurance vieillesse des travailleurs salaries*, C-103/94, ECLI:EU:C:1995:97

Judgment of 10 September 1996, *Taflan-Met and others*, C-277/94, ECLI:EU:C:1996:315

Judgment of 3 October 1996, *Hallouzi-Choho / Bestuur van de Sociale Verzekeringsbank*, C-126/95, ECLI:EU:C:1996:368

Judgment of 23 January 1997, *Tetik / Land Berlin*, C-171/95, ECLI:EU:C:1997:31

Judgment of 17 April 1997, *Kadiman / Freistaat Bayern*, C-351/95 ECLI:EU:C:1997:205

Judgment of 5 June 1997, *Kol / Land Berlin*, C-285/95, ECLI:EU:C:1997:280

Judgment of 30 September 1997, *Ertanir / Land Hessen*, C-98/96, ECLI:EU:C:1997:446

Judgment of 30 September 1997, *Günaydin and others / Freistaat Bayern*, C-36/96, ECLI:EU:C:1997:445

Judgment of 15 January 1998, *Babahenini / Belgian State*, C-113/97, ECLI:EU:C:1998:13

Judgment of 12 May 1998, *Martínez Sala / Freistaat Bayern*, C-85/96, ECLI:EU:C:1998:217

Judgment of 19 November 1998, *Akman / Oberkreisdirektor des Rheinisch-Bergischen-Kreises*, C-210/97, ECLI:EU:C:1998:555

Judgment of 26 November 1998, *Birden / Stadtgemeinde Bremen*, C-1/97, ECLI:EU:C:1998:568

Judgment of 2 March 1999, *Eddline El-Yassini*, C-416/96, ECLI:EU:C:1999:107

Judgment of 4 May 1999, *Sürül*, C-262/96, ECLI:EU:C:1999:228

Judgment of 11 November 1999, *Belgian State / Mesbah*, C-179/98, ECLI:EU:C:1999:549

Judgment of 16 March 2000, *Ergat*, C-329/97, ECLI:EU:C:2000:133

Judgment of 11 May 2000, *Savas*, C-37/98, ECLI:EU:C:2000:224

Judgment of 22 June 2000, *Eyüp*, C-65/98, ECLI:EU:C:2000:336

Judgment of 20 March 2001, *Fahmi and Esmoris Cerdeiro-Pinedo Amado*, C-33/99, ECLI:EU:C:2001:176

Judgment of 20 September 2001, *Grzelczyk*, C-184/99, ECLI:EU:C:2001:458

Judgment of 29 January 2002, *Pokrzeptowicz-Meyer*, C-162/00, ECLI:EU:C:2002:57

Judgment of 11 July 2002, *Carpenter*, C-60/00, ECLI:EU:C:2002:434

Judgment of 11 July 2002, *D'Hoop*, C-224/98, ECLI:EU:C:2002:432

Judgment of 25 July 2002, *MRAX*, C-459/99, ECLI:EU:C:2002:461

Judgments of 17 September 2002, *Baumbast and R*, C-413/99, EU:C:2002:493

Judgment of 19 November 2002, *Kurz*, C-188/00, ECLI:EU:C:2002:694
Order of 12 February 2003, *Alami*, C-23/02, ECLI:EU:C:2003:89
Judgment of 8 May 2003, *Deutscher Handballbund*, C-438/00, ECLI:EU:C:2003:255
Judgment of 23 September 2003, *Akrich*, C-109/01, ECLI:EU:C:2003:491
Judgment of 2 October 2003, *Garcia Avello*, C-148/02, ECLI:EU:C:2003:539
Judgment of 21 October 2003, *Abatay and others*, C-317/01 and C-369/01, ECLI:EU:C:2003:572
Judgment of 23 March 2004, *Collins*, C-138/02, ECLI:EU:C:2004:172
Judgment of 7 September 2004, *Trojani*, C-456/02, ECLI:EU:C:2004:488
Judgment of 30 September 2004, *Ayaz*, C-275/02, ECLI:EU:C:2004:570
Judgment of 19 October 2004, *Zhu and Chen*, C-200/02, ECLI:EU:C:2004:639
Judgment of 11 November 2004, *Cetinkaya*, C-467/02, ECLI:EU:C:2004:708
Judgment of 15 March 2005, *Bidar*, C-209/03, ECLI:EU:C:2005:169
Judgment of 12 April 2005, *Simutenkov*, C-265/03, ECLI:EU:C:2005:213
Judgment of 7 July 2005, *Aydinli*, C-373/03, ECLI:EU:C:2005:434
Judgment of 7 July 2005, *Gürol*, C-374/03, ECLI:EU:C:2005:435
Judgment of 7 July 2005, *Dogan*, C-383/03, ECLI:EU:C:2005:436
Order of 13 June 2006, *Echouikh*, C-336/05, ECLI:EU:C:2006:394
Judgment of 27 June 2006, *Parliament/Council*, C-540/03, ECLI:EU:C:2006:429
Judgment of 14 December 2006, *Gattoussi*, C-97/05, ECLI:EU:C:2006:780
Order of 17 April 2007, *El Youssfi*, C-276/06, ECLI:EU:C:2007:215
Judgment of 18 July 2007, *Derin*, C-325/05, ECLI:EU:C:2007:442
Judgment of 11 December 2007, *Eind*, C-291/05, ECLI:EU:C:2007:771
Judgment of 24 January 2008, *Payir and others*, C-294/06, ECLI:EU:C:2008:36
Judgment of 25 July 2008, *Metock and others*, C-127/08, ECLI:EU:C:2008:449
Judgment of 25 September 2008, *Er*, C-453/07, ECLI:EU:C:2008:524
Judgment of 19 February 2009, *Soysal and Savatli*, C-228/06, ECLI:EU:C:2009:101
Judgment of 4 June 2009, *Vatsouras and Koupatantze*, C-22/08 and C-23/08, ECLI:EU:C:2009:344
Judgment of 17 September 2009, *Sahin*, C-242/06, ECR 2009, ECLI:EU:C:2009:554
Judgment of 21 January 2010, *Bekleyen*, C-462/08, ECLI:EU:C:2010:30
Judgment of 4 February 2010, *Genc*, C-14/09, ECLI:EU:C:2010:57
Judgment of 23 February 2010, *Ibrahim and Secretary of State for the Home Department*, C-310/08, EU:C:2010:80
Judgment of 23 February 2010, *Teixeira*, C-480/08, EU:C:2010:83
Judgment of 4 March 2010, *Chakroun*, C-578/08, ECLI:EU:C:2010:117
Judgment of 29 April 2010, *Commission / Netherlands*, C-92/07, ECLI:EU:C:2010:228
Judgment of 18 November 2010, *Xhymshiti*, C-247/09, ECLI:EU:C:2010:698
Judgment of 9 December 2010, *Toprak and Oguz*, C-300/09 and C-301/09, ECLI:EU:C:2010:756
Judgment of 22 December 2010, *Bozkurt*, C-303/08, ECLI:EU:C:2010:800
Judgment of 8 March 2011, *Ruiz Zambrano*, C-34/09, ECLI:EU:C:2011:124

Judgment of 15 September 2015, *Alimanovic*, C-67/14, ECLI:EU:C:2015:597
Judgment of 19 November 2015, *Bukovansky*, C-241/14, ECLI:EU:C:2015:766
Judgment of 25 February 2016, *García-Nieto and others*, C-299/14, ECLI:EU:C:2016:114
Judgment of 12 April 2016, *Genc*, C-561/14, ECLI:EU:C:2016:247
Judgment of 21 April 2016, *Khachab*, C-558/14, ECLI:EU:C:2016:285
Judgment of 14 June 2016, *Commission / United Kingdom*, C-308/14, ECLI:EU:C:2016:436
Judgment of 6 September 2016, *Petruhhin*, C-182/15, ECLI:EU:C:2016:630
Judgment of 13 September 2016, *Rendón Marín*, C-165/14, ECLI:EU:C:2016:675
Judgment of 13 September 2016, *CS*, C-304/14 ECLI:EU:C:2016:674
Judgment of 21 September 2016, *Radgen*, C-478/15, ECLI:EU:C:2016:705
Judgment of 21 December 2016, *Ucar*, C-508/15 and C-509/15, ECLI:EU:C:2016:986 75
Judgment of 29 March 2017, *Tekdemir*, C-652/15, ECLI:EU:C:2017:239
Judgment of 4 April 2017, *Fahimian*, C-544/15, ECLI:EU:C:2017:255
Judgment of 10 May 2017, *Chavez-Vilchez and others*, C-133/15, ECLI:EU:C:2017:354
Judgment of 21 June 2017, *Martinez Silva*, C-449/16, ECLI:EU:C:2017:485
Judgment of 20 December 2017, *Gusa*, C-442/16, ECLI:EU:C:2017:1004
Judgment of 6 February 2018, *Altun and others*, C-359/16, ECLI:EU:C:2018:63
Judgment of 8 May 2018, *K.A. and Others*, C 82/16, EU:C:2018:308
Judgment of 28 June 2018, *Crespo Rey*, C-2/17, ECLI:EU:C:2018:511
Judgment of 7 August 2018, *Yön*, C-123/17, ECLI:EU:C:2018:632
Judgment of 7 November 2018, *C and A*, C-257/17, ECLI:EU:C:2018:876
Judgment of 7 November 2018, *K*, C-484/17, ECLI:EU:C:2018:878
Judgment of 14 March 2019, *Y.Z. and others*, C-557/17, ECLI:EU:C:2019
Judgment of 15 May 2019, *Çoban*, C-677/17, ECLI:EU:C:2019:408
Judgment of 19 September 2019, *Dakneviciute*, C-544/18, ECLI:EU:C:2019:761
Judgment of 2 October 2019, *Bajratari*, C-93/18, ECLI:EU:C:2019:809
Judgment of 3 October 2019, *A and others*, C-70/18, ECLI:EU:C:2019:823
Judgment of 3 October 2019, *X v Belgische Staat*, C-302/18, ECLI:EU:C:2019:830
Judgment of 20 November 2019, *Belgische Staat*, C-706/18, ECLI:EU:C:2019:993
Order of 13 February 2020, *Solak*, C-258/18, ECLI:EU:C:2020:98
Judgment of 27 February 2020, *Subdelegación del Gobierno en Ciudad Real v RH*, Case C-836/18, ECLI:EU:C:2020:119
Judgment of 2 April 2020, *Ruska Federacija*, C-897/19 PPU, ECLI:EU:C:2020:262
Judgment of 16 July 2020, *Belgian State*, C-133/19, C-136/19, and C-137/19, ECLI:EU:C:2020:577
Judgment of 6 October 2020, *Jobcenter Krefeld v JD*, C-181/19, ECLI:EU:C:2020:794
Judgment of 25 November 2020, *INPS*, C-302/19, ECLI:EU:C:2020:957
Judgment of 25 November 2020, *INPS*, C-303/19 ECLI:EU:C:2020:958
Judgment of 10 June 2021, *Land Oberösterreich*, C-94/20, ECLI:EU:C:2021:477
Judgment of 2 September 2021, *INPS*, C-350/20, ECLI:EU:C:2021:659

Judgment of 2 September 2021, *Udlændingenævnet*, C-379/20, ECLI:EU:C:2021:660

Judgment of 2 September 2021, *Belgian State*, C-930/19, ECLI:EU:C:2021:657

Judgment of 28 October 2021, *ASGI and others*, C-462/20, ECLI:EU:C:2021:894

Judgment of 20 January 2022, *Landeshauptmann von Wien*, C-432/20, ECLI:EU:C:2022:39

Judgment of 7 September 2022, *Staatssecretaris van Justitie en Veiligheid*, C-624/20, ECLI:EU:C:2022:639.

Judgment of 21 December 2023, *Chief Appeals Officer and others*, C-488/21, ECLI:EU:C:2023:1013

Opinions of Advocate Generals

Opinion of Advocate General Mancini delivered on 31 March 1987 in *Federal Republic of Germany and others v Commission of the European Communities*, Joined cases 281, 283, 284, 285, and 287/85, ECLI:EU:C:1987:169

Opinion of Advocate General Van Gerven delivered on 6 December 1990 in *Office national de l'emploi v Kziber*, C-18/90, ECLI:EU:C:1990:447

Opinion of Advocate General Jacobs delivered on 9 December 1992 in *Konstantinidis*, C-168/91 ECLI:EU:C:1992:504

Opinion of Advocate General Elmer delivered on 28 March 1995 in *Bozkurt / Staatssecretaris van Justitie*, C-434/93, ECLI:EU:C:1995:86

Opinion of Advocate General Fennelly delivered on 28 May 1998 in *Birden / Stadtgemeinde Bremen*, C-1/97, ECLI:EU:C:1998:262

Opinion of Advocate General La Pergola delivered on 17 December 1998 in *Sürül*, C-262/96, ECLI:EU:C:1998:55

Opinion of Advocate General Léger delivered on 19 May 1998 in *El-Yassini*, C-416/96, ECLI:EU:C:1998:243

Opinion of Advocate General Léger delivered on 9 July 1998 in *Akman*, C-210/97, ECLI:EU:C:1998:344

Opinion of Advocate General La Pergola delivered on 18 November 1999 in *Eyüp*, C-65/98, ECLI:EU:C:1999:561

Opinion of Advocate General Ruiz-Jarabo Colomer delivered on 6 April 2006 in *Gattoussi*, C-97/05, ECLI:EU:C:2006:243

Opinion of Advocate General Bot delivered on 19 January 2012 in *Commission v Netherlands*, C-508/10, ECLI:EU:C:2012:25

Opinion of Advocate General Mengozzi delivered on 30 April 2014 in *Dogan*, C-138/13, ECLI:EU:C:2014:287

Opinion of Advocate General Mengozzi delivered on 12 June 2014 in *Ben Alaya*, C-491/13, ECLI:EU:C:2014:1933

Opinion of Advocate General Bot delivered on 12 June 2014 in *Tümer*, C-311/13, ECLI:EU:C:2014:1997

Opinion of Advocate General Wahl delivered on 10 July 2014 in *Demirci and others*, C-171/13, ECLI:EU:C:2014:2073

Opinion of Advocate General Wathelet delivered on 4 June 2015 in *García-Nieto and others*, C-299/14, ECLI:EU:C:2015:366

Opinion of Advocate General Szpunar delivered on 28 January 2015 in *P and S*, C 579/13, ECLI:EU:C:2015:39

Opinion of Advocate General Szpunar delivered on 29 November 2016 in *Fahimian*, C-544/15, ECLI:EU:C:2016:908

Opinion of Advocate General Mengozzi delivered on 27 June 2018 in *C and A*, C-257/17, ECLI:EU:C:2018:503

Opinion of Advocate General Saugmandsgaard Øe delivered on 6 June 2019 in *X v Belgische Staat*, C-302/18, ECLI:EU:C:2019:469

Opinion of Advocate General Szpunar delivered on 19 June 2019 in *Bajratari*, C-93/18, ECLI:EU:C:2019:512

Opinion of Advocate General Pitruzzella delivered on 14 May 2020 in *JD*, C-181/19, ECLI:EU:C:2020:377

TABLE OF LEGISLATION

EU Law Material

EU Treaties

Treaty establishing the European Coal and Steel Community, 18 April 1951
Treaty establishing the European Economic Community, 25 March 1957
Single European Act [1986] OJ L 169/1
- General Declaration on Articles 13 to 19 of the Single European Act [1987] OJ L 169/24

Treaty on European Union, together with the complete text of the Treaty establishing the European Community [1992] OJ C 224/1
Treaty on European Union (Amsterdam consolidated version) [1997] OJ C 340/145
Treaty establishing the European Community (Amsterdam consolidated version) [1997] OJ C 340/173
Treaty of Nice amending the Treaty on European Union, the Treaties establishing the European Communities and certain related acts [2001] OJ C 80/1
Treaty establishing a Constitution for Europe [2004] OJ C 310/1
Consolidated version of the Treaty on European Union [2016] OJ C 202/13
Consolidated version of the Treaty on the Functioning of the European Union [2016] OJ C 202/47
- Protocol (No 2) on the application of the principles of subsidiarity and proportionality [2008] OJ C 115/206
- Protocol (No 21) on the position of the United Kingdom and Ireland in respect of the Area of Freedom, Security and Justice [2016] OJ C 202/295
- Protocol (No 22) on the position of Denmark [2016] OJ C 202/298

Charter of Fundamental Rights of the European Union [2016] OJ C 202/389

Accession Treaties

Treaty of Accession of Denmark, Ireland and the United Kingdom [1972] OJ L 73/3
- Joint declaration on the free movement of workers, Treaty of Accession of Denmark, Ireland and the United Kingdom [1972] OJ L 73/195

Treaty between the Kingdom of Belgium, the Kingdom of Denmark, the Federal Republic of Germany, the French Republic, Ireland, the Italian Republic, the Grand Duchy of Luxembourg, the Kingdom of the Netherlands, the United Kingdom of Great Britain and Northern Ireland (Member States of the European Communities) and the Hellenic Republic concerning the accession of the Hellenic Republic to the European Economic Community and to the European Atomic Energy Community [1979] OJ L 291/9

Treaty between the Kingdom of Belgium, the Kingdom of Denmark, the Federal Republic of Germany, the Hellenic Republic, the French Republic, Ireland, the Italian Republic, the Grand Duchy of Luxembourg, the Kingdom of the Netherlands, the United Kingdom of Great Britain and Northern Ireland (Member States of the European Communities) and the Kingdom of Spain and the Portuguese Republic concerning the accession of the Kingdom of Spain and the Portuguese Republic to the European Economic Community and to the European Atomic Energy Community [1985] OJ L 302/9

Act concerning the conditions of accession of the Kingdom of Norway, the Republic of Austria, the Republic of Finland and the Kingdom of Sweden and the adjustments to the Treaties on which the European Union is founded [1994] OJ C 241/9

- Joint declaration on the free movement of workers by Austria [1994] OJ C 241/388

Treaty between the Kingdom of Belgium, the Kingdom of Denmark, the Federal Republic of Germany, the Hellenic Republic, the Kingdom of Spain, the French Republic, Ireland, the Italian Republic, the Grand Duchy of Luxembourg, the Kingdom of the Netherlands, the Republic of Austria, the Portuguese Republic, the Republic of Finland, the Kingdom of Sweden, the United Kingdom of Great Britain and Northern Ireland (Member States of the European Union) and the Czech Republic, the Republic of Estonia, the Republic of Cyprus, the Republic of Latvia, the Republic of Lithuania, the Republic of Hungary, the Republic of Malta, the Republic of Poland, the Republic of Slovenia, the Slovak Republic, concerning the accession of the Czech Republic, the Republic of Estonia, the Republic of Cyprus, the Republic of Latvia, the Republic of Lithuania, the Republic of Hungary, the Republic of Malta, the Republic of Poland, the Republic of Slovenia and the Slovak Republic to the European Union [2003] OJ L 236/17

- Declarations no 6, 7, 10, 11, 13, 14, 15, 16, 18, 19 [2003] OJ L 236/955

Treaty between the Kingdom of Belgium, the Czech Republic, the Kingdom of Denmark, the Federal Republic of Germany, the Republic of Estonia, the Hellenic Republic, the Kingdom of Spain, the French Republic, Ireland, the Italian Republic, the Republic of Cyprus, the Republic of Latvia, the Republic of Lithuania, the Grand Duchy of Luxembourg, the Republic of Hungary, the Republic of Malta, the Kingdom of the Netherlands, the Republic of Austria, the Republic of Poland, the Portuguese Republic, the Republic of Slovenia, the Slovak Republic, the Republic of Finland, the Kingdom of Sweden, the United Kingdom of Great Britain and

Northern Ireland (Member States of the European Union) and the Republic of Bulgaria and Romania, concerning the accession of the Republic of Bulgaria and Romania to the European Union [2005] OJ L 157/11

- Joint declaration on the free movement of workers 1 and 2 [2005] OJ L 157/391

Treaty between the Kingdom of Belgium, the Republic of Bulgaria, the Czech Republic, the Kingdom of Denmark, the Federal Republic of Germany, the Republic of Estonia, Ireland, the Hellenic Republic, the Kingdom of Spain, the French Republic, the Italian Republic, the Republic of Cyprus, the Republic of Latvia, the Republic of Lithuania, the Grand Duchy of Luxembourg, the Republic of Hungary, the Republic of Malta, the Kingdom of the Netherlands, the Republic of Austria, the Republic of Poland, the Portuguese Republic, Romania, the Republic of Slovenia, the Slovak Republic, the Republic of Finland, the Kingdom of Sweden, the United Kingdom of Great Britain and Northern Ireland (Member States of the European Union) and the Republic of Croatia concerning the accession of the Republic of Croatia to the European Union [2012] OJ L 112/10

Association and Cooperation Treaties

Agreement establishing an Association between the European Economic Community and Greece [1963] OJ L 293/3

Convention d'association entre la Communauté économique européenne et les États africains et malgache associés à cette Communauté, Signée à Yaoundé le 20 juillet 1963 [1964] OJ L 93/1431

Convention d'association entre la Communauté économique européenne et les États africains et malgache associés à cette Communauté, Signée à Yaoundé le 29 juillet 1969 [1970] OJ L 282/2

Agreement between the European Economic Community and the Republic of Austria [1972] OJ L 300/2

Agreement between the European Economic Community and the Kingdom of Sweden [1972] OJ L300/9

Agreement between the European Economic Community and the Portuguese Republic [1972] OJ L 301/165

Agreement between the European Economic Community and the Swiss Confederation [1972] OJ L 300/189

- Declaration concerning workers, Agreement between the European Economic Community and the Swiss Confederation [1972] OJ L 300/189

Agreement between the European Economic Community and the Kingdom of Norway [1973] OJ L 171/2

Agreement establishing an Association between the European Economic Community and the Kingdom of Morocco [1973] OJ L 239

Agreement establishing an Association between the European Economic Community and the Tunisian Republic [1973] OJ L 239/125

Agreement establishing an Association between the European Economic Community and Turkey (signed at Ankara, 12 September 1963) [1977] OJ L 361/29

- Additional Protocol and Financial Protocol signed on 23 November 1970, annexed to the Agreement establishing the Association between the European Economic Community and Turkey and on measures to be taken for their entry into force [1972] OJ L 293/3
- Decision No 1/80 of the Association Council of 19 September 1980 on the development of the Association set up by the EEC–Turkey Agreement
- Decision No 3/80 of the Association Council of 19 September 1980 on the application of the social security schemes of the Member States of the European Communities to Turkish workers and members of their families

Cooperation Agreement between the European Economic Community and the People's Democratic Republic of Algeria [1978] OJ L 263/2

Cooperation Agreement between the European Economic Community and the Kingdom of Morocco [1978] OJ L 264/2

Cooperation Agreement between the European Economic Community and the Republic of Tunisia [1978] OJ L 265/2

Cooperation Agreement between the European Economic Community and the Socialist Federal Republic of Yugoslavia [1983] OJ L 41/2

Europe Agreement establishing an association between the European Communities and their Member States, of the one part, and the Republic of Poland, of the other part [1993] OJ L 348/2

Europe Agreement establishing an association between the European Communities and their Member States, of the one part, and the Republic of Hungary, of the other part [1993] OJ L 347/2

Agreement on the European Economic Area [1994] OJ L 1/3

Europe Agreement establishing an association between the European Economic Communities and their Member States, of the one part, and Romania, of the other part [1994] OJ L 357/2

Europe Agreement establishing an association between the European Communities and their Member States, of the one part, and the Republic of Bulgaria, of the other part [1994] OJ L 358/3

Europe Agreement establishing an association between the European Communities and their Member States, of the one part, and the Slovak Republic, of the other part [1994] OJ L 359/2

Europe Agreement establishing an association between the European Communities and their Member States, of the one part, and the Czech Republic, of the other part [1994] OJ L360/2

Agreement on Partnership and Cooperation establishing a Partnership between the European Communities and their Member States, of one part, and the Russian Federation, of the other part [1997] OJ L 327/3

Europe Agreement establishing an association between the European Communities and their Member States, of the one part, and the Republic of Latvia, of the other part [1998] OJ L 26/2

Europe Agreement establishing an association between the European Communities and their Member States, of the one part, and the Republic of Lithuania, of the other part [1998] OJ L 51/2

Euro-Mediterranean Agreement establishing an Association between the European Communities and their Member States, of the one part, and the Republic of Tunisia, of the other part [1998] OJ L 97/2

Europe Agreement establishing an association between the European Communities and their Member States, acting within the framework of the European Union, of the one part, and the Republic of Slovenia [1999] OJ L 51/3

Partnership and Cooperation Agreement establishing a partnership between the European Communities and their Member States, of the one part, and the Kyrgyz Republic, of the other part [1999] OJ L 196/48

Partnership and Cooperation Agreement establishing a partnership between the European Communities and their Member States, of the one part, and the Republic of Uzbekistan, of the other part [1999] OJ L 229/3

Partnership and Cooperation Agreement between the European Communities and their Member States, of the one part, and the Republic of Azerbaijan, of the other part [1999] OJ L 246/3

Euro-Mediterranean Agreement establishing an Association between the European Communities and their Member States, of the one part, and the Kingdom of Morocco, of the other part [2000] OJ L 70/2

Euro-Mediterranean Agreement establishing an Association between the European Communities and their Member States, of the one part, and the State of Israel, of the other part [2000] OJ L 147/3

Agreement between the European Community and its Member States, of the one part, and the Swiss Confederation, of the other, on the free movement of persons [2002] OJ L 114/6

Euro-Mediterranean Agreement establishing an Association between the European Communities and their Member States, of the one part, and the Hashemite Kingdom of Jordan, of the other part [2002] OJ L 129/3

Stabilisation and Association Agreement between the European Communities and their Member States, of the one part, and the former Yugoslav Republic of Macedonia, of the other part [2004] OJ L 084/13

Euro-Mediterranean Agreement establishing an Association between the European Communities and their Member States, of the one part, and the Arab Republic of Egypt, of the other part [2004] OJ L 304/39

Stabilisation and Association Agreement between the European Communities and their Member States, of the one part, and the Republic of Croatia, of the other part [2005] OJ L 26/3

Euro-Mediterranean Agreement establishing an Association between the European Community and its Member States, of the one part, and the People's Democratic Republic of Algeria, of the other part [2005] OJ L 265/2

Euro-Mediterranean Agreement establishing an Association between the European Community and its Member States, of the one part, and the Republic of Lebanon, of the other part [2006] OJ L 143/2

Stabilisation and Association Agreement between the European Communities and their Member States, of the one part, and the Republic of Albania, of the other part [2009] OJ L 107/166

Partnership and Cooperation Agreement establishing a partnership between the European Communities and their Member States, of the one part, and the Republic of Tajikistan, of the other part [2009] OJ L 350/3

Stabilisation and Association Agreement between the European Communities and their Member States, of the one part, and the Republic of Montenegro, of the other part [2010] OJ L 108/3

Stabilisation and Association Agreement between the European Communities and their Member States of the one part, and the Republic of Serbia, of the other part [2013] OJ L 278/16

Stabilisation and Association Agreement between the European Communities and their Member States of the one part, and Bosnia and Herzegovina, of the other part [2015] OJ L 164/2

Stabilisation and Association Agreement between the European Union and the European Atomic Energy Community, of the one part, and Kosovo, of the other part [2016] OJ L 71/3

Regulations

Règlement n° 3 concernant la sécurité sociale des travailleurs migrants [1958] OJ 30/561

Règlement n° 15 relatif aux premières mesures pour la réalisation de la libre circulation des travailleurs à l'intérieur de la Communauté [1961] OJ 57/1073

Règlement n° 38/64/CEE du Conseil du 25 mars 1964 relatif à la libre circulation des travailleurs à l'intérieur de la Communauté [1964] OJ 62/965

Regulation (EEC) No 1612/68 of the Council of 15 October 1968 on freedom of movement for workers within the Community [1968] OJ L 257/2

Regulation (EEC) No 1251/70 of the Commission of 29 June 1970 on the right of workers to remain in the territory of a Member State after having been employed in that State [1970] OJ L 142/24

Regulation (EEC) No 1408/71 of the Council of 14 June 1971 on the application of social security schemes to employed persons and their families moving within the Community [1971] OJ L 149/2

Council Regulation (EEC) No 312/76 of 9 February 1976 amending the provisions relating to the trade union rights of workers contained in Regulation (EEC)

No 1612/68 on freedom of movement for workers within the Community [1976] OJ L 39/2

Council Regulation (EEC) No 1247/92 of 30 April 1992 amending Regulation (EEC) No 1408/71 on the application of social security schemes to employed persons, to self-employed persons and to members of their families moving within the Community [1992] OJ L 136/1

Council Regulation (EEC) No 2434/92 of 27 July 1992 amending Part II of Regulation (EEC) No 1612/68 on freedom of movement for workers within the Community [1992] OJ L 245/1

Council Regulation (EC) No 3095/95 of 22 December 1995 amending Regulation (EEC) No 1408/71 on the application of social security schemes to employed persons, to self-employed persons and to members of their families moving within the Community, Regulation (EEC) No 574/72 fixing the procedure for implementing Regulation (EEC) No 1408/71, Regulation (EEC) No 1247/92 amending Regulation (EEC) No 1408/71 and Regulation (EEC) No 1945/93 amending Regulation (EEC) No 1247/92 [1995] OJ L 335/1

Council Regulation (EC) No 859/2003 of 14 May 2003 extending the provisions of Regulation (EEC) No 1408/71 and Regulation (EEC) No 574/72 to nationals of third countries who are not already covered by those provisions solely on the ground of their nationality [2003] OJ L 124/1

Regulation (EC) No 883/2004 on the coordination of social security systems in the EU [2004] OJ L 166/1

Regulation (EU) No 492/2011 of the European Parliament and of the Council of 5 April 2011 on freedom of movement for workers within the Union Text with EEA relevance [2011] OJ L 141/1

Regulation (EU) 2016/399 of the European Parliament and of the Council of 9 March 2016 on a Union Code on the rules governing the movement of persons across borders (Schengen Borders Code) (codification) [2016] OJ L 77/1

Directives

Directive du Conseil en matière de procédures et pratiques administratives relatives à l'introduction, l'emploi et le séjour des travailleurs d'un État membre, ainsi que de leur famille, dans les autres États membres de la Communauté [1961] OJ 80/1513

Council Directive 64/221/EEC of 25 February 1964 on the co-ordination of special measures concerning the movement and residence of foreign nationals which are justified on grounds of public policy, public security or public health [1964] OJ 56/850

Council Directive 64/240/EEC of 25 March 1964 on the abolition of restrictions on the movement and residence of Member States' workers and their families within the Community [1964] OJ 62/981

Council Directive 68/360/EEC of 15 October 1968 on the abolition of restrictions on movement and residence within the Community for workers of Member States and their families [1968] OJ L 257/13

Council Directive 73/148/EEC of 21 May 1973 on the abolition of restrictions on movement and residence within the Community for nationals of Member States with regard to establishment and the provision of services [1973] OJ L 172/14

Council Directive 75/34/EEC of 17 December 1974 concerning the right of nationals of a Member State to remain in the territory of another Member State after having pursued therein an activity in a self-employed capacity [1975] OJ L 14/10

Council Directive 80/987/EEC of 20 October 1980 on the approximation of the laws of the Member States relating to the protection of employees in the event of the insolvency of their employer [1980] 283/23

Council Directive 90/364/EEC of 28 June 1990 on the right of residence [1990] OJ L 180/2

Council Directive 90/365/EEC of 28 June 1990 on the right of residence for employees and self-employed persons who have ceased their occupational activity [1990] OJ L 180/28

Council Directive 90/366/EEC of 28 June 1990 on the right of residence for students [1990] OJ L 180/30

Council Directive 93/96/EEC of 29 October 1993 on the right of residence for students [1993] OJ L 317/59

Directive 96/71/EC of the European Parliament and of the Council of 16 December 1996 concerning the posting of workers in the framework of the provision of services [1997] OJ L 18/1

Council Directive 2003/109/EC of 25 November 2003 concerning the status of third-country nationals who are long-term residents [2003] OJ L 16/44

Council Directive 2003/86/EC of 22 September 2003 on the right to family reunification [2003] OJ L 251/12

Directive 2004/38/EC of the European Parliament and of the Council of 29 April 2004 on the right of citizens of the Union and their family members to move and reside freely within the territory of the Member States amending Regulation (EEC) No 1612/68 and repealing Directives 64/221/EEC, 68/360/EEC, 72/194/EEC, 73/148/EEC, 75/34/EEC, 75/35/EEC, 90/364/EEC, 90/365/EEC and 93/96/EEC [2004] OJ L 158/77

Council Directive 2004/114/EC of 13 December 2004 on the conditions of admission of third-country nationals for the purposes of studies, pupil exchange, unremunerated training or voluntary service [2004] OJ L 375/12

Council Directive 2005/71/EC of 12 October 2005 on a specific procedure for admitting third-country nationals for the purposes of scientific research [2005] OJ L 289/15

Council Directive 2009/50/EC of 25 May 2009 on the conditions of entry and residence of third-country nationals for the purposes of highly qualified employment [2009] OJ L 155/17

Directive 2011/98/EU of the European Parliament and of the Council of 13 December 2011 on a single application procedure for a single permit for third-country nationals to reside and work in the territory of a Member State and on a common set of rights for third-country workers legally residing in a Member State [2011] OJ L 343/1

Directive 2014/36/EU of the European Parliament and of the Council of 26 February 2014 on the conditions of entry and stay of third-country nationals for the purpose of employment as seasonal workers [2014] OJ L 94/375

Directive 2014/66/EU of the European Parliament and of the Council of 15 May 2014 on the conditions of entry and residence of third-country nationals in the framework of an intra-corporate transfer [2014] OJ L 157/1

Directive (EU) 2016/801 of the European Parliament and of the Council of 11 May 2016 on the conditions of entry and residence of third-country nationals for the purposes of research, studies, training, voluntary service, pupil exchange schemes or educational projects and au pairing (recast) [2016] OJ L 132/21

Directive (EU) 2021/1883 of the European Parliament and of the Council of 20 October 2021 on the conditions of entry and residence of third-country nationals for the purpose of highly qualified employment, and repealing Council Directive 2009/50/EC [2021] OJ L 382/1

Decisions

Commission Decision 85/381/EEC of 8 July 1985 setting up a prior communication and consultation procedure on migration policies in relation to non-member countries [1985] OJ L 217/25

Commission Decision 88/384/EEC of 8 June 1988 setting up a prior communication and consultation procedure on migration policies in relation to non-member countries [1988] OJ L 183/35

Council Decision 2011/407/EU of 6 June 2011 on the position to be taken by the European Union within the EEA Joint Committee concerning an amendment to Annex VI (Social Security) and Protocol 37 to the EEA Agreement [2011] OJ L 182/12

Council Decision 2011/863/EU of 16 December 2011 on the position to be taken by the European Union in the Joint Committee established under the Agreement between the European Community and its Member States, of the one part, and the Swiss Confederation, of the other, on the free movement of persons as regards the replacement of Annex II to that Agreement on the coordination of social security schemes [2011] OJ L 341/1

Council Decision 2012/776/ of 6 December 2012 on the position to be taken on behalf of the European Union within the Association Council set up by the Agreement establishing an association between the European Economic Community and Turkey, with regard to the adoption of provisions on the coordination of social security systems [2012] OJ L 340/19

Recommendations

Council Recommendation of 12 October 2005 to facilitate the admission of third-country nationals to carry out scientific research in the European Community [2005] OJ L 289/26

Council Resolutions

Council Resolution of 9 February 1976 on an Action Programme for Migrant Workers and Members of Their Families [1976] OJ C 34/2

Council Resolution of 16 July 1985 on Guidelines for a Community Policy on Migration [1985] OJ C 186/3

Council Resolution of 4 March 1996 on the status of third-country nationals residing on a long-term basis in the territory of the Member States [1996] OJ C 80/2

Council Resolution of 30 November 1994 relating to the limitations on the admission of third-country nationals to the territory of the Member States for the purpose of pursuing activities as self-employed persons [1996] OJ C 274/7

Council Resolution of 30 November 1994 on the admission of third-country nationals to the territory of the Member States for study purposes [1996] OJ C 274/10

Council Resolution of 20 June 1994 on limitation on admission of third-country nationals to the territory of the Member States for employment [1996] OJ C 274/31

Parliament Resolutions

Resolution embodying the Opinion of the European Parliament on the proposal from the Commission of the European Communities to the Council for a Directive on the education of the children of migrant workers [1975] OJ C 240/48

Resolution Doc. B2-881/86 on Community Policy on Migration of 9 October [1986] OJ C 283/52

Resolution on the Joint declaration against racism and xenophobia and an action programme by the Council of Ministers (Doc. A 2-261/88) [1989] OJ C 69/40

Resolution on migrant workers from third countries adopted on 14 June [1990] OJ C 175/150

Resolution on racism and xenophobia, adopted on 10 October [1991] OJ C 280/115

Resolution A3-0306/92 on economic and trade relations between the European Economic Community and the EFTA countries in the European Economic Area [1992] OJ C 305/564

Résolution du 3 avril 1998 sur les effets de l'élargissement de l'Union européenne sur la coopération dans le domaine de la justice et des affaires intérieures, A4-0107/98 [1998] OJ C 138/214

Résolution sur la communication de la Commission intitulé 'Agenda 2000 – Pour une Union plus forte et plus large' première partie, chapitre II, 'Cohésion économique et sociale' (COM(97)2000 – C4-0523/97), A4-0210/98, 1998-06-18, PE 270.314/15 [1998] OJ C 210/189

Résolution du Parlement Européen sur le rapport global de suivi sur le degré de préparation à l'adhésion à l'UE de la République tchèque, de l'Estonie, de Chypre, de la Lettonie, de la Lituanie, de la Hongrie, de Malte, de la Pologne, de la Slovénie et de la Slovaquie (COM(2003)675 – C5-0532/2003 – 2003/2201(1141)) A5-0111/2004 [2004] OJ C 102E/829

Résolution du Parlement européen sur le rapport global de suivi sur le degré de préparation à l'adhésion à l'UE de la République tchèque, de l'Estonie, de Chypre, de la Lettonie, de la Lituanie, de la Hongrie, de Malte, de la Pologne, de la Slovénie et de la Slovaquie A5-0111/2004 [2004] OJ C 102E/829

Resolution of 20 May 2021 on new avenues for legal labour migration (2020/2010(INI)) [2022] OJ C 15/196

Resolution of 25 November 2021 with recommendations to the Commission on legal migration policy and law (2020/2255(INL)) [2022] OJ C 224/69

Legislative resolution of 13 March 2024 on the proposal for a Recast Single Permit Directive (COM(2022)0655 – C9-0163/2022 – 2022/0131(COD))

European Economic and Social Committee Opinions

1984, Opinion of the Economic and Social Committee on Migrant Workers 84/C [1984] OJ C343/28

1989, Opinion of the European and Economic Social Committee on the Mediterranean policy of the European Community, 89/C 221/05, [1989] OJ C 221/16

1991, Own-initiative opinion on the Status of migrant workers from third countries (91/C 159/05) [1991] OJ C 159/12

1991, European Economic and Social Committee, Opinion on the status of migrant workers from third countries (91/C 339/15) [1991] OJ C 339/82

1992, Avis du Comite Économique et Social sur l'élargissement futur de la Communauté [1992] OJ C 313/40

1994, Opinion on the Communication from the Commission to the Council and the European Parliament on Immigration and Asylum Policies (94/C 393/13) [1994] OJ C 393/69

European Council Documents

Maastricht European Council, Presidency Conclusions, 16 December 1991

European Council in Copenhagen, Presidency Conclusions, 21–22 June 1993

Corfu European Council, Presidency Conclusions, 24–25 June 1994

Tampere European Council, Presidency Conclusions, 15 and 16 October 1999

European Council, Presidency Conclusions, Lisbon, 23–24 March 2000

European Council, Presidency Conclusions, Gothenburg, 15–16 June 2001, SN 200/1/01 REV 1

European Council, Presidency Conclusions, Barcelona, 15–16 March 2002, SN 100/1/02 REV 1

European Council, Presidency Conclusions, Brussels, 16–17 June 2005, 10255/1/05 REV 1

European Council, Conclusions, Brussels, 13 July 2010, EUCO 13/1/10 REV 1

European Council, The Hague Programme: strengthening freedom, security and justice in the European Union [2005] OJ C 53/1

European Council, The Stockholm programme, An open and secure Europe serving and protecting citizens [2010] OJ C 115/1

Council of the EU Documents

Council of the European Union, Press Release, 2370th Council meeting – Justice, Home Affairs and Civil Protection, Brussels, 27 and 28 September 2001, 12204/01 (Presse 334)

Council Document ST 13263 2003 ADD 1 – Projet d'exposé des motifs du Conseil 10/11/2003 Position commune arrêtée par le Conseil en vue de l'adoption d'une directive du Parlement européen et du Conseil relative au droit des citoyens de l'Union et des membres de leurs familles de circuler et de séjourner librement sur le territoire des États membres, modifiant le règlement (CEE) n° 1612/68 et abrogeant les directives 64/221/ CEE, 68/360/CEE, 72/194/CEE, 73/148/CEE, 75/34/CEE, 75/35/CEE, 90/364/CEE, 90/365/CEE and 93/96/CEE Orientations Communes Délai de consultation:14.11.20

Council of the European Union, First Euro-Med Ministerial meeting on migration (Algavre 18, 19 November 2007), Conclusions 15805/07

Joint declaration establishing a Mobility Partnership between the Kingdom of Morocco and the European Union and its Member States of 7 June 2013

Joint declaration establishing a Mobility Partnership between Tunisia and the European Union and its Member States of 3 March 2014

Joint declaration establishing a Mobility Partnership between the Hashemite Kingdom of Jordan and the European Union and its participating Member States of 9 October 2014

Council Document ST 16000 2023 INIT, Proposal for a Directive concerning the status of third-country nationals who are long-term residents (recast) – Mandate for negotiations with the Parliament, 28 November 2023

Parliament Documents

1975, Working Documents 1975–1976, Document 375/5, Report drawn up on behalf of the Committee on Cultural Affairs and Youth on the proposal from the Commission of the European Communities to the Council (Doc. 224/75) for a Directive on the education of the children of migrant workers, Rapporteur: Mrs T. Carettoni Romagnoli, PE 471.807 fin

1976, Opinion on the proposal for a Council Directive on the education of the children of migrant workers [1976] OJ C 45/6

1984, Parliament Working Documents 1983–1984, Document 1-811/83, Report drawn up on behalf of the Committee on Social Affairs and Employment on the problem of migrant workers, Rapporteur: Mrs Tove Nielsen, PE 84.870/fin

1985, Committee of Inquiry into the Rise of Fascism and Racism in Europe, Report on the findings of the inquiry – Evrigenis Report

1986, Report drawn up on behalf of the Committee on Social Affairs and Employment on the communication from the Commission of the European Communities to the Council (Doc. C2-6/85 – COM(85)48 final) on guidelines for a Community policy on migration together with a draft Council resolution, Working Documents 1985–86, Document A2-4/85

1990, Ford Glyn, Report drawn up on behalf of the Committee of Inquiry into Racism and Xenophobia on the findings of the Committee of Inquiry. Session Documents, A3-195/90, 23 July 1990

2020, Committee on Civil Liberties, Justice and Home Affairs, New avenues for legal labour migration (2020/2010((INI)) (rapporteur: Sylvie Guillaume)

2024, Final Compromise text, Directive (EU) 2024/. . . of the European Parliament and of the Council of. . .on a single application procedure for a single permit for third-country nationals to reside and work in the territory of a Member State and on a common set of rights for third-country workers legally residing in a Member State (recast), A9-0140/117

Commission Documents

COM(1988)640 final: Communication of the Commission on the Abolition of Controls of Persons at Intra-Community Borders

COM(1993)312 final: Avis de la Commission sur la demande d'adhésion de Malte à la Communauté,

COM(1993)313 final: Avis de la Commission sur la demande d'adhésion de la République Chypre à la Communauté

COM(1993)702 final: Report from the Commission on the citizenship of the Union

COM(1994)23 final: Communication from the Commission to the Council and the European Parliament, On immigration and asylum policies

COM(1994)427 final: Communication from the Commission to the Council and the European Parliament, Strengthening the Mediterranean Policy of the European Union: Establishing a Euro-Mediterranean Partnership

COM(1997)2000 final: Agenda 2000 pour une Union plus forte et plus large, Vol I and II

COM(1997)2001 final: Avis de la Commission sur la demande d'adhésion de la Hongrie à l'Union européenne

COM(1997)2002 final: Avis de la Commission sur la demande d'adhésion de la Pologne à l'Union européenne

COM(1997)2003 final: Avis de la Commission sur la demande d'adhésion de la Roumanie à l'Union européenne

COM(1997)2004 final: Avis de la Commission sur la demande d'adhésion de la Slovaquie à l'Union européenne

COM(1997)2005 final: Avis de la Commission sur la demande d'adhésion de la Lettonie à l'Union européenne,
COM(1997)2006 final: Avis de la Commission sur la demande d'adhésion de l'Estonie à l'Union européenne
COM(1997)2007 final: Avis de la Commission concernant la demande d'adhésion à l'Union européenne présentée par la Lituanie
COM(1997)2008 final: Avis de la Commission concernant la demande d'adhésion à l'Union européenne présentée par la Bulgarie,
COM(1997)2009 final: Avis de la Commission sur la demande d'adhésion de la République tchèque à l'Union européenne
COM(1997)2010 final: Avis de la Commission sur la demande d'adhésion de la Slovénie à l'Union européenne
COM(1998)459 final: Communication from the Commission, Towards an Area of Freedom, Security and Justice
COM(1999)0127 final: Report from the Commission to the Council and the European Parliament on the implementation of Directives 90/364, 90/365, and 93/96 (Right of residence)
COM(1999)69 final: Rapport de mise à jour de l'avis de la Commission sur la demande d'adhésion de Malte
COM(2000)757 final: Communication from the Commission to the Council and the European Parliament, On a Community immigration policy
COM(2001)0763 final: Communication from the Commission – Withdrawal of Commission Proposals which are no longer topical
COM(2001)264 final: Communication from the Commission, A Sustainable Europe for a Better World: A European Union Strategy for Sustainable Development, EU Sustainable Development Strategy (Commission's proposal to the Gothenburg European Council)
COM(2001)743 final: Commission working paper on the relationship between safeguarding internal security and complying with international protection obligations
COM(2002)0694 final: Communication from the Commission – Free movement of workers: achieving the full benefits and potential
COM(2002)82 final: Communication from the Commission to the European Parliament, the Council, the Economic and Social Committee and the Committee of the Regions, Towards a global partnership for sustainable development
COM(2004)178 final: Communication from the Commission to the Council and the European Parliament on the presentation of a proposal for a Directive and two proposals for recommendations on the admission of third-country nationals to carry out scientific research in the European Community
COM(2004)257 final: Avis sur la demande d'adhésion de la Croatie à l'Union européenne
COM(2005)0462 final: Communication from the Commission to the Council and the European Parliament – Outcome of the screening of legislative proposals pending before the Legislator

COM(2005)0669 final: Communication from the Commission – Policy Plan on Legal Migration

COM(2007)0780 final: Communication from the Commission to the European Parliament, the Council, the European Economic and Social Committee and the Committee of the Regions – Towards a Common Immigration Policy

COM(2010)2020 final: Communication from the Commission, EUROPE 2020 – A strategy for smart, sustainable and inclusive growth

COM(2011)0743 final: Communication from the Commission to the European Parliament, the Council, the European Economic and Social Committee and the Committee of the Region, The Global Approach to Migration and Mobility

COM(2011)292 final: Communication from the Commission to the European Parliament, the Council, the European Economic and Social Committee and the Committee of the Regions – A dialogue for migration, mobility and security with the southern Mediterranean countries

COM(2013)0837 final: Communication from the Commission to the European Parliament, the Council, the European Economic and Social Committee and the Committee of the Regions – Free Movement of EU Citizens and Their Families: Five Actions to Make a Difference

COM(2016)0184 final: Communication from the Commission to the European Parliament pursuant to Article 294(6) of the Treaty on the Functioning of the European Union concerning the Position of the Council on the adoption of a Directive of the European Parliament and of the Council on the conditions of entry and residence of third-country nationals for the purposes of research, studies, training, voluntary service, pupil exchange schemes or educational projects and au pairing

COM(2016)739 final: Communication from the Commission to the European Parliament, the Council, the European Economic and Social Committee and the Committee of the Regions, Next steps for a sustainable European future, European action for sustainability

COM(2020)274 final: Communication from the Commission to the European Parliament, the Council, the European Economic and Social Committee and the Committee of the Regions, European Skills Agenda for sustainable competitiveness, social fairness and resilience

COM(2020)609 final: Communication from the Commission to the European Parliament, the Council, the European Economic and Social Committee and the Committee of the Regions on a New Pact on Migration and Asylum

COM(2020)758 final: Communication from the Commission to the European Parliament, the Council, the European Economic and Social Committee and the Committee of the Regions, Action Plan on Integration and Inclusion 2021–2027

COM(2022)657 final: Communication from the Commission to the European Parliament, the Council, the European Economic and Social Committee and the Committee of the Regions, Attracting skills and talent to the EU

SEC(1991)1855 final: Commission Communication to the Council and the European Parliament on Immigration

SEC(1992)401 final: Communication from the Commission to the Council and the European Parliament, The future of relations between the Community and the Maghreb

SEC(2003)1293 final: Communication from the Commission to the European Parliament pursuant to the second subparagraph of Article 251 (2) of the EC Treaty concerning the common position of the Council on the adoption of a European Parliament and Council Directive on the right of citizens of the Union and their family members to move and reside freely within the territory of the Member States

SWD(2013)0138 final: Commission Staff Working Document Climate Change, Environmental Degradation, and Migration Accompanying the Document Communication from the Commission to the European Parliament, the Council, the European Economic and Social Committee and the Committee of the Regions – An EU Strategy on Adaptation to Climate Change

SWD(2019)1055 final: Commission Staff Working Document Executive Summary of the Fitness Check on EU Legislation on legal migration

SWD(2020)4000 final: Commission Staff Working Document, Delivering on the UN's Sustainable Development Goals – A comprehensive approach

Legislative Proposals

COM(1975)390 final: Proposal for a Council Directive on the Education of the Children of Migrant Workers [1975] OJ C 213/2

COM(1979)215 final: Proposal for a Council Directive on a Right of Residence for nationals of Member States in the territory of another Member State [1979] OJ C 207/14

COM(1980)358 final: Amended proposal for a Council Directive on a Right of Residence for nationals of Member States in the Territory of Another Member State OJ C 188/7

COM(1980)649 final: Amending of the proposal for a Council Directive on a Right of Residence for nationals of Member States in the Territory of Another Member State OJ C 292/3

COM(1985)292 final: Amended proposal for a Council Directive on a Right of Residence for Nationals of Member States in the Territory of Another Member State OJ C 171/8

COM(1988)815 final: Proposal for a Council Directive Amending Directive 68/360/EE on the abolition of restrictions on movement and residence within the Community for workers of Member States and their families, revised version [1989] OJ C 100/8

COM(1989)275 final: Proposal for a Council Directive on the Right of Residence [1989] OJ C 191/5

COM(1995)284 final: Amended proposal for a Council Regulation (EC) amending Regulation (EEC) No 1408/71 on the application of social security schemes to employed persons, to self-employed persons and to members of their families moving within the Community, Regulation (EEC) No 574/72 laying down the procedure for implementing Regulation (EEC) No 1408/71, Regulation (EEC) No 1247/92 amending Regulation (EEC) No 1408/71 and Regulation (EEC) No 1945/93 amending Regulation (EEC) No 1247/92

COM(1995)346 final: Proposal for a Council Directive on the right of third-country nationals to travel in the Community

COM(1997)0106 final: Amended proposal for a Council Directive on the right of third-country nationals to travel in the Community - CNS 95/0199

COM(1997)387 final: Proposal for a Council Act establishing the Convention on rules for the admission of third-country nationals to the Member States

COM(1998)0394 final: Proposal for a European Parliament and Council Directive amending Directive 68/360/EEC on the abolition of restrictions on movement and residence within the Community for workers of Member States and their families [1998] OJ C 344/12

COM(1999)0638 final: Proposal for a Council Directive on the right to family reunification

COM(2001)0257 final: Proposal for a European Parliament and Council Directive on the right of citizens of the Union and their family members to move and reside freely within the territory of the Member States [2001] OJ C 270E/150

COM(2001)0386 final: Proposal for a Council Directive on the conditions of entry and residence of third-country nationals for the purpose of paid employment and self-employed economic activities [2001] OJ C 332E/248

COM(2001)127 final: Proposal for a Council Directive concerning the status of third-country nationals who are long-term residents

COM(2002)0225 final: Amended proposal for a Council Directive on the right to family reunification

COM(2002)0548 final: Proposal for a Council Directive on the conditions of entry and residence of third country nationals for the purposes of studies, vocational training or voluntary service [2003] OJ C 45E/18

COM(2004)178 final: Proposal for a Council Directive on a specific procedure for admitting third-country nationals for purposes of scientific research

COM(2007)0637 final: Proposal for a Council Directive on the conditions of entry and residence of third-country nationals for the purposes of highly qualified employment

COM(2007)638 final: Proposal for a Council Directive on a single application procedure for a single permit for third-country nationals to reside and work in the territory of a Member State and on a common set of rights for third-country workers legally residing in a Member State

COM(2010)379 final: Proposal for a Directive of the European Parliament and of the Council on the conditions of entry and residence of third-country nationals for the purposes of seasonal employment

COM(2013)0151 final: Proposal for a Directive of the European Parliament and of the Council on the conditions of entry and residence of third-country nationals for the purposes of research, studies, pupil exchange, remunerated and unremunerated training, voluntary service and au pairing

COM(2016)0378 final: Proposal for a Directive of the European Parliament and of the Council on the conditions of entry and residence of third-country nationals for the purposes of highly skilled employment

COM(2022)650 final: Proposal for a Directive of the European Parliament and of the Council concerning the status of third-country nationals who are long-term residents (recast)

COM(2022)655 final: Proposal for a Directive of the European Parliament and of the Council on a single application procedure for a single permit for third-country nationals to reside and work in the territory of a Member State and on a common set of rights for third-country workers legally residing in a Member State (recast)

Other

Political Declaration by the Governments of the Member States on the Free Movement of Persons [1987] OJ L 169/24

Community Charter of Fundamental Social Rights of Workers adopted at the European Council in Strasbourg meeting on 8, 9 December 1989

Ad hoc Group Immigration, Resolution on the harmonization of national policies on family reunification, 1 June 1993, SN2828/1/93 WGI 1497 REV1

Report from the Ministers responsible for immigration to the European Council meeting in Maastricht on immigration and asylum policy, SN 4038/91 (WGI 930) 3 December 1991

Euro-Mediterranean Conference, 27 and 28 November 1995, Working Programme

Chris Patten, Javier Solana and Romano Prodi (2003) – Strengthening the EU's partnership with the Arab world, Paper for the attention of Franco Frattini, President of the Council, 4 December 2003 D(2003) 10318

Vienna Action Plan – Action plan of the Council and the Commission on how best to implement the provisions of the Treaty of Amsterdam on an area of freedom, security and justice [1999] OJ C 19/1

Answers given by Mr Verheugen on behalf of the Commission on 28 February 2003 to Written Question E-0113/03 by Mogens Camre (UEN) to the Commission (28 January 2003) with the subject: Migrant workers from the new Member States [2004] OJ CE 88/587

Commission, Directorate General for Migration and Home Affairs, Synthesis Report, Analysis of the responses to the public consultation on the future of legal migration, January 2021

International Law Material

Treaties

General Agreement on Trade in Services, 15 April 1994, Marrakesh Agreement Establishing the World Trade Organization, Annex 1B, 1869 U.N.T.S. 183, 33 I.L.M. 1167

Convention Relating to the Status of Refugees, 28 July 1951, UNTS, vol. 189, p. 137

Protocol Relating to the Status of Refugees, 31 January 1967, UNTS, vol. 606, p. 267

Vienna Convention on the Law of Treaties of 23 May 1969, UNTS, vol. 1155, p. 331

Soft Law Documents

UN General Assembly, Process of preparation of the Environmental Perspective to the Year 2000 and Beyond, 19 December 1983, A/RES/38/161

UN General Assembly 42/187 – Report of the WCED, A/RES/42/187, 11 December 1987

Rio Declaration on Environment and Development, 13 June 1992, adopted by the UNCED at Rio de Janeiro, UN Doc. A/CONF. 151/26, Vol.1, August 1992, ILM 874

Special Session of the UN General Assembly to Review and Appraise the Implementation of Agenda 21, 23–27 June 1997, New York

UN General Assembly, Transforming our world: The 2030 Agenda for Sustainable Development, 21 October 2015, A/RES/70/1

UN General Assembly, Compact for Safe, Orderly and Regular Migration, 19 December 2018, A/RES/73/195.

TABLE OF ARCHIVAL MATERIAL

Historical Archives of the EU

HAEU, CEUE _SEGE-SEC(1991)0803, Commission of the European Communities, Secretariat General, Communication from the President, Mr Bangemann and Mrs Papandreou in agreement with Mr Andriessen, Mr Marin and Mr Matutes, Communication to the Commission, Immigration, SEC(91)803

HAEU, CEUE_SEGE-SEC(1991)0803, Commission of the European Communities, Secretariat General, Communication from the President, Mr Bangemann and Mrs Papandreou in agreement with Mr Andriessen, Mr Marin and Mr Matutes, Communication to the Commission, Immigration, SEC(91)803 final

HAEU, CM2/1977-634.3, The Council, Note, Subject: Proposal for a Council Directive on the education of the children of migrant workers, Outcome of the discussions of the Working Party on Social Questions, Brussels, 31 March 1976, 377/76 (SOC 97)

HAEU, CM2/1977-634.4, The Council, Note, Subject: Proposal for a Council Directive on the education of the children of migrant workers, Report from the Working Party on Social Questions to the Permanent Representatives Committee, Brussels, 26 April 1976, R/987/76 (SOC 116) Annex – Attitude of the Italian delegation

HAEU, CM2/1977-634.5, The Council, Note, Subject: Proposal for a Council Directive on the education of the children of migrant workers, Report from the Working Party on Social Questions to the Permanent Representatives Committee, Brussels, 18 May 1976, R/1230/76 (SOC 131) B. Statement by the Commission Representative

HAEU, CM2/1977-634.5, The Council, Note, Subject: Proposal for a Council Directive on the education of the children of migrant workers, Report from the Working Party on Social Questions to the Permanent Representatives Committee, Brussels, 18 May 1976, R/1230/76 (SOC 131) C. Delegations' Position

HAEU, CM2/1977-634.7, European Communities, The Council, Note, Subject: Proposal for a Council Directive on the education of the children of migrant workers, Outcome of the meeting of the Working Party on Social Questions, Brussels, 9 November 1976, 1221/76 (SOC 253)

HAEU, CM2/1977-634.7, The Council, Note, Subject: Proposal for a Council Directive on the education of the children of migrant workers, Outcome of the discussions of the Permanent Representatives Committee, Brussels, 24 June 1976, R/1555/76 (SOC 167)

HAEU, CM2/1988-00024/001, 1237ème session du Conseil (marché intérieur), Bruxelles, 03.05.1988, DROIT DE SEJOUR, 5932/88 (Presse 53) Communication a la presse

HAEU, CM2/1989-00062/001, 1352ème session du Conseil (marché intérieur), Luxembourg, 10.10.1989, Projet de Procès-verbal, 9170/89 restreint

HAEU, DORIE-204, Annexe 2 à l'avis de la section des relations extérieures, de la politique commerciale et du développement du Comite économique et social sur 'L' élargissement de l'Union européenne' 24 Oct 1997: Rapporteur M Masucci CES 856/97 fin annexe 2 I-RD/CH/ic

HAEU, DORIE-205, Rapport sur la communication de la Commission 'Agenda 2000 - Pour une Union plus forte et plus large' (COM(97)2000 – C4-0371/97) A4-0368/97/ PARTIE C, Avis des commissions parlementaires et lettres des délégations du Parlement européen aux commissions parlementaires mixtes PE 224.339/Partie C/def, Avis (article 147 du règlement) à l'intention de la commission des affaires étrangères, de la sécurité et de la politique de défense, Rapporteurs: M. Oostlander et M Baron Crespo, Commission de l'emploi et des affaire sociales, Rapporteur pour avis: M Harald Ettl

HAEU, DORIE-205, Rapport sur la communication de la Commission 'Agenda 2000 - Pour une Union plus forte et plus large' (COM(97)2000 - C4-0371/97) A4-0368/97/ PARTIE C, Avis des commissions parlementaires et lettres des délégations du Parlement Européen aux commissions parlementaires mixtes PE 224.339/Partie C/def, Avis (article 147 du règlement) à l'intention de la commission des affaires étrangères, de la sécurité et de la politique de défense, Rapporteurs: M. Oostlander et M Baron Crespo, Commission de libertés publiques et des affaires intérieures, Rapporteur pour avis: M Maria Berger

HAEU, DORIE-207, Rapport sur la communication de la Commission 'Agenda 2000' - Première partie. Chapitre II COM(97)2000 C4-0371/97, A4-0210/98, PE 225.091/ def, Avis (article 147 du règlement) à l'intention de la commission de la politique régionale, commission de l' emploi et des affaires sociales, Rapporteur pour avis: M Hans Lindqvist, Point 9 et Avis (article 147 du règlement) à l'intention de la commission de la politique régionale, commission de la pèche, Rapporteur pour avis: M Pat the Cope Gallagher

HAEU, EM-87, Le Conseil, Association CEE-Turquie, Projet de Rapport du Comité 'Associations Pays Tiers' au Comité des Représentants Permanents (Document de travail établi par le Secrétariat et destiné à être examiné au cours de la réunion du 5 juillet 1968), Objet: Passage de la phase préparatoire à la phase transitoire de l'Accord d' Association avec la Turquie, S/595/68 (NT 24)

HAEU, EM-87, Secrétariat General, Rapport préliminaire de la Commission au Conseil au sujet du passage de la phase préparatoire à la phase transitoire de l'Accord d'Association avec la Turquie SEC(68)1386

HAEU, EM-88, Commission Parlementaire Mixte CEE-Turquie, Recommandation n° 2 sur le passage à la phase transitoire de l'association

HAEU, EM-89, Direction Général des Relations Extérieures, Bruxelles, 26.02.1969 10391, Note à l'attention de Monsieur Martino, Objet: Négociations avec la Turquie en vue du passage à la phase transitoire de l'Accord d'Ankara, session du conseil d'Association du 25 Février 1969

HAEU, EM-89, Le Conseil d'Association, Rapport du Comité d'Association au Conseil d'Association CEE-TR 25/69

HAEU, EM-89, Le Conseil d'Association, Sommaire des conclusions de la 19eme Réunion du Comité d'association CEE-Turquie qui s'est tenue à Bruxelles le mardi 11 mars 1969 CEE-TR 9/69 19

HAEU, EM-89, Le Conseil, Association CEE-Turquie, Aide-Mémoire du Secrétariat, Objet: Passage de la phase préparatoire à la phase transitoire de l'Accord d'Association avec la Turquie, Régime à prévoir en ce qui concerne le main d'œuvre, S/30/69 (NT 2)

HAEU, EM-89, Secrétariat Général, Projet de Communication au Conseil concernant l'état des négociations avec la Turquie sur le passage à la phase transitoire de l'Accord d'Ankara (présente par M.Martino) SEC(69)1601

HAEU, EM-91, Exposé de M Edoardo Martino, Membre de la Commission des Communautés européennes, Annex IV, Commission Parlementaire Mixte CEE-Turquie, Procès-Verbal de la VIIIe Session, du 27 au 30 Janvier 1970, Munich PE 24.098

HAEU, EM-130, Communication de la Commission au Conseil, Relations de la CEE avec les pays du Maghreb G(66)524 final

HAEU, EN-2228, Study group on enlargement formed within Directorate F of the Commission and produced a report called 'A strategy for enlargement', November 1991

HAEU, GJLA-180, Union Européenne, Le Conseil, Rapport du Groupe "Élargissement" en date du 2 Octobre 1997 au COREPER, Objet: Élargissement, Examen des avis de la Commission sur les demandes d'adhésion à l'Union présentées par les pays associés d'Europe centrale et orientale, 11125/97 LIMITE ELARG 18

HAEU, GJLA-204, European Commission, Directorate General Enlargement, Argumentaire on the Transitional Arrangement for the free movement of persons, For use in the candidate countries, Brussels, 31 May 2001, ELARG/FC D(2001)

HAEU, GJLA-204, Commission Information note by M Verheugen, The free movement of persons for the pursuit of economic activity in the context of Enlargement, 12 April 2000, SEC(2000)663/3, Section 3 Findings of academic research on enlargement; Commission, Information note on the Free Movement of Workers in the context of Enlargement, 6 March 2001

HAEU, GJLA-206, European Commission, Secretary General, The free movement of persons for the pursuit of economic activity in the context of Enlargement, Information note by M Verheugen addressed to the Members of the Commission, Directors Generals and Heads of service, 12 April 2000, O/139/2000 SEC(2000)663/3

HAEU, GJLA-206, Final version of Communication from Mr Verheugen in Agreement with Mrs Diamantopoulou, Essential elements for the draft Common Positions concerning 'Freedom of movement of persons', version of 6 April 2001 sent to the Secretary General for the college on 18.04.01

HAEU, GJLA-246, Commission of the European Communities, Directorate General External Relations, Task force Enlargissement, Enlargement and the Community's Relations with its Mediterranean Neighbours, Brussels 2 March 1992, RDM/m

HAEU, GJLA-246, Commission of the European Communities, Directorate General External Relations, Director General Note for the attention of MM Prat, Cadieux, Abbott, Avery, Benavides, Nuttall, Coher, Rhein, DG I, Burghardt, Secr. Gen, Brussels 05.03.1992, 003389

Centre virtuel de la connaissance sur l'Europe (CVCE)

1956, Note du ministère de la France d'Outre-mer sur l'Union française et le Marché commun (Paris, 3 mai 1956) and Note de Léon Pignon sur la France d'Outre-mer et le marché commun (Paris, 15 mai 1956) Archives Nationales d'Outre-Mer, Aix-en-Provence

1962, Speech by Hugh Gaitskell against UK Membership of the Common Market (3 October 1962), Britain and the Common Market, Texts of speeches made at the 1962 Labour Party Conference by the Rt. Hon Hugh Gaitskell M.P. and the Rt. Hon. George Brown M.P. together with the policy statement accepted by Conference (Labor Party 1962)

1968, Communication de la Commission au Conseil, Problèmes de renouvellement de la Convention de Yaoundé, COM(68)230

1974, Communique of European Summit in Paris on 9/10 December 1974

1993, Communication from the Commission, Growth, Competitiveness, and Employment. The challenges and ways forward into the 21st century, COM(93) 700 final.

1994, Communication de la Commission au Conseil, au-delà des accords européens: Préparation des pays d'Europe centrale et orientale à l'adhésion, COM(94)320 final

Archive of European Integration, University of Pittsburgh

1956, Communauté européenne du Charbon et de l'Acier, Obstacles à la mobilité des travailleurs et problèmes sociaux de réadaptation

1957, Bertrand M.A., Rapport complémentaire fait au nom de la Commission des Affaires sociales sur la migration et la libre circulation des travailleurs dans la Communauté, Exercice 1957–1958 Première session extraordinaire, Document 11

1957, Bertrand M.A., Rapport fait au nom de la Commission des affaires sociales sur la migration et la libre circulation des travailleurs dans la Communauté, Exercice 1957–1958, Première session extraordinaire, Document 5

1959, European Economic Community, Bulletin de La Communauté économique européenne 2, Professor Giuseppe Petrilli, Member of the Commission, Chairman of the Social Affairs Group, The Social Policy of the Commission

1960, Communauté économique européenne, Commission, Synthèse des rapports établis en 1960 sur la situation actuelle du service social des travailleurs migrants dans les six pays membres de la C.E.E.

1960, Commission of the European Economic Community, Bulletin of the European Economic Community 10

1960, Commission of the European Economic Community, Bulletin of the European Economic Community 5

1960, Commission of the European Economic Community, Bulletin of the European Economic Community 3

1960, Commission of the European Economic Community, Bulletin of the European Economic Community 10

1960, Commission of the European Economic Community, Bulletin of the European Economic Community 5

1960, Commission of the European Economic Community, Bulletin of the European Economic Community 4

1961, European Community Information Service, Press Notice, Common Market takes initial step toward free mobility for workers, 15 June 1961

1961, Commission of the European Economic Community, Bulletin of the European Economic Community 6, Lionello Levi Sandri, The free movement of workers in the countries of the European Economic Community

1964, Commission of the European Economic Community, Bulletin of the European Economic Community 9/10, Introduction to the survey of social developments in the Community in 1963 (Included in the Seventh General Report on the activities of the Community, in accordance with Article 122 of the Treaty)

1965, Communauté économique européenne, Commission, Libre circulation et migrations des travailleurs dans la Communauté, Bilan annuel des activités de compensation et de placement au sein de la Communauté, art. 25 §4 du règlement no 15/61, art. 36§4 du règlement no 38/64), SEC(65)2240 final

1965, Commission of the European Economic Community, Bulletin of the European Economic Community 3

1965, Commission of the European Economic Community, Bulletin of the European Economic Community 4

1966, Communauté économique européenne, Commission, La libre circulation de la main-d'oeuvre et les marches du travail dans la CEE

1966, Communauté économique européenne, Commission, La libre circulation de la main-d'œuvre et les marches du travail dans la CEE, Rapport établi en application des dispositions des articles 29 et 36 du règlement n° 38/64 relatif à la libre circulation des travailleurs

1966, Commission of the European Economic Community, Bulletin of the European Economic Community 8, Address introducing the Ninth General Report on the activities of the Community

1967, Communauté économique européenne, Commission, La libre circulation de la main-d'oeuvre et les marches du travail dans la CEE, Rapport 1967

1967, Communauté économique européenne, Commission, La libre circulation de la main-d'œuvre et les marches du travail dans la CEE, Rapport établi en application des dispositions des articles 29 et 36 du règlement n° 38/64 relatif à la libre circulation des travailleurs à l 'intérieur de la CEE

1967, Programme de politique économique à moyen terme (1966–1970) [1967] OJ 79/151

1968, Communauté économique européenne, Commission, La libre circulation de la main-d'oeuvre et les marches du travail dans la CEE. Rapport 1968

1968, Communauté économique européenne, Commission, La libre circulation de la main-d'œuvre et les marches du travail dans la CEE, Rapport établi en application des dispositions des articles 29 et 36 du règlement n° 38/64 relatif à la libre circulation des travailleurs à l 'intérieur de la CEE

1968, Commission of the European Communities (1968), Complete freedom of movement for workers now a reality. Information Memo P-50/68, July 1968

1969, Commission of the European Communities, Bulletin of the European Communities 6

1969, Commission of the European Communities, Bulletin of the European Communities 6

1969, Commission of the European Communities, Bulletin of the European Communities 6

1970, Commission of the European Communities, Bulletin of the European Communities 3

1971, Communication de la Commission au Conseil, Communication, Contenu possible d'Accords éventuels avec les États de l'AELE non candidats à l'adhésion, COM (71)701

1971, Vredeling H (1971), Migrants and the E.E.C, Full Text and Summary of a Speech by the Vice-President of the Commission of the E.C. for the Conference of the National Council of Social Services, London, 27 March 1971

1972, Commission of the European Communities, The relation between the Community and the Mediterranean Countries, Information Note P-48, October 1972

1974, Commission Communication, Action Programme in Favour of Migrant Workers and Their Families, COM(74)2250 final

1976, Commission of the European Communities, Cooperation Agreements between the European Community, Algeria, Morocco and Tunisia, Information Note P-14, March 1976

1976, Bulletin of the European Communities, Supplement 1/76, Report by Mr. Leo Tindemans, Prime Minister of Belgium, to the European Council

1977, Commission of the European Communities, Information Directorate-General, Information, Cooperation and Development, EEC/Tunisia Cooperation Agreement, 162/77 E

1978, Commission of the European Communities, Information Directorate-General, Information, Cooperation-Development, the European Community and the Arab World, 169/78

1978, Commission of the European Communities, General Considerations on the Problems of Enlargement, COM(78)120 final

1978, Commission of the European Communities, Communication to the Council, Economic and Sectoral Aspects, Commission Analysis supplementing its views on enlargement, COM(78)200 final

1978, Commission of the European Communities, Bulletin of the European Communities, Supplement 5/1978, Commission Opinion on Portugal's application for accession

1979, Commission Communication, Consultation on Migration Policies vis-à-vis Third Countries, COM(79)115 final

1980, Commission of the European Communities, Spokesman's Group and Directorate General for Information, Europe Information Development, EEC–Morocco Cooperation Agreement, February 1980

1982, Commission of the European Communities, Communication to the Council, On a Mediterranean policy for the enlarged Community, COM(82)353 final

1984, Commission of the European Communities, Directorate General for Information, Europe South-Dialogue, The Mediterranean Policy, 1984

1985, Bulletin of the European Communities, Supplement 9/85, Commission Communication transmitted to the Council on March 1985, Guidelines for a Community Policy on Migration, COM(85)48

1989, Bulletin of the European Communities, Supplement 1/89, Address by Jacques Delors to the European Parliament on 17 January 1989

1990, Commission Communication, Association Agreements with the Countries of Central and Eastern Europe – a general outline, COM(90)398 final

1990, Communication from the Commission to the Council and the Parliament, Association Agreements with the Countries of Central and Eastern Europe – a general outline, COM(90)398 final

1990, Commission of the European Communities, Policies on Immigration and the Social Integration of Migrants in the European Community, Experts' report drawn up on behalf of the Commission of the European Communities, SEC(90)1813 final

1991, Commission of the European Communities, Directorate General for Information, Europe Information Development, The countries of the Greater Arab and Maghreb and the European Community. DE 68, January 1991

1991, Commission of the European Communities, Directorate General, Employment, Industrial Relations and Social Affairs, Unit: Freedom of movement, migration policy, Immigration Policies in the Member States: Between the need for Control and the Desire for Integration, Working Document, Summary Report of the information network in migration from non-EC Countries (RIMET) year of reference 1991, V/1020/92

1992, Bulletin of the European Communities, Supplement 4/92, The Challenge of Enlargement, Commission Opinion on Austria's application for membership, Document drawn up on the basis of SEC(91)1590 final

1997, Second report from the Commission on citizenship of the Union [1994–1996], COM(97)230 final

Jean Monnet Archives

Mémorandum du comité Verret sur la participation des PTOM au Marché commun (Paris, 5 octobre 1956), Fondation Jean Monnet pour l'Europe, Lausanne, Archives Jean Monnet. Fonds ARM. 16/9/2

ABBREVIATIONS

ACP	African, Caribbean and Pacific Group of States
AEI	Archive of European Integration
AFSJ	Area of Freedom, Security and Justice
AG	Advocate General
CEAS	Common European Asylum System
CEECs	Central and Eastern European Countries
CJEU	Court of Justice of the European Union
CMLRev	Common Market Law Review
ColumJEurL	Columbia Journal of European Law
COREPER	Committee of Permanent Representatives
CVCE	Centre virtuel de la connaissance sur l'Europe
DukeJComp&IntlL	Duke Journal for Comparative and International Law
EA	Europe Agreement
EC	European Community
ECHR	European Convention on Human Rights
ECSC	European Coal and Steel Community
ECtHR	European Court of Human Rights
EEA	European Economic Area
EEC	European Economic Community
EESC	European Economic and Social Committee
EFTA	European Free Trade Association
EJIL	European Journal of International Law
ELJ	European Law Journal
ELR	European Law Review
ERT	Europarättslig Tidskrift
EU	European Union
HAEU	Historical Archives of the European Union
IJRL	International Journal of Refugee Law
JCMS	Journal of Common Market Studies
LIEI	Legal Issues of Economic Integration
OJ	Official Journal
SAA	Stabilisation and Association Agreement

SDG	Sustainable Development Goal
TCN	third country national
TEU	Treaty on European Union
TFEU	Treaty on the Functioning of the European Union
UN	United Nations
UNTS	United Nations Treaty Series
VCLT	Vienna Convention on the Law of the Treaties

1

Introduction

1.1 Scope

Sustainable migration is the new objective of the European Union (EU) migration policy. But what does this mean in terms of legal design? What instruments should be put in place to achieve it? And most importantly, what does it imply for migrants' rights? These were the questions that came to my mind upon the discovery that almost every EU migration policy document issued from 2015 onwards had the professed objective of shaping a 'fair, efficient, and sustainable' migration at EU level.[1]

As an EU law scholar, I first turned to the Treaties to see if primary law could inform the concept of an EU sustainable migration. I discovered that sustainable development can be found as an objective of the EU internal market under Article 3(3) Treaty on European Union (TEU); as an objective of the Union in its external action under Articles 3(5), 21(2)(d) and (f) TEU; and finally, that Article 11 Treaty on the Functioning of the European Union (TFEU) and Article 37 of the Charter of Fundamental Rights (CFR) demand the integration of environmental requirements in the EU policies in order to promote sustainable development. Unable to understand how this general framing, with more emphasis on environmental protection – an emphasis which is starkly absent from EU migration law and policy documents – could inform sustainable migration, I steered my investigation towards sustainability in law and scholarship, to understand if the concept has normative premises that could have implications for the rights of migrants under EU law.

As the reader will discover in Section 1.3, sustainability is a contested concept, whose premise, short history, and understanding can have very diverse implications for law and policy in general. What is not contested is that sustainability has three interdependent pillars – economic, social,

[1] The objective was confirmed in the New Pact on Migration and Asylum, COM(2020) 609 final.

and environmental – and that it entails a balancing between the pillars with a view to the long-term preservation of the whole, and under considerations of intergenerational and intra-generational justice. Subsequently, I turned to non-legal scholarship dealing specifically with sustainable migration to examine if extra-legal considerations could inform sustainable migration.

By that point, it had become clear to me that the concept of sustainable migration has little or no precedent. It implies the balancing of economic, social, and environmental considerations in the way the migration phenomenon unravels. How this balancing should take place; how the different interests of migrants, host states, and states of origin should be considered; and what kind of legal structures should operationalize it, is unclear. What is more, it also became apparent that such balancing has a very different meaning and takes into account very different parameters whether applied at the national, supranational, or global level. Therefore, as I have argued elsewhere, the recent branding of EU migration policy in the apparel of sustainability should be understood as an attempt to unite Member States behind a common slogan that sounds appealing, at times of extreme disagreement on the instruments and principles that should guide EU migration law.[2]

In attempt to go further than diagnosing the political function sustainable migration serves, and to imagine the potential implication of such an objective for EU migration law, I turned to EU legal history.[3] Through a critical historical study of different facets of EU migration law, this book traces the existence of economic and social sustainability in EU migration law long before sustainable migration was articulated as a goal for this area. Ultimately, I suggest that sustainable migration is not far from the legal framework currently in place for EU migrants. Pursuing sustainable migration in the Area of Freedom, Security and Justice (AFSJ) would mean reproducing the structures of economic exclusion that exist in free movement while attributing effective mobility rights to third country nationals (TCNs) and extending their social rights. Conceptualizing EU sustainable migration in this way would not do away with the exclusion

[2] See Alezini Loxa, 'Den Nya Migrations- och Asylpakten och Löftet om en Hållbar EU-Migration' [2022] ERT 175 on the New Pact; Alezini Loxa, 'An EU Sustainable Migration: Institutional Discourse and Migration Politics' (2024) JCMS on EU migration policy after 2015.

[3] On the importance of legal history in material areas of EU law, see Morten Rasmussen, 'Towards a Legal History of European Law' (2021) 6 European Papers – A Journal on Law and Integration 923.

of vulnerable migrants, which is after all attributed to the inherent limitations of a legal order structured around the objectives of growth and progress. It would, however, offer more extensive protection to migrants who contribute equally to the EU project of growth, thereby guaranteeing more socially sustainable societies.

After this short overview of the problem which inspired this research, Section 1.2 develops the argument guiding the development of the book. Section 1.3 presents the indeterminacy of sustainable migration and highlights the impossibility of using the term as a basis for EU legal imagination without further research. Section 1.4 argues for the necessity of addressing the problem by virtue of the critical legal historical study undertaken; it presents the material and the boundaries of the investigation. Finally, Section 1.5 outlines the structure of the book, its significance, and objectives.

1.2 Premises of the Argument

Taking the concept of an EU sustainable migration as the starting point of the analysis, a preliminary question to ask would be: migration that is sustainable for whom? The answer could vary: migration that is sustainable for the host states, for the states of origin, for the migrants involved, for the host communities, for the EU as a whole, for the planet, or for all of the above. Considering the diverse EU policy plans connected to sustainable migration, all these would be equally valid answers; indeed, each would frame a different investigation path. At the same time, not all these paths could and should be approached by means of legal research, as sustainable migration can be connected to different political approaches to growth and the role of human movement in it.[4] This project focuses on the EU legal order itself. Consequently, it will investigate what the past can tell us about the attribution of rights to migrants in

[4] On critical views, see Jane Briant Carant, 'Unheard Voices: A Critical Discourse Analysis of the Millennium Development Goals' Evolution into the Sustainable Development Goals' (2017) 38 Third World Quarterly 16; On the issues raised for human rights law by moving migration in the sustainable development discourse, see Elspeth Guild, 'The UN Global Compact for Safe, Orderly and Regular Migration: To What Extent Are Human Rights and Sustainable Development Mutually Compatible in the Field of Migration?' (2020) 16 International Journal of Law in Context 239; On a systematization of the different trade-offs involved in sustainable migration, see Judith Janker and Susan Thieme, 'Migration and Justice in the Era of Sustainable Development Goals: A Conceptual Framework' (2021) 16 Sustainability Science 1423.

a way that is sustainable for the EU legal order and that allows the maintenance of a 'common legal space that advances common aims under common values'.[5]

Turning to the Treaty text as a starting point of the investigation, we see that sustainability appears in primary law under Article 3(3) TEU. In this article the sustainable development of Europe appears an overarching objective of the internal market, and it is based on an interdependence of economic growth, social progress, and environmental protection. Article 3(3) TEU incorporates all three pillars of sustainability (economic, social, and environmental) and turns them into integral parts of the EU legal system. The inclusion of sustainability in EU primary law as an overarching objective which incorporates economic, social, and environmental considerations is recent. And while environmental considerations were first introduced with the Maastricht Treaty, the parallel pursuit of economic growth and social progress has formed part of the EU legal system from its inception.

Specifically, Article 2 of the Treaty of Rome referred to the aims of a harmonious development of economic activities, a continuous and balanced expansion, and an accelerated raising of the standard of living, among the objectives of the common market. In the Maastricht Treaty, Article 2 referred to harmonious and balanced development of economic activities, a high level of employment and of social protection, and the raising of the standard of living and quality of life. Under the Maastricht Treaty, these aims were to be accomplished not only through the internal market but also through the policies to be adopted on movement of persons in the internal market under Article 3(d) TEU. The Amsterdam Treaty changed the wording of Article 2 into harmonious, balanced, and sustainable development of economic activities next to the social objectives included in the Maastricht Treaty. Moreover, in the Amsterdam Treaty, these objectives were to be achieved not only through the internal market but also through measures on the entry and movement of persons in the context of the newly established AFSJ.

An overview of the evolution of the Treaties points to the persistence of economic and social objectives in primary law. Essentially the economic and social pillars of sustainability have been constantly reflected in

[5] Neil Walker, 'Legal and Constitutional Theory of the European Union' in Paul Craig and Gráinne de Búrca (eds), *The Evolution of EU Law* (Oxford University Press 2021) 111; Armin von Bogdandy, 'European Law Beyond "Ever Closer Union" Repositioning the Concept, Its Thrust and the ECJ's Comparative Methodology' (2016) 22 ELJ 519, 520.

EU primary law through these objectives. The term 'objectives' should be understood as the imperatives behind the adoption of EU secondary law. Secondary law is adopted as means to achieve the objectives expressed in primary law. Thus, as I argue in this book, to understand the potential legal implications of an EU sustainable migration for the rights of migrants, it is essential to investigate its history, that is, to investigate how economic, environmental, and social objectives have to this day been considered behind the attribution of rights to migrants under EU law. A challenge of this investigation is that environmental aspects have never been considered in EU migration law.[6] A single Commission Staff Working Document issued in 2013 suggested that environmental aspects should be taken into account in the planning of EU migration policy; however, the Commission held that there was not enough evidence at the time to evaluate how such migration could affect flows in the EU.[7] Therefore, due to lack of material, it is impossible to conduct a historical study on this aspect of an EU sustainable migration. In this sense, there can be no history of what has not existed.

As a result, my investigation into the past will be restricted to economic and social objectives, for these are the two pillars of sustainability that predate the appearance of the novel concept of sustainable migration, by being EU primary law objectives from the establishment of this legal order. In this, they must have affected how EU law creates rights for migrants. Investigating the way economic and social objectives have shaped EU migration law can point to the inherent limits and, perhaps, to the potentials of an EU sustainable migration for the rights of migrants. In light of the above, the historical investigation undertaken in this book traces the ways in which the economic and social pillars of sustainability, as historically conveyed in the EU primary law objectives of economic growth and social progress, have shaped the rights of migrants under EU law. Specifically, I investigate how the economic and social objectives of the EU legal order, as specific manifestations of the economic and social pillar of sustainability in EU law, have shaped a

[6] Unlike migration law scholarship; Matthew Scott, *Climate Change, Disasters, and the Refugee Convention* (Cambridge University Press 2020); Simon Behrman and Avidan Kent (eds), *Climate Refugees: Global, Local and Critical Approaches* (Cambridge University Press 2022).

[7] Commission Staff Working Document, "Climate Change, Environmental Degradation, and Migration Accompanying the Communication, An EU Strategy on Adaptation to Climate Change," SWD(2013)0138 final. See also Fitness Check on EU Legislation on legal migration, SWD(2019)1055 final, Part 2/2 149.

legal area where the national of a state becomes the subject of EU law rights by virtue of their cross-border movement and settlement (temporary or permanent) in a Member State. To explore how the parallel pursuit of growth and progress has affected the attribution, limitation, and extent of rights migrants enjoy under EU law, I focus more closely on law-making and adjudication at EU level.

The investigation of the role played by economic and social considerations entails exploring the factual elements examined by EU institutions when adopting a legal instrument or interpreting EU law. Economic considerations refer to factors related to the economy of the Member States more broadly, including, for example, labour market conditions, recession, trade. Social considerations refer to factors related to human life and society including, for example, human rights, social cohesion, education, social welfare. These considerations are taken into account in the negotiation and adoption of secondary legislation in order to steer the development of EU law in line with primary law objectives. In the interpretation of EU law by the Court of Justice of the EU, these considerations are taken into account in order to ensure that the effects of a decision will be aligned with primary law objectives. The examination of various legal instruments and case law in view of the social and economic purpose migrants' rights serve for the development of the EU legal order highlights the centrality of the economic and social pillars of sustainability in the historical evolution of EU migration law. Before going into the investigation, Section 1.3 will demonstrate why the knowledge that already exists on sustainability is not sufficient for understanding the legal implications of an EU sustainable migration.

1.3 The Indeterminacy of EU Sustainable Migration

According to the dictionary definition, sustainability means 'the quality of being able to continue over a period of time'.[8] A literal understanding of sustainability hints at the qualities of maintenance or continuity that are embedded in any application or interpretation of sustainability. However, this literal meaning is of little help in understanding the legal implications of the objective of shaping an EU sustainable migration. This is especially so, considering the many sectors that have been linked to sustainability and the many nouns that have followed the adjective

[8] See *Cambridge Dictionary* https://dictionary.cambridge.org/dictionary/english/sustainability.

'sustainable' from the 1970s onwards. To better tease out the problem we are up against, the following sections provide an overview of the concept of sustainability (Section 1.3.1), its appearance in EU law, policy, and scholarship (Section 1.3.2) as well as its recent connection to migration (Section 1.3.3).

1.3.1 Sustainability: An Overview

While the first recorded use of the term sustainability dates to the Enlightenment period, sustainability became popularized in the 1970s as a central part of environmental ethics, which at that time emerged as a distinct philosophical discipline.[9] The emergence of the concept was linked to concerns over the finite nature of planetary resources and the danger posed by human activities to the preservation of the environment.[10] Through a series of UN initiatives, sustainable development was proposed as a form of development better tailored to addressing the risks faced by humanity at the time.[11] By now sustainable development or sustainability has evolved into a concept of immense significance in international law and governance.[12] While there are scholars who distinguish between the two concepts, the distinction is

[9] Hans Carl von Carlowitz, *Sylvicultura Oeconomica, Oder Haußwirthliche Nachricht Und Naturmäßige Anweisung Zur Wilden Baum Zucht* (Leipzig 1713); Margaret Robertson, *Sustainability Principles and Practice* (3rd ed., Routledge 2021) 3; Marc Brightman and Jerome Lewis (eds), *The Anthropology of Sustainability: Beyond Development and Progress* (Palgrave Macmillan 2017) 3; Andrew Brennan and Lo YS Norva, 'Environmental Ethics' in Edward N Zalta and Uri Nodelman (eds), *The Stanford Encyclopedia of Philosophy* (Spring 2023 edition) https://plato.stanford.edu/archives/spr2023/entries/ethics-environmental/.

[10] Donella Meadows and others, *The Limits to Growth: A Report for the Club of Rome's Project on the Predicament of the Mankind* (Universe Books 1972).

[11] The central material shaping the contours of the concept in international law is the Brundtland Report, World Commission on Environment and Development, *Our Common Future* (Oxford University Press 1987) adopted by the United Nations General Assembly 42/187 – Report of the WCED, A/RES/42/187, 11 December 1987; Rio Declaration on Environment and Development, 13 June 1992, adopted by the UNCED at Rio de Janeiro, UN Doc A/CONF. 151/26, Vol.1, August 1992, ILM 874; Millennium Development Goals, Special Session of the UN General Assembly to Review and Appraise the Implementation of Agenda 21, 23–27 June 1997, New York; Transforming Our World: The 2030 Agenda for Sustainable Development, 21 October 2015, A/RES/70/1.

[12] See Margherita Pieraccini and Tonia Novitz, 'Sustainability and Law: A Historical and Theoretical Overview' in Margherita Pieraccini and Tonia Novitz (eds), *Legal Perspectives on Sustainability* (Bristol University Press 2020).

not uniform or consistent.[13] The convergence of these terms also appears in EU policy documents. For this reason, this work also addresses sustainability and sustainable development as entailing the same demands and considerations.

In general, it is widely accepted that sustainability is a three-pillar concept involving considerations related to the economy, the environment, and the society. The relationship among the three pillars, however, is rather less clear.[14] Initially the focus was on sustainable development or sustainability as an environmental concept. The evolution of the policy discourse set the basis for theoretical conceptions of sustainability as a more general concept which encompasses three interrelated pillars, which however can be 'independent dimensions and equally important goals in themselves'.[15] Much like sustainable development, there is no uniform understanding of the elements of social sustainability, which could be of relevance to migration.[16] Nevertheless, all the relevant works engage with questions of equity and social justice.[17] As Jacobs mentioned already in the 1990s, 'inequitable societies are prone to social conflict, they are therefore likely to be socially unsustainable'.[18]

International law scholarship has provided numerous contributions on the notion of sustainability, the different degrees of normativity under which the concept appears, as well as its potential to become a general

[13] See Andrew Dobson, *Justice and the Environment, Conceptions of Environmental Sustainability and Dimensions of Social Justice* (Oxford University Press 1998), who sees sustainable development as a form of theory of environmental sustainability; Klaus Bosselman, *The Principle of Sustainability: Transforming Law and Governance* (Ashgate 2008), addressing sustainability as an ethical principle predating sustainable development.

[14] Michael Jacobs, 'Sustainable Development as a Contested Concept' in Andrew Dobson (ed), *Fairness and Futurity: Essays on Environmental Sustainability and Social Justice* (Oxford University Press 1999).

[15] Henrik Åhman, 'Social Sustainability – Society at the Intersection of Development and Maintenance' (2013) 18 Local Environment 1153, 1155; See Tonia Novitz, 'Social Sustainability, Labour and Trade: Forging Connections' in Margherita Pieraccini and Tonia Novitz (eds), *Legal Perspectives on Sustainability* (Bristol University Press 2020) on different connections forged between the pillars of sustainability.

[16] Åhman (n 15); Beate Littig and Erich Griessler, 'Social Sustainability: A Catchword between Political Pragmatism and Social Theory' (2005) 8 International Journal of Sustainable Development 65; Jesse F Dillard, Veronica Dujon and Mary C King (eds), *Understanding the Social Dimension of Sustainability* (Routledge 2009).

[17] Andrew Dobson (ed), *Fairness and Futurity: Essays on Environmental Sustainability and Social Justice* (Oxford University Press 1999) for theoretical discussions on justice and sustainability.

[18] Jacobs (n 14) 38.

principle of international law.[19] Most of the relevant literature engages with sustainability and sustainable development in relation to economic growth and environmental considerations.[20] In the past decade, scholarly work has also paid attention to social considerations and their interplay with sustainable development, with no connection whatsoever with migration.[21] After this general overview of sustainability as a concept of relevance in international governance, the next sections turn to the EU policy field.

1.3.2 The Disconnect of Migration from Sustainability in EU Policy and Scholarship

Sustainability as a concept pertinent to law and policy considerations first appeared in the EU legal order in the 1990s. Sustainable development has formed part of EU primary law since the Maastricht Treaty.[22] Specifically, the Maastricht Treaty referred to sustainable development in the field of development cooperation in Article 130u TEC. The notion of sustainable development was also alluded to in Article B TEU and Article 2 TEC, by reference to the economic, environmental, and social pillars of the notion being connected *in abstracto* with progress and growth. The Amsterdam Treaty was the first instrument to explicitly introduce sustainable development as an EU objective, encompassing all the pillars of the notion and adding a special reference to the relation of

[19] Vaughan Lowe, 'Sustainable Development and Unsustainable Arguments' in Alan E Boyle and David Freestone (eds), *International Law and Sustainable Development: Past Achievements and Future Challenges* (Oxford University Press 1999) on sustainable development as a meta-principle; See Vaughan Lowe, *International Law* (Oxford University Press 2007) on sustainable development as an interstitial norm; See Pieraccini and Novitz (n 12) 22–24 for an overview of how sustainable development appears in International Law litigation; Nicolas de Sadeleer, 'Environmental Principles, Modern and Post Modern Law' in Richard Macrory, Ian Havercroft, and Ray Purdy (eds), *Principles of European Environmental Law, Proceedings of the Avosetta Group of European Environmental lawyers* (Europa Law Publishing 2004).

[20] For a critique, see Federico Demaria and Ashish Kothari, 'The Post-Development Dictionary Agenda: Paths to the Pluriverse' (2017) 38(12) Third World Quarterly 2588; Giacomo D'Alisa, Federico Demaria, and Giorgos Kallis (eds), *Degrowth: A Vocabulary for a New Era* (Routledge 2015).

[21] Margherita Pieraccini and Tonia Novitz (eds), *Legal Perspectives on Sustainability* (Bristol University Press 2020); Littig and Griessler (n 16) is considered as a turning point for the beginning of engagement with social sustainability.

[22] Treaty on European Union, together with the complete text of the Treaty establishing the European Community [1992] OJ C 224/1.

the concept to environmental protection.[23] The reference to and inclusion of sustainable development as a primary law objective that relates to economic growth, social progress, environmental protection, and external action was maintained in the Lisbon Treaty and creates a link between this concept and virtually every area of EU policies.

In terms of policy evolution, in the beginning of the new millennium, the EU started shaping an autonomous Sustainable Development Strategy.[24] Throughout the evolution of the relevant policy, no link with migration ever appeared.[25] The first time the EU Sustainable Development Strategy became connected with migration was under the von der Leyen Commission. Specifically, von der Leyen's political programme aimed at integrating the UN 2030 Agenda on Sustainable Development in all Commission proposals, thus streamlining sustainability in EU policy, instead of having an autonomous EU Sustainable Development Strategy.[26] In a working document issued in 2020, the Commission elaborated on the different policies adopted with the aim of implementing the Sustainable Development Goals (SDGs) at EU level. In that working document, and in the SDGs' mapping tool developed by the Commission, it appears as if all the EU policies currently pursued, and all the legal acts adopted by the EU, relate to one or more SDGs.[27] Among all the different policies, the Commission mentions the New Pact on Migration and Asylum as linked to the EU's pursuit of sustainability.[28] It is safe to assume that this newly established link relates more to the diffusion of sustainability-related goals across all areas of the Commission, rather than to a conceptual connection between the Agenda and the EU migration policy. Despite this recent link, over the previous twenty years, the EU Sustainable Development Strategy had

[23] Preamble, Article 2, Treaty on European Union (Amsterdam consolidated version) [1997] OJ C 340/145; Articles 2, 6, and 177, Treaty establishing the European Community (Amsterdam consolidated version) [1997] OJ C 340/173.

[24] European Council, Presidency Conclusions, Lisbon, 23–24 March 2000; Communication, A Sustainable Europe for a Better World: A European Union Strategy for Sustainable Development, EU Sustainable Development Strategy, COM(2001)264 final.

[25] Ibid; Towards a global partnership for sustainable development, COM(2002)82 final; EUROPE 2020, A strategy for smart, sustainable and inclusive growth, COM(2010)2020 final; Next steps for a sustainable European future, European Action for Sustainability, COM(2016)739 final.

[26] Commission Staff Working Document, Delivering on the UN's Sustainable Development Goals – A comprehensive approach, SWD(2020)4000 final.

[27] SDG policy mapping tool at https://knowsdgs.jrc.ec.europa.eu/intro-policy-mapping.

[28] Commission Staff Working Document (n 26) Box 1 at 6.

evolved in silo from the EU migration policy. The recent connection of sustainability with every aspect of EU action, and thus also with migration, obfuscates the concept's meaning and implications. A similar siloed approach exists in EU scholarly research in sustainability.

Specifically, sustainability-related research in EU law has not hitherto engaged with the links between sustainability and migration. Rather, EU law scholars have investigated sustainability in relation to environmental law, competition law, and, more recently, labour law. In the literature, there have been two broad ways of engagement with sustainability over the last twenty years. The first is scholarship that looks at how EU law can be used as a tool to address environmental problems. By emphasizing the need to equip the EU legal system with tools that can address environmental challenges, scholars looked at if and how EU law could be interpreted or applied to address such challenges. This strand includes research mostly in the fields of environmental law and competition law.[29]

Second, in more recent years, we see a shift in the perception of sustainability, such that more recent works discuss how EU law can be used as a tool to achieve more sustainable societies. The second strand of scholarship developed later in time and is tied to the conceptual evolution of sustainability during the 2000s, the evolution of EU law itself, especially after the Lisbon Treaty, and different events that have taken place in the European region. Sustainability as a concept that includes three pillars (economic, social, and environmental) finds explicit expression in Article 3(3) TEU. After the adoption of the Lisbon Treaty, many different crises have been experienced at EU level (economic/financial crisis, Brexit, migration crisis, public health crisis), which have pointed to

[29] In environmental law, see Richard Macrory, Ian Havercroft, and Ray Purdy (eds), *Principles of European Environmental Law* (Europa Law Publishing 2004); Nicolas de Sadeleer, *Environmental Principles: From Political Slogans to Legal Rules* (Oxford University Press 2002); Christina Voigt and Hans Christian Bugge (eds), *Sustainable Development in National and International Law* (Europa Law Publishing 2008); Beate Sjåfjell and Anja Wiesbrock (eds), *The Greening of European Business under EU Law: Taking Article 11 TFEU Seriously* (Routledge 2015); Matthew Humphreys, *Sustainable Development in the European Union: A General Principle* (Routledge 2017). In competition law, see Marios Iacovides and Christos Vrettos, 'Falling through the Cracks No More? Article 102 TFEU and Sustainability: The Relation between Dominance, Environmental Degradation, and Social Injustice' (2022) 10 Journal of Antitrust Enforcement 32; Edith Loozen, 'Strict Competition Enforcement and Welfare: A Constitutional Perspective Based on Article 101 TFEU and Sustainability' (2019) 56 CMLRev; F Oles Andriychuk, 'The Concept of Sustainability in EU Competition Law: A Legal Realist Perspective' (2021) 23 Yearbook of Antitrust and Regulatory Studies 11.

the inability of the existing system to achieve sustainability objectives.[30] In light of these crises, different scholars have suggested how different fields of EU law should be developed or applied as means to achieve more just and sustainable societies. This strand of scholarship continues to investigate the meaning of sustainability.[31] While most of these works are focused on fields related to economic law, some research has also emerged in the field of labour law.[32] Such a broadening of the field of enquiry follows the evolution of sustainability in international and EU policy as a concept related to every aspect of human life.

However, this conceptual opening of sustainability still does not provide much clarity as to the meaning or implications of the concept for sustainable migration. Three key lines of argument can be identified in the relevant research. First, sustainability is viewed as a concept comprised of economic, environmental, and social pillars, although not all scholarship agrees on whether these pillars are interdependent or autonomous. Second, sustainability demands the continuity or maintenance of something for the future, although not all scholars agree on what is the value to be maintained. Third, sustainability involves considerations of intergenerational and intra-generational justice, which take differentiated expression in different areas of law. In spite of the aforementioned analyses, the relevant scholarship has not yet addressed the relation of sustainability to EU migration law. Section 1.3.3 thus engages with the connection between sustainability and migration in EU policy.

30 Takis Tridimas, 'Foreword' in Beate Sjåfjell, Georgina Tsagas, and Charlotte Villiers (eds), *Sustainable Value Creation in the European Union: Towards Pathways to a Sustainable Future through Crises* (Cambridge University Press 2022).

31 Alexandros Kyriakidis, 'Sustainability and Eurozone 2.0: Still Impossible?' in Beate Sjåfjell, Charlotte Villiers, and Georgina Tsagas (eds), *Sustainable Value Creation in the European Union: Towards Pathways to a Sustainable Future through Crises* (Cambridge University Press 2022); Tonia Novitz and Margherita Pieraccini, 'Agenda 2030 and the Sustainable Development Goals: "Responsive, Inclusive, Participatory and Representative Decision-Making?"' in Margherita Pieraccini and Tonia Novitz (eds), *Legal Perspectives on Sustainability* (Bristol University Press 2020).

32 Novitz (n 15); Tonia Novitz, 'The Paradigm of Sustainability in a European Social Context: Collective Participation in Protection of Future Interests?' (2015) 31 International Journal of Comparative Labour Law & Industrial Relations 243; Tonia Novitz, 'Addressing Social Dumping and Unfair Competition – An Analysis of EU Pillar Initiatives from a Sustainability Perspective' in Ann-Christine Hartzén, Andrea Iossa, and Eleni Karageorgiou (eds), *Law, Solidarity and the Limits of Social Europe* (Edward Elgar 2022); Konstantinos Alexandris Polomarkakis, 'The European Pillar of Social Rights and the Quest for EU Social Sustainability' (2020) 29 Social & Legal Studies 183.

As will be argued in the section, the lack of coherence in the way this connection is made renders the scholarly gap particularly salient.

1.3.3 The Incoherent Appearance of Sustainability in EU Migration Policy

Migration was first linked to sustainability in the 2030 Agenda on Sustainable Development. Among the seventeen SDGs and under the umbrella of reducing inequalities, goal 10.7 targets the facilitation of 'orderly, safe, regular and responsible migration and mobility of people, including through the implementation of planned and well-managed migration policies'.[33] Following the adoption of the Agenda, the UN Global Compact on Migration was adopted in December 2018.[34] The Compact was the first intergovernmental effort to holistically address migrant protection. Specifically, and building on already binding human rights obligations, the Compact addressed issues of migrant protection at all stages of their journey (origin, transit, and destination countries).[35]

The EU discourse on sustainable migration predated the adoption of the Compact and has developed in complete disconnect to the international policy on the matter. Specifically, after 2015, sustainable migration became the new buzzword describing the future of EU migration policy.[36] In different documents issued by the Commission from 2015 to this day, sustainability appears as a central goal of EU migration policy. Nevertheless, the connection made between sustainability and migration is nowhere elaborated in a manner which would clarify its legal implications. In previous research, I have offered a typology of the various ways in which sustainable migration appears in EU policy documents.[37] Specifically, sustainable migration appears first with a literal meaning related to the reduction in the numbers of incoming migrants. Second, the term appears with an abstract meaning as an undefined goal

[33] See Michele Klein Solomon and Suzanne Sheldon, 'The Global Compact for Migration: From the Sustainable Development Goals to a Comprehensive Agreement on Safe, Orderly and Regular Migration' (2019) 30 IJRL 584.

[34] UN General Assembly, Compact for Safe, Orderly and Regular Migration, 19 December 2018, A/RES/73/195.

[35] Ibid, point 2. On countries of origin, see objectives 2, 4; On transit countries, see objectives 5, 8, 9; On destination countries, see objectives 16-2.

[36] For a detailed analysis of the relevant policy discourse, see Loxa, 'An EU Sustainable Migration' (n 2), Section 3.

[37] Ibid, Table 1.

or characteristic for the future of EU migration policy. Finally, sustainable migration appears closely related to specific areas. These are partnerships with third countries and returns and reintegration, the creation of sustainable legal pathways, and sustainable sharing of responsibility. Even if we were to accept that these policies form part of an EU sustainable migration, they lack coherence and create challenges for the EU legal order, making them unsuitable to use as a basis for the legal implementation of a sustainable EU migration.[38]

At the same time, scholarly research on sustainable migration has still not engaged with the potential legal implications of the concept. While the link between sustainability and migration under the Global Compact prompted scholarly investigation, the literature focused on the legal value of the Compact and its interaction with international human rights law.[39] Moreover, authors have used the term 'sustainable migration' in a declaratory manner, as a demand for a type of migration policies, without any clear definition of what these should entail.[40] Outside legal scholarship, migration studies have been investigating the relation between development and migration for a long time.[41] From the 1960s to this day, migration has been connected to development by outlining how the flow of people and, consequently, of money (through remittances), as well as of knowledge (acquired in the host country and employed in the country of origin upon return) can impact the development of host countries and countries of origin of migrants.[42]

[38] Ibid, Section 3.

[39] See Alan Desmond, 'A New Dawn for the Human Rights of International Migrants? Protection of Migrants' Rights in Light of the UN's SDGs and Global Compact for Migration' (2020) 16 International Journal of Law in Context 222; Elspeth Guild and Raoul Wieland, 'The UN Global Compact for Safe, Orderly and Regular Migration: What Does It Mean in International Law?' in Giuliana Ziccardi Capaldo (ed), *The Global Community Yearbook of International Law and Jurisprudence 2019* (Oxford University Press 2020); Peter Hilpold, 'Opening up a New Chapter of Law-Making in International Law: The Global Compacts on Migration and for Refugees of 2018' (2020) 26 ELJ 226.

[40] Klein Solomon and Sheldon (n 33); Eva Dick and others, 'Regional Migration Governance: Contributions to a Sustainable International Migration Architecture' (2018) Briefing Paper Deutsches Institut für Entwicklungspolitik (DIE); Tesseltje de Lange, 'A New Narrative for European Migration Policy: Sustainability and the Blue Card Recast' (2020) 26 ELJ 274.

[41] See Thomas Faist, Margit Fauser, and Peter Kivisto (eds), *Migration-Development Nexus: A Transnational Perspective* (Palgrave Macmillan 2011).

[42] For an overview of the evolution of the scholarly analysis, see Thomas Faist and Margit Fauser, 'The Migration–Development Nexus: Toward a Transnational Perspective' in

In this regard, it should not come as a surprise that research into potential definitions of the term 'sustainable migration' have been explored outside the field of legal science and with an emphasis on development considerations.[43] Specifically, the Peace Research Institute of Oslo produced two papers which offered definitions of sustainable migration from the perspective of migration studies and human geography. In these papers, it was acknowledged that the concept of sustainable migration, especially without an established definition, is a powerful one in the sense that its rhetorical effects can be seen as fitting both liberal and restrictive migration agendas.[44]

The relevant definitions offer a starting point for conceptualizing sustainable migration policies, but they cannot provide much guidance on legal design. Their emphasis lies on the distribution of costs and benefits and evaluation of long-term interests between the individuals, states, and societies affected, a distribution which cannot be easily translated in law, let alone EU law, which would have to consider the very different ways in which Member States are affected by migration. Moreover, these definitions encounter another obstacle, namely the position of individuals and their agency as rights-bearers in law. On this matter, Guild has highlighted the risk that arises from linking sustainable development and migration and has argued that migration should be applied within the framework of human rights standards

Thomas Faist, Margit Fauser, and Peter Kivisto (eds), *The Migration-Development Nexus* (Palgrave Macmillan 2011).

[43] See Pierre Picard and Tim Worrall, 'Sustainable Migration Policies' (2011) Université catholique de Louvain, Center for Operations Research and Econometrics 2011/40, where sustainability of migration is examined in light of the development of formulas examining the costs and benefits of labour migration under different schemes; Janker and Thieme (n 4) have tried to develop a framework for sustainable migration based on trade-offs between costs and benefits at different levels (individual, household, community/regional, national); Mohammed Al-Husban and Carl Adams, 'Sustainable Refugee Migration: A Rethink towards a Positive Capability Approach' (2016) 8 Sustainability 451, where alternative governance models are proposed on the basis of ethnographic field studies.

[44] Jørgen Carling and Marta Bivand Erdal, 'Is "Sustainable Migration" a Valuable Concept?' (PRIO Policy Brief 2018) 5; Marta Bivand Erdal and others, 'Defining Sustainable Migration', EMN Norway Occasional Papers; Alexander Betts and Paul Collier, 'Sustainable Migration: A Framework for Responding to Movement from Poor to Rich Countries' (2018) EMN Norway Occasional Papers; Cf Christina Voigt, 'From Climate Change to Sustainability: An Essay on Sustainable Development, Legal and Ethical Choices' (2005) 9 Worldviews 112, 120; See also John S Dryzek, *The Politics of the Earth: Environmental Discourses* (3rd ed., Oxford University Press 2012) 132 for similar discussions on the politics of environmental sustainability.

rather than SDGs.[45] The aforementioned analysis points to the difficulty of identifying and operationalizing elements that can inform a legal framework structured around the objective of an EU sustainable migration.

1.4 EU Legal History as a Precondition for Understanding Sustainable Migration

Section 1.3.3 has provided an overview of sustainability as a concept of relevance to law and policy, tracing its appearance in EU policy and scholarship and its recent connection to EU migration policy. The numerous inconsistencies and divergent objectives of EU migration policy all huddle together under the umbrella of sustainable migration. These inconsistencies suggest the need to reach back into the past in the remainder of this book, in order to problematize for the future.

To put it in simply, looking at EU policy documents does not allow us to understand what sustainable migration is or how it would be different from the action that was already shaped under the EU Agenda on Migration, and previously under the Global Approach to Migration and Mobility.[46] Yet turning to law and legal scholarship does not help either, as there is no apparent link between migration law and sustainability, contrary to the link between sustainability and environmental law, competition law and, more recently, labour law. Extra-legal scholarship on sustainable migration hints at a balancing of costs and benefits on the design of migration policies, yet cannot provide guidance as to how such balancing could take place in EU law or what implications it would have for migrants' rights. In one way or another, we are in unchartered territory.

Two theoretical propositions on sustainability are of value in this unchartered territory. Under the first, sustainable migration could be understood as a political concept put forward by the Commission to unite Member States in a period of contentious migration politics, as I have argued elsewhere.[47] Already in the 1990s, Baker suggested that the commitment of the EU to sustainable development was a symbolical political act and she pointed to the function of symbols in politics as 'stimulators of change' which have transformative potential for the *status*

[45] Guild (n 4) 249.
[46] Loxa (n 2), Section 3.
[47] Ibid.

quo.[48] In order to explore the transformative potential (if any) of sustainable migration, we need to first explore how the *status quo* under EU law engages in balancing economic and social considerations in the regulation of migration. Only after doing so can we evaluate if the symbolical commitment of the EU to sustainable migration has potential of transformation or continuity with past policies.[49] Indeed, as the remainder of the book will show, EU migration law has been developing under very specific legal structures and principles over the course of many years drawing on considerations related to the parallel – though not always interdependent – pursuit of economic and social objectives.

Under the second theoretical proposition, sustainability could be seen through the lens of system theory. In the relevant scholarship, sustainability is seen as entailing a balancing exercise between conflicting demands and based on interdependence. Building on ecology and systems theory, Lélé has argued that sustainability encompasses the attributes of dynamic equilibrium, reliability, resilience, and adaptability.[50] Similarly, in ecological economics, Constanza has proposed that sustainability of an ecosystem is the system's ability to maintain its structure and function over time in the face of external stress.[51] This system-theoretical understanding of sustainability has also been applied at EU level by Barbier who suggested that sustainability is a quality of the European Social Model.[52] By suggesting that the European Social Model is the system in question, his approach fails to conceptualize sustainability in the overarching way in which it appears as an EU primary law objective.

Following the demand set by primary law that sustainability is the objective of this legal order, I argue in this book that sustainable migration can be perceived as being connected to EU law as the system

48 Susan Baker, 'Sustainable Development as Symbolic Commitment: Declaratory Politics and the Seductive Appeal of Ecological Modernisation in the European Union' (2007) 16 Environmental Politics 297, 314.

49 Cf Natasja Reslow, 'Transformation or Continuity? EU External Migration Policy in the Aftermath of the Migration Crisis' in Sergio Carrera, Juan Santos Vara, and Tineke Strik (eds), *Constitutionalising the External Dimensions of EU Migration Policies in Times of Crisis* (Edward Elgar 2019).

50 Sharachchandra M Lélé, 'Sustainability: A Plural, Multi-Dimensional Approach' [1993] Working Paper, Pacific Institute for Studies in Development, Environment, and Security.

51 Robert Costanza and Michael Mageau, 'What Is a Healthy Ecosystem?' (1999) 33 Aquatic Ecology 105.

52 Jean-Claude Barbier, Ralf Rogowski, and Fabrice Colomb (eds), *The Sustainability of the European Social Model: EU Governance, Social Protection and Employment Policies in Europe* (Edward Elgar 2015) 9.

in question. For migration to be sustainable, EU migration law would need to align with the sustainability objective of the EU legal order. Plainly put, it would need to respect the structure of the EU legal system in terms of horizontal and vertical division of competences, the function of the system in delivering the promised objectives of growth and social progress, and to have resilience against external stress. Chapter 10 will reflect on the findings of the historical analysis and it will connect them with the theoretical propositions presented here, to discuss if and how EU law can deliver the objective of sustainable migration. Sections 1.4.1 and 1.4.2 will in turn discuss the material and delimitations of the research carried.

1.4.1 Material

The remainder of the book develops by a historical investigation on both free movement and regulation of migration from third countries. The embeddedness of economic and social sustainability throughout the history of EU migration law is demonstrated after a historical investigation analysing the negotiation, adoption, and interpretation of various instruments regulating residence and social rights of EU and TCN migrants from the European Coal and Steel Community (ECSC) to the present day. This approach to EU migration law as a broader category of examination is rarely encountered in EU law literature any longer.[53] Migration law research and teaching under EU law is dichotomized along two distinct categories: free movement and migration from third countries.[54] There is a presumed difference in the normative foundations of the attribution of rights to each category of migrants under these frameworks.[55] Tracing the history of economic and social sustainability in the development of EU migration law by including both EU and TCN

[53] In the 1990s, various authors examined the potential convergence between the two frameworks. See David O'Keeffe, 'The Free Movement of Persons and the Single Market' (1992) 17 ELR 3; Elspeth Guild, *Immigration Law in the European Community* (Brill Nijhoff 2001).

[54] As attested by the recent publication of two separate handbooks: Daniel Thym, *European Migration Law* (Oxford University Press 2023) and Niamh Nic Shuibne, *EU Citizenship Law* (Oxford University Press 2023).

[55] The presumption has been developed and perfected in the work of Thym. See Daniel Thym, '"Citizens" and "Foreigners" in EU Law, Migration Law and Its Cosmopolitan Outlook' (2016) 22 ELJ 296; Daniel Thym, 'EU Migration Policy and Its Constitutional Rationale: A Cosmopolitan Outlook' (2013) 50 CMLRev 709.

migration does not contest this differentiation. However, by conclusively examining both these frameworks, the book reveals that there exists a thread that in fact links them in light of economic and social considerations.

In terms of doctrinal material, the fields of free movement of workers, Accession Treaties, Association Agreements, and regulation of regular migration from 1951 to 15 March 2024 are examined. The investigation extends over forty-four Association Agreements, out of which twenty-eight contain labour migration or equal treatment related clauses, all the seven Accession Treaties, eleven Regulations, and seventeen Directives, next to case-law of the Court regarding migrants' security of residence, free movement, enjoyment of the right to family life, and social rights under the relevant instruments.[56]

To demonstrate how EU institutions took into account economic and social sustainability aspects in the negotiation and adoption of the relevant instruments, the analysis is enriched by the inclusion of archival material from the Historical Archives of the EU (HAEU), the University of Pittsburgh Archive on European Integration (AEI), the CVCE, a digital research infrastructure run by the University of Luxembourg, as well as material accessed after information requests to the Commission and the Council. It should be noted that historical and geopolitical events surrounding legal evolutions are presented as they appear in analyses carried by the EU institutions, as the purpose of the investigation is to demonstrate how different EU institutions, based on their perception of factual economic and social reality, attempted to align EU migration law to the social and economic objectives of the EU legal order. Further, when going through the analysis, one might notice that the material invoked from the Commission (and hence the Commission's approach to migration) exceeds the material related to the Council (and relatedly its approach). The reason for this discrepancy relates to the very different practice of the two institutions. As Thym has pointed out, the Commission has used its monopoly of initiative 'skilfully by presenting itself as the source of technical expertise and as a repository of

[56] Social rights refer to equal treatment on access to social security, social assistance, and other state-supported facilities like education and healthcare. See similar use of the term in Karin de Vries, 'The Integration Exception: A New Limit to Social Rights of Third-Country Nationals in European Union Law?' in Daniel Thym (ed), *Questioning EU Citizenship Judges and the Limits of Free Movement and Solidarity in the EU* (Hart 2017).

knowledge'.[57] In contrast, the Council – especially in the area of AFSJ – operates under a veil of secrecy, making it almost impossible to access the discussions that preceded the negotiation of different instruments.[58] Through the investigation of the relevant material, the book conclusively reconstructs the history of EU labour migration and shows the role of economic and social sustainability from its inception to its most recent manifestation.

1.4.2 Delimitations

What is not covered in the investigation is aspects of EU migration law related to border management, illegal migration, and asylum. The regulation regarding posted workers and intra-corporate transferees is also excluded from the examination. Finally, I engage only partially with external aspects of EU migration. These choices are made for three reasons.

First, border management and illegal migration instruments are part of the legal apparatus of the EU which is shaped by security-related considerations, and which emphasizes supranational administrative and police management.[59] In the relevant area, the EU regulates the movement of individuals by the coordination of networks of cooperation between Member States. The individual and their movement are the object, but not the subject of EU law.[60] This is also behind the exclusion of a full analysis of the external aspects of migration policy. While I examine Agreements between the EU and third countries which create EU law rights for migrants, I do not investigate more recent elements of the

[57] Daniel Thym, 'Institutional and Constitutional Framework' in Evangelia Tsourdi and Philippe De Bruycker (eds), *Research Handbook on EU Migration and Asylum Law* (Edward Elgar 2022) 60.

[58] Ibid 63.

[59] Didier Bigo, Rob BJ Walker, and Sergio Carrera, *Europe's Twenty-first Century Challenge: Delivering Liberty* (Routledge 2010); Ferruccio Pastore, 'Visas, Borders, Immigration: Formation, Structure, and Current Evolution of the EU Entry Control System' in Neil Walker (ed), *Europe's Area of Freedom, Security, and Justice* (Oxford University Press 2004); Dora Kostakopoulou, 'The Area of Freedom, Security and Justice and the Political Morality of Migration and Integration' in Hans Lindahl (ed), *A Right to Inclusion and Exclusion?: Normative Fault Lines of the EU's Area of Freedom, Security and Justice* (Hart 2009).

[60] The Court has emphasized the protection of rights even in these frameworks. See Moraru Madalina, 'EU Return Directive: A Cause for Shame or an Unexpectedly Protective Framework?' in Evangelia Tsourdi and Philippe De Bruycker (eds), *Research Handbook on EU Migration and Asylum Law* (Edward Elgar 2022).

cooperation that are focused on returns and irregular migration, or Agreements that institute transnational cooperation in migration without creating rights for individual migrants.[61]

Second, regarding asylum, there are two reasons why it is excluded from this study; one is connected to the empirical legal reality, while the second is connected to normative demands. On the empirical legal reality, the regulation of asylum has historically been disconnected from broader economic and social considerations in the EU.[62] While EU migration policy documents from 2000 onwards mix migration and asylum, and asylum has not escaped the sustainability discourse, I suggest that it is better if we stick to a clear division between EU asylum law and sustainable migration.[63] International humanitarian obligations should not be balanced against the social and economic demands constantly pursued by EU law, as this would risk of undermining the nature of international protection.[64]

Finally, posted workers and migrants falling under the Intra-Corporate Transfers Directive are excluded, not for lack of social and economic considerations in the relevant instruments, but because in this type of

[61] I do not investigate soft law in the context of the EU–Africa cooperation (EU–Africa Partnership on Migration, Mobility, and Employment, AU–EU Migration and Mobility Dialogue, Rabat process, Khartoum process, Valetta summit); the Euro-Mediterranean Agreements that refer to cooperation on social matters or migration but do not set up concrete obligations for the parties as regards migrant workers like the Agreements with Jordan, Lebanon, Israel, and Egypt; and the agreements put in place in the context of the Eastern Partnership or with Western Balkans on visa liberalization, as these refer to temporary movements.

[62] Refugees fell under the scope of EU instruments adopted in the 1950s and 1960s, long before the creation of the CEAS. See Article 4(1), Règlement n° 3 concernant la sécurité sociale des travailleurs migrants [1958] OJ 30/56; Article 2, Regulation 1408/71 on the application of social security schemes to employed persons and their families moving within the Community [1971] OJ L 149/2. They were also excluded from national policies geared towards halting migration after the 1970s oil crisis – see Communication, On Immigration, SEC(91)1855 final. Rather, CEAS was harmonized initially with a view to ensure Member States' compliance with their international obligations. See also the approach of the Commission until the end of 1990s, demanding differentiated treatment of asylum and migration expressed for the last time in the Action plan of the Council and the Commission on how best to implement the provisions of the Treaty of Amsterdam on an area of freedom, security and justice [1999] OJ C 19/1.

[63] Loxa, 'An EU Sustainable Migration' (n 2).

[64] A risk that has been materializing. See Lilian Tsourdi and Cathryn Costello, 'The Evolution of EU Law on Refugees and Asylum' in Paul Craig and Gráinne de Búrca (eds), *The Evolution of EU Law* (Oxford University Press 2021) who refer to 'flight from law'; See also Guild (n 4) where her arguments could apply by analogy for the case of EU asylum law.

movement, migrants are not the subject of rights individually; rather, they draw such rights from their employer, who is the subject EU law seeks to protect. Their mobility is tied to the operational needs of international companies, and thus, their movement becomes absorbed by the transnational business transactions they serve.[65] Despite these limits, the investigation will reveal that sustainable migration has a very concrete expression in the history of EU labour migration. The concept of sustainable migration might be a recent one, but the objectives it serves can be traced back to the origins of EU law.

1.5 Structure and Objectives

In tracing the history of economic and social sustainability in the past of EU migration law, the book develops in three parts, which examine chronologically all the different areas of EU migration law from 1951 to the present. Part I begins with an examination of the period from 1951 to the Single European Act. Part II continues by reviewing material from the Single European Act to the failed Constitutional Treaty. Part III concludes the analysis by looking at the evolution of the relevant areas from 2004 to the present day. The material is categorized in the respective parts based on the following factors: legal instruments are categorized based on the date of their adoption, while case-law is categorized based on a combination of the Treaty framework applicable at the time the dispute was heard by the Court, and the secondary law applicable to the dispute. During the analysis, it will become clear that the three periods are framed not only by a Treaty framework that guided and transformed the EU structure, but also by broadly similar economic and geopolitical circumstances with specific repercussions for EU legal imagination. Once the linear historical investigation is concluded, the centrality of the economic and social pillars of sustainability in the development of EU migration law will become apparent. Finally,

[65] Cf Georg Menz, 'Employers and Migrant Legality: Liberalization of Service Provision, Transnational Posting, and the Bifurcation of the European Labour Market' in Cathryn Costello and Mark Freedland (eds), *Migrants at Work: Immigration and Vulnerability in Labour Law* (Oxford University Press 2014); Alexander Somek, 'From Workers to Migrants, from Distributive Justice to Inclusion: Exploring the Changing Social Democratic Imagination' (2012) 18 ELJ 711. Recital 15, Article 18, Directive 2014/66/EU which refers to Directive 96/71/EC concerning the posting of workers in the framework of the provision of services [1997] OJ L 18/1 to assimilate the degree of protection of migrants falling under these instruments.

Chapter 10 concludes the book by presenting the findings of the historical investigation and fleshing out how the history of EU migration law informs the contemporary objective of an EU sustainable migration.

As to the significance and objectives of the book, my analysis shows that the overt emphasis on growth cannot sustain the EU legal order anymore. This conclusion is based on the premise that the impossibility of delivering unhindered growth for twenty-seven Member States, with extremely diverse industrial, economic, and social conditions, has led to a diverse and incoherent legal framework on migration, which in turn negatively impacts both growth and social progress. However, an academic analysis, let alone a legal one, cannot hope to convince the hundred million EU voters whose resistance to migration in view of its assumed economic implications underpins the inability of current EU migration law to deliver on the promise of growth for Member States, and on the issue of social and mobility rights for migrants.[66] Instead, in this scholarly contribution, I wish to make clear three things on different levels.

On the first level, I demonstrate that the novel concept of sustainable migration comes with specific limitations. Highlighting the close ties of EU migration law to economic development would mean that an EU sustainable migration is migration that supports the EU project of growth. If migrants are not a burden to national economies, and if they contribute to growth, then their residence and rights in Member States will not cause tensions. In one way or another, migration law, and especially in the EU, has always been exclusive. The non-mobile [citizen], the economically inactive, the vulnerable, the migrant whose value cannot be monetised, have always been excluded from legal protection.[67] By tracing economic sustainability in the past of EU migration law, we can make sense of the exclusionary politics of the EU towards more

[66] See Gregor Noll, 'Viciously Circular: Will Ageing Lock the European Union into Immigrant Exclusion?' in Stijn Smet and Vladislava Stoyanova (eds), *Migrants' Rights, Populism and Legal Resilience in Europe* (Cambridge University Press 2022).

[67] Cf Noreen Burrows, 'The Promotion of Women's Rights by the European Economic Community' (1980) 17 CMLRev 191; Charlotte O'Brien, 'Social Blind Spots and Monocular Policy Making: The ECJ's Migrant Worker Model' (2009) 46 CMLRev 1107; Tamara Hervey, 'Migrant Workers and Their Families in the European Union: The Pervasive Market Ideology of Community Law' in Jo Shaw and Gillian More (eds), *New Legal Dynamics of European Union* (Clarendon Press 1995); Clare McGlynn, 'Reclaiming a Feminist Vision: The Reconciliation of Paid Work and Family Life in European Union Law and Policy' (2001) 7 ColumJEurL; Isabella Moebius and Erika Szyszczak, 'Of Raising Pigs and Children' (1998) 18 Yearbook of European Law 125.

vulnerable categories of migrants. EU migration law will always be geared towards prioritizing the utility of migrants to the internal market. Sustainable migration thus captures the need to ensure the sustaining of the EU internal market and, relatedly, the disconnection of the individual from the market operates as a basis for exclusion.

On a second more theoretical level, I connect two strands of scholarship – free movement and migration law – and challenge the mainstream scholarly paradigm that insists on the disconnect between the rights of EU and TCN migrants.[68] The Court has indeed used free movement provisions and economic considerations to shape an EU constitutional architecture, long before these were ingrained in a Treaty text. However, since the EU legal architecture shifted due to closer integration and the adoption of the Charter, the Court has interpreted secondary law on migration in light of the Charter, in order to consolidate the rights of TCN migrants and further the social objectives of the EU project. I suggest that this judicial move does not come under a different cosmopolitan paradigm that would apply to TCN migrants, but rather utilizes secondary law on TCN migration to furnish a more complete constitutional structure after the Lisbon Treaty.

In doing so, the Court can be seen as a political actor continuing the path of using law as a means of integration.[69] In a way, the judicial approach to migrants' rights mirrors economic and social considerations in different points in time, so as to further the construction of the EU legal order. The economic considerations behind migrants' rights were highlighted by the Court before the Maastricht Treaty with the purpose of furthering the constitutional elements of the EU legal order via the construction of legal principles. This was the case not only as regards free movement provisions but also in the case-law on Association Agreements. The social considerations behind migrants' rights were highlighted by the Court after the Lisbon Treaty with the purpose of furthering the constitutional elements of EU legal order via the fortification of the Charter. To put it simply, the Court has used both economic and social objectives at different points in time to furnish a more complete constitutional structure for EU law.

[68] Above (n 55).

[69] Cf Mark Dawson, 'The Political Face of Judicial Activism: Europe's Law-Politics Imbalance' in Bruno de Witte, Elise Muir, and Mark Dawson (eds), *Judicial Activism at the European Court of Justice* (Edward Elgar 2013).

On a more abstract level, pointing to the unsustainability of the current system, I ask the reader to imagine how an EU sustainable migration could be informed by a legal design grounded in legal rules and principles, which form part of the EU *acquis*, but which have nevertheless been sidelined in the legal instruments adopted to this day. My suggestions cannot overcome the structural limitations that characterize the EU legal order and, relatedly, EU migration law. Rather, taking a pragmatic approach on the current form of the EU legal system, I make some practical suggestions that could better align migration law to the economic and social objective of the EU project.

PART I

Aligned Paths from the Treaty of Paris to the Single European Act

This part begins the investigation in the past and examines how economic and social objectives shaped the regulation of migration in the period from the Treaty of Paris to the Single European Act. In doing so, it proves that while the concept of sustainable migration is a recent one, the social and economic pillars of sustainability have been constantly guiding the development of EU migration law. Specifically, the balancing between economic and social considerations shaped the regulation of migration already from the establishment of Community law. The analysis further shows that during the years of post-war growth, the Community institutions' approach to the regulation of migration was aligned for both Community and third country national (TCN) migrants. Contemporary analyses of EU migration law emphasize the different rationales behind free movement and regulation of migration from third countries. In contrast to this, the investigation shows that during the early years of Community law, all migrants were perceived as having the same function for the collective project of growth.

The demand for labour necessary for economic development in the Member States conditioned the extensive attribution of social rights at least until the 1970s. Following the 1970s oil crisis, the disruptive potential of surplus migrant labour for the economy lay behind the limitation of rights for migrant workers. Looking more closely at the regulation of migration in light of the economic and social objectives of Community law and the economic circumstances in the Member States until the end of the 1980s, one thing becomes clear. The attribution or limitation of rights to migrants is dictated by the need to ensure the smooth functioning of the economy in the Member States. In parallel, social progress is pursued in the form of equal rights for all migrant workers and their families. During this period, the regulation of migration could be found in four legal areas: in the free movement of workers framework as regards Community workers; in Accession Treaties regulating how migrants from acceding states should become part of the free movement framework; in Association and Cooperation Agreements with specific countries granting rights to their nationals; and, finally, through the Community labour and employment policy aiming to generally raise the living standards of all population within the Community territory. This legal framework of migration, which is analysed in detail in this chapter, developed at a time of shifting economic and social circumstances. The 1950s and 1960s were characterized by rapid economic development and increased need for labour migration.[1] During that time, migration movements mainly comprised guest workers, and these were regarded by Member States as a short-term phenomenon, regulated by the demands of the market.[2] In contrast, during the 1970s, the Community underwent a period of economic crisis and a declining need for manpower. After the 1973 oil crisis, the economic situation in most Member States was characterized by stagnation, unemployment, and inflation.[3] This led to a decline in migration flows from third countries, and many Member States tried to completely ban migration.[4] However, a significant number of migrants remained on Community territory.[5] What is more, while in 1959 TCN workers accounted for 51.9 per cent of the migrant working population, by 1973, and despite the persistent economic stagnation, the share of TCN workers had risen to 73 per cent of the migrant working population in the Community.[6] This created the impetus to coordinate national migration policies.[7]

Perhaps the hope of return to the 1950s and 1960s paradigm, or the resilience of the legal framework to quickly shifting circumstances, meant that the considerations behind the legal instruments adopted during this period did not immediately reflect the bleak economic realities on the ground. Rather, the effects of the recession and national unemployment

[1] Programme de politique économique à moyen terme (1966–1970) [1967] OJ 79/1513; Bulletin of the European Communities (1969)6 23.

[2] Communication, On Immigration, SEC(91)1855 final, para 9; James Hollifield, *Immigrants, Markets, and States: The Political Economy of Postwar Europe* (Harvard University Press 1992) 72.

[3] Consultation on Migration Policies Vis-à-Vis Third Countries, COM(79)115 final, Annex, para 5.

[4] Ibid, point 6; Communication Transmitted to the Council on March 1985, Guidelines for a Community Policy on Migration, COM(85)48 final, II.5.

[5] Consultation on Migration Policies, COM(79)115 final, Annex, para 4 estimates 6 million, which could be around 12.5 million with their families.

[6] Ibid, para 5.

[7] See also point 10 of the Communique of European Summit in Paris on 9/10 December 1974, which calls for a 'stage by stage harmonization of legislation affecting aliens'.

for Community legal instruments were felt later, during the 1990s when it became clear that growth would never again achieve the levels enjoyed during the initial years of the Community project.

The scholarly analysis conducted during this period was mostly doctrinal and did not extend to all the areas reviewed in this part. The initial examination of the free movement framework consisted of purely doctrinal studies until the late 1970s, providing an overview of the relevant primary and secondary law of the field in this novel supranational area.[8] At this stage, certain authors suggested that free movement could also include TCN workers.[9] In light of judicial and legislative evolution from the 1980s onwards, scholarship in the field of free movement of workers became theoretically denser and started to explore the rights attributed to workers as an incipient form of European citizenship.[10] At the same time, while these evolutions clarified the personal scope of free movement to Community nationals, they spawned limited output on the relation of Community law to migrants from third countries.[11] As a result, scholarly research identifies the beginning of an EU migration policy in the late 1980s or early 1990s, starting with the intergovernmental cooperation of Member States discussed in Part II.

Regarding accession, the elements of flexibility and differentiation introduced in the 2004 enlargement enjoyed considerable academic attention, which is reviewed in Part III. Before that point, there is little literature on the issue of regulating migration in the context of accession. The only work that stands out is a book published by Böhning, who engaged with the Community rules on migration to diffuse misconceptions about the potential threats to the UK economy posed by foreign

[8] ED Brown, 'Recent Developments in the Social Policy of the European Economic Community' (1966) 3 CMLRev 184; K Lewin, 'The Free Movement of Workers' (1965) 2 CMLRev 300; H ter Heide, 'The Free Movement of Workers in the Final Phase' (1969) 6 CMLRev 466; Jean-Claude Séché, 'Free Movement of Workers under Community Law' (1977) 14 CMLRev 384; David O'Keeffe, 'Practical Difficulties in the Application of Article 48 of the EEC Treaty' (1982) 19 CMLRev 35; Derrick Wyatt, 'The Social Security Rights of Migrant Workers and Their Families' (1977) 14 CMLRev 411.

[9] DF Edens and Schelto Patijn, 'The Scope of the EEC System of Free Movement of Workers' (1972) 9 CMLRev 322; Allan Campbell, *Common Market Law* (Supplement 2/71, Longmans 1971).

[10] Richard Plender, 'An Incipient Form of European Citizenship' in Francis Geoffrey Jacobs (ed), *European Law and the Individual* (Elsevier/North-Holland 1976); Louis Singer, 'Free Movement of Workers in the European Economic Community: The Public Policy Exception' (1977) 29 Stanford Law Review 1283, 1284.

[11] Peter Oliver, 'Non-Community Nationals and the Treaty of Rome' (1985) 5 Yearbook of European Law 57.

workers during the period of UK accession.[12] Similarly, on international agreements and the rights they created for migrant workers, scholarly attention was only drawn later to the extensive interpretations of the Court on the rights of migrants under the EEC–Turkey Association Agreement.[13] Migrants from third countries and the potential of their enjoyment of rights during this period were largely overlooked.

Against this backdrop, this part looks at the period before the adoption of the Single European Act to investigate how economic and social objectives shaped the regulation of migrants' rights under Community law. Specifically, Community primary and secondary law, as well as Accession Treaties and Association Agreements that include provisions regulating labour movement, are examined in order to investigate how economic and social considerations appeared in their negotiation and eventual adoption. In this examination, I show how economic considerations conditioned the attribution or limitation of rights for migrants across different instruments already in the early years of Community law. The Community institutions had a clear view on the function of Community and TCN migrants for the project of growth, and relatedly they also considered the rights that migrants should enjoy because of their contribution to growth. The material examined in this part includes legal instruments, agreements, and case-law that were in place before the Single European Act was signed.

Chapter 2 analyses how free movement of workers was included in the Treaty of Paris and the Treaty of Rome and outlines the framework that was put in place to operationalize it for the completion of the internal market. Next, Chapter 2 engages with case-law and investigates how the CJEU took into account economic and social considerations in its adjudication of rights of Community workers. Chapter 3 provides an overview of (mostly) soft-law material and highlights the aspiration of Community institutions to extend the protection offered by Community law to all migrants legally resident in the Community. Finally, Chapter 4 turns to the focus on International Agreements negotiated by the Community that created rights for migrant workers, whose power was only felt later, through rulings of the Court in the 1990s.

From the analysis, it will become clear that the attribution and/or limitation of migrants' rights under Community law followed a single

[12] WR Böhning, *The Migration of Workers in the United Kingdom and the European Community* (Oxford University Press for the Institute of Race Relations 1972).

[13] The first judgment was issued in 1987, Case 12/86, *Demirel*, ECLI:EU:C:1987:400.

logic across the different instruments adopted in this period. According to this logic, migrant workers, regardless of origin, contributed to the Community development project. For this reason, they were to be granted rights. At the same time, the wide-ranging attribution of rights (with an emphasis on residence rights) could lead to market distortions and hinder growth. Thus, the legal framework needed to include clauses allowing for the smooth distribution of labour force in the Member States, while limiting potential distorting effects. In parallel, the attribution of social rights to all legally resident migrants was without question. Granting social rights was the central means to guarantee social progress to the population engaged in the Community development project, and to ensure that no unfair competition took place between the Member States, which were all involved in the same project. Arguably, across the different periods and shifts that took place in different areas of EU law, the attribution or limitation of migrants' rights did not follow a single logic based on the origin of the migrant. It rather followed a logic based on the function of the migrant for the collective development project. Behind this logic lies a balancing act between economic and social considerations aimed at shaping a sustainable migration framework that could support Community growth.

2

Migrant Workers Finding Their Way into Community Law

2.1 The Initial Free Movement Framework Aimed at the Optimal Allocation of Manpower

Free movement of all factors of production (worker, goods, capital, and services) is so fundamental to our understanding of Community law that it is scarcely questioned whether the inclusion of migrant workers in the Treaties was an automatic element of the intended closer cooperation between the founding Member States. On this matter, Christian had suggested that free movement found its way into the Treaty framework due to Italy's pressure for the use of Italian workers in the rest of the Member States.[1] The countries negotiating the European Project in the aftermath of World War II joined with different interests and posed different threats to the stability of the European future.[2] Italy was the only emigration country of the founding six and, at that time, was experiencing problems related to overpopulation and unemployment.[3] Positioning its overpopulation problem in combination with the political threats of this period, Italy managed to secure labour positions for its unemployed population in the form of free movement of workers within the ECSC under Article 69 ECSC.[4] In this initial framework, free

[1] David Christian, 'Resistance to International Worker Mobility: A Barrier to European Unity' (1955) 8 Industrial and Labor Relations Review 379, 379–389; Daniel Thym, '"Citizens" and "Foreigners" in EU Law: Migration Law and Its Cosmopolitan Outlook' (2016) 22 ELJ 296, 300; Luuk van Middelaar, *The Passage to Europe: How a Continent Became a Union* (Yale University Press 2013) 256.

[2] David Arter, *The Politics of European Integration in the Twentieth Century* (Dartmouth 1993).

[3] Francesca Fauri (ed), *The History of Migration in Europe: Perspectives from Economics, Politics and Sociology* (Routledge 2015).

[4] Christina Blanco Sío-López and Paolo Tedeschi, 'Migrants and European Institutions: A Study on the Attempts to Address the Economic and Social Challenges of Immigration in EU Member States' in Francesca Fauri (ed), *The History of Migration in Europe: Perspectives from Economics, Politics and Sociology* (Routledge 2015).

movement was not open to all workers, but only to qualified workers in the coal and steel industries, and under a specific procedure on vacancies.[5] By limiting the personal scope of free movement, the founding Member States wanted to ensure that no massive migratory waves would be caused by this concession to Italian interests.[6]

The abolition of the requirement of qualifications as a prerequisite for enjoying the right to free movement came with the Treaty of Rome.[7] Under this Treaty, the optimal allocation of manpower and its integration in the national societies was the objective of free movement, which was focused on abolishing the hardships deriving from the migrant status of the workers in the European industries.[8] Member States did not perceive the Treaty of Rome as creating an obligation for them to employ Community migrants.[9] Instead, the prevailing understanding was that nationals should always be chosen first to fill vacancies. If nationals were not in need of employment or were not sufficient, then a Member State could turn to Community migrants through a specifically designed procedure. If Community migrants did not suffice, then Member States could resort to TCNs. This national perception of the Treaty framework is not very different from what is in place today regarding the principle of Union preference in the labour market.[10] At the same time, this perception of free movement was nowhere close to a teleological reading of a scheme that would eventually foster a true political community. On the contrary, Member States perceived free movement as a labour migration framework that created obligations of preferential treatment to Community migrant workers only as long as national workers were not sufficient to fulfil labour needs.

What is more, at that point in time, there was nothing distinguishing the migrant workers employed in the Member States depending on

[5] Articles 69 (1) and (4), ECSC Treaty. Under Article 69 (2) and (3) of the ECSC Treaty, Member States would also draft a list of the skilled trades and their qualifications, which could be revisited in case of labour shortage.

[6] Blanco Sío-López and Tedeschi (n 4) 118.

[7] Article 48, EEC Treaty.

[8] Bertrand MA (1957), Rapport complémentaire fait au nom de la Commission des Affaires sociales sur la migration et la libre circulation des travailleurs dans la Communauté, Exercice 1957–1958 Première session extraordinaire, Document 5 et 11; Communauté européenne du Charbon et de l'Acier (1956), *Obstacles à la mobilité des travailleurs et problèmes sociaux de réadaptation.*

[9] European Community Information Service, Press Notice, Common Market takes initial step toward free mobility for workers, 15 June 1961.

[10] See 1994 Council Resolution, discussed in detail in Section 6.1.1.

whether or not they held Community nationality. On this matter, Thym points out:

> It would be wrong, however, to assume that the Rome Treaty wanted to establish universal free movement irrespective of nationality. During negotiations, there was agreement that only nationals of the member states should be covered; an explicit nationality clause was discarded in reaction to Franco-Italian disputes about the status of workers from Algeria and German concerns about the status of citizens from communist East Germany.[11]

Regardless of the intentions of the drafters, institutional practice pointed to a uniform approach towards both TCN and Community migrants. Specifically, the first Commission reports on free movement of workers generally discussed the number of labour migrants employed in Community Member States, regardless of their origin.[12] Even after the adoption of a framework that prioritized Community workers, the relevant Commission Reports looked at the labour market situation in Member States and examined how national manpower demand was covered by migrant workers in general, and not exclusively by Community migrants.[13]

At the time, the importance of labour mobility as a means to increase the production capacities of national industries was so prominent that there were discussions on including TCNs in the Community scheme of

[11] The quote appears verbatim in Thym (n 1) 303; Daniel Thym, 'Institutional and Constitutional Framework' in Evangelia Tsourdi and Philippe De Bruycker (eds), *Research Handbook on EU Migration and Asylum Law* (Edward Elgar 2022) 57. The same point is also raised in Daniel Thym, 'Ambiguities of Personhood, Citizenship, Migration and Fundamental Rights in EU Law' in Loïc Azoulai, Ségolène Barbou des Places, and Etienne Pataut (eds), *Constructing the Person in EU Law: Rights, Roles, Identities* (Hart 2016) 122; In all works, the author refers to Simone AW Goedings, *Labor Migration in an Integrating Europe: National Migration Policies and the Free Movement of Workers; 1950–1968* (Sdu Uitgevers 2005).

[12] Bertrand (n 8), Document 5.

[13] Commission (1965), Libre circulation et migrations des travailleurs dans la Communauté. Bilan annuel des activités de compensation et de placement au sein de la Communauté (art. 25 § 4 du règlement no 15/61 art. 36 § 4 du règlement no 38/64), 48ff; Commission (1966), La libre circulation de la main-d'œuvre et les marches du travail dans la CEE, Rapport établi en application des dispositions des articles 29 et 36 du règlement n° 38/64 relatif à la libre circulation des travailleurs, 36 ff; Commission (1967), La libre circulation de la main-d'œuvre et les marches du travail dans la CEE, Rapport établi en application des dispositions des articles 29 et 36 du règlement n° 38/64 relatif à la libre circulation des travailleurs à l 'intérieur de la CEE, 16–19; Commission (1968), La libre circulation de la main-d'œuvre et les marches du travail dans la CEE, Rapport établi en application des dispositions des articles 29 et 36 du règlement n° 38/64 relatif à la libre circulation des travailleurs à l 'intérieur de la CEE, 34 ff.

mobility in order to meet Community labour needs.[14] Any opening up of the Community labour markets in this way would always take place with oversight so as to not risk the unlimited access of foreign workers to national markets, which was seen as possibly limiting the quality of life for nationals.[15]

In Section 2.1.1, I turn to the secondary law adopted in successive steps in 1961, 1964, and 1968 to operationalize the free movement provisions. The analysis shows that free movement was structured as a labour mobility scheme aimed at addressing the uneven distribution of manpower between the Member States. The economic expansion of the Community was pursued through the 'optimum valorization of the technical abilities of human beings' residing in the Member States.[16] At the same time, the social aims of the Community, namely improving living standards, were to be realized through strategies related to achieving the full potential of labour mobility in order to maximize productive activities in Community industries, and were not reflected in an extensive attribution of rights in legal instruments.[17] Section 2.2 examines how this framework was interpreted by the CJEU whose judgments revolutionized the rights of EU migrant workers.

2.1.1 The 1961 Framework

The original framework regulating free movement in the Community was provided in Regulation 15/1961 and the Directive of the same year.[18] The 1961 Regulation was adopted with an emphasis on prioritizing national markets. Specifically, the 1961 Regulation gave preference to free movement of workers towards Member States that could not satisfy

[14] Bertrand (n 8) Document 11; Commission (1960), Synthèse des rapports établis en 1960 sur la situation actuelle du service social des travailleurs migrants dans les six pays membres de la CEE.

[15] Bertrand (n 8) Document 11, para 55.

[16] Giuseppe Petrilli, Member of the Commission, Chairman of the Social Affairs Group, The Social Policy in Bulletin de la Communauté économique européenne (1959)2 6.

[17] An example is mass unemployment, to which the response was rapid occupational training to maximize labour mobility. See Bulletin of the European Economic Community (1960)10 40.

[18] Règlement n° 15 relatif aux premières mesures pour la réalisation de la libre circulation des travailleurs à l'intérieur de la Communauté [1961] OJ 57/1073; Directive du Conseil en matière de procédures et pratiques administratives relatives à l'introduction, l'emploi et le séjour des travailleurs d'un État membre, ainsi que de leur famille, dans les autres États membres de la Communauté [1961] OJ 80/1513.

their labour needs by recourse to national workers.[19] Simply put, Community workers could take up work in another Member State if such work could not be carried by national workers.[20] What is more, they could exercise their free movement rights only after obtaining a specific job offer.[21] This was in order to avoid an 'invasion of workers from other countries' that could 'upset the economic and the social order of the national markets'.[22]

The scheme initiated by the 1961 Regulation was based on cooperation between national authorities and the Commission to ensure that national vacancies would be occupied by Community workers. In this regard, national employment offices were tasked with sending information to the Commission on such vacant positions in each Member State as needed to be filled by international labour.[23] Simultaneously, the Community set up a European Office on the coordination of this scheme.[24] Migrant workers moved following authorization to work in another Member State. Such authorization could be prolonged for one year in case of employment in the same profession.[25] After three years, the workers were provided with the possibility of exercising another profession for which they were qualified, while after four years they had the possibility to pursue regular employment in any profession.[26]

The aim of this Regulation was to replace the traditional migratory schemes between Member States based on bilateral or multilateral agreements.[27] In this regard, it granted migrant workers the right to equal treatment with respect to their working conditions and the right to vote in their respective trade unions.[28] In addition, migrant workers could be joined by their spouses and children under the age of twenty-one, who were also given access to the labour market.[29]

[19] Preamble, Regulation 15/1961.
[20] Articles 1(1) and 2.
[21] Article 2, Regulation 15/1961.
[22] Lionello Levi Sandri, The free movement of workers in the countries of the European Economic Community in Bulletin of the European Economic Community (1961)6 5–9.
[23] Cf Articles 3, 16, Regulation 15/1961. Article 18 mentions that 'les informations concernant le nombre d'offres et de demandes d'emploi par profession, enregistrées par leurs services en vue d'une *compensation internationale*' [emphasis added].
[24] Articles 22, 23, Regulation 15/1961.
[25] Article 6(1), Regulation 15/1961.
[26] Article 6(2) and (3), Regulation 15/1961.
[27] Levi Sandri (n 22) 5.
[28] Article 8, Regulation 15/1961.
[29] Article 11, Regulation 15/1961.

The right to equal treatment was introduced as a necessary part of the Community framework. It was not based on considerations regarding human rights guarantees for migrant workers, but rather derived from the 'new spirit of European solidarity'.[30] It was presented as a concession made by the Member States with a view to creating a labour market that would ensure the best use of the 'Community's human potential'.[31] It was the capacity of migrants as workers (not as human beings, or as nationals of the Member States) that ensured them the right to equality of treatment. This also ensured that native workers would be protected from unfair competition that could be caused from migrants taking up work for lower wages and less favourable working conditions.[32]

This first regulation was pronounced by Levi Sandri as 'an element of economic integration in its own right' and an 'important step towards the integration of Europe'.[33] The rights attributed to Community workers reflected a vision of social progress going hand-in-hand with economic development. These rights 'without representing such a direct return for progress in the individual worker's productivity, are nevertheless useful on a broader view, and satisfy requirements which progressive societies cannot evade'.[34] These words reflect the continuous balance of economic and social considerations behind the attribution of rights for Community migrants. They are attributed to migrants because of their function for growth, but also with a view to raising living standards for both nationals and migrants within the Member States. The Commission's vision of free movement was guided by the interdependence of economic growth and social progress in a way that today we would call economic and social sustainability of migration.

2.1.2 The 1964 Framework

At the second stage, Regulation 38/64 and Directives 220 and 221/64 were adopted.[35] The 1964 framework abolished the clauses on the

[30] Levi Sandri (n 22) 6.

[31] Ibid.

[32] Ibid 9.

[33] Ibid 5–6.

[34] Bulletin of the European Economic Community (1964)9/10, Introduction to the survey of social developments in the Community in 1963, 6.

[35] Règlement n° 38/64/CEE relatif à la libre circulation des travailleurs à l'intérieur de la Communauté [1964] OJ 62/965; Directive 64/240/EEC on the abolition of restrictions on the movement and residence of Member States' workers and their families within the

priority of the national labour market. It did, however, maintain Member State discretion to restrict free movement rights, 's'il existe un excédent de main-d'œuvre ou si l'équilibre du marché de l'emploi est mis en grave danger'.[36] This possibility was used by the Netherlands, Belgium, and France with respect to specific regions of their countries or specific professions.[37] The scheme put in place by the 1961 Regulation, whereby vacant positions were notified and coordinated by national employment offices in cooperation with the Commission, was maintained.[38] However, the rights of Community workers were now assimilated with those of national workers after two years of employment following their original entry to another Member State.[39] Migrant workers under the 1964 Regulation maintained the equal treatment rights with respect to their working conditions. In parallel, their rights to participation in trade unions were extended to include the right to be elected as well, upon condition of employment in the same company for at least three years.[40] The conditions on family admission also evolved to include all dependent relations of the worker.[41]

At this stage, human mobility among the Member States was restricted in an instrumental use of people as a resource on the path to economic development of Europe. In a report on the economic situation of the Community in 1964 and the outlook for 1965, this instrumentality is pronounced as follows: 'It is of course essential that each worker should

Community [1964] OJ 62/981. See also Directive 64/221/EEC on the co-ordination of special measures concerning the movement and residence of foreign nationals which are justified on grounds of public policy, public security or public health [1964] OJ 56/850.

36 Preamble, Regulation 38/64/ Such suspension took place upon notification under Articles 2 and 4–6, which also provided for exceptions.

37 Commission (1965), Libre circulation et migrations des travailleurs dans la Communauté. Bilan annuel des activités de compensation et de placement au sein de la Communauté, 48–50; Commission (1966), La libre circulation de la main-d'œuvre et les marches du travail dans la CEE, 57–58; Commission (1967), La libre circulation de la main-d'œuvre et les marches du travail dans la CEE, Rapport 1967, 24–25; Commission (1968), La libre circulation de la main-d'œuvre et les marches du travail dans la CEE. Rapport 1968, 65–67. Bertrand (n 8) Document 11; Commission (1960), Synthèse des rapports établis en 1960 sur la situation actuelle du service social des travailleurs migrants dans les six pays membres de la C.E.E.; H ter Heide, 'The Free Movement of Workers in the Final Phase' (1969) 6 CMLRev 466, 467.

38 Articles 1, 24 and 32, Regulation 38/64.

39 Article 1, Regulation 38/64.

40 Articles 8, 9(2), Regulation 38/64.

41 Article 17, Regulation 38/64.

have a job, but it is also necessary that he should be employed where the economy most needs his contribution, and where he can make the best use of his abilities.'[42] Free movement rights were not tied to the individual agency of the people of Europe, but were rather conditioned by the workers' contribution to economic development.[43]

2.1.3 *The 1968 Framework*

The third and final phase of harmonization came with Regulation 1612/68 and Directive 68/360.[44] The 1968 Regulation, in its preamble, points to the links between mobility and development both for the individual and for the states involved:

> [W]hereas mobility of labour within the Community must be one of the means by which the worker is guaranteed the possibility of improving his living and working conditions and promoting his social advancement, while helping to satisfy the requirements of the economies of the Member States.[45]

The connection of mobility to national economies further implied that such mobility should be restricted in cases where Member States experienced or foresaw disturbances in their labour market which could threaten the standard of living and level of employment in a specific region or industry.[46] In any case, the phrasing of this Regulation was more open and guaranteed access to the labour market of Member States to every Community worker under the same conditions as nationals of the host Member States.[47] The 1968 framework also provided more enhanced protection for workers against potential discriminatory practices.[48]

[42] Bulletin of the European Economic Community (1965)3 11.
[43] See also Bulletin of the European Economic Community (1965)4 18; Bulletin of the European Economic Community (1966)8, Address introducing the Ninth General Report on the activities of the Community 7.
[44] Regulation 1612/68 on freedom of movement for workers within the Community [1968] OJ L 257/2; Directive 68/360/EEC on the abolition of restrictions on movement and residence within the Community for workers of Member States and their families [1968] OJ L 257/13.
[45] Preamble, Regulation 1612/68.
[46] Ibid.
[47] Preamble, Article 1, Regulation 1612/68.
[48] Articles 3, 4 and 7–9, Regulation 1612/68.

Despite the right to access Community labour markets, the scheme was still based on a mechanism of exchange of information between Member States and the European Co-ordination office regarding vacancies that could not be filled by the national labour market, but also applicants who were willing to undertake employment in another Member State.[49] The scheme thus aimed to match vacancies in one Member State to the surplus of manpower in another.[50] Vacancies could also be announced to non-Member States, if it was considered that Member States could not provide a sufficient number of workers.[51] This further serves to point out that labour migration under the free movement framework was intimately connected to the production needs of the time.

Even though the 1968 Regulation was a lot more progressive in terms of workers' rights compared to the previous ones, the extension of free movement rights was still balanced by the mechanism foreseen in Title III of the Regulation. This mechanism provided for an analysis to be carried out by the Member States and the Commission twice per year on the labour positions occupied by TCNs, the expected developments of the labour market, and the manpower movements in the Community.[52] Member States had to give priority to Community workers in order to ensure a balance between vacancies and employment applications.[53] Nevertheless, Article 20 of the 1968 Regulation provided that, upon approval by the Commission, Member States could partially or totally suspend the mechanisms provided for vacancy clearance, in case of existent or expected disturbances in the national labour market that could threaten the standard of living or level of employment in a specific region or occupation.[54] It should be noted, however, that unlike the 1964 Regulation, Member States could not adopt these measures unilaterally.

The analysis of secondary law shows that free movement was progressively opened to ensure orderly migration of workers and to avoid negative effects to national economies. The demand of primary law to ensure free movement of workers was gradually achieved via secondary law that evolved through the incorporation of clauses related to national

[49] Article 15, Regulation 1612/68.

[50] Article 16, Regulation 1612/68.

[51] Article 16(2), Regulation 1612/68.

[52] Article 19(1), Regulation 1612/68.

[53] Article 19(2), Regulation 1612/68.

[54] Articles 15–17 and 20(1), Regulation 1612/68.

labour market priority and the possibility to restrict free movement for economic reasons. This shows how economic considerations shaped the applicable legal framework that operationalized Article 48 EEC.

The three phases of liberalization of movement were all connected to different concerns as to how national labour markets operate in relation to a Community-wide free movement objective. In essence, the institutional build-up of free movement was shaped with a view to addressing manpower mismatches between the national labour markets, mismatches which posed dangers for the unhindered pursuit of growth.[55] At that stage of industrialization, the productive capacities of Member States and availability of manpower were codependent.[56] The Commission therefore had to set up a system that could address the disequilibrium between national labour markets (shortage of labour in Germany and the Netherlands which had greater productive capacities and surplus of unskilled labour in Italy) to make the best of the human capital of the Community Member States.[57]

The adoption of the 1968 Regulation marked the end of the transitional period provided under Article 8 EEC for the establishment of the common market. According to the Commission, the provisions of this Regulation along with the Directive of the same year would serve to create European awareness by attributing identical rights to all Community migrants.[58] Moreover, the Commission envisioned the extension of these rights with the eventual purpose of making the free movement framework an element of geographic and vocational mobility for a single Community labour market.[59] In this setting, migration was perceived as a means of a functioning common market, which should be able to cover shortages in the respective national markets. Community workers were first and foremost manpower, and their movement was directed towards the optimal allocation of resources within the common market. Even though there was an attempt to present free movement 'as something more important and more exacting than the free movement of

[55] Bulletin of the European Economic Community (1960)5.

[56] Bulletin of the European Economic Community (1960)3 39.

[57] Bulletin of the European Economic Community (1960)10 40; Bulletin of the European Economic Community (1960)5 35; Bulletin of the European Economic Community (1960)4 43. See also Levi Sandri (n 22) 6.

[58] Commission Information Memo P-50/68, Complete freedom of movement for workers now a reality.

[59] Ibid.

a factor of production',[60] the attribution of rights to migrants in this context was dictated by their economic contribution. At this stage, there was no perception of migrant workers as Europeans with connected historical and political identities.

In what was presented as an achievement towards the end of a political union, Levi Sandri stated that 'all the citizens of the Member States are placed on an equal footing and therefore possess the same status'.[61] This equal footing, however, was framed in the pursuit of what he called 'man's most important practical activity' – work, and not on the basis of their political existence in the Community.[62] At this stage of liberalization of free movement, we see an unlimited emphasis on worker status as the core source of the social and human rights tied to migration. With this in mind, Section 2.2 turns to the Court and examines the way in which it revolutionized the protection enjoyed by migrant workers.

2.2 Social Rights of Community Migrants: A Judicial (R) Evolution

In the secondary law adopted to implement free movement of workers' provisions, the set of rights enjoyed by Community workers was dictated by Regulation 1612/68.[63] Article 7 of the Regulation implemented the non-discrimination principle of Article 48 EEC. It provided that migrant workers should enjoy equal treatment in relation to their working conditions and equal access to the social and tax advantages that are available to national workers. The Regulation also provided for the right of migrant workers to be joined by their family in the host Member State (Article 10), the right of family members to pursue employment (Article 11), and the right of migrant children to access education in the host Member State (Article 12).

In addition to this, Regulations 3 and 4 of 1958 and later Regulation 1408/71 were adopted under Article 51 EEC to coordinate social security between the Member States. Social security rights were harmonized to facilitate free movement of workers, and this objective conditioned the

60 Lionello Levi Sandri, Free movement of workers in the European Community, Bulletin of the European Economic Community (1968)11 7.
61 Ibid.
62 Ibid 6.
63 Until 2011 when it was repealed by Regulation 492/2011.

interpretation of the relevant regulations.[64] The Court developed a rich case-law on social security dealing primarily with the calculation of pension rights or accident costs.[65] By focusing on the abolition of barriers to ensure the greatest possible free movement for migrant workers and their families, it ensured the protection of Community workers.[66] However, in cases where the Court assessed that the rights of Community workers could not be protected under the more specific scope of application of Regulation 1408/71 on social security rights, it did not exclude the relevant rights from the scope of Community law. Rather, it used the principle of non-discrimination and created extensive rights, by recourse to the concept of social advantages under Article 7 Regulation 1612/68.

By reviewing of the case-law of the Court on the social rights granted to migrant workers (Section 2.2.1) and their families (Section 2.2.2), we can see how economic considerations conditioned the consolidation of social rights for migrant workers. Section 2.2.3 will demonstrate how this reasoning played out in relation to access to education by migrant workers and their families. The *ratio* underlying the judgments is that granting social protection to migrants and thereby improving their living and working conditions can guarantee labour mobility that will in turn lead to the development of the Member States' economies. The achievement of growth was considered to bring about social progress as a by-product, by the raising of living standards for the worker in the form of social rights.

2.2.1 Social Advantages Extending the Scope of Equal Treatment

During the 1970s and 1980s, the Court addressed many different aspects of Regulation 1612/68 and developed a rich case-law that extended the

[64] Case 75/63 (*Hoekstra*) *Unger*, ECLI:EU:C:1964:19, 184.

[65] Case 92/63, *Nonnenmacher*, ECLI:EU:C:1964:40; Judgment of 15 July 1964, Case 100/63, *Van der Veen*, ECLI:EU:C:1964:65; Case 24/64, *Dingemans*, ECLI:EU:C:1964:86; Case 31/64, *Bertholet*, ECLI:EU:C:1965:18; Case 33/64, *Van Dijk*, ECLI:EU:C:1965:19; Case 33/65, *Dekker*, ECLI:EU:C:1965:118.

[66] Case 44/65, *Singer et Fils*, ECLI:EU:C:1965:122; Case 61/65, *Vaassen-Goebbels*, ECLI:EU:C:1966:39; Case 4/66, *Hagenbeek*, ECLI:EU:C:1966:43; Case 1/67, *Ciechelsky*, ECLI:EU:C:1967:27; Case 2/67, *De Moor*, ECLI:EU:C:1967:28; Case 6/67, *Guerra*, ECLI:EU:C:1967:29; Case 9/67, *Colditz*, ECLI:EU:C:1967:30; Case 11/67, *Couture*, 11/67, ECLI:EU:C:1967:52; Case 14/67, *Welchner*, ECLI:EU:C:1967:48; Case 18/67, *Cossutta*, ECLI:EU:C:1967:46; Case 19/67 *Van Der Vecht*, ECLI:EU:C:1967:49; Case 22/67, *Goffart*, ECLI:EU:C:1967:47; Case 19/68, *De Cicco*, ECLI:EU:C:1968:56.

rights granted to migrant workers beyond what might be imagined under a literal reading of the Regulation. The logic behind this approach can be found in the 5th Recital of Regulation 1612/68, which prescribes, *inter alia*, that free movement should be exercised in freedom and dignity, and that worker and their families should be integrated in the host country. The economic benefits of migration and its position as means to achieve further development of the Union were tied to an improvement in the living and working conditions of the migrant and eventual social progress of the Community.

The provision of Article 7(2) Regulation 1612/68 provided that migrant workers should enjoy equal treatment in relation to their working conditions, and equal access to the social and tax advantages that are available to national workers. This provision was central to the development of the relevant case-law. In all cases where the Court dealt with discriminatory practices against migrant workers, it resolved them by recourse to the non-discrimination principle of Article 48 EEC, and Article 7 of Regulation 1612/68, which was held to be a more specific application of Article 7 EEC.

The Court interpreted the concept of social advantages broadly and found that they did not have to be directly linked to a contract of employment. Specifically, it defined social advantages as all the advantages

> which, whether or not linked to a contract of employment, are generally granted to national workers primarily because of their objective status as workers or by virtue of the mere fact of their residence on the national territory and the extension of which to workers who are nationals of other Member States therefore seems suitable to facilitate their mobility within the Community.[67]

Already in 1969, the Court examined its first free movement case, which concerned protection against disadvantages resulting from fulfilment of military service.[68] *Ugliola*, an Italian worker in Germany, who had completed his military service in Italy, claimed the protection of a German law which provided that military service should be taken into account for the calculation of benefits related to the conditions of work and employment. Germany put forward an argument related to the economic burden it would have to bear if it were to apply the national

[67] Case 207/78 *Ministère public v Even*, ECLI:EU:C:1979:144.

[68] Case 15/69, *Ugliola*, ECLI:EU:C:1969:46.

benefits to workers who performed their military service in other Member States. Essentially, it suggested that in such a case, it 'would be indirectly relieving the defence budget of those States'.[69] AG Gand's Opinion in the case reflected the economic integration basis of the Community and highlighted that free movement of workers was promoted and protected due to the multilateral advantages drawn by all members of the Community.[70] The Opinion implied that workers were not seen as full subjects of the Community.[71] They were rather protected in a format similar to bilateral migration treaties: the nationals of a state of origin should enjoy protection in a host state because the host state's nationals enjoy equal protection in the state of origin. The Court found that national law should extend to migrant workers in light of the principle of equal treatment under Article 48 EEC and 7 Regulation 1612/68.

Following this case, the Court's docket consisted of cases on different national benefits and their classification under Community law. In most cases, where the benefits could not be classified under social security coordination, the Court used Article 7(2) of Regulation 1612/68 and declared them to be social and tax advantages. Thus, it established an extensive reading that fortified the social protection offered to workers.[72]

At the same time, this reasoning was applied as regards discriminatory practices in Member States which were completely unrelated to employment. In *Marsman*, the Court found that Community workers were entitled to the special protection against dismissal. Such a protection was granted under German law only to workers who were resident in Germany. The Court held that the protection should extend to all migrants who work in Germany, even if they reside in another Member State.[73] In *Mutsch*, the Court held that the right to be heard by a Court in one's own language was a social advantage under Article 7 (2) of Regulation 1612/68.[74]

Then, in *Netherlands v Reed*, the Court held that the right of a Community worker to be accompanied by his unmarried partner also

[69] Case 15/69, *Ugliola*, ECLI:EU:C:1969:46, p. 367.

[70] Opinion of AG Gand in Case 15/69, *Ugliola*, ECLI:EU:C:1969:38.

[71] In contrast to what was stated in Case 26/62, *Van Gend & Loos*, ECLI:EU:C:1963:1 that referred to the individual as a full subject of Community law.

[72] Case 65/81, *Reina*, ECLI:EU:C:1982:6; Case 249/83, *Hoeckx*, ECLI:EU:C:1985:139, para 22.

[73] Case 44/72, *Marsman v Rosskamp*, ECLI:EU:C:1972:120.

[74] Case 137/84, *Mutsch*, ECLI:EU:C:1985:335.

constituted a social advantage.[75] Article 10(1) Regulation 1612/68 provided the right of migrant workers to be joined by their spouse. The wording of the provision could not be stretched to incorporate family reunification rights for the unmarried partner.[76] Despite this, the Court held that the right to be accompanied by an unmarried partner fell within the scope of Community law. This right was recognized as a social advantage for the purposes of Regulation 1612/68 in light of the economic function of the Regulation.[77] The Court found that the residence permit of the unmarried partner supports the integration of the migrant worker in the host state and thereby contributes to the free movement of workers framework.[78]

In conclusion, the Court's case-law at the early stages of the EU project dealt with discriminatory practices against migrant workers in the Member States. Such cases were resolved by recourse to the non-discrimination principle of Article 48 EEC and Article 7 of Regulation 1612/68, which was held to be a more specific application of Article 7 EEC. As the Community developed, the Court attempted to guarantee the more human aspects of free movement. However, the competence of the Community on the market could not go further than the prescriptions of Article 51 EEC on the harmonization of social security systems. Where the Court saw that the rights of Community workers could not be protected under the more specific scope of application of Regulation 1408/71 on social security rights (due to the personal nature of certain rights or the relation to specific benefits in kind), it used the principle of non-discrimination and created a set of rights under the concept of social advantages under Regulation 1612/68.

2.2.2 Extensive Interpretation of Social Advantages for the Families of Migrant Workers

In parallel with this broad interpretation of social advantages for migrant workers, the Court developed a line of case-law on benefits for workers' families. This extension was affected by employing a similar line of reasoning. In most cases, the Court recognized derivative rights for migrant workers' families as social advantages under Article 7(2) Regulation 1612/68. In the relevant case-law, the Court always clarified

[75] Case 59/85, *Netherlands v Reed*, ECLI:EU:C:1986:157.
[76] Ibid, para 16.
[77] Ibid, para 28.
[78] Ibid, para 38.

that social advantages granted to the worker's family were in all cases derivative rights, and they were enjoyed by virtue of the person's association to the migrant worker. This is because the members of a worker's family were granted the right to move in order to join the worker and ensure that they migrate in dignity.[79] Thus, the status of the migrant worker was the source of rights for the worker's family. The migrant worker was the only one engaged in the process of economic development of the Community and, as a result, the only subject that could draw rights directly from Community law. In this context, the Court recognized the right of workers' families to fare reduction cards for large families that were available to nationals of the host Member State,[80] handicap allowance for dependent children,[81] and the right of dependent family members to old people's benefit.[82]

The protection afforded to workers' families was further extended in *Deak*, where the Court held that unemployment benefits could be granted to TCN family members of Community workers as social advantages under Article 7(2) of Regulation 1612/68.[83] The Court held that Deak could not draw rights to a benefit under Regulation 1408/71 on social security, as this Regulation applied to benefits related to personal rights of Community workers, and he was a TCN associated to a worker.[84] In this context, the Court went on to examine whether protection could stem from Article 7(2) Regulation 1612/68, and it found that under this provision, advantages of this kind should be attributed to the worker's family. An unemployment benefit for the worker's child should be recognized as a social advantage of the worker themself due to the objective of effective exercise of free movement rights:

> A worker anxious to ensure for his [sic] children the enjoyment of the social benefits provided for by the legislation of the Member States for the support of young persons seeking employment would be induced not to remain in the Member State where he had established himself and found employment if that State could refuse to pay the benefits in question to his children because of their foreign nationality.[85]

79 5th Recital and Article 10, Regulation 1612/68.
80 Case 32/75, *Cristini*, ECLI:EU:C:1975:120, para 16.
81 Case 63/76, *Inzirillo*, ECLI:EU:C:1976:192.
82 Case 261/83, *Castelli*, ECLI:EU:C:1984:280; similar in Case 157/84, *Frascogna*, ECLI:EU:C:1985:243.
83 Case 94/84, *Deak*, ECLI:EU:C:1985:264.
84 Ibid, paras 15–16.
85 Ibid, para 23.

Subsequently, the Court held that the principle of non-discrimination, which migrant workers enjoy in relation to their employment, also extended to their TCN spouses. In *Gül*, a Cypriot doctor married to a British worker in Germany was denied the renewal of his temporally limited authorization to practice medicine due to the fact that there was an increasing level of unemployment among doctors of German nationality.[86] The Court held that the right of access to the employment market enjoyed by the spouse of the migrant worker under Articles 10 and 11 Regulation 1612/68 was linked to the rights enjoyed by the worker under Article 48 EEC.[87] As long as the spouse relies on such 'secondary rights', their access to employment should take place under the same conditions of non-discrimination as those enjoyed by the migrant worker beneficiary of free movement.[88]

Later, the Court built on *Hoeckx* and the entitlement of workers to minimex, a Belgian minimum subsistence benefit, finding that dependent family members were also entitled to this benefit. Lebon, a French national, lived in Belgium with her father, who received a retirement pension there.[89] She received minimex, which was discontinued on the ground of lack of evidence that she was looking for a job. The Court considered that Lebon came under the scope of Community law, since her father was a retired Community worker. It thus confirmed the extension of equal treatment regarding social advantages under Article 7 Regulation 1612/68 to members of the worker's family.[90] It also emphasized that this extension of equal treatment referred to rights derivative from the worker and extended to family members only to relieve the migrant worker from undue burden. As a result, the descendants of migrant workers can rely on equal treatment only to the extent that they are dependent on the worker.[91]

Such rights as are enjoyed without regard to the nationality of the family members required an association with the worker. This means that benefits that are attributed in the form of personal rights could not be claimed under Article 7(2) of Regulation 1612/68.[92] It is the association to a worker, or the dependency on them in certain cases, that forms

[86] Case 131/85, *Gül*, ECLI:EU:C:1986:200, para 6.
[87] Ibid, para 20.
[88] Ibid.
[89] Case 316/85, *Lebon*, ECLI:EU:C:1987:302.
[90] Ibid, para 12.
[91] Ibid, para 13.
[92] Case C-243/91, *Taghavi*, ECLI:EU:C:1992:306, para 12.

the basis of the rights of family members. At this stage of Community law, families and family members were not protected independently out of considerations of humanity; instead, they were situated within the functional logic of the Community. They were granted rights because they facilitated migration in dignity.[93] What is more, when the association with the worker ends, there is no longer a basis to claim the rights under Community law. This was confirmed in *Diatta*, where the Court implicitly held that an official divorce would take away residence rights of a TCN spouse of a migrant worker.[94]

2.2.3 The Social Protection of Migrant Workers and Their Families in Education

The case-law analysed in Section 2.2.2 shows how the Court interpreted the concept of social advantages broadly as a means to facilitate free movement and to promote the economic objectives served by labour mobility. The economic progress supported by labour migration would bring about social progress for the migrant as a by-product. This section turns to how this reasoning played out in relation to access to education. It shows that equal access to education was guaranteed for Community workers and their families because it supported personal development that could make them more competitive in the internal market. Non-discrimination and the effective exercise of free movement rights have been examined in a series of preliminary rulings related to enrolment fees for access to education or grants related to maintenance while in education.[95] Sections 2.2.3.1 and 2.2.3.2 will look at how the effective protection of social rights developed in the case-law related to access to education of children of Community workers (Section 2.2.3.1) as well as of Community workers themselves (Section 2.2.3.2). The analysis will highlight the close link between economic and social objectives also in relation to this type of social rights.

93 For a different focus, see Clare McGlynn, 'Families and the European Union Charter of Fundamental Rights: Progressive Change or Entrenching the Status Quo' (2001) 26 ELR 582, 587.

94 Case 267/83, *Diatta*, ECLI:EU:C:1985:67, whereas separation and residence in different houses does not take away such rights.

95 Case 152/82, *Forcheri*, ECLI:EU:C:1983:205; Case 293/83, *Gravier*, ECLI:EU:C:1985:69; Case 235/87, *Matteucci*, ECLI:EU:C:1988:460; Case C-357/89, *Raulin*, C-357/89, ECLI:EU:C:1992:87; Case 39/86, *Lair*, ECLI:EU:C:1988:322; Case 309/85, *Barra*, ECLI:EU:C:1988:42; Case 24/86, *Blaizot*, ECLI:EU:C:1988:43.

2.2.3.1 The Double Objective of Access to Education for Children of Community Workers

The case-law of the Court during the 1970s made groundbreaking steps in relation to the protection of children of migrant workers and their access to education. Article 12 of Regulation 1612/68 provided for the equal access of migrant children to education in the host Member State. This provision was interpreted by the Court in relation to benefits of different kind and the rights of access to education for children of migrant workers under Article 12 of Regulation 1612/1968.

The first line of cases examined disability benefits for children of migrant workers. In *Michel S*, the Court recognized that the child of a Community worker was entitled to access any benefits aimed at improving the fitness for work of disabled individuals under Article 12 Regulation 1612/68.[96] Subsequently, in *F*, the Court found that benefits under Article 12 could also be granted to children of migrant workers, even when such children had no prospect of employability.[97] In that case, Belgium, where the migrant family resided, argued that the only reason why disability benefits should be granted to children of migrant workers was to improve the children's fitness for employment. This could not be the case for F's child, who had no prospect of employment due to their disability. The Court did not accept this argument. Similar to *Deak*, the Court put forward the effective enjoyment and exercise of free movement rights and emphasized that if this benefit was not recognized,

> [A] worker anxious to ensure to his child the lasting enjoyment of the benefits necessitated by his condition as a handicapped person, would be induced not to remain in the Member State where he has established himself and has found his employment.[98]

In these first cases, the derivative rights of children were interpreted in an instrumental manner. Children of migrant workers should enjoy social rights in the host Member State because otherwise the worker would not be able to move and become an active part of the Community labour market. The second line of case-law of the Court developed by reference to the right of migrant children to equal access to education in the host Member State.

In *Casagrande*, the Court addressed the question whether migrant children of Community workers should have access to education grants

[96] Case 76/72, *Michel S*, ECLI:EU:C:1973:46.

[97] Case7/75, *Mr and Mrs F*, ECLI:EU:C:1975:80.

[98] Ibid, para 20; Case 63/76, *Inzirillo*, para 17.

available to children of German nationals. The case was resolved in favour of the migrant children with reference to the fifth recital of Regulation 1612/68,[99] which enshrined the intended purpose of integration of the migrant family in the host country. This reasoning was confirmed in *Alaimo*.[100] As a result, migrant children were entitled to equality not only in terms of admission to education but also, more broadly, with respect to all measures, adopted by Member States, that could facilitate their course of education.

The issue was developed by the Court in *di Leo*, which concerned a German educational grant for attendance of courses outside Germany.[101] The daughter of an Italian worker was refused this grant, because under national law, even though the grant could be provided to children of Community nationals, the education could not be provided in the state of which they were nationals. Despite the clear case-law on Article 12 of Regulation 1612/68 and its application to educational grants, the German and Dutch governments argued that if the children of a migrant worker were to study in their state of origin, the objective of the Regulation, which is to promote integration, would not be pursued.[102]

The Court rejected these arguments. It emphasized that integration of migrant workers in the host country should take place in respect of liberty and dignity.[103] To that end, it was essential that children of migrant workers, who resided with them in the host country, should be able to choose their education in the same way that children of nationals did.[104] As a result, Article 12 of Regulation 1612/68 also extended to grants for training or education abroad. However, Article 12 imposed obligations only on the Member State in which migrant workers resided. In *Humbel and Edel*, the Court held that protection from discrimination in relation to access to education could not be extended to create obligations for a third Member State in relation to any migrant worker within the Community.[105]

[99] Case 9/74, *Casagrande*, ECLI:EU:C:1974:74, para 6.
[100] Case 68/74, *Alaimo*, ECLI:EU:C:1975:11.
[101] C-308/89, *Di Leo*, ECLI:EU:C:1990:400.
[102] Ibid, para 11; Case 9/74, *Casagrande*.
[103] C-308/89, *Di Leo*, para 13.
[104] Ibid.
[105] Case 263/86, *Humbel and Edel*, ECLI:EU:C:1988:45, 1, para 10. In that case, French workers in Luxembourg claimed the repayment of 'minerval' [enrolment fee] for their sons' education, arguing that Luxembourgish nationals are not required to pay such fee when they access education in Belgium.

Overall, in the aforementioned case-law, the Court acknowledged various objectives underlying the broad interpretation of secondary law. First, the rights of children were meant to facilitate the function of their worker parent in the internal market. Especially when it comes to children with no prospect of employment, the central idea was that the worker should be facilitated in the host Member State; otherwise, they would be less willing to migrate. This reason is a primarily economic one tied to providing incentives for labour migration. Second, equal access to education for migrant children is ensured in order to achieve integration. Integration in this case is sought as a purely social objective. It is a recognition that the common historical and cultural background of Community workers is not enough in itself. Rather, action needs to be taken to promote the social advancement of migrant families by facilitating their incorporation into national societies. Section 2.2.3.2 turns to migrant workers themselves and their rights to education to investigate how economic and social objectives appear in their protection under Community law with regard to education.

2.2.3.2 Migrants' Rights While in Education: Protection Dependent on an Effective Market Link

The Court's extensive interpretation of social advantages presented earlier in Section 2.2.1 also applied to maintenance grants for students, insofar as they could qualify as workers. This was confirmed in *Lair*, which concerned training grants requested by a French national in Germany.[106] Germany refused to award the grants on the ground that the worker had not been engaged in occupational activity in Germany for five years prior to their studies. The Court took this opportunity to clarify the difference between access grants and maintenance grants. It reiterated that grants related to registration and tuition fees, insofar as they concerned access to education, came within the scope of the Treaty as conditions of access to vocational training, and Article 7 EEC was thus applicable.[107] In contrast, grants attributed by Member States to students for maintenance during their education fell outside the scope of Community law as they fell under educational policy, which was a competence retained by the Member States.[108]

[106] Case 39/86, *Lair*.
[107] Ibid, para 14; Case 293/83, *Gravier* and 24/86, *Blaizot*.
[108] Case 39/86, *Lair*, para 15.

The Court could have concluded the case at this stage – but it did not. It tried to examine whether that type of assistance could fall under the notion of social advantage for migrant workers under Article 7 of Regulation 1612/68. In this regard, Article 7(3) provided for access to training in vocational schools and retraining centres. But the school in question did not fall in either of these categories. This did not preclude the Court from qualifying the training grant at issue as a general social advantage under Article 7(2) of Regulation 1612/68.[109] During the proceedings, Member States argued that once a person became a student, they lost their status as workers and, accordingly, the entitlement to social advantages in the host Member State.[110] The Court resisted such a limitation of the right to equal access to social advantages. Specifically, the Court held that as regards grants for university education, the status of worker could form the basis of entitlements as long as there was a relationship between the previous employment and the course of study.[111]

This function of studies as a means of developing a worker's capacities can only be invalidated if 'a migrant has involuntarily become unemployed and is obliged by conditions on the job market to undertake occupational retraining in another field of activity'.[112] Hence, the granting of entitlements to migrant students presupposes that it takes place in the context of professional development that could reinforce their professional mobility. If the course of study had no link with one's occupational activities, then the status of worker and the benefits that come attached to it could not be retained.[113]

In *Brown*, the Court additionally held that when a Community national entered in an employment relationship for a short period (eight-month traineeship in this case) with a view to undertaking studies in the same field, and where his employer employed him only because he was already accepted for admission, that person qualified as a worker under the Treaty, but he did not qualify for maintenance benefits related to study under Article 7(2) of Regulation 1612/68.[114] This created a 'legal

[109] Ibid, para 22.
[110] Ibid, para 29.
[111] Ibid, para 37.
[112] Ibid.
[113] C-357/89, *Raulin*, para 22.
[114] Case 197/86, *Brown*, ECLI:EU:C:1988:323, paras 23, 28.

loophole' according to O'Keeffe and Johnson.[115] Prospective students could take up casual work in the country where they intend to study and qualify as workers.[116] In such cases, they would be eligible for all the benefits available to workers in that state under Regulation 1612/68. This issue was clarified in *Raulin*.[117] There the Court held that enjoying benefits related to education through the concept of social advantages under Article 7(2) of Regulation 1612/68 required an independent employment relationship prior to pursuing studies. The nature and duration of the prior employment had to be taken into account and the migrant needed to show that there was an effective and genuine exercise of economic activity.[118]

Finally, in *Matteucci*, the Court held that equal treatment of migrant workers should also apply in relation to scholarships awarded pursuant to a bilateral agreement between two specific Member States.[119] Specifically, the Court observed that even if such types of agreement fell under the cultural sphere, they could not jeopardize the rights of Community workers to equal treatment.[120] What is more, similarly to the case-law on access to education,[121] the Court held that Article 7(2) of Regulation 1612/68 created a responsibility in the social sphere on each Member State to ensure equality of treatment for every Community migrant worker whether they pursued training in the territory of their host Member State or abroad.[122]

This case-law shows that the Court proceeded in far-reaching interpretation and application of Community law in the educational sphere. This led to a significant enlargement of equal treatment rights when it comes to maintenance while in education. Nevertheless, this was never disconnected from the functional logic of education in the Community legal order. The Community worker was not attributed rights on the grounds of human dignity and freedom of choice on how to pursue life, or at least the Court's reasoning does not point to such bases for

115 David O'Keeffe and Esther Johnson, 'From Discrimination to Obstacles to Free Movement: Recent Developments Concerning the Free Movement of Workers 1989–1994' (1994) 31 CMLRev 1313, 1318.

116 Ibid.

117 C-357/89, *Raulin*.

118 Ibid, para 14.

119 Case 235/87, *Matteucci*, ECLI:EU:C:1988:460.

120 Ibid, para 14.

121 C-308/89, *Di Leo*.

122 Case 235/87, *Matteucci*, para 16.

justification. Rather, they were attributed rights to survive while better tailoring themselves to serve the market. This close interdependence of social rights for migrants and economic growth under Community law points to considerations that would nowadays fall under the economic and social pillars of sustainability.

Overall, the analysis in this chapter demonstrated how free movement was progressively opened up to ensure orderly migration of workers and to avoid detrimental effects on national economies from lack of labour migrants. The demand of primary law to allow free movement of workers was gradually achieved via secondary law that evolved with the incorporation of clauses related to national labour market priority and the possibility to restrict free movement for economic reasons. This highlights the presence of economic sustainability considerations driving the applicable legal framework that operationalized Article 48 EEC. Next to the legal framework, the rulings of the Court revolutionized the social rights of Community migrants by an extensive application of the free movement provisions. The analysis in this section revealed the centrality of economic objectives in the reasoning of the Court as a basis for broader interpretations facilitating free movement. By promoting such objectives, the Court also guaranteed social progress for the Community migrants and their families in the form of rights they were entitled to. Against this background, Chapter 3 engages with the material related to migrants from third countries and investigates whether and how similar considerations drove the Commission's and the Council's agenda to coordinate national labour migration policies.

3

The Ambition of Extending the Scope of Protection to All Migrants

3.1 The Prelude to an Admission Policy: Coordination of National Positions on TCN Migration

By the time of the completion of the common market by the adoption of Regulation 1612/68, it was clear that the Community's workforce would not be enough to cover its labour needs and to ensure the productive capacity of Member States. Member States continued to employ workers from non-member countries at high rates to fill their vacancies. The First Medium-term Economic Policy Programme issued by the Commission in 1967 showed that recourse to workers from non-member countries would become necessary as the years passed.[1] Essentially, it was at this stage that the Commission started pushing for comparison of national recruitment policies to establish whether there existed common interests that could form the basis for closer cooperation in this field.[2]

The change in the economic situation and the declining need for labor forces in the 1970s did not alter the Community approach. In this regard, the first explicit articulation of the need for a Community migration policy appeared in the 1974 Action Programme in Favour of Migrant Workers and their Families.[3] In this Programme, the Commission emphasized the benefits of migration for the economies of the Member States:

> The influx of migrant workers on this scale has profound consequences for the economics of the Member States. First, their presence has contributed to a *faster rate of economic growth* than would otherwise have been attainable – least without much greater rates of capital investment.

[1] Programme de politique économique à moyen terme (1966–1970) [1967] OJ 79/1513; Bulletin of the European Communities (1969)6 23.

[2] Ibid; Bulletin of the European Communities (1970)3 39.

[3] Action Programme in Favour of Migrant Workers and Their Families, COM(74) 2250 final.

> Second, they have given the system a greater degree of *flexibility* than it would otherwise have had. The fact that migrants are available in such large numbers and are usually engaged in short term-contracts – typically one year – has facilitated the adjustment of the labour force, both in individual enterprises and in the economy as a whole, to short-term changes in demand, and has therefore, facilitated anti-cyclical policies. Third there is evidence that the ready availability of a relatively cheap source of unskilled manpower *has retarded the search for greater productivity* in Community industries.[4]

Despite the economic problems that co-occurred with migration during a period of stagnation, the Commission highlighted what should be the driver of a Community migration policy. In this, the 1974 Action Programme mentions that '[t]hese solutions must take account of the migrant workers' needs and their rightful place in a society to whose prosperity and well-being they contribute'.[5] The contribution of the migrant workers to the economic development of the host society set the basis for the need to attribute rights. In this alignment between the treatment of Community and TCN workers, we see the implicit attempt of the Commission to frame a sustainable migration policy, that is, a migration policy that supports the economic development of the Community and attributes rights to migrants in view of securing their social progress and relatedly social cohesion.

Against this backdrop, this section presents and evaluates the first binding measure adopted by the Community on coordination of national migration policies in 1985, a measure that should be seen as the prelude to a Community policy on admission that was completed a lot later, in the new millennium. Subsequently, the analysis of soft-law instruments and legislative measures in Sections 3.2 and 3.3 will show that, in this early period, emphasis was placed on shaping a migration policy characterized by full extension of equal treatment to TCN workers and their families. Overall, this chapter shows the desire of the Community, as expressed via its institutions, to fully coordinate labour-migration policies and to assimilate the rights of migrant workers, so as to support economic growth in the Member States and to raise the living standards of the population legally resident in the Community, regardless of their nationality.

In 1979, the Commission started encouraging the coordination of national migration policies in order to ensure the better functioning of

[4] Ibid 11, emphasis in the original.

[5] Ibid.

the labour market, as well as the harmonious development of Member States. The attempt was initiated by presenting the coordination of admission of migrants from third countries as corollary to the Community free movement framework:

> Insofar as the terms and conditions under which Third Country citizens are admitted to a State, the decision on admission is related fundamentally to labour market policy, at national as well as at Community level. It is, in fact, labour market policy which generally determines the conditions and terms under which a non-Community migrant is admitted or allowed to remain, and, in this regard, consultation on migration policies vis-a-vis Third Countries, constitutes a corollary to the Community policy of free movement of Community workers.[6]

In this light, the Commission presented the need for action to maximize the effects of migration for economic growth. As it suggested, the lack of coordination of national migration policies did not allow for the most effective use of workers, while at the same time the lack of central planning had led to the concentration of migration in the central industrialized areas of the Community and to the creation of economic and social problems for the periphery.[7] The Council also recognized the need for a policy that would allow consultation between the Member States on their national migration policies with third countries.[8]

In a Resolution on the matter, the Council mentioned Article 117 of the EEC Treaty, which referred to the need to promote improved working and living conditions for all the workers in the Community as a legal basis for such action.[9] Eventually, Commission Decision 85/381/ EEC was adopted, which set up a prior communication and consultation procedure on national migration policies in relation to third countries.[10] The legal basis used was Article 118 EEC, which provided that the Commission should promote the close cooperation of Member States in the social field and particularly with regard to employment and working conditions. The Decision required Member States to inform the Commission on draft measures and agreements related to migration from third countries and provided for consultations with the

6 Consultation on Migration Policies vis-à-vis Third Countries, COM(79)115 final, para 3.2.

7 Action Programme, COM(74)2250 final 22.

8 Council Resolution of 9 February 1976 on an Action Programme for Migrant Workers and Members of Their Families [1976] OJ C 34/2, Recital 6 and point 5(a).

9 Council Resolution of 16 July 1985 on Guidelines for a Community Policy on Migration [1985] OJ C 186/3, Recital 1.

10 Commission Decision 85/381/EEC.

Commission, to coordinate common positions and ensure that national action does not compromise the Community labour market policy.

This Decision was met with resistance from Member States for fear of encroachment on national competences. Several turned against it and requested that it be declared void. In *Germany a.o. v Commission*, five Member States claimed that the Commission did not have competence to adopt a binding decision in the field of migration, which field fell within the exclusive competence of States.[11] Matters related to migration from third countries were, they argued, part of their sovereign core and went beyond the social field mentioned in Article 118 EEC.[12] The Court found that

> [M]igration policy is capable of falling within the social field within the meaning of Article 118 only to the extent to which it concerns the situation of workers from non-member countries as regards their impact on the Community employment market and on working conditions.[13]

In this finding, the Court aligned the rationale behind the Community competence with the points of Commission Communication of 1979, which mentioned that the coordination of migration policies is corollary to free movement.[14] As AG Mancini noted on the same matter,

> The admission of foreigners, which is haphazard and ill-planned and often implemented illegally, seriously risks jeopardizing that policy. A series of measures should therefore be studied jointly with a view to adopting a coherent approach to the immigration of workers from non-member countries by safeguarding and strengthening the 'priority for Community nationals' in the Community labour market.[15]

The Court confirmed the Commission's competence to legislate and held that national migration policies should take into account action at Community level and specifically in the context of the labour market policy in order to not undermine its results.[16] It further held that such competence had the nature of procedural coordination. This means that

[11] Joined cases 281, 283, 284, 285, and 287/85, *Federal Republic of Germany and others v Commission of the European Communities*, ECLI:EU:C:1987:351.

[12] Ibid, para 8.

[13] Ibid, para 23.

[14] Consultation on Migration Policies, COM(79)115 final, para 3.2.

[15] Ibid; Opinion of AG Mancini in Joined cases 281, 283, 284, 285, and 287/85, *Federal Republic of Germany and others v Commission of the European Communities*, ECLI:EU:C:1987:169, p. 3225.

[16] Joined cases 281, 283, 284, 285, and 287/85, *Federal Republic of Germany and others v Commission of the European Communities*, para 16.

Community action had to be restricted in coordination and could not involve the adoption of substantive measures that would create obligations for Member States or rights for TCN workers. The Court upheld Article 118 EEC as the basis of the Decision; however, it declared the decision void as regards two specific provisions extending Community powers.[17] The Commission then adopted Decision 88/384/EEC, which reproduced the provisions of Decision 85/381/EEC and included amendments to comply with the Court's judgment.[18]

In this early case-law, the Court confirmed both the Community competence on TCN migration and the rationale for such competence. In line with the Commission's reasoning for the need for such a Decision, it became clear that national migration policies were not only related to the sovereign core of Member States and their right to control population movement; they also played a significant function at Community level. That is, they served the economic objective of ensuring the harmonious development of economic activities in the Community through a functional Community labour market. Both the EU institutions, in preparing and adopting the Decision, and the Court, confirmed the corollary nature of migration to free movement. This is apparent in the need to ensure that Community workers are not in a less competitive position because of national (lack of) planning. But most importantly, it appears in the alignment of objectives between free movement and migration coordination; they are both necessary means to ensure the economic objective of the Community.

In what follows, we shall see how similar objectives appear in parallel with social considerations in a series of attempts to grant rights to migrant workers. Unlike Community workers, TCN workers who did not fall under Association Agreements did not enjoy rights under primary or secondary law. However, by looking at soft-law instruments issued at that time, we will see that the progressive achievement of equal treatment between Community workers and TCN workers as regards their working and living conditions was the constant goal of the Community migration policy before the Single European Act. TCN

[17] One related to the scope of consultation extending to matters of cultural integration and one related to the objective of the consultation to ensure that draft measures are in conformity with Community policies.

[18] Commission Decision 88/384/EEC of 8 June 1988 setting up a prior communication and consultation procedure on migration policies in relation to non-member countries [1988] OJ L 183/35.

workers and Community workers were thought of as facing the same problems in their social and working life.[19]

3.2 The Case for Abolition of Discrimination between All Migrant Workers

As early as the 1974 Action Programme, the Commission had suggested that discrimination between TCN workers and Community workers as regards living and working conditions should be eliminated.[20] In the 1979 Communication that predated the Decision reviewed previously, the Commission stated that,

> The social situation which arises from inequality of treatment, and the failure to insert migrant workers and their families into the economic and social life of the host country, leads to tensions and discriminations which are potentially dangerous.[21]

This shows the interdependence of economic and social considerations behind the Commission's approach. The demand for labour migration necessary to achieve economic growth would need to be paired with social rights to ensure what we would call today social sustainability. Relatedly, it was considered self-evident that TCN migrants who live and work in the Community should enjoy equal treatment.[22]

The 1985 Commission guidelines for a Community Policy on migration set the goal of horizontal equality between Member States nationals, Community and TCN migrants, and required the extension of equal treatment to the social security field. In this regard, the Commission noted that '[f]rom the social standpoint, workers in the same objective situation cannot be treated differently on the sole basis of nationality'.[23] Even though the Commission realized that, especially as regards social security, this would also require the involvement of third countries (for aggregated periods of insurance and transfer of benefits), it still promoted the establishment of such agreements based on Community

[19] Guidelines for a Community Policy on Migration, COM(85)48 final; Council Resolution (n 9); Commission Decision 85/381/EEC, para 3.

[20] Action Programme, COM(74)2250 final 13.

[21] Consultation on Migration Policies, COM(79)115 final, para 2.3.

[22] Vredeling Henk, Migrants and the EEC, Full Text and Summary of a Speech by the Vice-President of the Commission for the Conference of the National Council of Social Services, London, 27 March 1971.

[23] Guidelines for a Community Policy on Migration, COM(85)48 final, para 40.

principles.[24] Similarly to the Commission, the Parliament was also insistent on achieving full equality between Community workers and TCN workers.[25]

Aside from the economic contribution of migrant workers as the basis for equal treatment, the need for active measures to advance their social position also appears in the relevant material. During the rapid economic development of the 1950s and 1960s, Community institutions focused solely on employment policy as means to ensure the social advancement of migrant workers. Nevertheless, in the context of the economic stagnation and unemployment that persisted throughout the 1970s and 1980s, it became clear that the social advancement of migrant workers would need to go further than employment policies to be successful.[26] In this context, more emphasis was put on equal treatment as a principle that should guide integration policies related to access to residence, education, vocational training, housing, and working environment.[27] Social advancement via integration was also connected to the civic rights of migrant workers. During the period under review, the Commission, the Parliament, and the Economic and Social Committee were demanding the granting of the right to vote in local elections for all migrant workers and their families living and working on the Community territory, regardless of nationality.[28]

However, this ambition of securing equal treatment was met with resistance from the Council. Under a more restrictive approach, the 1985 Council resolution on the Guidelines for a Community Policy on

[24] Ibid.

[25] Parliament Resolution on Migrant Workers from Third Countries adopted on 14 June [1990] OJ C 175; Parliament Working Documents 1983–1984, Document 1-811/83, Report drawn up on behalf of the Committee on Social Affairs and Employment on the problem of migrant workers, Rapporteur: Mrs Tove Nielsen, PE 84.870/fin.

[26] Policies on Immigration and the Social Integration of Migrants in the European Community, SEC(90)1813 final, para 101.

[27] Ibid, para 19.

[28] Opinion of the Economic and Social Committee on Migrant Workers 84/C 343/07, point 3.2.9; Policies on Immigration and the Social Integration of Migrants in the European Community, SEC(90)1813 final, paras 76–79; Parliament Resolution Doc. B2–881/86 on Community Policy on Migration of 9 October [1986] OJ C 283; Report drawn up on behalf of the Committee on Social Affairs and Employment on the Communication (Doc. C2–6/85-COM(85)48 final) on Guidelines for a Community Policy on Migration Together with a Draft Council Resolution, Working Documents 1985–1986, Document A2–4/85, points 2, 3(b); Guidelines for a Community Policy on Migration, COM(85)48 final, para 19; Resolution on the Joint Declaration against Racism and Xenophobia and an Action Programme by the Council of Ministers (Doc. A 2-261/88) [1989] OJ C 69 point 9.

Migration confirmed the desire that 'everyone within it [the Community] should have an equal opportunity of deriving advantages and making a contribution'.[29] A right of TCN migrant workers to equal opportunity is far from the Commission and the Parliament vision of full application of the free movement regime to TCN workers, voting rights in local elections, and equal access to the social security systems of Member States. The different approach of the Council can be explained by its proximity to national politics. After all, this was a time characterized by national bans on migration due to prevailing unemployment. The sensitivity of extending rights to migrants in such a national political climate will be seen more clearly in Chapter 6, where the analysis focuses on how national fears sealed the fate of many of the Commission's plans to promote the rights of migrant workers.[30]

In any case, a review of the relevant soft-law instruments shows that both economic and social objectives were tied to the demand of equal treatment for TCN workers. Equal treatment was linked to the contribution of the individual migrant to the project of growth. At the same time, we see an emphasis on the need to advance the living conditions of the population resident in the Community and to maintain social cohesion. The social considerations behind the promotion of migrant rights will become clearer in Section 3.3, which considers measures devised to ensure equal access to education for children of migrant workers.

3.3 The Social Imperative of Granting Access to Education to Migrant Children

Access to education for children of migrant workers was one of the first migration-related measures adopted at the Community level. The issue had been on the agenda since the 1960s, and gained the attention of Member States during the 1970s and 1980s. At this point it was becoming clear that migrant workers had set up family lives in the host countries, leading to a new generation of migrant children that had to be integrated in Member States to ensure their social advancement and avoid marginalization.

[29] Council Resolution (n 9), point 5.

[30] See David O'Keeffe, 'The Free Movement of Persons and the Single Market' (1992) 17 ELR 3, who criticizes the intergovernmental initiatives in the Council and acknowledges the political and nationalistic overtones migration was subject to during this period.

In 1975, the Commission published a proposal for a Directive on the education of children of migrant workers.[31] The considerations behind the proposal were twofold. First, the 1974 Council Resolution concerning a social action programme prioritized actions related to the reception and education of children in order to improve free movement of workers.[32] And second, in the same resolution, the Council set the objective of achieving equal treatment between EC and TCN workers and their families as regards their living and working conditions.[33] In this context, the proposed Directive would establish a right to tuition-free compulsory education in the host country, and promote the teaching of the language and culture of origin. The system was conceived to improve the living and working conditions in the Community, and it was suggested that the right to education provided in the proposal should cover all migrant children residing in the Community, regardless of their country of origin.[34] The Directive sought on the one hand to assist in the social and personal advancement and integration in the host country, and on the other to ensure the maintenance of the possibility of repatriation. Specifically, the Commission wanted to ensure that, by having access to courses in their mother tongue and their national culture, migrant children would maintain the possibility of reintegration into the country of origin.[35]

This proposal was approved by the European Parliament, which considered it an essential part of the educational aspects of the Community's Social Policy.[36] Showcasing the interdependence of economic and social objectives behind the proposed instrument, the Parliament Committee on Cultural Affairs and Youth suggested that migrant recruitment to cover labour demands should also be followed by measures that ensure the social well-being of the migrants.[37] The European Economic and

[31] Proposal for a Directive on the Education of the Children of Migrant Workers [1975] OJ C 213/2.

[32] Ibid, Recital 1.

[33] Ibid, Recital 2.

[34] Ibid, Recital 7, Article 1(2) of the proposed Directive.

[35] Ibid, Recital 6.

[36] Resolution embodying the Opinion of the Parliament on the proposal from the Commission for a Directive on the education of the children of migrant workers [1975] OJ C 240/48, point 2.

[37] Parliament, Working Documents 1975–1976, Document 375/5, Report drawn up on behalf of the Committee on Cultural Affairs and Youth on the proposal from the Commission to the Council (Doc. 224/75) for a Directive on the education of the children of migrant workers, Rapporteur: Mrs T. Carettoni Romagnoli, PE 471.807 fin p. 12, para 6.

Social Committee (EESC) also welcomed the inclusion of all migrant children in the scope of the directive.[38]

The initial proposal was based on Article 49 and Article 235 EEC. Article 49 EEC concerned the adoption of Directives or Regulations on measures necessary to ensure the realization of free movement of workers. Article 235 EEC, on the other hand, was a general clause providing for the adoption of measures necessary to achieve the objectives of the Community in cases where the Treaty did not provide necessary powers. Due to this, the Commission put forward Article 49 EEC as the legal basis for social measures concerning Community workers. Then, in line with the Council resolutions that provided for the objective of gradually establishing equal treatment for all migrant workers, the Social Action Programme, and the objective of Article 117 EEC to promote an improved standard of living of workers, the Commission argued that Article 235 EEC should be used as a legal basis to extend protection to TCN workers.[39]

The proposal of the Commission was not welcomed by the Member States for various reasons. The Danish, Italian, and French delegations in the Council disagreed with the choice of legal basis. The Danish delegation insisted that the Community had no jurisdiction in matters affecting TCNs and that, as a result, no binding instrument could be adopted on the matter.[40] The Italian delegation objected to the joint use of Articles 49 and 235 EEC. The Italians did not contest the Community competence on TCNs. Rather, they suggested that the Directive should only cover EC nationals and be based on Article 49 EEC, whereas a different binding measure should be put forward under Article 235 EEC for TCN workers.[41] Eventually, the French delegation joined the opposition, and

[38] Opinion on the proposal for a Directive on the education of the children of migrant workers [1976] OJ C 45/6, point 3.1.2.

[39] HAEU, CM2/1977-634.3, The Council, Note, Subject: Proposal for a Directive on the education of the children of migrant workers, Outcome of the discussions of the Working Party on Social Questions, Brussels, 31 March 1976 377/76 (SOC 97) 3; HAEU, CM2/1977-634.5; The Council, Note, Subject: Proposal for a Directive on the education of the children of migrant workers, Report from the Working Party on Social Questions to the Permanent Representatives Committee, Brussels, 18 May 1976 R/1230/76 (SOC 131), B. Statement by the Commission Representative.

[40] HAEU, CM2/1977-634.5 (n 39), C. Delegations' Position.

[41] HAEU, CM2/1977-634.4, The Council, Note, Subject: Proposal for a Directive on the education of the children of migrant workers, Report from the Working Party on Social Questions to the Permanent Representatives Committee, Brussels, 26 April 1976 R/987/76 (SOC 116) Annex – Attitude of the Italian delegation.

suggested that Article 49 EEC could not serve as the basis for covering TCN workers, but that similar measures could be extended to TCN workers by means of a non-binding act.[42] Besides these countries, Luxembourg, the UK, and Germany were in favour of a single instrument for both Community and TCN workers, but suggested that such an instrument should be non-binding.[43] Their disagreement did not relate to the personal scope of the instrument but with its material one. These states considered educational policy to be part of national competence.

Eventually, a compromise was reached: the Directive maintained Article 49 as its sole basis, and excluded children of TCN workers from its scope. At the same time, a declaration was added to the minutes of the Council Meeting of 25 July 1977. The declaration confirmed the Council's intention that the measures adopted in compliance with the Directive should also apply to children of TCN migrants. This would allow the delegations that were in favour of a single instrument for all migrant children to introduce higher standards of protection while implementing the Directive.[44]

In the negotiation of this instrument, we see how national disagreements over the personal and material scope of Community law led to the exclusion of children of TCN workers from the text of the Directive. Despite this exclusion, it is worth reflecting on the intimate link between the social and economic objectives of measures attributing rights to migrant workers' families. As it appears in later documents of the Commission, the education of migrant children was a measure aimed at addressing the underachievement and marginalization of immigrant groups. On the economic side, education was connected to the growing realization on behalf of the Community that migrant communities would be necessary for future demands of the labour market and, as a result, education could play a central role in that.[45] The social advancement of

[42] HAEU, CM2/1977-634.5 (n 39).

[43] Ibid. This related mostly to objections on education policy as part of national competence.

[44] HAEU, CM2/1977-634.7, The Council, Note, Subject: Proposal for a Directive on the education of the children of migrant workers, Outcome of the discussions of the Permanent Representatives Committee, Brussels, 24 June 1976 R/1555/76 (SOC 167); HAEU, CM2/1977-634.7 European Communities, The Council, Note, Subject: Proposal for a Directive on the education of the children of migrant workers, Outcome of the meeting of the Working Party on Social Questions, Brussels, 9 November 1976 1221/76 (SOC 253).

[45] Policies on Immigration and the Social Integration of Migrants in the European Community, SEC(90)1813 final, para 59.

migrant workers' families was set in the context of improving the living and working conditions of the people residing in the Community regardless of their nationality. At the same time, a utilitarian approach to their education was adopted to ensure that the labour market demands will be covered by the offspring of migrant workers, so there is no need to recourse to more migration.

3.4 The Double Economic and Social Objective of the Community Migration Policy

During this period, the growing percentage of TCN workers present in Member States created the impetus for the adoption of a first set of legislative instruments, as means to create an incipient Community migration policy. The projected economic and social objectives of the Community dictated a need for coordination of national migration policies and attribution of rights to migrant workers. These objectives have been presented previously in this chapter in the following way.

First, there was the economic objective of ensuring the proper functioning of the Community labour market. Member States were required to safeguard free movement for Community workers and respect their obligations towards the Community manpower before hiring TCN workers.[46] This is closely related to a liberal trade theory on international migration that presupposes that in the long term, economic growth will reduce the need for factor mobility.[47] Insofar as the Community had labour demands that could not be covered by the regional labour force, there was a preference to adopt measures that would make the TCN workers already resident on the Community territory more appropriate for the market, rather than opening the door to more TCN migration. The initiatives related to the education of migrant children and the coordination of national positions on migration, which were reviewed in Sections 3.1 and 3.3, can be seen to fall under this economic objective.

Second, there was the social objective linked with TCN workers' contribution to growth. Due to their status as workers, migrants had to be treated with respect and the Community had to take action for the improvement of their living and working conditions. The measures related to education of migrant children and the emphasis on equal

[46] Consultation on Migration Policies, COM(79)115 final, para 2.10.

[47] James Hollifield, *Immigrants, Markets, and States: The Political Economy of Postwar Europe* (Harvard University Press 1992) 24.

treatment, as the central principle guiding integration were linked to the pursuit of this objective which is identical for all migrants regardless of their origin. At the stage of Community law under examination, the Commission envisioned a policy on labour migration that would cover both TCN workers and Community workers without discrimination. Both these categories of migration were necessary for the economic development of the Community, and both should be attributed rights to ensure social progress in the Community. This grounding of the Commission's approach on the parallel pursuit of economic and social objectives is essentially an attempt to ensure a system of sustainable migration.

This aspiration did not meet much resistance from the Council, as long as there were national labour demands to be filled. While the Commission consistently backed this aspiration in the years that followed, the economic effects of the oil crisis and the increase in unemployment gave rise to a more restrictive approach in the Council as we shall see in detail in Chapter 6. In the meantime, Chapter 4 investigates the regulation of migration in the context agreements concluded by the EU with third countries either with the aim of instituting closer cooperation (like Association Agreements) or with the aim of accession.

4

Special Arrangements for Migrants Whose State of Origin Is (About to Be) Implicated in the Development Project

4.1 Turkish Workers under the EEC–Turkey Association Agreement

After the examination of the evolution of the free movement framework in Chapter 2, and the ambition of extending rights to TCN workers regardless of their country of origin in Chapter 3, this chapter addresses the special arrangements made to regulate migration from specific third countries. First, it will be shown how social and economic objectives, paired with favourable economic circumstances, laid the foundation for the extensive protection of Turkish workers under the EEC–Turkey Association Agreement. Then, Section 4.2 shows how economic cooperation with specific countries that were crucial for supplying migrant labour led to the attribution of rights to third-country nationals, despite their exclusion from primary and secondary law. Finally, Section 4.3 turns to enlargement processes and investigates how Accession Treaties concluded during this period were framed in light of ensuring the promotion of economic objectives, while limiting migration rights for nationals of acceding states. The analysis reveals the constant attempts by EU institutions to ensure that migration policy is aligned with the objectives of growth and progress, and thereby with the economic and social pillars of sustainability.

The EEC–Turkey Agreement was concluded in 1963 with a view to preparing Turkey for eventual accession to the EU. Such an evolution has not materialized to this day.[1] Despite the fact that the accession has not occurred, the rights granted by this agreement to Turkish workers are quite extensive, especially as judicially interpreted, as we will see in Chapter 7. Due to this, their privileged status compared to other third

[1] EEC–Turkey Association Agreement (signed at Ankara, 12 September 1963) [1977] OJ L 361/29.

country-national workers has been acknowledged in scholarship.[2] The aim of the EEC–Turkey Agreement enshrined in Article 2 was the continuous and balanced strengthening of economic relations between the parties, taking into account the need to ensure both the economic and social development of Turkey. In addition, the importance of Turkish workers for the development of the EU and for the functioning of the Turkish economy was acknowledged by all parties.[3]

Labour migration was regulated in the Agreement in the following way. Article 12 provided that the parties should be guided by Articles 48, 49, and 50 EC Treaty for the purpose of progressively securing free movement of workers. Article 36 of the Additional Protocol to the Agreement provided that free movement of workers between Turkey and the Community must be secured by progressive stages in the period between the end of the twelfth and the twenty-second year after the entry into force of the agreement subject to rules adopted by the Association Council.[4] Article 37 provided that Turkish nationals employed in the Member States should enjoy equal treatment as regards conditions of work and remuneration. Finally, under Article 38, the Association Council had the possibility to return to issues related to the geographical and occupational mobility of Turkish workers in order to facilitate their employment in the Member States as the association progressed. Article 39 provided that the Association Council would eventually adopt social security measures for the workers and their families, whereas under Article 40, it could make recommendations for the exchange of young workers guided by Article 50 EC.

In the progressive development of the Association, the Association Council adopted specific decisions in order to implement Article 12 of the Agreement and Article 36 of the Additional protocol.[5] During the process of negotiating these decisions, the Turkish side put continued emphasis on the need to ensure priority for its nationals in the EU labour

[2] Narin Idriz, 'Hierarchies of Privilege: Juxtaposing Family Reunification Rights, Integration Requirements, and Nationality in EU Law' in Moritz Jesse (ed), *European Societies, Migration, and the Law: The 'Others' amongst 'Us'* (Cambridge University Press 2020).

[3] HAEU, EM87 Secrétariat General, Rapport préliminaire de la Commission au Conseil au sujet du passage de la phase préparatoire à la phase transitoire de l'Accord d'Association avec la Turquie, SEC(68)1386.

[4] Additional Protocol and Financial Protocol signed on 23 November 1970, annexed to the EEC–Turkey Association [1972] OJ L 293.

[5] Decisions 2/76, 1/80 and 3/80.

market.[6] The Community resisted this prioritization as inconceivable, since, in parallel to this Agreement, it was negotiating Association Agreements with all the countries from which it received migrant workers. Next to the Association concluded with Greece, it was negotiating with the Maghreb countries and Yugoslavia, which were also labour-exporting countries.[7] Thus, giving priority to Turkish workers would necessarily mean giving priority to all the other countries under negotiation, which would make the provision pointless.[8] At the same time, Member State delegations invoked issues of political (in relation to antagonisms with other Mediterranean countries with which they had historical bonds), economic (in relation to the effects such a priority would have in case of a potential recession in the Community economies), and technical nature (in relation to the practical procedure of recruitment).[9]

Despite this, the Community sought to find a solution for a rational use of Turkish workers that could assist in the harmonious economic development of both the Community and Turkey.[10] What could be offered to achieve this was the implementation of the principle of non-discrimination by an analogous application of Article 48(2) EC, and the easing of restrictions to professional and geographic mobility within the Member States in a more preferential way compared to other migrant

[6] HAEU, EM87, Secrétariat General (n 3), point 11.

[7] Association Agreement with Greece presented in Section 4.3. See Articles 44–46 of Cooperation Agreement with Yugoslavia [1983] OJ L 41/2.

[8] HAEU, EM87, Le Conseil, Association CEE-Turquie, Projet de Rapport du Comité 'Associations Pays Tiers' au Comité des représentants permanents (Document de travail établi par le Secrétariat et destine à être examine au cours de la réunion du 5 juillet 1968), Objet: Passage de la phase préparatoire à la phase transitoire de l'Accord d'Association avec la Turquie, S/595/68 (NT 24) 20; HAEU, EM87, Secrétariat Général (n 3) point 12; HAEU, EM89, Le Conseil, Association CEE-Turquie, Aide-Mémoire du Secrétariat, Objet: Passage de la phase préparatoire à la phase transitoire de l'Accord d'Association avec la Turquie, Régime à prévoir en ce qui concerne le main d'œuvre, S/30/69 (NT 2).

[9] HAEU, EM89, Le Conseil (n 8) 6; HAEU, EM89, Le Conseil d'Association, Sommaire des Conclusions de la 19eme Réunion du Comité d'association CEE-Turquie qui s'est tenue à Bruxelles le mardi 11 mars 1969 CEE-TR 9/69, 19.

[10] HAEU, EM88, Commission Parlementaire Mixte CEE-Turquie, Recommandation no 2 sur le passage à la phase transitoire de l'association, point 9. For an overview of the negotiating positions see HAEU, EM89, Le Conseil d'Association, Rapport du Comité d'Association au Conseil d'Association CEE-TR 25/69; HAEU, EM89, Direction Général des relations extérieures, Bruxelles, 26.02.1969 10391, Note à l'attention de Monsieur Martino, Objet: Négociations avec la Turquie en vue du passage à la phase transitoire de l'Accord d'Ankara, session du conseil d'Association du 25 Février 1969.

workers.[11] In this regard, the position of economic and social considerations and their effects on the rights granted to migrant workers in the context of International Agreements was correctly conceptualized by Edoardo Martino, the Community Commissioner for External Relations in the period of 1967–1970, during a speech to the EEC–Turkey Joined Parliamentary Committee.

> Il convient de remarquer, a cet égard, que le problème de la libre circulation des travailleurs turcs à l'intérieur de la Communauté parait avoir été jusqu'à présent quelque peu surestimé. En effet, ce qui compte n'est pas seulement le statut juridique en tant que tel des travailleurs turcs, mais aussi la conjoncture économique favorable, d'une part, l'expérience et la qualification technique des travailleurs turcs, d'autre part. Dans la mesure où ces deux conditions sont réalisées le problème de la libre circulation des travailleurs turcs à l'intérieur des états membres de la Communauté pourrait apparaitre en quelque sorte un peu théorique.[12]

In this passage, Mr Martino suggested that the issue of granting rights to Turkish workers was very much dependent on what these workers brought to the Community markets in terms of technical expertise, and the prevailing economic conditions in the Member States. As long as there was a favourable economic climate, experienced workers would be needed to cover labour demands, and the question of granting them free movement rights became theoretical. The legal protection to be accorded to migrant workers should then be seen as closely tied to the economic conditions existing at the time when the relevant legal instruments are negotiated.

Ultimately, the rights of Turkish workers were established in Decision 2/76 adopted as the first stage in securing free movement of Turkish workers, and Decision 1/80 intended to improve the treatment of workers and their families in the social field. These Decisions provided that Turkish workers duly registered as belonging to the labour force of a member would be entitled, after a specified period of legal employment, to free access to any employment of their choice. What is more, Turkey

[11] HAEU, EM89, Le Conseil (n 8) 4; HAEU, EM89, Secrétariat General, Projet de Communication au Conseil concernant l'état des négociations avec la Turquie sur le passage à la phase transitoire de l'Accord d' Ankara (présente par M. Martino) SEC(69) 1601, 11.

[12] HAEU, EM91, Exposé de M Edoardo Martino, Membre de la Commission, Annex IV, Commission Parlementaire Mixte CEE-Turquie, Procès-verbal de la VIIIe session, du 27 au 30 Janvier 1970, Munich PE 24.098, 17.

succeeded in securing a priority status in the Community labour market, a provision which, together with the aims of the Agreement and the function of Turkish workers, can be seen as the basis for the differentiated treatment of Turkish workers compared to other TCN workers as we shall see in Section 7.1.1.[13]

These Decisions also included safeguard clauses. Article 6 of Decision 2/76 and Article 12 of Decision No 1/80 provided that in cases where a Member State experienced or anticipated disturbances in the labour market which could affect the standard of living or level of employment in a region, branch of activity, or occupation, it could refrain from granting rights to Turkish workers and their families. This safeguard clause should be seen in parallel to Article 15 of Decision 1/80, which provided that the Association Committee should exchange information on the economic and social situation in Turkey and the outlook of the labour market to ensure that the provisions of the Decision do not cause the danger of disturbance of the Member States' employment markets. Decision 3/80 was also adopted to coordinate social security for Turkish workers.[14]

It should be noted that EEC–Turkey Agreement and its implementing Decisions did not create a right of residence for Turkish migrant workers. Member States maintained competence on regulating the admission of Turkish workers and their families under national law. What was regulated was the progressive access of Turkish workers to the Community labour market by a system based on attribution of rights depending on the period the migrant workers had spent under employment. Arguably, rights were earned by Turkish workers to the extent that they contributed to the Community project of growth by their long participation in national labour markets. The specific provisions that regulated this attribution of rights are examined in more detail in Chapter 7, together with the case-law which interpreted them. In the relevant analysis, it becomes apparent that not only the aim of the agreement but also the function of the individual migrant was taken into account by the Court in interpreting the provisions of the EEC–Turkey Agreement and its implementing Decisions.

[13] Article 8, Decision 1/80.

[14] Decision 3/80 of the Association Council of 19 September 1980 on the application of the social security schemes of the Member States of the European Communities to Turkish workers and members of their families [unpublished].

4.2 A Minimum Right to Non-discrimination in Association Agreements

Provisions granting rights to TCN workers were also included in agreements concluded by the EU with countries from which it traditionally imported labour. Next to the Association Agreements concluded with Greece and Turkey, which foresaw the possibility of Accession, the first Cooperation Agreements that included labour migration clauses were signed with Morocco, Algeria, and Tunisia in the 1970s.[15] These Agreements had the purpose of contributing to the economic and social development of these third countries.[16] They established cooperation in the field of labour, which was guided by similar provisions in all three Agreements. At the time of their negotiation, workers from Morocco, Algeria, and Tunisia were employed in large numbers in various Member States.[17] The countries of origin of TCN migrants were suffering extreme demographic pressures and had no means to finance the creation of new employment.[18] Migrant work in the Community was crucial for their development, as it both eased pressure in the local employment markets and supported national economies through remittances. This support raised the purchasing power of the countries of origin, which was then used to the benefit of Europe.[19]

For this reason, the third counties tried to ensure some type of preferential access to employment for their nationals.[20] The interdependence created between their economies and the Community, due to the labour export from the former to the latter, meant that it would be inconceivable for any cooperation not to cover labour-related questions.[21]

[15] Prior to these, the Community had set in place time-limited Association Agreements with no labour-related provisions: Association Agreement with Morocco [1973] OJ L 239; Association Agreement with Tunisia [1973] OJ L 239/125.

[16] Preamble, Recital 2 and Article 1, Cooperation Agreement with Morocco [1978] OJ L 264/2; Cooperation Agreement with Algeria [1978] OJ L 263/2; Cooperation Agreement with Tunisia [1978] OJ L 265/2.

[17] Commission, Information DG, EEC–Morocco Cooperation Agreement, February 1980, 25; Commission, Information DG, Cooperation and Development, EEC–Tunisia Cooperation Agreement, 162/77 E, 20.

[18] HAEU, EM130, Communication to the Council, Relations de la CEE avec les Pays du Maghreb, G(66) 524 final, 4–10.

[19] Commission, Information DG, Europe-South Dialogue, The Mediterranean Policy, 1984, 5.

[20] HAEU, EM130 (n 18) points 64–65.

[21] Commission Information Note P-48, The relation between the Community and the Mediterranean Countries, October 1972, 2.

However, the Community was not willing to grant preferential treatment to workers from Morocco, Algeria, and Tunisia, mostly because Greece and Turkey were negotiating similar advantages at the time, and they too had a large number of workers employed in the Member States. The Commission held that any advantage for Maghreb countries would have to be extended to Greece and Turkey.[22]

However, the Commission also held that it that was 'natural' for any cooperation to include a guarantee of non-discrimination on working conditions and remuneration.[23] After all, these migrants had 'contributed, and continue to contribute to Europe's economic development'.[24] The final version of the Agreements eventually provided for equal treatment of Moroccan, Algerian, and Tunisian nationals as regards working conditions and remuneration.[25] Further, the Agreements provided that TCNs of the associated countries and their family members would enjoy equal treatment in the field of social security.[26]

The changing economic and political circumstances that existed in the EU in the late 1970s called for a reconsideration of its approach to its Mediterranean partners. Specifically, the rise in unemployment in Member States, the introduction of restrictive migration policies to stem the inflow of foreign workers, in order to address both the lack of jobs and the need to integrate existing migrant labour and the completion of the South enlargement, whose candidates traditionally supplied migrant labour to the Community, limited the potential of large-scale migration from the Mediterranean region, as the relevant labour supply could not be absorbed.[27]

During this period, the Community suggested an approach to its cooperation with South Mediterranean that would emphasize both the rights of TCN workers employed in the Community and their function in

[22] HAEU, EM130 (n 18) 4–10.

[23] Commission Information Note P-14, Cooperation Agreements between the European Community, Algeria, Morocco and Tunisia, March 1976, Section IV Cooperation in the field of labour.

[24] Commission, Information DG, The European Community and the Arab World, 169/78, 16.

[25] Article 40, EEC–Morocco Cooperation Agreement; Article 38, EEC–Algeria Cooperation Agreement; Article 39, EEC–Tunisia Cooperation Agreement.

[26] Article 41, EEC–Morocco Cooperation Agreement; Article 39, EEC–Algeria Cooperation Agreement; Article 40, EEC–Tunisia Cooperation Agreement.

[27] Communication, On a Mediterranean policy for the enlarged Community, COM(82)353 final 2–3; Opinion of the European and Economic Social Committee on the Mediterranean policy of the European Community, 89/C 221/05 [1989] OJ C 221/16.

the development process in their country of origin. A Commission Communication on the matter mentions: 'The Community owes much of its prosperity to migrant workers – it cannot now refuse its responsibility for their future. It should increase its efforts to give them true equality in their conditions of life and work.'[28] The Commission also mentioned the need for measures to support integration of workers and their families in the host countries.[29] Once more in this context we see that the functional role of the migrant sets the basis for the attribution of rights at the Community level in a discourse that is identical to the Commission's approach for both Community and third-country nationals.

At the same time, clauses like the ones found in the Association Agreements with the Mediterranean were not included in the agreements regulating the cooperation of the EU with the African, Caribbean and Pacific Group of States (ACP). At the time of conclusion of the Treaty of Rome, decolonization was under way, and the founding states set up a framework that would allow them to maintain trade with their former colonies, while excluding nationals of these countries from free movement.[30] Scholars have engaged with how this exclusion privileged the interests of European states over the rights of former colonial subjects.[31] These interests were indeed privileged, with no consideration given to obligations of the Member States towards their former colonies. Archival material shows that underdevelopment of these states and the unskilled nature of their labour force were the reasons put forward for this exclusion.[32] As the Community states had no need for unskilled labour, the inclusion of the former colonial subjects in the free movement regime would only bring economic risks.

[28] On a Mediterranean policy for the enlarged Community, COM(82)353 final, para 19.

[29] Ibid. The Opinion of the European and Economic Social Committee (n 27), point 9.29 also calls for full application of social legislation and collective bargaining in light with ILO Convention 143.

[30] Fourth part, Treaty of Rome, Article 135. Under the pressure of France, Note du ministère de la France d'Outre-mer sur l'Union française et le Marché commun (Paris, 3 mai 1956) and Note de Léon Pignon sur la France d'Outre-mer et le Marché commun (Paris, 15 mai 1956) Archives Nationales d'Outre-Mer, Aix-en-Provence accessed in the digital collection of CVCE.

[31] Thomas Spijkerboer, 'Coloniality and Recent European Migration Case Law' in Stijn Smet and Vladislava Stoyanova (eds), *Migrants' Rights, Populism and Legal Resilience in Europe* (Cambridge University Press 2022) 117–138.

[32] Mémorandum du comité Verret sur la participation des PTOM au Marché commun (Paris, 5 octobre 1956), Fondation Jean Monnet pour l'Europe, Lausanne, Archives Jean Monnet, Fonds ARM. 16/9/2.

As decolonization proceeded and the Overseas Countries and Territories (OCTs) gained independence, various Conventions were put in place to establish trade cooperation with no mention of migrant's rights.[33] It was not until late 1970s, in the Lomé II Convention, that the parties attached a Declaration on the matter. The Declaration provided that states would accord migrant workers legally employed in their territory equal treatment as regards working conditions and pay. The Declaration also provided that migrant workers and their families were entitled to enjoy equal treatment as regards social security benefits linked to employment.[34] A similar Declaration was attached to Lomé III, supplemented by another Declaration acknowledging that migrant workers and their families would enjoy in the host state the fundamental freedoms derived from general principles of international law as well as treatment free from discrimination on the basis of race, religious, cultural, and social differences.[35] Under Article 31 VCLT, Declarations are to be taken into account for the purposes of interpretation of international agreements. Given that no provision of Lomé included any obligation as regards migrant workers and the non-binding status of the declarations, they were unlikely to directly confer rights to migrant workers.[36] Equal treatment eventually made it into the Agreement in Lomé IV. Article 5, which made extensive references to human rights in the context of development and cooperation of the parties, provided under paragraph 2 that migrant workers must not be discriminated against on the basis of racial, religious, cultural, or social differences not only as regards employment but also as regards housing, education,

[33] Yaoundé Convention [1964] OJ L 93/1431; Second Yaoundé Convention [1970] OJ L 282/2; Absence of considerations is also attested in Communication, Problèmes de Renouvellement de la Convention de Yaoundé, COM(68)230 final 32, which mentions the intention to abolish discrimination on freedom of establishment and provisions of services but lacks any consideration on free movement of workers.

[34] Annex XV, Joint Declaration on workers who are nationals of one of the contracting parties and are residing legally in the territory of a Member State or an ACP State, Second ACP-EEC Convention signed at Lomé on 31 October 1979 [1980] OJ L 347/2.

[35] Annex X, Joint Declaration on workers who are nationals of one of the Contracting Parties and are legally resident in the territory of a Member State or an ACP State and Annex IX, Joint Declaration on ACP migrant workers and ACP students in the Community, Third ACP-EEC Convention signed at Lomé on 8 December 1984 [1986] OJ L 86/3.

[36] See Katharina Eisele, *The External Dimension of the EU's Migration Policy: Different Legal Positions of Third-Country Nationals in the EU: A Comparative Perspective* (Brill 2014) 261, who argues that there can be direct effect of these with reference to the direct effect of provisions of Annexes to International Agreements.

healthcare, and other social services.[37] In parallel to this, the Joint Declaration specifying the equal treatment rights of migrant workers and their families was maintained as formulated in Lomé III.[38]

Overall, these agreements were not framed with the aim of creating rights for migrant workers to enter Member States. Rather they demanded the effective protection of workers who were already resident and employed in Member States under national law. Given the significant presence of migrants from the associated states in the Community labour market, the guarantee of equal treatment was inserted to ensure their social advancement by an entitlement to a certain level of protection as regards working conditions, remuneration, and social security, as compensation for their contribution to the common market. Behind such rights is the demand that migration does not only support the growth of Community industries but also the fair treatment of the migrants, thereby ensuring social progress at the individual level and social cohesion at the Member State level. The way the demands for rights were incorporated in these Agreements showcases a balancing between economic and social objectives similar to what would be conveyed today in the concept of economic and social sustainability.

4.3 Avoiding the Presumed Negative Effects of Migration in Accession Treaties

Previous sections have examined the frameworks creating rights of different extent for migrant workers from third countries (from progressive access to employment and security of residence for Turkish nationals to social rights for migrants under Association Agreements). This section considers the in-between category of migrants whose states of origin were about to become a part of the Community growth project.

Accession to the Community did not take place in an unregulated manner. Various clauses were inserted in different Accession Treaties, and the enlargement process became differentiated over the years, to minimize the economic risks that could be caused by extending free

37 The non-discrimination demand applies also to students and foreign nationals legally found in the territory of Member States or ACP States.

38 Annex V, Joint Declaration on ACP migrant workers and ACP students in the Community and ANNEX VI, Joint Declaration on workers who are nationals of one of the Contracting Parties and are legally resident in a territory of a Member State or an ACP State, Fourth ACP-EEC Convention signed at Lomé on 15 December 1989 [1991] OJ L 229/3.

movement of workers to all nationals of the acceding states. This differentiation took into account the circumstances of the acceding states in terms of economic development, as well as the extent to which they were already labour-exporting countries to the other Member States.

The first enlargement took place through the accession of the United Kingdom, Ireland, and Denmark in the 1970s. The relevant Accession Treaty provided the nationals of the acceding Member States with direct access to the free movement of workers framework. During the decade of negotiation that led to this enlargement, issues related to migration did not come up. From the perspective of the founding six, the UK, Denmark, and Ireland did not pose any risk in that respect, as they were not emigration countries. As a result, there was no prospect of migration flows that could cause any disruption to the Community labour market. From the perspective of the acceding states, the issue of migration appeared in a marginal way in the negotiations, and was of relevance solely in the internal politics of the UK.[39] In this regard, no transitional period was set as to the application of free movement of workers provisions. This meant that UK, Irish, and Danish nationals immediately enjoyed free movement rights as Community workers.

Despite the fact there was no migration-related risk, the Accession Treaty included a general safeguard clause under Article 135(1), which allowed both old and new Member States to apply for authorization to take protective measures in case of difficulties 'which are serious and liable to persist in any sector of the economy or which could bring about serious deterioration in the economic situation of a given area'. Such an application was subject to the review of the Commission under Article 135(2). This general safeguard clause was similar to that of Article 226 of the Treaty of Rome. In this respect, it added nothing novel to the Community framework. The first free movement regulations examined in Section 4.1 also had clauses allowing derogations by Member States in case of national unemployment.[40] Finally, the Member States also attached a declaration to the Accession Treaty, where they acknowledged

[39] See speech by Hugh Gaitskell against UK Membership of the Common Market (3 October 1962), Britain and the Common Market, Texts of speeches made at the 1962 Labour Party Conference by the Rt. Hon Hugh Gaitskell M.P. and the Rt. Hon. George Brown M.P., together with the policy statement accepted by Conference (Labour Party 1962); WR Böhning, *The Migration of Workers in the United Kingdom and the European Community* (Oxford University Press for the Institute of Race Relations 1972).

[40] Regulation 15/1961; Preamble and Articles 2, 4–6, Regulation 38/64; Article 20, Regulation 1612/1968.

that free movement of workers might potentially create difficulties for the social situation of Member States.[41] As a result, they reserved the right to bring the matter before the Community institutions, should such difficulties arise, in order to tackle it from within Community law.

In contrast to this first enlargement, which included safeguards despite the absence of risks, the Accession Treaties signed with Greece in 1979 and Spain and Portugal in 1985 were differentiated to take into account risks related to potential migration flows. In these cases, the risks stemmed from the fact that the candidate states were traditional emigration states and were less economically developed compared to the other members of the Community club. In the first enlargement, there existed a level of homogeneity between the founding and the acceding Member States.[42] Their level of development and industrialization was similar, allowing a smooth transition in a common market focused on promoting economic growth and social progress. Greece, Spain, and Portugal, on the other hand, were considered developing countries.[43] Despite individual differences, they had recently transitioned to democracy and were all lagging behind the Community in terms of economic development.[44] Their economies were primarily based on agriculture, their rate of economic growth was not as high as that of the Community Member States, they were facing problems with unemployment, and they were already countries of origin of labour migration to the Community.[45] In this context, a Commission analysis on labour migration from Greece, Spain, and Portugal noted:

> During the period of high economic growth up to 1973, these [labor migration] links created a source of interdependence between the three applicant countries and the Community, with the Community being able to make up its labor shortage from labor surpluses in the applicant

[41] Joint Declaration on the free movement of workers, Treaty of Accession of Denmark, Ireland and the United Kingdom [1972] OJ L 73.

[42] Communication, General Considerations on the Problems of Enlargement, COM(78)120 final, points 4–6.

[43] Bulletin of the European Communities, May 1978, Supplement 5/1978, Commission Opinion on Portugal's application for accession, paras 4,11.

[44] General Considerations on the Problems of Enlargement, COM(78)120 final, points 1, 6.

[45] Ibid, points 4–6. Greece had also concluded an Association Agreement with the Community in 1961 that provided for the creation of a customs union after a twenty-two-year transitional period and a free movement regime after a twelve-year transitional period. Due to political changes in Greece (military occupation), the Association Agreement was blocked, and the country applied for accession after the restoration of democracy in 1975.

> countries. Since the emergence of high and continuing levels of unemployment in the Community, this interdependence has gradually changed into a relationship of unilateral dependence of the three applicant countries on the Community, particularly France and Germany.[46]

The difference in economic and social conditions between the acceding countries and the Member States created the risk of high concentration of migrant workers in the more developed regions of the Community. This concern was particularly connected with anticipated migration from Spain.[47] There, the demographic prediction showed an anticipated growth in young population seeking their first job. As the Commission stated in its Opinion on the Spanish Accession, this created 'some justification for the fear that there would be a sudden flood of immigrants if access to employment were to be made completely free upon accession'.[48] This, in connection with the higher unemployment in the Community, created the necessity for extended transitional periods in order to allow the gradual and 'orderly' introduction of free movement.[49] Safeguard clauses were also considered next to the progressive liberalization of free movement to address 'erratic movements of labour'.[50]

Against this backdrop, the accession of the southern Member States was differentiated by the introduction of transitional arrangements specific to free movement of workers.[51] In the case of Greece, for a fixed period of six years, Greek workers would not be able to participate in the free movement framework.[52] During that period, Member States were allowed to regulate labour migration under national law, and thereby require prior authorization for migration of Greek workers to their territories. The members of the workers' family were equally excluded from access to the labour market, albeit for a shorter period of five years.[53] As for Greek labour migrants who were already employed in Member States at the time of accession, members of their family would be allowed to independently take up work, if they had already resided

[46] Communication, Economic and Sectoral Aspects, Commission Analysis supplementing its views on enlargement, COM(78)200 final, Part I, point 46.
[47] Opinion on Spain's Application for Membership, COM(78)630 final, point 44.
[48] Ibid, point 117.
[49] Ibid, points 60, 117.
[50] Ibid, point 44.
[51] Article 44, Act concerning the conditions of accession Greece (1979 Accession Treaty) [1979] OJ L 291.
[52] Article 45, 1979 Accession Treaty.
[53] Article 45(2), 1979 Accession Treaty.

with the worker for three years in the territory of the Member State where they sought employment.[54] From 1984 onwards, this requirement would be limited to eighteen months prior residence. This Accession Treaty also included the general safeguard clause that appeared in the first accession, allowing for protective measures to be adopted by the old Member States or Greece in case of serious problems which could bring deterioration in the economic situation in any given area for a period of six years.[55]

Similar transitional measures were adopted in the Portuguese and Spanish accession of 1985. The accession envisaged a fixed period of seven years, during which labour migration from the acceding countries would be regulated under national law or bilateral agreements.[56] With respect to Luxembourg, the relevant transitional period was extended to ten years.[57] A new element, added for the first time in this Accession Treaty, is that the Community could subsequently review the transitional period and adjust the measures in place for Spanish and Portuguese workers within five years following the accession.[58] As for migrant workers employed prior to accession, members of their families residing with them would be allowed to immediately take up employment. Nevertheless, the Accession Treaty provided that such a right could be limited where special bilateral agreements put in place before the Accession Treaty provided for a different treatment.[59] As for Spanish and Portuguese workers who moved after the accession, their family members would be allowed to independently take up work if they had already resided with the worker for three years in the territory of the Member State where they sought employment. From 1989 onwards, this requirement would be limited to eighteen months prior residence.[60] This accession also included the same general safeguard clause, which allowed for protective measures to be adopted for a period of seven years and which was extended to ten years for Luxembourg due to the difficulties related specifically to its employment market.[61]

54 Ibid.
55 Article 130, 1979 Accession Treaty.
56 Articles 56 and 216, Act concerning the conditions of accession of Spain and Portugal (1985 Accession Treaty) [1985] OJ L 302.
57 Ibid.
58 Articles 56(2) and 216(2), 1985 Accession Treaty.
59 Articles 57(1)(a) and 217(1)(a), 1985 Accession Treaty.
60 Articles 57(1)(b) and 217(1)(b) Act, 1985 Accession Treaty.
61 Article 379, 1985 Accession Treaty.

The Accession Treaties did not make any differentiation as to how migrant workers who had been employed in Member States prior to accession should be treated during the transitional period. This gap was filled by the Court. In *Peskeloglou* and *Lopes da Veiga*, the Court dealt with restrictive policies against migrant workers and their family members who were nationals of Greece and Portugal.[62] The migrant workers were already employed in Germany in the case of *Peskeloglou,* and in the Netherlands in the case of *Lopes da Veiga*, prior to the accession of their states of origin to the Community. In both the cases, the Court confirmed that the aim of the derogation from free movement during the transitional period prescribed in the Accession Treaties was to prevent the disruption of the labour markets caused by the potential massive influx of migrants from the acceding Member States.[63] In this context, the Court held that derogations from free movement should be interpreted strictly, and should not be applied to the detriment of the migrant workers already residing in the Community Member States.[64] In contrast to this, in *Tsiotras v Landeshauptstadt Stuttgart*, the Court held that an unemployed national from an acceding Member State for whom it has become objectively impossible to find employment could not enjoy any rights under Community law during the transitional period. An ex-worker national of an acceding Member State who could no longer pursue work represented a category of migration that could pose adverse effects to economic growth.[65] Thus, only migrants actively engaged in the objective of growth and who could not pose a risk to the disruption of the labour market could enjoy Community rights during the transitional periods.

In light of this, and under a combined reading of the Accession Treaties and Regulation 1612/68 applicable to free movement of workers at the time of the Greek, Spanish, and Portuguese accession, we can infer the following. All labour migrants from the acceding states who were employed in Community Member States before or after accession would immediately benefit from the principle of equal treatment. Specifically, Article 48 EEC was subject to the transitional provisions laid down in the

[62] Case 77/82, *Peskeloglou*, ECLI:EU:C:1983:92; Judgment of 27 September 1989, Case 9/88, *Lopes da Veiga*, ECLI:EU:C:1989:346.

[63] Case 77/82, *Peskeloglou*, para 12; Case 9/88, *Lopes da Veiga*, para 10; See also Case C-113/89, *Rush Portuguesa*, ECLI:EU:C:1990:142, para 19.

[64] Case 77/82, *Peskeloglou*, para 13; Case 9/88, *Lopes da Veiga*, para 10.

[65] Case C-171/91, *Tsiotras*, ECLI:EU:C:1993:215.

Accession Treaties and analysed in this section. At the same time, Regulation 1612/68, which implemented and specified how this freedom was to be enjoyed, was subject to transitional arrangements with respect to specific articles mentioned in the Accession Treaties. Article 7 of the Regulation, which constitutes a specific expression of the non-discrimination principle, was not mentioned as a provision whose application could be derogated during the transitional period. This meant that labour migrants of the acceding states who were employed in Community Member States during the transitional period fully enjoyed equal treatment.

In essence, the transitional arrangements set in place aimed at restricting free movement rights only for soon-to-be Community nationals who were suspected of seeking work in Community Member States. The fear of economic repercussions from a potential mass exodus to the north, which was a core rationale of the transitional arrangements, was unsubstantiated for one group of individuals from the acceding Member States. These were migrants who had established themselves in the Community prior to the accession and who were actively contributing to the development of the Community by participating in national labour markets as workers. Such migrants had acquired rights which should not be restricted during the transitional period.

Overall, in the regulation of accession, but also in the rest of the legal instruments which were negotiated and adopted in this period, the following characteristics can be identified. As the period was primarily characterized by demand for migrant labour, the Community agenda was quite liberal in the sense of demanding the extensive attribution of rights to migrant workers as a compensation for their participation in the project of growth. This was without consideration of nationality. Equal treatment in working conditions and social security was a bare minimum to be enjoyed by all migrant workers implicated in the Community project. In parallel, instruments which could lead to the creation of entry rights for migrants incorporated safeguard clauses to ensure that Member States can close the valve and limit potential adverse effects in case of change of economic conditions. Such safeguard clauses could not be adopted unilaterally and were instead submitted for review to the Community institutions. These were the ways in which social and economic objectives shaped the law-making during this period with due regard for parallel pursuit of growth and progress in a way which today would be called the pursuit of social and economic sustainability.

4.4 The Incorporation of Safeguards and the Attribution of Rights

Part I has engaged in a historical study of different areas of Community law that concerned the rights of migrant workers from the Treaty of Paris to the Single European Act and it highlighted the way economic and social considerations shaped the attribution of rights to migrants. The analysis has shown how economic and social objectives have affected the attribution of rights to migrants already from the establishment of Community law. It also showed that labour demand and positive economic circumstances were behind an aligned approach to both Community and TCN migrants. During the early years of the Community project and before the oil crisis, it would not have been an understatement to say that the Commission had the objective of shaping a sustainable migration. Such a plan was envisaged as based on social rights for all migrants contributing to the post-war project of growth.

Overall, the analysis showed that until the 1970s, there was nothing distinguishing Community workers and TCN workers, as both groups provided the same contribution to the Community project, and the different action plans put forward were meant to cover both.[66] The position of the migrant in the Community legal order was based on their market participation. By being actively engaged in the Community project of growth, Community migrants 'earned' social rights in return. Similarly, the Community institutions were determined to extend these rights to all other migrants engaged in this project. At the same time, the archival material revealed a link between the economic benefits of migration for the Community market and the social advancement of migrants in their capacity as workers. Social progress came in the form of rights as the result of the economic function of migrants. As long as the economy continued to develop, all migrants within the territory should draw benefits from this progress. In circumstances of unhindered economic growth, the paths of regulating migration were aligned for both Community and TCN migrants.

In the early 1980s, and with the effects of the oil crisis experienced in the Member States, the category of 'workers' slowly became differentiated based on nationality. Member States hesitated to extend rights to all, for

[66] Action Programme in Favour of Migrant Workers and Their Families, COM(74)2250 final; Council Resolution of 9 February 1976 on an Action Programme for Migrant Workers and Members of Their Families [1976] OJ C 34/2.

fear that they could not guarantee social progress for their own citizens. And while extending rights to Community migrants is supposed by a form of solidarity between the different Member States that are all implicated in the same development project, this type of solidarity cannot extend to migrants whose state of origin is not implicated in the project at all. In that context, we do see the attribution of rights to migrants in trade and cooperation agreements, but once the crisis hit, Member States hesitated to maintain such treatment. Indeed, clauses were embedded in all frameworks and controlled by Community institutions to ensure that, in all cases, economy did not collapse under the weight of the rights granted.

In general, during this period, considerations related to economic imperatives determined the limitation, the temporal attribution, and the extension of rights for migrant workers. Depending on these economic considerations, social progress came as a by-product in the form of personal rights for the migrants and derivative rights for their family. The same considerations will continue to appear throughout the regulation of migration in Parts II and III. What changes is that during the period examined in Part II, political ambitions enter the picture in relation to the rights of Community migrants, whereas thicker perceptions of social progress in the form of rights are also found in the legal system. The interdependence and parallel pursuit of economic and social objectives via the regulation of migration framed both free movement and Association Agreements as the first manifestations of a Community sustainable migration. Similar considerations also lay behind the pursuit of coordinating national migration policies and in the transitional clauses inserted in the Accession Treaties concluded in this period. Part II will investigate how such considerations evolved after the adoption of the Single European Act and until the failed Constitutional Treaty.

PART II

Differentiation from the Single European Act to the Failed Constitutional Treaty

Part I has demonstrated the importance of migration for the Community project of post-war growth as the main reason behind the attribution of rights to migrants. Most importantly, the analysis unveiled an aligned approach on the part of the Community institutions regarding the attribution of rights to all migrants, shaped by an understanding that both Community and TCN migrants contributed with their labour to the development of the Member States, and because of this they were to enjoy equal treatment rights. The balancing of economic and social considerations behind the regulation of migration at that time was explicit, uniform, and clear-cut. Sustainability did not exist as concept for the greater part of the period examined. However, economic and social considerations driving the regulation of migration are identical to what the economic and social pillars of sustainability would demand, namely pursuing economic and social development by the regulation of migration.

During the period examined in this part, the approach to EU and TCN migrants was differentiated. The political ambition behind the transformation of the EU framework after the Single European Act framed an institutional discourse that emphasized the special status of EU migrants as EU citizens, and the lesser status of TCN migrants, whose status and rights were left in the realm of intergovernmental cooperation. However, a closer investigation of archival material and case-law undertaken in this part proves that the need to balance the economic and social objectives of the Treaties continued to appear and condition the rights of all migrants. Essentially this part shows that economic and social sustainability objectives continued to exist as the end to be served by the regulation of migration, even when the prevalent institutional discourse highlighted different considerations. Adding another building block to the historical investigation, this part demonstrates that while the EU sustainable migration objective is a recent one, its underlying considerations have constantly found their way in EU secondary law and case-law.

The late 1980s and early 1990s found the Community up against diverse challenges. The growth of the 1950s and 1960s was long forgotten, while global changes pointed to the potential of bigger population movements towards the Community Member States. Specifically, increased unemployment and political instability pointed to potential movements from the Mediterranean.[1] In addition to this, the fall of the Soviet Union and the process of accession of the Central and Eastern European Countries (CEECs) pointed to the potential of increase in labour migration.[2] This was at a time when the Community industries were not in need of extra labour, and the Member States continued to employ the restrictive policies that began in the 1970s in order to permanently halt migration.[3] Towards the mid-1990s, growth began to slowly resume, and this created extra demand for labour in specific sectors.[4] In parallel, a new challenge appeared – that of an ageing population which would no longer be able to support the EU development needs.[5] All these were taking place in a period of continued national unemployment combined with settled migrant communities that were increasingly facing racism and xenophobia.[6] The need to resort to labour migration to cover labour needs would become complicated for the EU, as it took place in a highly politicized climate around migration,[7] and a constantly changing legal framework.

In parallel, Member States engaged in an ambitious project of incorporating political elements into their cooperation, and consequently the

1 See Commission, Information DG, The Countries of the Greater Arab and Maghreb and the European Community, DE68, 1991.

2 HAEU, GJLA-246, Commission, DG External Relations, Task Force Enlargissement, Enlargement and the Community's Relations with its Mediterranean Neighbours, Brussels 2 March 1992, RDM/m 4.

3 Communication, On Immigration, SEC(91)1855 final, para 3.

4 See retrospective description of the 1990s trends in Communication, On a Community Immigration Policy, COM(2000)757 final, Annex 1.

5 Communication, On Immigration and Asylum Policies, COM(94)23 final, para 9.

6 Ibid, para 10; See Evrigenis Report and Parliament Resolution on Racism and Xenophobia, adopted on 10 October [1991] OJ C 280; Maastricht European Council, Presidency Conclusions, 16 December 1991, Annex 3; Corfu European Council 24–25 June 1994, Presidency conclusions, Annex III.

7 On Immigration and Asylum Policies, COM(94)23 final, foreword; HAEU, CEUE _SEGE-SEC(1991)0803, Commission, Secretariat General, Communication from the President, Mr Bangemann and Mrs Papandreou in agreement with Mr Andriessen, Mr Marin and Mr Matutes, Communication to the Commission, Immigration, Annex I, Annex 6.

Treaty framework was repeatedly transformed during the years under review. The Single European Act demanded the completion of the internal market, defined as an area without internal frontiers, in which, among others, free movement of persons should be guaranteed under Article 13. The completion of the internal market moved border controls between Member States to the external frontiers of the EU territory. This first change was followed by the Maastricht Treaty, which came with the grand promise of political integration between Member States. The citizenship of the Union was established, which created a generalized right of nationals of Member States to move and reside freely within the territory of the EU. At the same time, migration policy came into the EU framework under the intergovernmental pillar of Justice and Home Affairs. During these developments, there seemed to be an ambition to create political bonds between nationals of the Member States and the EU, whereas the status of TCNs was to be regulated through intergovernmental cooperation. The changes were completed with the Amsterdam Treaty, which moved migration to the Community pillar and created a specific competence basis for the adoption of legislation on migration under Title IV of the Treaty. The Amsterdam Treaty established the AFSJ, under which measures would be adopted in different areas to guarantee the free movement of persons within EU borders. While the incorporation of migration in the Community framework was welcomed, the creation of an AFSJ was thought to perfect a legal structure whereby Europeans are the primary recipients of rights from the EU legal order and all other persons would come into the picture either by their association with a European citizen or with very limited rights guarantees.[8]

As for scholarly research during this period, it became much more theoretically dense as regards European migrants and their rights. This was due not only to the Treaty changes but also to the Court's case-law which began to employ grand phrasing and emphasized the importance of the newly created citizenship status, as we will see in Chapter 5. Different scholars emphasized the *telos* of an ever-closer Union between the peoples of Europe, and engaged with different theoretical frameworks

[8] Steve Peers, 'Towards Equality: Actual and Potential Rights of Third-Country Nationals in the European Union' (1996) 33 CMLRev; David O'Keeffe, 'Recasting the Third Pillar' (1995) 32 CMLRev; Steenbergen, 'All the King's Horses. . .: Probabilities and Possibilities for the Implementation of the New Title IV EC Treaty' (1999) 1 European Journal of Migration and Law 29.

that would permit a conceptualization of this *sui generis* citizenship.[9] Others emphasized the continuum and natural evolution between the rights afforded to EU workers and the rights protected by EU citizenship.[10] At the same time, scholarship also examined the deficiencies of the new status and emphasized a perceived lack of social direction of the internal market.[11] In addition, some authors reflected on more specific exclusions (on the basis of gender, nationality, class) which, in their view, EU law privileged.[12]

Research on TCN migrants and their rights under EU law remained much more doctrinal and to a large extent descriptive.[13] Authors engaged in case-law analyses on the right to family reunification of EU migrants and on Association Agreements.[14] What is more, different scholars engaged with the deficits and potentials of the changing Treaty framework for TCN migrants, and criticized the intergovernmental elements of

[9] See Dora Kostakopoulou, 'Ideas, Norms and European Citizenship: Explaining Institutional Change' (2005) 68 The Modern Law Review 233 for an overview.

[10] Elspeth Guild, *The Legal Elements of European Identity: EU Citizenship and Migration Law* (Kluwer Law International 2004), Chapter 5.

[11] Antoine Jacobs, 'Social Europe in Delay' (1990) 6 International Journal of Comparative Labour Law and Industrial Relations 26; Miguel Poiares Maduro, 'Europe's Social Self: "The Sickness Unto Death"' in Jo Shaw (ed), *Social Law and Policy in an Evolving European Union* (Hart 2000); Noreen Burrows, 'The Promotion of Women's Rights by the European Economic Community' (1980) 17 CMLRev 191; Charlotte O'Brien, 'Social Blind Spots and Monocular Policy Making The ECJ's Migrant Worker Model' (2009) 46 CMLRev 1107.

[12] Tamara Hervey, 'Migrant Workers and Their Families in the European Union: The Pervasive Market Ideology of Community Law' in Jo Shaw and Gillian More (eds), *New Legal Dynamics of European Union* (Clarendon Press 1995); Clare McGlynn, 'Reclaiming a Feminist Vision: The Reconciliation of Paid Work and Family Life in European Union Law and Policy' (2001) 7 ColumJEurL; Isabella Moebius and Erika Szyszczak, 'Of Raising Pigs and Children' (1998) 18 Yearbook of European Law 125.

[13] Daniel Duyssens, 'Migrant Workers from Third Countries in the European Community' (1977) 14 CMLRev; Kenneth R Simmonds, 'The Fourth Lomé Convention' (1991) 28 CMLRev; Jan Niessen, 'European Community Legislation and Intergovernmental Cooperation on Migration' (1992) 26 International Migration Review 676; Peter-Christian Müller-Graff, 'The Legal Bases of the Third Pillar and Its Position in the Framework of the Union Treaty' (1994) 31 CMLRev 493.

[14] Willy Alexander, 'Free Movement of Non-EC Nationals A Review of the Case-Law of the Court of Justice' (1992) 3 EJIL 53; Henry G Schermers, 'Case C-192/89, *S.Z. Sevince v. Staatssecretaris van Justitie*, Preliminary Ruling of 20 September 1990 Requested by the Raad van State of the Netherlands' (1991) 28 CMLRev; A Weber, 'Case C-18/90, *Bahia Kziber v. Office National de l'Emploi (ONEM)*, Preliminary Ruling of 31 January 1991, Requested by the Cour du Travail de Liège (5th Chamber)' (1991) 28 CMLRev.

cooperation on migration.[15] Finally, some engaged with the question of whether and how the EU could extend free movement rights to TCNs and to create a coherent migration policy.[16] In this context, different authors mapped the rights TCN migrants enjoyed under the different legal frameworks (family reunification for Community workers, Turkish workers, and other Association Agreements); they pointed out inconsistencies and legal conflicts arising from the treatment of TCNs under Community law and proposed different solutions.[17]

Against this backdrop, this part develops as follows. Chapter 5 presents the institutional ambition to disconnect economic objectives from the exercise of free movement rights, in an attempt to create a political community of European nationals. It shows how this ambition was reflected in the case-law, underlining that economic considerations were never detached from secondary law. Chapter 6 focuses on the regulation of migration from third countries. The usual lens for this period in the scholarship is a critique of intergovernmentalism and of the creation of Fortress Europe. The examination undertaken in the section does not contest that. However, the analysis draws a more nuanced picture and demonstrates that the Commission and the Council had divergent approaches as to the regulation of migration and its relation to the economic and social objectives of the EU. Finally, Chapter 7 evaluates the case-law on Association Agreements and highlights the Court's significance as an actor of European integration. This approach of the Court was not well received. Rather, Member States tried to employ more conservative wording in the Agreements concluded during this period precisely with the purpose of avoiding the application of the case-law.

15 Kay Hailbronner, 'Perspectives of a Harmonization of the Law of Asylum after the Maastricht Summit' (1992) 29 CMLRev 917; Steve Peers, 'Building Fortress Europe: The Development of EU Migration Law' (1998) 35 CMLRev; Ferruccio Pastore, 'Visas, Borders, Immigration: Formation, Structure, and Current Evolution of the EU Entry Control System'; and Steve Peers, 'Family Reunion and Community Law' in Neil Walker (ed), *Europe's Area of Freedom, Security, and Justice* (Oxford University Press 2004).

16 See David O'Keeffe, 'The Free Movement of Persons and the Single Market' (1992) 17 ELR 3; Elspeth Guild, European Community Law from a Migrant's Perspective (Katholieke Universiteit Nijmegen 2000).

17 Marise Cremona, 'Citizens of Third Countries: Movement and Employment of Migrant Workers within the European Union' (1995) 22 LIEI 87; Kay Hailbronner and Jorg Polakiewicz, 'Non-EC Nationals in the European Community: The Need for a Coordinated Approach' (1992) 3 DukeJComp&IntlL 49; Joseph HH Weiler, 'Thou Shalt Not Oppress a Stranger: On the Judicial Protection of the Human Rights of Non-EC Nationals – A Critique' (1992) 3 EJIL 65; Thomas Hoogenboom, 'Integration into Society and Free Movement of Non-EC Nationals' (1992) 3 EJIL 36.

The chapter finally examines EU action in enlargement and association with European developed countries, where the extension of rights to migrants was easily accepted.

Overall, the period under review in this part adds to the evolution of EU law by the element of differentiation. Unlike the previous period, where there were seeds for a common single migration policy that would cover all migrants, now a mix of economic recession and political ambition shaped differentiation. This differentiation came with the aspiration of making something more of the EU migrants, overcoming the function of their labour and shaping a set of rights they should enjoy as members of a new political community of a kind. That aspiration was matched by disagreement on what to do with other migrants and on how to regulate their rights. This disagreement blocked the proactive stance of the Commission, that had a specific vision of how migrants could play a part, even in this political project, and how their rights could be aligned with the economic and social objectives of the EU, thereby service economic and social sustainability. Both ambitions were undermined due to diverse historical events experienced in the new millennium, as will be shown in Part III.

5

Shifting Political Ambitions and Persistent Economic Considerations in the Free Movement Framework

5.1 Economic Considerations Limiting Residence Rights

The regulation of residence and movement of EU migrants was subject to many changes during the period under examination. During the early 1990s, the Commission highlighted that the citizenship provisions shaped a political link between Member States nationals and the EU with the purpose of fostering a sense of identity with the EU.[1] In this regard, the Commission emphasized that the rights EU migrants already enjoyed under Community law were now 'fundamentally altered'.[2] It suggested that Articles 8 and 8a EC Treaty combined could directly generate entry and residence rights for EU nationals, even though they were supplementary and could not replace the more specific legal bases for residence found in the Treaties.[3] The relevant Treaty bases, however, restricted residence to people engaged in economic activity.[4] As a result, during the first years after the introduction of the EU citizen status, residence rights for EU migrants continued to be regulated by sectoral Directives which predated the adoption of the citizenship status in primary law. This section analyses the relevant secondary law framework and different suggestions to amend it, before turning to the case-law of the

[1] Communication, Report from the Commission on Citizenship of the Union, COM(93) 702 final.

[2] Second report from the Commission on Citizenship of the Union [1994–1996], COM(97) 230 final.

[3] Ibid, 14.

[4] In the meantime, a framework was put in place for self-employed and retired workers: Regulation 1251/70 on the right of workers to remain in the territory of a Member State after having been employed in that State [1970] OJ L 142/24; Directive 73/148/EEC on the abolition of restrictions on movement and residence within the Community for nationals of Member States with regard to establishment and the provision of services [1973] OJ L 172/14; Directive 75/34/EEC concerning the right of nationals of a Member State to remain in the territory of another Member State after having pursued therein an activity in a self-employed capacity [1975] OJ L 14/10.

period in Section 5.2. The analysis shows the tension behind the ambition to create a shared political identity and the economic unsustainability of extending social rights without limitations to all EU migrants.

The first time the Commission tried to disconnect residence rights under secondary law from economic activity was in 1979. The proposal was put forward under Article 3(c) of the EEC Treaty, which provided for the abolition of obstacles to free movement of persons, in the context of the first discussion on more political aspirations for the Union.[5] The attribution of residence rights under the relevant initiative would allow Member States to require proof of sufficient resources as a condition for residence.[6] This proposal was on the table for almost a decade, during which time the Council avoided discussing the matter.[7] From archival material, it appears that Member States could not reach an agreement on the parts of the proposal that could pose risks to their national economies. Among the points of contestation were the requirement of resources for students, the difference between insurance systems of Member States, and the legal basis and scope of application of the Directive.[8] The attribution of a general residence right to all EU migrants could pose risks to national economies, especially because of the various social rights such migrants would enjoy in the different social security and social assistance systems of the Member States. Such a generalization carried the risk of making the EU free movement system economically unsustainable.[9]

In parallel, the case-law of the Court on Regulation 1612/68 substantially extended the categories of EU migrants falling under the scope of free movement as workers, as well as the rights they were to enjoy under

[5] Proposal for a Directive on a right of residence for nationals of Member States in the territory of another Member State, COM(79)215 final [1979] OJ C 207/14.

[6] Recital 4, Article 4(2) the proposed Directive.

[7] There were several amendments following comments by the Parliament and the ECOSOC. See Amended proposal for a Directive on a right of residence for nationals of Member States in the territory of another Member State, COM(80)358 final [1980] OJ C 188/7; Amending of the proposal for a Directive on a right of residence for nationals of Member States in the territory of another Member State, COM(80)649 final [1980] OJ C 292/3; Amended Proposal for a Directive on a Right of residence for nationals of Member States in the territory of another Member State, COM(85)292 final [1985] OJ C 171/8.

[8] HAEU, CM2/1988-00024/001, 1237ème session du Conseil (marché intérieur), Bruxelles, 03.05.1988, Droit de séjour, 5932/88 (Presse 53) Communication á la presse.

[9] See Catherine Barnard and Emilija Leinarte, 'The Creation of European Citizenship: Constitutional Miracle or Myopia?' (2022) 24 Cambridge Yearbook of European Legal Studies 24, who argue that in the initial political discussions on EU citizenship, the practical extension of rights under equal treatment was not envisioned.

secondary law.[10] Due to this, in 1988 the Commission proposed an amendment to Regulation 1612/68 and Directive 68/360 aimed at extending their provisions on equal treatment and family reunification, thereby promoting the social objectives of the Community.[11] The Council could not reach an agreement on the matter.[12] The Commission presented another proposal in 1998, framed in terms of promoting competitiveness and the economic objectives of the Union.[13] Still, the Council failed to discuss the relevant proposal.

With the impetus created by the Single European Act, the Commission presented three sectoral proposals in order to extend residence rights to students, retired persons, and others not engaged in economic activity. For the Commission, the extension of residence rights should be viewed in light of Article 8A EC Treaty, which established a general right of residence to the Member States nationals.[14] During the negotiation of these instruments, Member States were concerned that an unrestricted extension of residence rights would lead to migration flows solely driven by financial considerations due to the lack of harmonization of social security and social assistance systems.[15] To avoid the perceived negative economic impact of such type of migration, a principle was put forward, which still determines the residence rights of EU migrants – that is, that whoever wishes to reside in a country other than their own should not constitute an unreasonable burden on the public finances of the host

[10] See Section 2.2.

[11] Proposal for a Regulation amending Regulation 1612/68 on Freedom of Movement for workers within the Community, COM(88)815 final, Revised Version [1989] OJ C 100/6; Proposal for a Directive amending Directive 68/360/EE on the abolition of restrictions on movement and residence within the Community for workers of Member States and their families, COM(88)815 final, Revised Version [1989] OJ C 100/8.

[12] Communication from the Commission, Free movement of workers: achieving the full benefits and potential, COM(2002)0694 final. There is no information available on whether this proposal was ever discussed by the Council.

[13] Proposal for Regulation amending Regulation 1612/68 on freedom of movement for workers within the Community, COM(98)0394 final [1998] OJ C 344/9, Recitals 3 and 10; Proposal for a Directive amending Directive 68/360/EEC on the abolition of restrictions on movement and residence within the Community for workers of Member States and their families, COM(98)0394 final [1998] OJ C 344/12.

[14] Report from the Commission on the implementation of Directives 90/364, 90/365 and 93/96, COM(99)0127 final.

[15] Proposal for a Directive on the right of residence, COM(89)275 final [1989] OJ C 191/5 mentioning the concerns expressed by the ad hoc Committee on a People's Europe in its report to the European Council in Brussels on 29 and 30 March 1985.

country.[16] In line with this, the relevant Directives provided for the attribution of residence rights to EU migrants who could demonstrate sufficient resources and insurance, so as not to become a burden for the social security systems of the Member States.[17] These texts continued to regulate residence rights of EU migrants until the adoption of Directive 2004/38, while Regulation 1612/68 was not amended but rather codified to incorporate amendments caused to it by other instruments over the years.[18] At this stage, it should be noted that there was no single Community view on how to proceed with EU migrants' rights even under the changed institutional setting, especially because of the need to safeguard the economic and social sustainability of the EU.

The political aspirations were reflected in Treaty changes and various soft-law instruments, but the Council was not able to agree on how migration rights could be generalized without risks to national economies. The overview of the proposals by the Commission and their deflection by the Council are indicative of the constant motivation to safeguard the economic objective of growth. The Council preferred to negotiate different instruments for different categories of movement while maintaining safeguard clauses in all of them. Contribution to the economy could no longer be set as the reason behind attribution of rights to EU migrants. The aspiration to shape a true political community would not justify that. However, this political aspiration was matched with the constant historical aspiration of the EU project to promote

16 HAEU, CM2/1989-00062/001, 1352ème session du Conseil (marché intérieur), Luxembourg, 10.10.1989, Projet de Procès-verbal, 9170/89 restreint.

17 Article 1, Directive 90/364/EEC of 28 June 1990 on the right of residence [1990] OJ L 180/2; Article 1, Directive 90/365/EEC of 28 June 1990 on the right of residence for employees and self-employed persons who have ceased their occupational activity [1990] OJ L 180/28; Directive 90/366/EEC of 28 June 1990 on the right of residence for students [1990] OJ L 180/30 annulled by Case C-250/90, *Parliament v Council*, ECLI:EU: C:1992:294 and reproduced in Directive 93/96/EEC of 29 October 1993 on the right of residence for students [1993] OJ L 317/59, which adapted the text to comply with the appropriate legal basis.

18 By Regulation 312/76 of 9 February 1976 amending the provisions relating to the trade union rights of workers contained in Regulation 1612/68 on freedom of movement for workers within the Community [1976] OJ L 39/2; Regulation 2434/92 of 27 July 1992 amending Part II of Regulation 1612/68 on freedom of movement for workers within the Community [1992] OJ L 245/1 and eventually Directive 2004/38/EC on the right of citizens of the Union and their family members to move and reside freely within the territory of the Member States amending Regulation 1612/68 and repealing Directives 64/221/EEC, 68/360/EEC, 72/194/EEC, 73/148/EEC, 75/34/EEC, 75/35/EEC, 90/364/EEC, 90/365/EEC and 93/96/EEC [2004] OJ L 158/77.

growth and progress. This growth and progress could be guaranteed by excluding from the attribution of rights those EU migrants who could negatively affect growth. Relatedly, we see the goal of economic sustainability as conveyed in the primary law objective of harmonious and balanced development of economic activities behind the limitation of the rights of EU migrants. In Section 5.2, we will see how the Court approached the relevant limitations in the case-law by extensive invocation of primary law.

5.2 The Judicial Aspiration to Overcome the Economic Foundations

During the period under review, the Court consistently invoked the broad framing of primary law to consolidate the rights of EU migrants beyond the limits prescribed in secondary law analysed in Section 5.1. This was celebrated in scholarship as an indication of the potential of EU citizenship as an independent status, disconnected from statist limitations.[19] In the relevant case-law, the Court did not invalidate the limitations prescribed in secondary law. Rather, while acknowledging the economic considerations that preclude the unlimited enjoyment of rights by EU migrants, it tried to expand protection by focusing on how such limits should be reviewed in light of the social and political objectives of primary law that established the legal status of EU citizenship.

First, in *Martínez Sala*, the Court suggested that EU migrants lawfully residing in a Member State should enjoy equal treatment on access to family benefits. The Court could not establish if Martínez Sala fell under the category of worker or self-employed and, hence, whether she enjoyed an EU law residence right.[20] Despite this, the Court held that when an EU migrant lawfully resided in another Member State, their situation fell within the scope of EU law by virtue of the provisions on EU citizenship.[21] This is regardless of whether the legal basis of their residence rights is from EU or national law. As a result, EU migrants lawfully resident in another Member State could rely on equal treatment under

[19] Jo Shaw, 'View of the Citizenship Classics: *Martínez Sala* and Subsequent Cases on Citizenship of the Union' in Loïc Azoulai and Miguel Poiares Maduro (eds), *The Past and Future of EU Law: The Classics of EU Law Revisited on the Fiftieth Anniversary of the Rome Treaty* (Hart 2010).

[20] Case C-85/96, *Martínez Sala*, ECLI:EU:C:1998:217, paras 34, 45.

[21] Ibid, para 61.

Article 6 of the EC Treaty in order to claim family benefits and were not limited to enjoying such rights only as social advantages under secondary law on free movement of workers.[22]

The Court went even further in *Baumbast*, where it held that EU migrants could rely directly on Article 18(1) EC Treaty as a basis for residence rights in a Member State. In that case, Baumbast did not satisfy the conditions of secondary law to claim a right of residence due to lack of comprehensive insurance,[23] even though he did have sufficient resources. The Court suggested that residence rights under secondary law can be limited due to legitimate interests of Member States. Such a legitimate interest would be avoiding the negative economic effects of migration by not granting residence rights to EU migrants who became an unreasonable burden in light of Recital 4 of Directive 90/364.[24] The Court further held that the limitations imposed due to such legitimate interests should comply with the principle of proportionality and should be subject to judicial review for compliance with the rights attributed to individuals under Article 18 EC.[25]

The Court evaluated the limitation to the residence rights of Baumbast as a limitation based on the legitimate interests of Member States. However, this limitation was based on the requirements of EU secondary law and should rather be perceived as a consideration of the EU legislature, in light of the attempt to minimize the effects of free movement to the project of growth. Since sufficiency of resources does not appear as an exception to the free movement rule, but rather as the condition behind the attribution of free movement rights under secondary law, it is problematic to suggest that judicial review refers to the compliance of state action and the legitimate interests of Member States with primary law. Rather, the Court could have considered whether such limitations, as expressed in the Directive conditioning the right to reside, are in compliance with primary law, and whether secondary law should be reviewed against primary law in light of the objectives it seeks to pursue.

In any case, at this stage of evolution of the case-law, scholars suggested that this approach was employed by the Court to consolidate the rights of EU migrants in line with the Maastricht Treaty and to limit the restrictions of the residence Directives adopted before the establishment

[22] Ibid, para 63.

[23] Case C-413/99, *Baumbast and R*, ECLI:EU:C:2002:493, paras 80, 88.

[24] Ibid, para 91.

[25] Ibid, paras 85–86, 91.

of the citizenship status.[26] The Court carried on with similar interpretations in *Grzelczyk* concerning the rights of residence of a student who claimed a subsistence benefit as a former worker.[27] In this case, the Court developed a formula, which has been repeated in the case-law and quoted in literature with great hopes.[28] Therein the Court held that

> Union citizenship is destined to be the fundamental status of nationals of the Member States, enabling those who find themselves in the same situation to enjoy the same treatment in law irrespective of their nationality, subject to such exceptions as are expressly provided for.[29]

This quote has been seen as setting the backdrop against which the rights of EU migrants should be developed, in line with a new fundamental status, disentangled from economic considerations.[30] This decoupling of economic considerations and migrant movement in the EU does not appear throughout the rest of the judgment, where the Court repeated that Member States could withdraw the residence permit of an EU migrant if they found that, in having recourse to social assistance, the said migrant no longer had sufficient resources, which is the precondition of their residence right.[31] The greater protection for EU migrants in this case actually lay in the fact that the Court suggested that expulsion measures could not be an automatic consequence of having recourse to social assistance.[32] By shaping a system in a way which limits the rights of residence to holders of sufficient resources, while also providing access to social assistance under equal treatment conditions, the economic and social objectives of primary law are channelled into secondary law. As the Court held,

[26] Christian Timmermans, '*Martínez Sala* and *Baumbast* Revisited' in Loïc Azoulai and Miguel Poiares Maduro (eds), *The Past and Future of EU Law: The Classics of EU Law Revisited on the Fiftieth Anniversary of the Rome Treaty* (Hart 2010); For a critique, see Agustín José Menéndez, 'European Citizenship after *Martínez Sala* and *Baumbast*: Has European Law Become More Human but Less Social?' in Loïc Azoulai and Miguel Poiares Maduro (eds), *The Past and Future of EU Law: The Classics of EU Law Revisited on the 50th Anniversary of the Rome Treaty* (Hart 2010).

[27] Case C-184/99, *Grzelczyk*, ECLI:EU:C:2001:458.

[28] Perhaps as many as the 'civis europeaus sum' in the Opinion of AG Jacobs in Case C-168/91, *Konstantinidis*, ECLI:EU:C:1992:504.

[29] C-184/99, *Grzelczyk*, para 31.

[30] Dora Kostakopoulou, 'Ideas, Norms and European Citizenship: Explaining Institutional Change' (2005) 68 The Modern Law Review 233; Shaw (n 19).

[31] C-184/99, *Grzelczyk*, para 42.

[32] Ibid, para 43.

> Whilst Article 4 of Directive 93/96 does indeed provide that the right of residence is to exist for as long as beneficiaries of that right fulfil the conditions laid down in Article 1, the sixth recital in the directive's preamble envisages that beneficiaries of the right of residence must not become an unreasonable burden on the public finances of the host Member State. Directive 93/96, like Directives 90/364 and 90/365, thus accepts a certain degree of financial solidarity between nationals of a host Member State and nationals of other Member States, particularly if the difficulties which a beneficiary of the right of residence encounters are temporary.[33]

Jesse and Carter have rightly suggested that, in this finding, the Court introduced a distinction between reasonable and unreasonable burden, with the latter capable of breaking the bond of financial solidarity between a host state and a migrant.[34] *Trojani* and *Bidar* followed a similar inconsistent line.[35]

In *Trojani*, which concerned the claim of a French national to subsistence benefit in Belgium, the Court confirmed that EU migrants could claim a general residence right under the Treaty citizenship provisions. But at the same time, the Court found that such right to residence could not be established for Trojani, for want of sufficient resources under secondary law.[36] Contrary to *Baumbast*, where the EU migrant had sufficient resources and family members with him in the UK, and only lacked comprehensive health insurance, Trojani had none of these. Thus, failure to recognize a residence right was not found to be disproportionate in light of the objective of the Directive to avoid EU migrants becoming a burden.[37] The Court then repeated the approach of *Martínez Sala*, where it had held that residence under national law is sufficient to claim equal access to social benefits under Article 12 EC.[38]

Essentially, the Court made a differentiation between EU residence rights, which could be limited for economic reasons, and social rights

[33] Ibid, para 44.

[34] Moritz Jesse and Daniel Carter, 'Life after the "Dano-Trilogy": Legal Certainty, Choices and Limitations in EU Citizenship Case Law' in Nathan Cambien, Dimitry Kochenov, and Elise Muir (eds), *European Citizenship under Stress, Social Justice, Brexit and Other Challenges*, vol 16 (Brill Nijhoff 2020) with reference to Dora Kostakopoulou, 'European Union Citizenship: Writing the Future' (2007) 13 ELJ 623 and Charlotte O'Brien, *Unity in Adversity: EU Citizenship, Social Justice and the Cautionary Tale of the UK* (Hart 2017).

[35] C-456/02, *Trojani*, ECLI:EU:C:2004:488; Case C-209/03, *Bidar*, ECLI:EU:C:2005:169.

[36] C-456/02, *Trojani*, para 36.

[37] Ibid.

[38] Ibid, paras 39–44.

stemming from EU citizenship, once a migrant finds themselves in a host state. Member States can deny residence to economically inactive EU migrants who do not possess sufficient resources, in order to protect their national welfare systems from collapse. However, if they recognize a right of residence under national law, by virtue of this lawfulness of residence, EU nationals need to be protected under equal treatment provisions, furthering the objectives of social cohesion in the Member States. In this balancing of economic considerations as a limit to residence and social considerations behind treatment in the host state, the Court acknowledged the discretion of Member States to remove EU migrants who had recourse to the social assistance system; however, such removal should not be the automatic consequence of having recourse to the social assistance system.[39]

Bidar continued down the path of this case-law. Bidar was a student, lawfully resident in the UK, where he completed his secondary education and claimed assistance for the tuition fees of his university education. The Court found that the student enjoyed a right of residence on the basis of Article 18 EC and Directive 90/364, even though he did not have sufficient resources and did not fulfil the conditions of secondary law.[40] In order to qualify how the balancing act should take place between granting social assistance under equal treatment and preserving the public finances of Member States, the Court came up with the criterion of integration. Specifically, it stated that Member States can legitimately grant assistance covering maintenance costs to students who have demonstrated a certain degree of integration in the host state.[41] In so doing, the Court attempted to ground its expansionist protection of EU citizens' right in the fact that they were already part of the host societies. It further tried to dissociate access to such benefits from market participation by differentiating from the criterion it applied to the case-law on jobseekers.[42]

Specifically, in cases regarding jobseekers who did not have residence rights under EU law and claimed benefits, the Court had suggested the existence of a genuine link between the applicant and the geographical market in question as a condition to be taken into account in order to examine whether the denial of access to such benefits would be

[39] Ibid, para 45.
[40] C-209/03, *Bidar*, para 36.
[41] Ibid, para 57.
[42] Ibid, para 58 with reference to Case C-224/98, *D'Hoop*, ECLI:EU:C:2002:432, para 38, and Case C-138/02, *Collins*, ECLI:EU:C:2004:172, para 67.

discriminatory for EU migrants under primary law.[43] In the relevant case-law, it is true, as Jesse and Carter have suggested, that

> On paper, these formulas recognized the legitimate interest of Member States to protect the financial sustainability of their welfare system. However, in practice they strengthened the position of individual applicants vis-à-vis the State, again arguably circumventing conditions contained in applicable secondary legislation.[44]

Looking at the legislative and case-law developments of the relevant period, the ambition to reshape the rights of migrants under EU law is clear. The Council was hesitant to operationalize a general residence right without safeguards for national economies, despite the Commission proposals on the table. At the same time, the Court went much further in consolidating the protection of EU migrants under primary law. Besides *Baumbast*, the Court did not go as far as accepting an EU residence right stemming directly from the Treaties without regard to the conditions of secondary law. Nevertheless, it did use primary law as a ground for review of Member State action, limiting the grounds that could allow removal of EU migrants from a Member State.

At the same time, it extended the application of equal treatment provisions to all EU migrants who had lawful residence in Member States, regardless of whether that residence stemmed from EU or national law. Next to the Court, the Commission had the ambition that 'Union citizens should, *mutatis mutandis*, be able to move between Member States on similar terms as nationals of a Member State moving around or changing their place of residence or job in their own country'.[45] While such an evolution of migrants' rights eventually materialized as regards entry and residence, this is only the case for a short period of time.[46] Security of residence and family reunification are not generally applicable to all EU migrants. Rather, economic considerations dictate their limitation only to those who have sufficient resources not to become a burden on the public finances of the host states.

43 C-138/02, *Collins*, and Case C-22/08 and C-23/08, *Vatsouras and Koupatantze*, C-22/08 and C-23/08, ECLI:EU:C:2009:344, para 38.

44 Jesse and Carter (n 34) 141.

45 Proposal for a Directive on the right of citizens of the Union and their family members to move and reside freely within the territory of the Member States, COM(2001)0257 final [2001] OJ C 270E/150, Section 1.3; Communication on the follow-up to the recommendations of the High-level panel on the free movement of persons, COM(98)403 final.

46 Right to residence up to three months under Article 6, Directive 2004/38.

In this way, the economic objectives of the Treaty are pursued by ensuring that free movement rights are not unlimited. Relatedly, economic sustainability dictates the limitation of EU migrants' rights. The challenges in setting up a system of residence and social rights for EU migrants and the different views of institutional actors accurately reflect the development of a legal framework with due regard to a balance between different objectives of the EU project. In this framework, we see the intention to support the economy by promoting mobility of EU migrants who can positively affect growth (via their work). In parallel to this, the ambition of closer political integration and social cohesion necessitates rights for those who do not negatively impact economic growth (those not being unreasonable burden). Having shown in this chapter that the development of EU migrants' rights is closely connected to a continuous balancing of the economic and social objectives of EU law, and thus to economic and social sustainability, Chapter 6 will investigate how similar objectives played out in relation to TCN migrants.

6

National Contestation over the Aspiration of Long-Term Solutions to Migration

6.1 The Complicated Issue of a Harmonized Admission Policy

To achieve the intended objective of an internal market without frontiers, actions were required by both the Community and the Member States in their respective areas of competence.[1] What this objective would mean for the rights of TCN migrants was not conceived in a uniform way by the Commission and the Council. Specifically, during this period, Member States were coordinating action outside the framework of EU institutions. Intergovernmental meetings of different kinds took place from the late 1980s to the end of the 1990s with the aim of setting an agenda for closer cooperation in what they considered to be sensitive areas.[2] The discussions that occurred in these groups were shrouded with a veil of secrecy and their outcome contained technical goals related to specific areas.[3] To the extent that these technical goals were incorporated

[1] Communication of the Commission on the Abolition of Controls of Persons at Intra-Community Borders, COM(88)640 final, para 9.

[2] Indicatively see the ad hoc group on immigration set up at the initiative of the UK presidency, Coordinator's group on the free movement of persons set up following the Rhodes European Council, Trevi ministers' group, and Immigration ministers group under the Belgian Presidency.

[3] Ford Glyn (1990), Report drawn up on behalf of the Committee of Inquiry into Racism and Xenophobia on the findings of the Committee of Inquiry, Session Documents, A3-195/90, 23 July 1990 criticized these groups for deflecting community competence and democratic control from the Parliament; Communication, Towards an Area of Freedom, Security and Justice, COM(98)459 final in retrospect on the absence of transparency and the inadequacy of the achievements of the period before the Amsterdam Treaty. On the goals on migration, see Statewatch European Monitoring and Documentation Centre on Justice and Home Affairs in the European Union, Compilation no 3, Maastricht Immigration Programme (1991) and Follow up (1993), Supplement to: 'Key texts on justice and home affairs in the European Union, Volume 1 (1976–1993)', 1. Report from the Ministers responsible for immigration to the European Council meeting in Maastricht on immigration and asylum policy, SN 4038/91 (WGI 930) 3 December 1991.

in Council Resolutions regarding migration, they form part of the analysis that follows.

The Commission's agenda on migration, in contrast, was more transparent. For this institution, the abolition of border controls should entail the elimination of legal obstacles to access to employment in other Member States and the harmonization of policies on admission.[4] Aware of the constantly changing socio-economic circumstances, the Commission emphasized the need to create a system that could accommodate the fluctuation of population movements and, relatedly, labour demand and supply in Member States, while promoting the social advancement for legally resident migrants.[5] Behind this demand lay the acknowledgement that migration had brought economic and cultural benefits to the European societies, and such benefits needed to be preserved.[6] The approach of the Commission constantly attempted to align migration with economic and social sustainability. Against this background, the analysis will develop as follows.

In Sections 6.1.1 and 6.1.2, we see how social and economic considerations played out in attempts to harmonize admission, before looking at proposals to grant rights to TCN workers in Section 6.2. Unlike the period examined in Chapter 3, where the Community institutions emphasized the need to align the regulation of migration for TCNs to that of EU migrants, the politicization of migration precluded a uniform approach to the regulation of TCN migrants' rights.

6.1.1 Reactive Approach of the Council Shaped by Economic Fears and Unwillingness to Yield Competence

Already with the adoption of the Single European Act, Member States issued a Declaration, in which they acknowledged their intention to cooperate on matters of entry, movement, and residence of TCNs on the one hand and terrorism, crime, and trafficking on the other hand.[7] They also added a General Declaration to Article 13 SEA stating that they retained competence on measures related to controlling migration.[8]

4 On Immigration, SEC(91)1855 final, para 62.

5 Ibid, paras 3, 69.

6 On Immigration and Asylum Policies, COM(94)23, Section I.2.

7 Political Declaration by the Governments of the Member States on the Free Movement of Persons [1987] OJ L 169/24.

8 General Declaration on Articles 13 to 19 of the Single European Act [1987] OJ L 169/24.

In line with this emphasis on national competence, the Council paid little attention to issues of harmonizing admission or granting rights to TCN migrants.

Contrary to the Commission's emphasis on the need to ensure the development of the EU project via a regulated system of admission shaped around long-term considerations, discussed in detail in Section 6.1.2, the Council adopted a series of resolutions stemming from intergovernmental cooperation, which stressed national competence over admission. The 1994 Resolutions touched upon admission of different categories of migrants. One resolution was issued on migrant workers, while two more followed on self-employed migrants and students.[9] The Resolution on TCN workers was extremely restrictive. At a time when Member States were struggling with high national unemployment and had no immediate need for migrant workers, the Resolution on TCN workers was restrictive and only addressed the issue of admission for temporary employment.[10] Member States reserved the right to allow family reunification for people admitted for temporary employment.[11] Finally, failing to take into account long-term considerations, the resolution emphasized that the restrictive measures on admission implemented in Member States should be maintained and, if necessary, reinforced.[12] These principles set out to govern admission were meant to represent the stricter standards and were not intended to be relaxed by Member States.[13]

The overall approach of the Council was that Member States should in principle refuse entry to all TCN workers. Entry should only be considered in case of vacancies that could not be filled by Community workers or TCN workers already permanently residing in a Member State.[14] Such admission was to take place for workers who had specialist

[9] Council Resolution of 30 November 1994 relating to the limitations on the admission of third-country nationals to the territory of the Member States for the purpose of pursuing activities as self-employed persons [1996] OJ C 274/7; Council Resolution of 20 June 1994 on Limitations on Admission of Third-Country Nationals to the Member States for employment [1996] OJ C 274/3; Council Resolution of 30 November 1994 on the admission of third-country nationals to the territory of the Member States for study purposes [1996] OJ C 274/10.

[10] Council Resolution on admission of TCNs for employment [1996] OJ C 274/3, paras ii and iii.

[11] Ibid, para v.

[12] Ibid, para vi.

[13] Ibid.

[14] Ibid, I. general criteria.

qualifications or if there was a temporary manpower shortage in national or Community labour markets, which can affect the operation of employers.[15] Authorizations to reside should be restricted to employment in a specific job and with a specific employer.[16] Further, the Resolution provided that admission for temporary employment might be offered to seasonal workers, in strictly controlled numbers, who undertook specific jobs and fulfilled a 'traditional need' in a Member State, trainees; frontier workers; and intra-corporate transferees. Finally, the Resolution included restrictions as to the maximum period of admission for employment, arguably to avoid the settlement of migrant workers.[17] As a result, extension of temporary stays was to be denied to seasonal workers over the six-month employment period, whereas for regular TCN workers, extension of permits could be considered only if the criteria for initial admission continued to be met, that is special skills, vacancies unfilled by Community labour, and jeopardizing the function of an undertaking.

Were economic considerations the reason for such a restrictive policy? While there is not much information in the text of the resolution to draw definite conclusions, if we compare this with the resolutions that followed on self-employed TCNs and students, the economic fears behind labour migration become clear. Specifically, the resolution on self-employed TCNs was not restrictive, and the Council acknowledged therein that the reason for differentiation was that admission of people pursuing independent economic activity added value to the economy of the host state, and thus was, as such, of benefit.[18] To the extent that the economic activity was of no benefit to Member States, then TCNs should not be admitted.[19] Similarly, regarding students, the Council emphasized the importance of ensuring that their migration was time-limited and did not turn into permanent immigration via employment.[20]

In times of national contestation of immigration, with local unemployment and the possibility of employing workers already residing in EU

[15] Ibid.

[16] Ibid, para iii restrictions as to the scope of employment.

[17] Ibid, para iv restrictions as to the period of admission to employment; for seasonal workers, a maximum six months in a twelve-month period; for trainees, a maximum of one year, which might be extended for the time needed to obtain a professional qualification, and a general ban on admission for more than four years in the first instance.

[18] Council Resolution on admission of self-employed TCNs [1996] OJ C 274/7, para 4.

[19] Ibid, para 5.

[20] Council Resolution on the admission of TCN students [1996] OJ C 274/10, para 4.

territory, the slowly resurging economies of Member States had no need for migration from outside the EU to continue to perform. This restrictive approach, although based on economic considerations, did not take into account the constantly changing economic circumstances and their relation to labour migration. What was missing was a long-term understanding of migration for achieving economic sustainability. Towards the end of the 1990s and in the years following, the Council continued to engage very sporadically with economic migration and the need to harmonize conditions of admission and residence. According to the Tampere Council, such harmonization should take place based on a shared assessment of economic and demographic developments within the EU, as well as the situation in the countries of origin.[21] It is not clear why the Council did not refer to the fact that the Commission had tried to issue an instrument which would embed such assessment within the EU framework, as we will see in Section 6.1.2.

6.1.2 The Persistent Ambition of the Commission to Align Migration with the Project of Growth

With an emphasis on the need to shape a system that has inbuilt guarantees to ensure the development of the Member States in changing economic and demographic circumstances, the Commission submitted a proposal on a Convention to harmonize the rules of admission of TCNs in 1997.[22] The proposed Convention was submitted under Article K3(2) of the Maastricht Treaty, and the Commission was prepared to redraft it into a Directive after the entry into force of the Amsterdam Treaty, should there be agreement. Despite its title, the proposal went a lot further than the harmonization of conditions of admission. It suggested a framework for the conclusive regulation migration at EU level by regulating the admission of migrants for employment, independent economic activity, training, study, non-gainful activity, family reunification, and the attribution of progressive rights for long-term residents. This section evaluates how economic and social objectives appeared behind the regulation of admission, while the parts of the proposal that dealt with the attribution of rights to migrant workers form part of the analysis under Section 6.2. The analysis highlights how the Commission

[21] Tampere European Council, Presidency Conclusions, 15 and 16 October 1999, para 20.
[22] Proposal for a Council Act establishing the Convention on rules for the admission of third-country nationals to the Member States, COM(97)387 final.

envisioned a migration system deeply rooted in economic and social sustainability.

Acknowledging that the economic growth of the 1950s and 1960s would not return, and that the current labour market situation would not allow for a liberal migration policy, the Commission remained realistic as to the fact that the zero immigration target envisioned by Member States could not be realized.[23] In the explanatory memorandum, the Commission set the Convention within the context of shaping a system that could ensure the continued benefits of migration for the EU development project. This would materialize as follows: admission would be granted to TCN workers if there existed a vacancy that could not be filled by a Community worker or by a legally resident TCN worker. The idea behind this system was to allow the market to function, while avoiding an increase in labour force via migration at a time when unemployment was already a problem in the Member States.[24]

TCN workers would need to have an offer of employment for at least one year in order to enter, and they could be admitted with a maximum four-year authorization at the first entry.[25] The renewal of their permit would be dependent on the continuation of the conditions behind their initial entry. This meant that, if there was labour demand, migrants would be able to continue to reside, whereas, in the case of recession and unemployment, the conditions of their initial entry would not be fulfilled, and they would not be able to prolong their stay, as their labour would no longer be needed. As for seasonal workers, they would be granted admission for six months, and TCNs who had already been admitted as seasonal workers would have priority in future applications for a seasonal work permit.[26] The idea behind the prioritization was to counter the risk of seasonal workers staying illegally, as they would benefit from preferential treatment in future applications.[27] The emphasis on the function of labour migration, and more specifically on a harmonized admission system for achieving the economic objectives of

[23] Ibid, Section 2.

[24] Ibid, Explanatory memorandum.

[25] Ibid, Article 8.

[26] Ibid, Article 9.

[27] This was channelled into Directive 2014/36/EU on the conditions of entry and stay of third-country nationals for the purpose of employment as seasonal workers [2014] OJ L 94/375.

the EU, is also apparent if we compare the admission criteria for workers to those of students and trainees.[28]

Finally, Article 22 of the proposed Convention attested the cost-benefit analysis behind the regulation of admission of TCNs in the EU. Specifically, the Commission suggested that there were certain categories of TCNs who were not covered by the proposal but who should not be denied stay, namely pensioners, people living on capital income, writers receiving royalties, and au pair students. Since such people do not seek to join the labour market and create no economic burden, but are rather consumers and investors, their admission should be considered favourably. This proposal was eventually withdrawn in 2001.[29]

At this point, the Commission issued another proposal under Article 63(3)(a) of the Amsterdam Treaty suggesting that the role of TCNs in the EU labour market had been disregarded in comparison with other areas, related to the single market.[30] The 2001 proposal sought to regulate the admission of TCNs for the purpose of paid employment and self-employed activities.[31] The aim was to provide rights to TCN migrants, while allowing Member States to limit admission for economic migration in case of limited labour demand. Specifically, the framework would permit a quick reaction to changing economic and demographic circumstances, and admission would be allowed only if there was an economic need on behalf of the Member States, or if such TCN migrants had a beneficial effect to the national economies.[32]

The proposed Directive provided for equal treatment on a set of basic rights enshrined in Article 11.[33] More specific provisions regulated the admission of seasonal workers, trans-frontier workers, intra-corporate transferees, trainees, and au pairs.[34] Further, Article 32 of the proposed Directive introduced a general non-discrimination provision regarding its application, with a wording based on Article 13 EC Treaty and Article

[28] Articles 17–19 Proposal, COM(97)387.

[29] Communication, Withdrawal of Commission Proposals which are no longer topical, COM(2001)0763 final.

[30] On a Community Immigration Policy, COM(2000)757 final, 13.

[31] Proposal for a Directive on the conditions of entry and residence of third-country nationals for the purpose of paid employment and self-employed economic activities, COM(2001)0386 final [2001] OJ C 332E/248.

[32] Ibid, Explanatory Memorandum, Section 3, points 5, 6, 8.

[33] Housing could be limited to only apply to workers with minimum stay. Article 11 of the Explanatory Memorandum refers to Article 12 of the Long-term Residents Draft Directive which was issued around the same time.

[34] Articles 12–16 Proposal, COM(2001)0386 final.

21 CFR.[35] Under Article 26 of the proposed Directive, Member States were allowed to maintain horizontal measures in addition to the economic needs test to regulate access to the labour market. Such measures would have to be communicated to the Commission, which would evaluate whether they were justified.[36] Finally, Member States could introduce exceptions for employment in public service under Article 28 of the proposed Directive.[37] This proposal was eventually withdrawn in 2006, after failing to gather support from the Council, which did not want to address the matter of horizontal admission for all categories of TCN migrants.[38]

In addition to this failed proposal, the Commission had proposed an instrument on admission of students and an instrument on family reunification, which were supposed to be complementary and to meet the Tampere demand for conclusive regulation of migration. Admission for TCNs for reasons other than these (employment, independent economic activity, family reunification, and studies) was deemed as adequately regulated under domestic law due to the low number of people falling in this category.[39]

The regulation of student admission was presented as disconnected from the labour market and linked to social enrichment and the exchanges between cultures promoted by student mobility.[40] The instrument was much more socially oriented, insofar as it aimed at promoting the EU as a global centre of excellence for education which would support the dissemination of human rights values, and sought to contribute to the objective of promoting quality education under Article 149 EC.[41] In the end, the Directive adopted covered the admission of students, and Member States were given discretion on extending its application to school pupils, unremunerated trainees, and volunteers. The Directive included general and

[35] Ibid, Explanatory memorandum, Article 26.

[36] Ibid, Article 30.

[37] Ibid, Explanatory memorandum Article 28 proposed to have the same wording as 39(4) and 46(1) TFEU on employment in public service.

[38] Communication, Outcome of the screening of legislative proposals pending before the Legislator, COM(2005)0462 final; Withdrawal of Commission proposals following screening for their general relevance, their impact on competitiveness and other aspects [2006] OJ C 64/3.

[39] Proposal for a Directive on the conditions of entry and residence of third country nationals for the purposes of studies, vocational training or voluntary service, COM (2002)0548 final [2003] OJ C 45E/18, Section 1.1.

[40] Ibid, Section 1.2 and Recital 7.

[41] Ibid, Section 1.3 and Recital 6.

specific conditions of admission for the different categories.[42] Regardless of the category, though, comprehensive insurance and sufficient resources during the migrants' stay were required.[43]

Following the national practice of allowing students to remain in Member States in order to address skilled manpower shortages, the Commission also proposed the possibility of change of status from student to worker without having to leave the host state and reapply.[44] The proposal provided for the right to work to both students and trainees. In the text adopted, this right was only limited to students under Article 17, which also allowed Member States discretion to determine for how many hours students could be employed. Additionally, Member States were allowed to restrict access to employment for the first year of residence under Article 17(3). Finally, Article 12(2)(a) of the Directive provided that a refusal to renew or withdrawal of a permit could be justified based on a failure on the part of the student to respect the limitations regarding access to economic activities.

Essentially, all the proposals by the Commission to horizontally regulate admission for all the categories of TCN migrants failed. It is not easy to determine with certainty why these proposals were rejected by the Council, that is, whether the issue was the need of Member States to maintain competence on regulating migration, the assumed risks for their economies, or the fact that the proposals, especially the 1997 one, would lead to a system of residence and movement equally extensive to that applicable to EU migrants. In any case, in the period under review, the only measure that was eventually adopted regulated the admission of students, which came with no economic cost, and which still incorporated specific limits to avoid the possibility of students entering the EU to find employment.

6.2 Laying the Groundwork for Fragmentation and Differentiation

Unlike the previous period, the claim for migrant rights in the transformed EU legal order drew on a stronger perception of social objectives

[42] Directive 2004/114/EC of 13 December 2004 on the conditions of admission of third-country nationals for the purposes of studies, pupil exchange, unremunerated training or voluntary service [2004] OJ L 375/12.

[43] Sickness in Article 6(1)(c), resources for students in 7(1)(b), for pupils Article 9(1)(d) and (e), for trainees Article 10(b), for volunteers 11(b) and (c), Directive 2004/114.

[44] Proposal, COM(2002)0548 final, Section 1.4. This change of status was to be regulated under the Proposed Directive on self-employed third country nationals, COM(2001) 386 final.

and the importance of TCN rights for social cohesion. Equal treatment continued to be the central principle guiding the Community approach to legally resident TCNs during the 1990s.[45] Both social and economic considerations lay behind the demand for equal treatment. Economic considerations were included with reference to contradictory practices at national level having the potential of distorting the EU labour market, and of social dumping within the EU.[46] At the same time, the granting of equal rights was perceived as having the potential to lead to an increase in the workforce, and to affect beneficially the social security systems of Member States, which were experiencing difficulties due to negative population growth.[47] The emphasis on the value of the migrant worker for the project of growth diminished, and equal treatment became part of broader social objectives of the EU through a link between the treatment of migrants and a social agenda for a functioning EU society.[48]

Against this backdrop, equal treatment was demanded in a series of initiatives to advance the rights of migrant workers. In 1995, the Commission suggested extending the personal scope of Article 22 of Regulation 1408/71 to TCNs in order to ensure their right to immediately necessary healthcare when staying for a short time in another Member State.[49] This proposal did not go through in the adoption of the Regulation 3095/95.[50] However, social protection for TCN migrants

[45] On Immigration, SEC(91)1855 final, para 42.

[46] Ibid, para 43; Economic and Social Committee, Own-initiative opinion on the Status of migrant workers from third countries (91/C 159/05) [1991] OJ C 159/12, para 3.2.2.

[47] Ibid, para 3.2.3.

[48] On Immigration, SEC(91)1855 final, para 59. See also European Economic and Social Committee, Opinion on the status of migrant workers from third countries (91/C 339/15) OJ C 339/82, para 2.4.1 on equal rights as an independent political choice; On Immigration and Asylum Policies, COM(94)23 final, para 130; HAEU, CEUE _SEGE-SEC(1991)0803, Commission, Secretariat General, Communication from the President, Mr Bangemann and Mrs Papandreou in agreement with Mr Andriessen, Mr Marin and Mr Matutes, Communication to the Commission, Immigration, 10.

[49] Amended proposal for a Regulation amending Regulation 1408/71 on the application of social security schemes to employed persons, to self-employed persons and to members of their families moving within the Community, Regulation 574/72 laying down the procedure for implementing Regulation 1408/71, Regulation 1247/92 amending Regulation 1408/71 and Regulation 1945/93 amending Regulation 1247/92, COM(95)284.

[50] Regulation 3095/95 of 22 December 1995 amending Regulation 1408/71 on the application of social security schemes to employed persons, to self-employed persons and to members of their families moving within the Community, Regulation 574/72 fixing the procedure for implementing Regulation 1408/71, Regulation 1247/92 amending Regulation 1408/71 and Regulation 1945/93 amending Regulation 1247/92 [1995] OJ L 335/1. See Caroline Laske, 'The Impact of the Single European Market on Social

was eventually achieved with the adoption of Regulation 859/2003.[51] Moreover, TCN workers were included in the scope of the Community Charter on Fundamental Rights of workers, a non-binding instrument, adopted by a declaration in 1989 by all the Member States, with the exception of the UK.[52] Similarly, the Agreement on Social Policy annexed to the Maastricht Treaty, which sought to set up closer cooperation among all Member States with the exception of the UK, provided that the Council could take action in the area of conditions of employment of legally resident TCNs. Having these in mind, Sections 6.2.1 and 6.2.2 look at the development of family reunification rights and the progressive attribution of rights to long-term residents.

6.2.1 Towards an Autonomous Protection of Migrant Workers' Families

The attribution of family reunification rights to legally resident TCN migrants was very controversial. Despite the restrictive admission policies prevalent in the 1980s, Member States had maintained exceptions for humanitarian reasons, among which was also family reunification. This led to substantial migration movements, and, as a result, in the 1990s, Member States started to impose tighter conditions for family reunification.[53] According to an ILO working paper, economic considerations influenced both the law and practice of Member States, as foreign family members were viewed as a potential economic liability, searching for work at times of high unemployment.[54]

Protection for Migrant Workers' (1993) 30 CMLRev; Herwig Verschueren, 'EC Social Security Coordination Excluding Third Country Nationals: Still in Line with Fundamental Rights after the *Gaygusuz* Judgment?' (1997) 34 CMLRev.

51 Regulation 859/2003 of 14 May 2003 extending the provisions of Regulation 1408/71 and Regulation 574/72 to nationals of third countries who are not already covered by those provisions solely on the ground of their nationality [2003] OJ L 124/1.

52 Community Charter of Fundamental Social Rights of Workers adopted at the European Council in Strasbourg meeting on 8, 9 December 1989.

53 On Immigration, SEC (91) 1855 final, para 17; Commission, DG Employment, Industrial Relations and Social Affairs, Unit: Freedom of movement, Migration policy, Immigration Policies in the Member States: Between the Need for Control and the Desire for Integration, Working Document, Summary Report of the information network in migration from non-EC Countries (RIMET) year of reference 1991, V/1020/92, 23.

54 WR Böhning and J Werquin, *Some Economic, Social and Human Rights Considerations Concerning the Future Status of Third-Country Nationals in the Single European Market* (International Labour Office 1990) 41.

During this period, the ad hoc Group on Immigration tabled a resolution on harmonization of national policies on family reunification, which was adopted in Copenhagen in June 1993.[55] The resolution did not provide much harmonization. Rather, it suggested that family reunification should apply to TCNs legally resident in a Member State 'on a basis which affords them an expectation of long-term residence'.[56] The definition of what constituted an expectation of long-term residence was left to national law. Member States were allowed to make entry and stay conditional on the availability of adequate accommodation, sufficient resources, and the existence of health insurance, to avoid placing a burden on public funds.[57] What is more, the authorization to family members could be made conditional on a continued fulfilment of the criteria for admission for a period, which the Member States would define.[58] Within a reasonable time following admission, family members could be authorized to stay on an independent basis in accordance with the provisions of national law.[59] This restrictive approach is in stark contrast with the Opinion of the Economic and Social Committee, which suggested that family reunification should take place under the same conditions as applicable to Community workers.[60]

The 1997 Commission proposal on a Convention regulating the admission of TCN migration discussed earlier, also included provisions on family reunification. In the proposal, the issue was disconnected from economic considerations, and instead it was linked with obligations to consolidate the rights of migrant workers.[61] Under Article 24 of the proposed Convention, family reunification rights would be granted to TCNs who were resident for one year and had a prospect of valid residence for two more years. Article 28 of the proposed Convention provided that the applicant should have sufficient material conditions to support their family and to ensure that reunification would not place a burden on state expenditure. Article 30 enshrined a limitation for family members' access to employment for a period of six months, as the admission was granted

55 Ad hoc Group Immigration, Resolution on the harmonization of national policies on family reunification, 1 June 1993, SN2828/1/93 WGI 1497 REV1.

56 Ibid, point 1.

57 Ibid, 16.

58 Ibid, 11.

59 Ibid, 12.

60 European Economic and Social Committee, Opinion on the Communication, On Immigration and Asylum Policies (94/C 393/13) [1994] OJ C 393/69, para 3.2.2.

61 Proposal, COM(97)387 final, Section 2.

for human rights reasons and not for economic ones. Finally, Article 31 provided that family members would be entitled to an autonomous right to reside subject to the fulfilment of the specified conditions.

After the failure to adopt the proposed Convention, the Commission issued a specific proposal on family reunification for both TCNs and EU nationals who did not fall under the free movement rules.[62] By this proposal, the Commission sought to consolidate the protection of family life in the EU, as means to promote the living conditions of everyone in the territory, rather than specific migration-related rights. Specifically, the harmonization of family reunification was suggested because of the function of family for integration in the host state.[63] By analogy to family reunification rights for EU nationals, the Commission suggested that fair treatment of TCNs was 'indispensable' if they were to lead a normal life in the host states.[64] However, this horizontal regulation of family life for both TCN and EU nationals who had not moved from their state of origin was not accepted by the Council.[65]

Eventually, the Family Reunification Directive was adopted in 2003.[66] It applies to all legally resident TCNs and excludes all migrants whose status is considered uncertain or temporary.[67] Under the current framework, the right to family reunification for TCNs is regulated and harmonized to promote economic and social cohesion under Article 3 TEU, as acknowledged in Recital 4 of the Directive. Even though Article 3 TEU is not explicitly referred to, the recital mentions the central role of family reunification in the creation of sociocultural stability and integration for TCNs, and explains that such outcome serves to promote economic and social cohesion as fundamental objectives stated in the Treaty. The Directive creates a right to family reunification for the nuclear family of TCN migrants. The 1999 proposal for this Directive provided for a larger scope of family members entitled to reunification.[68] This was met

[62] Proposal for a Directive on the right to family reunification, COM(99)0638 final, Article 1, Article 3(c).

[63] Ibid, Section 2.2.

[64] Ibid, Section 7.2.

[65] Amended proposal for a Directive on the right to family reunification, COM(2002)0225 final, Section 2.4.

[66] Directive 2003/86/EC of 22 September 2003 on the right to family reunification [2003] OJ L 251/12.

[67] Article 3, Directive 2003/86; See also Amended proposal, COM(2002)0225 final.

[68] Proposal, COM(99)0638 final, Article 5 with obligation for spouse and unmarried partner in line with Case59/85, *Netherlands v Reed*, 59/85, ECLI:EU:C:1986:157, ascendants and children of full age.

with resistance by the Council, which suggested as a compromise that the Family Reunification Directive should create an obligation on the part of the Member States for family reunification for members of the nuclear family, and allow discretion for the rest.[69] Thus, Article 4 of the Family Reunification Directive provides family reunification rights for the spouse of the TCN and the minor children (including adopted children) of the TCN or the spouse as long as the TCN has custody and the children are dependent on them. The age of majority for reunification of children is set by national law and the children must not be married. Apart from the spouse and minor children, Member States have discretion to authorize the reunification of other family members under Article 4(2) and (3) of the Directive. Similarly, the provisions as to the age of children were revised as Member States requested room for manoeuvre to examine whether children met the conditions of integration beyond a certain age before authorizing family reunification.[70]

The Directive also provides family members with rights that are dependent on economic considerations. All family members enjoy entry and residence rights in the host Member State.[71] The Directive also provides rights of access to vocational guidance. This should not come as a surprise, since access to vocational guidance means that family members will be ready and trained for work when labour demand might arise. They should indeed eventually enjoy access to employment. However, the Directive allows Member States to limit such right for up to twelve months, during which they may examine the situation of their labour market, and they may also restrict access to the employment market for the dependent relatives and adult children entitled to reunification under Article 4(2). This type of limitation of family members' right to access the labour market should also not come as a surprise. The purpose served by such restrictions is the following: family reunification is introduced as a social measure to ensure better living conditions for the migrant worker. If family members are allowed to access the labour

[69] See Council of the European Union, Press Release, 2370th Council meeting – Justice, Home Affairs and Civil Protection, Brussels, 27 and 28 September 2001, 12204/01 (Presse 334).

[70] Amended proposal, COM(2002)0225 final, Section 2.4 and Article 4. See Article 4(6) and (5), Directive 2003/86.

[71] In the Blue Card Directive 2009/50 and Directive 2021/1883, the Intra-Corporate Transfers Directive 2014/66 and Researchers Directive 2005/71 the duration of their residence permits is altered to match the duration of the sponsor permit.

market with no restriction, this has the potential of negatively impacting the economy at times when there is no labour demand.

Finally, the Directive provides for the possibility that family members establish an autonomous right of residence.[72] Specifically, such an autonomous right shall be granted after maximum five years of residence in the host state. Member States are allowed to limit the autonomous rights of the spouse or unmarried children in the case of breakdown of the family relationship. They have the discretion of granting such a right to adult children and dependent relatives under Article 4(2) and the possibility to providing it in cases of widowhood, divorce, separation, or death of first-degree relatives in the direct ascending or descending line, as well as in cases of particularly difficult circumstances. Family members of workers also enjoy a set of procedural rights, which have been consolidated in the case-law.[73]

The Directive includes limitations to the right to entry and grounds for non-renewal of the permit in case the conditions set by the Directive are no longer satisfied, in case of fraud, public policy threat, fake marriage, or marriage of convenience; in case family members no longer have a real relationship with the sponsor; in case the sponsor has no right to reside; and, finally, in case the sponsor does not have sufficient resources.[74] The requirement of sufficient resources applies as a condition of entry but is explicitly repeated as a reason to withdraw the permit upon application for renewal.[75] The difference is that, on renewal, Member States can also take into account the potential contribution of the family member.

Thus, in the field of family reunification, while economic considerations appeared behind restrictive national policies, the Commission's approach was socially oriented. Essentially, the demand for securing rights to family reunification was aligned with a need to protect the human rights of people residing in EU territory and fit with the promotion of the social objectives of the EU project.[76] This is unlike family reunification for EU migrants, where the stated objective of regulation

[72] The 1999 Proposal granted such rights after four years, but in the 2002 Proposal it was suggested to change this to improve consistency with the long-term resident status.

[73] Joined Cases C-133/19, C-136/19, and C-137/19, *Belgian State*, ECLI:EU:C:2020:577.

[74] See Case C-557/17, *Y.Z. and others*, ECLI:EU:C:2019:203 on fraud as a ground of withdrawal when such fraud has been conducted by the sponsor and the family member has no knowledge.

[75] This clause was not included in the original proposal of 1999, but upon deadlock, it became part of the revised proposal of 2002.

[76] On Immigration and Asylum Policies, COM(94)23 final, para 125.

was to support the migrant worker in the performance of their task, as discussed in Chapter 2. At the same time, economic considerations condition the attribution of rights to migrant families to ensure that the family members will not pose risks to Member States' economy. This is achieved through the introduction of requirements related to sufficient resources of the sponsor as a precondition for enjoyment of the family reunification right. The economic conditioning of the relevant rights has been interpreted in a restrictive way by the Court, as we will see in Chapter 9. Overall, in the regulation of family reunification, we see a shift that places migration closer to the social objectives of the EU, which were redefined during this period and were consolidated in the post-Amsterdam framework. At the same time, it is clear that the parallel pursuit of economic and social sustainability also conditions the attribution and limitation of migrants' rights in this field.

6.2.2 From a By-product of Economic Progress to a Means of Integration: The Case for Progressive Attribution of Rights

During this period, the rights of legally resident TCNs appear in concrete legislative proposals. As should be expected at this stage of the analysis, the ambition to attribute rights to TCN migrants was subject to conflicting ideas between different actors. Specifically, the Commission suggested the extension of free movement and access to employment across all Member States for resident migrants.[77] The need to extend freedom of movement to TCN migrants was also supported by the Parliament and the Economic and Social Committee, with reference to the contribution of TCN workers to the development of the EU project, and to the aim of creating an EU labour market.[78] Regarding the Commission's position, it appears that the internal market logic lay behind such a demand. Absent any differentiation between EU and

[77] On Immigration, SEC(91)1855 final, para 62. The Commission suggested the application of free movement, first for certain categories of TCNs (permanent residents, refugees, frontier workers, staff of firms providing cross border services).

[78] Resolution on the Joint Declaration against racism and xenophobia and an action programme by the Council of Ministers (Doc. A 2-261/88) [1989] OJ C 69; Economic and Social Committee own-initiative opinion on the status of migrant workers from third countries [1991] OJ C 159 point 3.4; European Economic and Social Committee, Opinion on the status of migrant workers from third countries (91/C 339/15) OJ C 339/82, paras 2.6.3, 2.6.4; European Economic and Social Committee, Opinion on the communication, on immigration and asylum policies (94/C 393/13) [1994] OJ C 393/69 para 3.1.3.

TCN workers' contribution to growth, there was a demand to grant access to employment in another Member State to the latter.[79] In this context, the Commission envisioned the priority of legally resident TCNs after EU nationals in accessing employment in other Member States.[80] That would be the first step, while a 1994 Commission Communication suggested a second step of allowing TCN workers to enter another Member State to respond to offers of employment.[81] Leaving some leeway to the intergovernmental cooperation taking place at the ad hoc group on migration, the Commission suggested that it would pursue the conditions of movement in the EU for legal migrants if the relevant initiatives did not move forward.[82]

Free movement of TCNs did not materialize at that time, but instead the Commission submitted a proposal that would grant rights to legally resident TCNs to travel within the Community.[83] The attribution of a right to travel was based on Article 100 EC, which provided for the coordination of national laws in matters affecting the functioning of the common market. While such a right would advance the position of TCNs, the central aim was to ensure the full economic benefits of a single market. As the Commission suggested in the relevant proposal, such a right to travel between the Member States for short stays was both useful from an economic point of view and legally necessary.[84] For the Commission, it did not make sense to have labour demand that can be filled internally, that is, by other EU workers and TCN workers resident in other Member States, and to still preclude TCNs from such employment, which would lead to more external recruitment.

At the same time, security of residence became a demand related to the social advancement of the migrant, and hence there was call for a common permanent residence scheme granted after a fixed period across

[79] On Immigration, SEC(91)1855 final, para 62.

[80] On Immigration and Asylum Policies, COM(94)23 final, para 129.

[81] Ibid, para 129.

[82] HAEU, CEUE _SEGE-SEC(1991)0803, Commission, Secretariat General, Communication from the President, Mr Bangemann and Mrs Papandreou in agreement with Mr Andriessen, Mr Marin and Mr Matutes, Communication to the Commission, Immigration, 6.

[83] Proposal for a Directive on the right of third-country nationals to travel in the Community, COM(95)346 final.

[84] Ibid, para 12; The proposal was amended, Amended proposal for a Directive on the right of third-country nationals to travel in the Community, COM(97)0106 final, and then implicitly withdrawn, Withdrawal of Commission Proposals which are no longer topical, COM(2001)0763 final.

the Member States, as well as for the progressive attribution of extra rights to settled migrants.[85] While the Council seemed to recognize the social significance of integration of legally resident TCNs, its approach to granting rights to long-term resident TCN workers remained restrictive.[86] In a 1996 Resolution, the Council held that long-term residents should be defined as TCN migrants who have stayed in the territory of a Member State for a period of ten years.[87] While the resolution provided that Member States should ensure security of residence for at least ten more years to long-term resident workers, it suggested that when an application was made to this end, Member States should be able to assess whether the applicant had a certain and stable level of means of subsistence, in particular health insurance, and whether they fulfilled the conditions for exercising an occupation.[88] As to the question of rights, the resolution provided that long-term residents and their family members should enjoy 'no less favourable' treatment than nationals of the Member States as regards working conditions, membership in trade unions, public policy in the housing sector, social security, emergency healthcare, and compulsory schooling.[89] Moreover, the resolution suggested that it should be possible for long-term residents and their family members to be granted non-contributory benefits.[90]

Unlike the restrictive approach of that Resolution, the 1997 proposed Convention discussed earlier placed security of residence in light of integration, as necessary to safeguard an equilibrium in European societies.[91] Under Article 32 of the proposed Convention, long-term resident status would be granted to TCNs who had been resident in a Member State for five years and who held a residence permit that ensured that on expiry they would have lived in that Member State for a total period of ten years. The rights for long-term residents would be guided by non-discrimination compared to EU nationals and a greater protection against expulsion.[92] In Article 35, the proposed Convention provided

[85] On Immigration, SEC(91)1855 final, para 59; On Immigration and Asylum Policies, COM(94)23 final, para 124.

[86] Recital 3, Council Resolution of 4 March 1996 on the status of third-country nationals residing on a long-term basis in the territory of the Member States [1996] OJ C 80/2.

[87] Ibid, III.1.

[88] Ibid, III.2 and IV.2

[89] Ibid, V.2

[90] Ibid.

[91] Proposal, COM(97)387 final, Section 2.

[92] Ibid, Article 34.

them the right to apply for vacancies in other Member States, and to study throughout the EU. The reasoning behind the attribution of such rights was both economic and social. According to the Commission, the possibility to take up work in another Member State would not affect the labour market, as it would not increase the number of migrants employed in the EU.[93] Moreover, with the aim of moving towards a broader EU social space, the Commission mentioned that long-term residents were seeking integration not in the particular Member State where they resided but rather in the frontier-free area of the EU.[94] As the new millennium began, the Commission also used the Charter as a point of reference, perhaps in an attempt to consolidate a direct link of rights between TCNs and the EU legal order. Specifically, it mentioned that the Charter could be a reference point for the development of a civic citizenship that would comprise of common rights and obligations.[95]

Relatedly, a proposal was issued by the Commission with the aim of consolidating the rights of long-term residents.[96] The proposal suggested that full integration for long-term residents should necessarily imply their right to move between Member States. Specifically, the Commission claimed that '[a] genuine area of freedom, security and justice, a fundamental objective of the European Union, is unthinkable without a degree of mobility for third-country nationals residing there legally, and particularly for those residing on a long-term basis'.[97] Free movement rights for long-term residents were demanded in light of Article 45 CFR, which provides for the possibility of extending free movement rights to TCNs. Apart from suggesting such rights to free movement, the Commission insisted on the economic need behind such attribution which would allow for 'better utilisation of employment reserves available in different Member States'.[98]

The Commission managed to gather support and adopted the Long-term Residents Directive in 2003, as means to promote the social objectives of the EU by ensuring fair treatment to legally resident TCNs and to put in place an integration policy that would grant TCNs rights and

93 Ibid, Explanatory Memorandum, Article 35(1).

94 Ibid.

95 On a Community Immigration Policy, COM(2000)757 final, 19–20.

96 Proposal for a Directive concerning the status of third-country nationals who are long-term residents, COM(2001)127 final.

97 Ibid, Section 5.6.

98 Ibid, Section 5.8.

obligations comparable to those of EU migrants.[99] Recital 4 of the Directive mentions that the integration of TCNs who have had a long residence in the EU is key in promoting the economic and social cohesion of the Union. Under Article 4(1), the status is attributed to all migrants who have lawfully resided in a Member State for a period of five years. Under Article 14, long-term residents can move to another Member State for periods longer than three months for any purpose (study, economic activity, other purposes). What is more, they have access to the labour market of the second Member States under equal treatment conditions under Article 21. However, Articles 13 and 21(2) allow Member States to set restrictions and conditions to the exercise of such rights which can significantly limit their effectiveness by making it extremely hard to move to take up employment in another Member State. Thus, even though free movement found its way in the Directive, the practical effect of the relevant right is significantly limited.

The Long-term Residents Directive is a clear example of the ways in which economic considerations can frame legislation at EU level: the aspiration of extending rights to migrants in order to boost the economy is limited and made ineffective due to economic fears of what might happen to the economy if migrants actually enjoy rights. The long-term approach of the Commission and its emphasis on the positive function of long-term residents for the EU economy was the reason for attribution of free movement rights to this category of TCNs. In parallel, the economic fears connected to potential negative effects of such movement for national labour markets were expressed by the Council as a reason to set substantive limitations to such movement making it practically ineffective.[100]

This ineffectiveness led to a demand for the revision of this instrument. In December 2022, the Commission issued a proposal for revision with the aim of strengthening the rights of long-term residents and their families and drawing them closer to the rights of EU nationals.[101] The

[99] Directive 2003/109/EC of 25 November 2003 concerning the status of third-country nationals who are long-term residents [2003] OJ L 16/ 44; Tampere European Council, Presidency Conclusions, 15 and 16 October 1999; Proposal, COM(2001)127 final, Explanatory memorandum 1.1.

[100] See Sara Iglesias Sánchez, 'Free Movement as a Precondition for Integration of Third-Country Nationals in the EU' in Elspeth Guild, Kees Groenendijk, and Sergio Carrera (eds), *Illiberal Liberal States: Immigration, Citizenship, and Integration in the EU* (Ashgate 2009).

[101] Proposal for a Directive concerning the status of third-country nationals who are long-term residents (recast), COM(2022)650 final. See also the similar demands in

Commission demanded consolidation of free movement rights for long-term residents once again, based on the idea that such movement can improve labour market effectiveness.[102] The negotiations of the relevant proposal have shown that Member States are unwilling to take away economic limitations from the exercise of mobility rights.[103] When it comes to the protection of social rights of long-term residents, which were also limited in the original formulation of the Directive, these have been extensively interpreted by the Court, which has limited state discretion behind their limitation, as we will see in Section 9.3. Once again economic and social considerations appear in the approach of different actors and affect the shaping of the EU migration policy. The lack of long-term considerations on the part of the Council limiting the attribution of both mobility and social rights to long-term residents lies behind the unsustainability of this instrument and its failure to achieve the economic and social objectives of primary law in the regulation of migration.

6.3 National Contestation Limiting the Rights of TCN Workers and Social Considerations behind New Demands

Unlike the period reviewed in Part I, the way economic and social objectives appear behind the regulation of labour migration becomes differentiated in the 1990s, leading to paradoxical results. Long-term economic planning dictated the Commission's effort to pursue harmonization of admission for TCN migrants. It put forward various proposals to align migration with the economic and social objectives of the Community under a long-term strategy. Behind these proposals, there was a need to shape a migration policy that could match national labour demand with the TCN workforce resident in the EU, and that would allow admission of TCNs to cover potential labour needs with a long-

Parliament, Committee on Civil Liberties, Justice and Home Affairs, Report on new avenues for legal labour migration (2020/2010((INI)) (rapporteur: Sylvie Guillaume) and of public stakeholders in Commission, DG for Migration and Home Affairs, Synthesis Report, Analysis of the responses to the public consultation on the future of legal migration, January 2021.

102 Proposal for revision of Long-term Residents Directive, COM(2022)650 final, Explanatory memorandum, Articles 16–18.

103 Article 6, Council Document, Proposal for a Directive concerning the status of third-country nationals who are long-term residents (recast) – Mandate for negotiations with the Parliament ST 16000 2023 INIT, 28 November 2023.

term perspective. In parallel, the various Commission proposals sought to align migration to the social objectives of the EU, referencing the need to guarantee a minimum core of rights to migrant workers and a progressive attribution of extra rights to long-term residents, who would eventually be protected similarly to Community workers. At a point of closer political integration, the rights of migrants became tied to a positive vision of what EU societies should look like.

The Council's stance was determined by economic considerations, but unlike the Commission, its approach to EU law-making was reactive.[104] During the period examined, Member States were facing high national unemployment, and in this context labour migration was viewed as an aggravating factor. This created a political sensitivity around migration that precluded any consideration regarding the contribution of migrants as a reason for harmonizing admission. Instead, the Council focused on measures that would reinforce a feeling of control for Member States over their territories and shared borders.[105]

Regarding measures that guarantee rights for migrants, such as family reunification and security of residence, equal treatment for TCNs was dictated under both a socially oriented and an economic logic. On the social side, the EU was promoting an identity that was socially and culturally pluralistic, based on respect of human rights and human dignity.[106] At the same time, equality for TCN workers was linked to observance of labour law, as a precondition for attracting migrants for highly skilled jobs, a demand the EU population could not meet.[107] As the Commission stated, granting such equality in terms of wages and working conditions was in the interest of society, which could benefit fully from the contribution of migrants to the economic and social life, while at the same time this would ensure that economic exploitation would not fuel unfair competition.[108]

The difference between the Council and the Commission as regards economic and social considerations behind migration appears on two

[104] Neil Walker, 'In Search of the Area of Freedom, Security and Justice: A Constitutional Odyssey' in Neil Walker (ed), *Europe's Area of Freedom, Security, and Justice* (Oxford University Press 2004) suggests that the AFSJ developed as a reactive policy domain.

[105] Giuseppe Callovi, 'Regulation of Immigration in 1993: Pieces of the European Community Jig-Saw Puzzle' (1992) 26 The International Migration Review 353 mentions that the obstacles are not technical but purely political.

[106] On a Community Immigration Policy, COM(2000)757 final, 19.

[107] Ibid.

[108] Ibid, 13.

levels. First, the Council focused these considerations on a domestic level and the relation of migration to the circumstances and labour needs of each Member State, while the Commission was looking at the EU as a whole. Second, the Council, perhaps due to its touch with national politics, took a short-term approach to economic and social objectives, while the Commission took a long-term one. It is in this long-term approach to the pursuit of economic development and social progress that the demand of economic and social sustainability finds implicit expression in the regulation of migration.

In any case, these different approaches on the function of migrants for EU economies blocked every attempt to harmonize admission, but they did allow the adoption of instruments guaranteeing a set of rights to some migrants. The rights were not as ambitious as the Commission had planned, as we saw in both the case of the Family Reunification Directive and in the case of the Long-term Residents Directive. However, they did put in place minimum guarantees which, as we shall see in Chapter 9, were significantly extended by the Court.

7

The Uneven Evolution of Association Agreements

7.1 The Unstoppable(?) Social Orientation of the Court

In its early case-law on free movement of workers, the Court extended the protection of migrants falling under the scope of Regulation 1612/68 by teleological interpretations, related to the need to remove obstacles to free movement and to assist workers in migrating in dignity. With an emphasis on the economic considerations behind personal rights, the Court pioneered the protection of rights of migrant workers in ways that could not have been envisioned under a literal reading of the text of the relevant provisions. From the 1980s onwards, the Court followed a similar approach as regards the rights of migrants falling under Association Agreements. This chapter will review the relevant case-law starting from the EEC–Turkey Agreement in Section 7.1.1 and moving to other Association Agreements in Sections 7.1.2 and 7.1.3, and it will highlight the extensive protection of social rights demanded by the Court. Section 7.2 will look at how Member States tried to bypass the relevant interpretations for fear that the extensive granting of social rights would prove unsustainable. Section 7.3 turns the focus to Association Agreements developed with full extension of the free movement framework to migrants of associated counties. That was the case when the relevant economic and demographic situation of the associated states showed no risk for the continued development of the EU project from the migrant populations. Overall, this chapter demonstrates first how social sustainability considerations have appeared behind an extensive interpretation of the relevant framework in the case-law. Second, Association Agreements provide the ideal example of how rights are attributed, extended, or limited depending on the economic sustainability challenges posed by the associated states.

7.1.1 *Economic and Social Considerations behind the Attribution and Consolidation of the Rights of Turkish Workers*

The EEC–Turkey Agreement created a special status for Turkish workers, which distinguished them from other third-country national workers. The adoption of the Agreement and its implementing decisions took place in years characterized by significant socio-economic changes. Throughout these years, the presence and importance of Turkish workers on Member States' territory was massive for the economic development of the EU. This allowed a better negotiating position for Turkey during the development of the Association. The aim of the Agreement and the initial – yet never materialized – purpose of eventual accession has been acknowledged as a basis of analogous interpretation in the case-law.[1] However, this aim has not been the only consideration in the reasoning of the Court. Before going into the relevant analysis, a reminder is due: the EEC–Turkey Agreement did not affect Member States' competence in regulating entry of migrants, nor did it impose obligations regarding family reunification. Rather, under different implementing decisions, the Agreement sought to advance the social position of Turkish workers and their families by ensuring the consolidation of their position after a certain time in the national labour market.

The most crucial part of the Decisions implementing the Agreement, and one which differentiates Turkish workers to this day, when the EU has put in place a separate migration policy, is the standstill clauses that were included in them. Specifically, Decision 1/80, which specified the rights that should be granted to migrant workers and their families, included a standstill clause under Article 13. The clause provided that Member States should not introduce new restrictions on the conditions of access to employment of Turkish workers and their families who are legally residents and employed in the Member States. Early on, the Court held that Article 13 of Decision 1/80, much like the similar clause of Article 41 of the Additional Protocol to the Agreement, had direct effect and could grant rights to individuals.[2] The Article was interpreted as meaning that Member States were not allowed to adopt new measures having the object or effect of making the conditions of access to

[1] See, however, mentions to a purely economic or essentially economic aim of the Agreement in Cases C-371/08, *Ziebell*, ECLI:EU:C:2011:809 and C-221/11, *Demirkan*, ECLI:EU:C:2013:583.

[2] See C-37/98, *Savas*, ECLI:EU:C:2000:224, paras 54, 71. On Article 13, see Case C-192/89, *Sevince*, ECLI:EU:C:1990:322, para 26.

employment for Turkish nationals more restrictive.[3] The Court further held that the standstill was intended to protect Turkish nationals who were not already lawfully employed and residing in the host state.[4] Those who were lawfully employed were protected via the provision of Article 6 of Decision 1/80.[5] What is more, the Court held that this also applied to Turkish workers and their families who were not in paid employment.[6] How to reconcile this with the fact that the wording of the provision refers to 'legally resident and employed' Turkish nationals? The Court held that this should be taken to mean that the provision benefited Turkish nationals only if they complied with the host state's rules on entry, residence, and employment.[7] The similar standstill clause of Article 41 of the Additional Protocol to the Agreement also shaped the Court's case-law on practices of Member States which could limit family reunification rights.[8]

Overall, the standstill clause was interpreted as follows: the adoption of new rules by Member States would either have to benefit the Turkish workers or, if these were more restrictive, they would have to apply equally to both Turkish and EU nationals, and would have to be proportionate in light of the pursuit of a reason of overriding public interest.[9] The Court has found several legitimate reasons falling under this concept: the aim of preventing illegal entry and residence, the prevention of forced marriages, ensuring successful integration, effective management of migration flows, and preventing and combatting entry fraud.[10]

3 Joined Cases C-317/01 and C-369/01, *Abatay and others*, ECLI:EU:C:2003:57, paras 74, 80. This was taken to mean more restrictive compared to what the framework was when the Agreement was adopted. See, however, Joined Cases C-300/09 and C-301/09, *Toprak and Oguz*, ECLI:EU:C:2010:756, where the Court found that the standstill prohibited more restrictive measures also compared to more lenient practices adopted by Member States after the adoption of Decision 1/80.

4 C-317/01 and C-369/01, *Abatay and others*, para 81.

5 Ibid, para 78; Case C-242/06, *Sahin*, ECLI:EU:C:2009:554, para 51.

6 C-317/01 and C-369/01, *Abatay and others*, para 81.

7 Ibid, para 84; C-242/06, *Sahin*, para 53.

8 Case C-138/13, *Dogan*, ECLI:EU:C:2014:2066; Case C-561/14, *Genc*, ECLI:EU:C:2016:24; Case C-379/20, *Udlændingenævnet*, ECLI:EU:C:2021:660.

9 In all cases it should not lead to a situation where a Turkish national would be in a position more advantageous than an EU one. See Article 59 of the Additional Protocol interpreted in conjunction with Article 13, Case C-228/06, *Soysal and Savatli*, ECLI:EU:C:2009:101, para 61; C-242/06, *Sahin*, paras 67 and 71. Similarly, in Case C-92/07, *Commission/Netherlands*, ECLI:EU:C:2010:228.

10 Case C-225/12, *Demir*, ECLI:EU:C:2013:725 para 41; C-138/13, *Dogan*; C-561/14, *Genc*, paras 43–44, 55; C-379/20, *Udlændingenævnet*; Case C-652/15, *Tekdemir*, ECLI:EU:

The system set up by Decision 1/80 and the progressive attribution of rights to migrant workers under Article 6 allowed the Court to infer a residence right from an effective protection of a right to work.[11] Specifically, the Decision set up a system of progressive attribution of rights to Turkish workers on access to employment. Turkish workers were entitled to renewal of their permit to work for the same employer after one year of legal employment. After three years of legal employment, they could respond to any offers of their choice for the same occupation, subject to priority for Community workers. After four years of employment, they were entitled to free access to any paid employment. This Article regulated the conditions under which Turkish workers would progressively enjoy greater access to employment in the Member States. By engaging with the different criteria that needed to be met for a Turkish national to acquire the relevant EU law rights, the Court extended the scope of protection of the Decision and consolidated the rights of Turkish workers to security of residence.

Overall, for Turkish nationals to enjoy rights under Decision 1/80, they would have to be workers, duly registered in the labour force of a Member State, and in legal employment for a specified period of time. The Court aligned the interpretation of 'worker' with that provided under the free movement case-law.[12] Specifically, the Court held that the Agreement aimed at progressively extending access of Turkish nationals to the EU labour market, and that this was similar to the aim pursued by free movement of workers. The result was that the scope of the Decision was aligned with the extensive scope of protection under the free movement framework.[13] Migrant workers who continuously contributed to a national labour market ought to enjoy full protection of the rights granted in Decision 1/80, and those who could no longer do so

C:2017:239, para 39; Case C-123/17, *Yön*, ECLI:EU:C:2018:632, para 77; C-70/18, *A and others*, ECLI:EU:C:2019:823, para 49.

11 Case C-192/89, *Sevince*; Case C-237/91, *Kus*, ECLI:EU:C:1992:527 paras 22–25; Case C-268/11, *Gülbahce*, ECLI:EU:C:2012:695; Case C-187/10, *Unal*, ECLI:EU:C:2011:623, para 50; Case, C-294/06, *Payir and others*, ECLI:EU:C:2008:36; Case C-36/96, *Günaydin and others*, ECLI:EU:C:1997:445, paras 37–38; Case C-98/96, *Ertanir*, ECLI:EU:C:1997:446, paras 31, 25; Case C-14/09, *Genc*, ECLI:EU:C:2010:57, para 40.

12 See Opinion of AG Fennelly in Case C-1/97, *Birden*, ECLI:EU:C:1998:262, para 23.

13 See Case C-355/93, *Eroglu*, ECLI:EU:C:1994:369; Case C-188/00, *Kurz*, ECLI:EU:C:2002:694, para 44; *Genc*, C-14/09, paras 23–28; Case C-1/97, *Birden*, ECLI:EU:C:1998:568 where the Court differentiated from Case 344/87, *Bettray*, ECLI:EU:C:1989:226 and found that work under publicly subsidized scheme also fell under the agreement.

could not secure a right to remain.[14] With no EU competence on regulating entry of TCN migrants, the admission and residence of Turkish nationals were based on national law and the sovereign right of states to manage population. However, once Turkish nationals were engaged in economic activity that fulfilled the criteria of the decisions implementing the Association Agreement, they proved themselves worthy of rights attributed under EU law. Due to this, security of residence should be guaranteed in order to allow them to continue their engagement in the activity, by which they personally contributed to the EU development project. The Court drew both on the purpose of the Agreement and on the agency and contribution of the individual migrant as a way to secure residence rights for Turkish migrants. A need to secure the effective exercise of the right to work became the basis for attribution of residence rights to Turkish workers who could not secure such residence under national law. The significance of the functional role of Turkish workers for the EU development project became a basis for attribution of rights in ways very similar to EU workers. Similar considerations of economic and social sustainability as expressed in the parallel pursuit of economic growth and social progress underpin the rights of both these categories of migrants.

As regards the protection of family life, the Court has been very explicit about the social purpose served by family reunification and has ensured an extensive protection for family members. The EEC–Turkey Agreement did not establish a right to family reunification. Rather, the implementing decisions secured rights for family members, who were authorized under national law to join the Turkish worker in the host state.[15] Article 7 of Decision 1/80 secured rights for family members of Turkish workers in the following way. Family members were entitled to respond to offers of employment after residing in the host state for more than three years. After five years of residence, they could enjoy an autonomous employment right and a corresponding residence right, flowing from EU law. After the establishment of such an autonomous right, family life need not be maintained.[16] The Court's case-law has

[14] Opinion of AG Elmer delivered on 28 March 1995 in Case C-434/93, *Bozkurt*, ECLI:EU:C:1995:86, para 31 and C-434/93, *Bozkurt*, ECLI:EU:C:1995:168, para 40.

[15] Case C-451/11, *Dülger*, ECLI:EU:C:2012:504, 62; Case C-467/02, *Cetinkaya*, ECLI:EU:C:2004:708.

[16] Case C-329/97, *Ergat*, ECLI:EU:C:2000:133, para 40 with reference to C-192/89, *Sevince*, paras 29, 31; Case C-171/95, *Tetik*, ECLI:EU:C:1997:31, paras 26–31 by analogy, as regards the third indent of Article 6(1), Decision No 1/80; C-355/93, *Eroglu*, para

engaged at great length with the purpose served by the rights granted to family members and has held that this gradual attribution of rights pursued a dual objective.[17]

The first objective of Article 7 Decision 1/80 (for the first three years of common residence) was to support migrant workers by means of family reunification in their employment and residence in the host state.[18] During these first three years, family members played a supportive function to the worker, and their rights promoted cohesion in the host societies.[19] In light of this function of family as conducive to the enjoyment of the worker's life in the host state, the Court interpreted the notion of family under Article 7 Decision 1/80 in ways similar to Regulation 1612/68. The analogous interpretation stemmed from an understanding that the purpose of Article 7 Decision 1/80 and Regulation 1612/68 was similar, that is, protecting family unity as conducive to the enjoyment of the worker's life in the host state.[20] This led to a significant limitation of restrictions on entry and residence in light of the importance of family life for the enjoyment of work-related rights.

The second objective of the protection of family life appears in relation to free access to any employment and the corresponding residence rights for family members after a period of five years. These rights were conferred in order to consolidate the social integration of the Turkish worker's family in the host state by allowing family members to earn their own living and become independent of the migrant worker.[21] The individualization of protection of the family member is put forward by

20 and Case C-210/97, *Akman*, ECLI:EU:C:1998:555, para 24 as regards Article 7(2), Decision 1/80.

[17] Case C-303/08, *Bozkurt*, ECLI:EU:C:2010:800, para 32.

[18] Ibid, para 33; Case C-351/95, *Kadiman*, ECLI:EU:C:1997:205 33–34; Case C-65/98, *Eyüp*, ECLI:EU:C:2000:336; C-467/02 *Cetinkaya*, para 25; Case C-484/07, *Pehlivan*, ECLI:EU:C:2011:395, 54.

[19] C-451/11, *Dülger*, para 42. The Court has been lenient in interpreting the common residence condition; see C-351/95, *Kadiman*, paras 48–49; C-467/02, *Cetinkaya*, para 32.

[20] Case C-275/02, *Ayaz*, ECLI:EU:C:2004:570, paras 46–47. In some cases, the Court went even further than the interpretation it had given to Regulation 1612/68. See C-65/98, *Eyüp*, where cohabitation could also qualify for protection under family life going further than Case 59/85, *Netherlands v Reed*, ECLI:EU:C:1986:157. This extensive interpretation could be attributed to the circumstances of the family in question rather than in an attempt of the Court to extend the rights of Turkish workers further than those of Community workers.

[21] C-351/95, *Kadiman*, para 35; C-303/08, *Bozkurt*, para 34 with reference inter alia to C-65/98, *Eyüp*, para 26; C-467/02, *Cetinkaya*, para 25; C-373/03, *Aydinli*, para 23; Case C-325/05, *Derin*, ECLI:EU:C:2007:442, paras 50, 71.

the Court in light of the purpose of Decision 1/80 to improve the social situation of Turkish migrants by promoting the gradual integration of those covered by the Decision in the Member State.[22] In this regard, the Court held that residence rights of family members who have been residing with the worker in a host state for a period of five years should be maintained in cases where such family members were not actively pursuing employment. In *Er*, the Court held that the grounds for exclusion from the rights granted under Decision 1/80 were specific: they referred exhaustively to public policy limitations and absence from territory.[23] Member States no longer enjoyed discretion in adding restrictive conditions on the exercise of the relevant rights.[24] The reasoning for proceeding in such a finding followed the acknowledgement of a link between the unconditional right to access employment and the right of residence.[25] The right of free access to employment was granted to family members of Turkish workers in order to ensure their permanent integration in the host state.[26] Such permanent integration would be jeopardized where family members did not enjoy an effective right to reside and thereby to eventually exercise employment.[27]

In developing this case-law, the Court put a lot of emphasis on the objective of Decision 1/80 to improve the situation of migrant workers in the social field. Does this mean that economic considerations should not affect the attribution of rights to family members? This seems to be the approach followed by the Court. Although not explicitly acknowledged by the Court, AG La Pergola, in his Opinion in *Eyüp*, suggested that a balancing of interests between protection of family life and protection of national employment markets had already taken place in the design of the provisions of Decision 1/80.[28] Thus, it was assumed that no further restrictions should be imposed in a system designed to progressively attribute rights to family members of migrant workers.

Relatedly, in the case of children of Turkish workers, we see how access of a specific cohort of migrant children to vocational education

[22] C-303/08, *Bozkurt*, para 39 with reference inter alia to C 329/97, *Ergat*, paras 43 and 44; C-325/05, *Derin*, para 53; C-337/07, *Altun*, paras 28–29.

[23] Case C-453/07, *Er*, C-453/07, ECLI:EU:C:2008:524, para 30.

[24] Ibid, para 27.

[25] Ibid, para 29.

[26] Ibid, paras 29, 34.

[27] No matter how unlikely the prospect of finding employment would be. See the referring court's framing of the factual background in C-453/07, *Er*, para 23.

[28] Opinion of AG La Pergola in C-65/98, *Eyüp*, ECLI:EU:C:1999:561, paras 17–24.

becomes the basis for autonomous residence rights. Children of Turkish workers who had completed vocational training in the host state were granted a right to respond to offers of employment independent of the length of their residence there, as long as one of their parents had been already legally employed in the Member State for at least three years. This autonomous right, granted under Article 7(2) Decision 1/80 to children trained in the host country, was linked to the presumption that they had the expertise necessary to immediately participate in the labour market of the state that had trained them.[29] Children of Turkish workers are not only significant as family members. They are also significant as part of a future labour force that is trained in the host state at its expense.[30]

In addition to these rights, Article 9 Decision 1/80 required that children of Turkish workers be granted access to education, apprenticeship, and vocational training under the same conditions as children of Community nationals. In *Gürol*, the Court held that Article 9 Decision 1/80 is an application of the general principle of non-discrimination in the sphere of education and vocational training. Specifically, the Court held that this provision is a specific iteration not only of the principle of non-discrimination laid down in Article 9 of the Agreement but also of the general non-discrimination principle of Article 7 of the EC Treaty.[31] The right to equal access to education is independent of residence with the parents during the period of education.[32] What is more, children also have access to advantages related to education.[33] Essentially, the purpose of Article 9 Decision 1/80 is to guarantee equal opportunities to Turkish children and nationals of the host state.

Overall, in the relevant case-law, the Court consolidated the rights of Turkish workers and their families. The consistently broad interpretations

[29] C-355/93, *Eroglu*, para 22. The fact that the right to enter might have been given for the purpose of study and not for the purpose of family reunification is irrelevant. Further, in C-210/97, *Akman*, para 38, the Court held that this right could also be granted to children of migrant workers, even after the Turkish worker was no longer employed or resident in the host country. See also Case C-462/08, *Bekleyen*, ECLI:EU:C:2010:30 on the residence rights of a child born in Germany in a family of Turkish workers, where the family returned to Turkey, and then upon adulthood, the child returned to Germany and attended higher education courses.

[30] See also Opinion of AG Léger in C-210/97, *Akman*, ECLI:EU:C:1998:344, paras 33, 37 with reference to Case 197/86, *Brown*, ECLI:EU:C:1988:323 and Joined Cases 389/87 and 390/87, *Echternach and other*, ECLI:EU:C:1989:130, paras 48–52.

[31] C-374/03, *Gürol*, ECLI:EU:C:2005:435.

[32] Ibid, para 30.

[33] Ibid, para 44.

took place not only in light of the purpose of the Association Agreement, whose main elements shifted over the years, for reasons that are related to geopolitical evolutions and circumstances external to legal reasoning. The interpretation of the Court was also driven by the function of migrant workers for the host state and the corollary need for social advancement of migrants in host societies. These considerations implicitly convey the pursuit of economic and social sustainability in the regulation of migration. To what extent similar considerations play out in relation to Agreements signed by the EU, where eventual accession was never foreseen, will be traced in Section 7.1.2.

7.1.2 Non-discrimination in the Field of Social Security

In the field of social security, *Kziber* stands out as the case which provided the foundation for a full extension of equal treatment to migrant workers and their families covered by Association Agreements.[34] The case concerned the refusal of Belgian authorities to grant an unemployment allowance to the daughter of a Moroccan pensioner in Belgium. She claimed that she was entitled to this allowance as a family member of a former Moroccan worker under the equal treatment provisions of the EEC–Morocco Association Agreement.

The benefit at stake was also the subject of the *Deak* case, where a family member of a former Community migrant worker claimed access to it.[35] There the Court held that the specific benefit could not be attributed to family members of migrant workers as a derived right. It was rather granted to former workers due to their own personal situation. Despite this, the Court found that the children of Community workers, to the extent that they were dependent on the Community worker, were entitled to this benefit under Article 7(2) Regulation 1612/68 as a social advantage.

Contrary to the conservative approach of AG Van Gerven,[36] the Court resolved the case with reference to the provisions of the Cooperation Agreement. It found that the principle of non-discrimination as provided for in Article 41(1) of the Agreement had direct effect.[37] What is more, it

[34] Case C-18/90, *Kziber*, ECLI:EU:C:1991:36.

[35] Examined in Section 2.2, Case 94/84, *Deak*, ECLI:EU:C:1985:264.

[36] Opinion of AG Van Gerven delivered in C-18/90, *Kziber*, ECLI:EU:C:1990:447, para 18; See also Case 40/76, *Kermaschek v Bundesanstalt für Arbeit*, ECLI:EU:C:1976:157.

[37] C-18/90, *Kziber*, paras 20–22.

found that social security benefits under Article 41(1) of the Agreement were identical to those provided under Regulation 1408/71 and that the unemployment benefit at issue fell under them. By basing the attribution of the respective rights directly on Regulation 1408/71, the Court took the social rights of TCN workers and their families a step further than those of Community workers. The findings of the Court in *Kziber* have been consistently applied in a series of cases covering various social security benefits, Association Agreements, and family members.[38]

The extensive application of non-discrimination in the field of social security was also confirmed with regard to Turkish workers. Decision 3/80 regulated the application of social security schemes to Turkish workers.[39] Article 3 of the Decision provided for equal treatment of Turkish workers and nationals of the Member State. The Court established the direct effect of provisions of the Decision and held that its purpose was similar to that of Regulation 1408/71, which applied to Community workers.[40] In *Sürül*, the Court addressed the question of whether a Turkish national covered by Decision 3/80 would have to hold a specific residence permit in order to be granted family allowances in a case where residence was the only requirement applicable to nationals of the state.[41] In resolving the case, the Court aligned the application of non-discrimination to Turkish workers and their families to the interpretation it had provided on other Association Agreements.[42] Specifically, the Court found that non-discrimination, as it appears in

[38] See Case C-58/93, *Yousfi*, ECLI:EU:C:1994:160; Case C-23/02, *Alami*, ECLI:EU:C:2003:89; Case C-276/06, *El Youssfi*, ECLI:EU:C:2007:215; Case C-103/94, *Krid*, ECLI:EU:C:1995:97 on Article 39 (1) of the EEC–Algeria Agreement; Case C-113/97, *Babahenini*, ECLI:EU:C:1998:13 where the Court rejected the Belgian government's attempt to reopen the question of distinguishing between personal and derived rights as in the case-law on Community workers; Case C-126/95, *Hallouzi-Choho*, ECLI:EU:C:1996:368; Case C-179/98, *Mesbah*, ECLI:EU:C:1999:549.

[39] Decision no 3/80 of the Association Council of 19 September 1980 on the application of the social security schemes of the Member States of the European Communities to Turkish workers and members of their families.

[40] Case C-277/94, *Taflan-Met and others*, ECLI:EU:C:1996:315, paras 37–38, where the Court held that provisions of the decision might have direct effect but found that Articles 12 and 13 of the Decision which were applicable did not have direct effect. Then the direct effect of Article 3(1) was established in Case C-262/96, *Sürül*, ECLI:EU:C:1999:228, para 64.

[41] C-262/96, *Sürül*, para 64.

[42] Ibid, paras 62–74 where the Court held that in light of the aim of the EEC–Turkey Association Agreement, its relevant findings from the interpretation of Association Agreements with Mediterranean neighbours should apply *a fortiori*.

Article 3(1) of Decision 3/80, was a specific expression of the general non-discrimination principle laid in Article 9 of the EEC–Turkey Agreement, which referred to the general non-discrimination principle under Article 7 of the EEC Treaty.[43] As a result, it held that national legislation requiring Turkish workers to possess specific residence document to access family allowances, where such documents were not required for Germans, constituted an unjustified discrimination under the Decision.[44]

The extensive protection of migrant workers under the principle of non-discrimination is not limitless. Rather its limits should be seen in relation to the purpose served by its attribution. In this respect, in *Fahmi and Esmoris Cerdeiro-Pinedo Amado*, the Court held that the prohibition of discrimination regarding access to social security did not cover workers who returned home and claimed child allowance benefits for children who studied in the state of origin.[45] Article 41(3) of the EEC–Morocco Agreement, which was applicable to the facts of the case, provided that family allowances were granted for family members who resided in the Community. In light of this, and the fact that the purpose of the Agreement was to consolidate the positions of workers and their families living in the Member States, the Court found that the right to non-discrimination could not extend as far as providing access to entitlements to those outside its territory.[46] After all, non-discrimination ensures the social advancement of the migrant worker and the members of their family in the host state, and is granted to support the migrant in the provision of their work. If the migrant worker is no longer engaged in economic activity in the EU, there is no reason why non-discrimination should apply and support their life outside the exercise of such activity.

After an overview of the relevant case-law, one is left wondering why equal treatment as provided under all the different Association Agreements examined in this section is protected by the Court in such an extensive manner. The special purpose of the EEC–Turkey Agreement is always emphasized by the Court, but the Association Agreements with Mediterranean countries did not foresee eventual accession and, unlike the EEC–Turkey Agreement, did not make any reference to guidance by the provisions of the EU free movement framework. Despite this, the

[43] Ibid, para 64.
[44] Ibid, paras 103–104.
[45] Case C-33/99, *Fahmi and Esmoris Cerdeiro-Pinedo Amado*, ECLI:EU:C:2001:176.
[46] Ibid, para 56.

Court made the link between non-discrimination in all the relevant Agreements and the general non-discrimination principle enshrined in the Treaty. What the Court added by its interpretation is that, regardless of state competence on the regulation of migration, whoever falls within the scope of EU law must not be discriminated against in the specific economic activity that they pursue. Based on this, it can be argued that the significant advancement of the social position of the migrant workers covered under these Agreements by the interpretation of the Court is closely connected to the migrants' contribution to the EU development project, which is also the reason why they fall under social security schemes in the first place. This close connection reveals the interdependence of economic development and social progress behind the rights of migrants in a way which would be demanded today by economic and social sustainability in the regulation of migration.

7.1.3 A Permanent Safeguard: Non-discrimination behind a Limited Right to Remain

The significance of the principle of non-discrimination for migrant workers is further highlighted through the case-law of the Court in *El Yassini*.[47] In this case, the Court addressed non-discrimination regarding working conditions as the source of legal certainty, which demanded that a residence right should be ensured for as long as someone was granted a right to employment, subject to clearly construed limitations. El Yassini, a Moroccan national, entered the UK as a visitor and was granted leave to remain, due to a subsequent marriage to a British national. The marriage was eventually dissolved, and he was engaged in lawful employment in the UK. Upon refusal by the UK authorities to grant him leave to remain, El Yassini claimed that the equal treatment provision of the EEC–Morocco Agreement should guarantee his right to continue his employment, by the creation of a derivative residence right for the remaining time of his employment contract.

In his Opinion, AG Léger set out to compare three types of legislation that were relevant for migrant workers' rights, and the different purposes non-discrimination served in each of them, namely the Community free movement framework, the EEC–Turkey Agreement and the EEC–Morocco Agreement.[48] In light of the purpose of the EEC–Morocco

[47] Case, C-416/96, *Eddline El-Yassini*, ECLI:EU:C:1999:107.

[48] Opinion of AG Léger in C-416/96, *El-Yassini*, ECLI:EU:C:1998:243, paras 36–50.

Agreement to contribute to the economic and social development of Morocco and of the absence of any rights regulating the personal situation of Moroccan workers in the Agreement, the AG suggested that Community law had no relevance in the specific dispute as to the treatment of Moroccan workers, who belonged to the labour force of Member States.[49] The AG supported this exclusion from Community law not only on the basis of the sovereign right of states to decide their immigration policy, but also on the EU law obligation to ensure priority access to national labour markets for Community workers in the first place and Turkish workers in the second.[50] The Opinion could have concluded at that stage. But it did not. Instead, the AG held that the principle of non-discrimination demanded that when a worker was authorized by a Member State to take up employment for a specific period of time, the effectiveness of that principle implied that he should have a right to reside in the host state during that time.[51] In light of this, he suggested that, while Member States can in principle terminate a residence permit before an employment contract has expired, they cannot do so in order to address economic problems.[52]

The Court, following the AG Opinion, acknowledged the distinction in terms of purpose and rights of migrant workers under the different schemes and held that the Agreement did not in principle prohibit the refusal of Member States to grant a right to reside despite the existence of paid employment.[53] It then qualified the statement by holding that such discretion on the part of Member States was allowed only if the initial reason for granting leave to remain no longer existed by the time the right to reside expired.[54] If, however, a person was granted a work permit for a specific duration of time and a residence permit for a shorter period, then potential non-renewal of the residence permit would have to be justified by the protection of legitimate national interest, such as public policy, public security, or public health.[55]

In so doing, the Court construed a limited right to reside from the effective enjoyment of non-discrimination regarding working conditions. This right exists only if legitimate employment is ongoing, and only for

[49] Ibid, paras 51–54.
[50] Ibid, para 60–61.
[51] Ibid, para 64 with reference to C-237/91, *Kus*.
[52] Ibid, para 66.
[53] C-416/96, *El-Yassini*, paras 57–62.
[54] Ibid, para 67.
[55] Ibid, paras 65, 67.

migrants who initially entered the host state as workers. In practice, this means that Member States are allowed to terminate the right to reside of workers covered by Association Agreements who are in ongoing employment, but only where this termination is unrelated to economic considerations. Where Member States proceed in premature termination of the right to reside, non-discrimination leads to the application by analogy of the case-law on Turkish workers, as there is nothing differentiating foreign workers engaged in gainful employment of the same kind in a host state.[56] Non-discrimination cannot be a basis of the right to remain on its own, but, as the Court held, in specific circumstances it might have effects on the right to remain by imposing specific limits on state discretion as regards migration.[57]

7.2 The Backlash to Extensive Judicial Protection

This emphasis of the Court on safeguarding the effective application of equal treatment for migrant workers and their families in the field of social security was not welcomed by Member States. A potential application of the *Kziber* line of case-law to TCN workers coming under other Association Agreements could have significant financial repercussions for the social security systems of the Member States, as AG La Pergola insinuated in his Opinion on a case related to similar issues under the EEC–Turkey Agreement.[58] For this reason, all the Agreements negotiated and concluded after *Kziber* was issued avoid providing for the application of non-discrimination in the field of social security. *Kziber*, next to the EEC–Turkey Agreement case-law, showed the teeth of the non-discrimination principle. The Member States tried to limit the power of this principle by drafting the Agreements that were concluded in the 1990s a lot more carefully. Sections 7.2.1 and 7.2.2 investigate the evolution of different Association Agreements in light of the preceding

[56] Opinion of AG Léger in C-416/96, *El-Yassini*, para 68.

[57] See also Case C-97/05, *Gattoussi*, ECLI:EU:C:2006:780, para 43.

[58] Opinion of AG La Pergola in C-262/96, *Sürül*, ECLI:EU:C:1998:55, para 45. See also Daniel Thym, 'Constitutional Foundations of the Judgments on the EEC-Turkey Association Agreement' in Daniel Thym and Margarite Zoeteweij-Turhan (eds), *Rights of Third-Country Nationals under EU Association Agreements: Degrees of Free Movement and Citizenship* (Brill Nijhoff 2015) 35, who claimed that this was the effect of the case-law on Turkish workers according to discussions with the German negotiating Team; Jan Niessen, 'European Community Legislation and Intergovernmental Cooperation on Migration' (1992) 26 International Migration Review 676, 680.

case-law, showing that the scope of equal treatment was renegotiated in Agreements with Mediterranean countries and construed in a limited manner in the Europe Agreements signed with the CEECs.

7.2.1 Renegotiating Cooperation to Limit the Scope of Equal Treatment

Given the economic and political circumstances of the 1990s, new objectives of regulation of migration in the Euro-Mediterranean region were formulated in the Barcelona conference.[59] These sought to reduce migratory pressures through assistance to the host states, to ensure the rights of all migrants legally residing in the territories of Member States and to address illegal immigration.[60] At this stage, the contribution of the migrant workers to the development of the EU meant that their rights could not be sidelined where they were employed in the Member States.[61] However, this economic contribution was no longer enough to allow support for the attribution of more extensive rights.

Against this backdrop, the new generation of Agreements signed with third countries in the region aimed at cooperation that would support 'harmonious economic and social relations' between the parties.[62] Among the agreements concluded, the ones with Morocco, Tunisia, and Algeria were the only ones including clauses that attributed rights

[59] The future of relations between the Community and the Maghreb, SEC(92)401 final; Strengthening the Mediterranean Policy of the European Union: Establishing a Euro-Mediterranean Partnership COM(94)427 final; HAEU, GJLA-246, Commission, DG External Relations, Task Force Enlargissement, Enlargement and the Community's Relations with its Mediterranean Neighbours, Brussels 2 March 1992, RDM/m, 4.

[60] Euro-Mediterranean Conference, 27 and 28 November 1995, Working Programme.

[61] Chris Patten, Javier Solana, and Romano Prodi (2003), Strengthening the EU's partnership with the Arab world, Paper for the attention of Franco Frattini, President of the Council, 4 December 2003 D(2003) 10318.

[62] Art 1(2) Euro-Mediterranean Agreement with Tunisia [1998] OJ L 97/2; Article 1(2), Euro-Mediterranean Agreement with Morocco [2000] OJ L 70/2; Article 1(2), Euro-Mediterranean Agreement with Algeria [2005] OJ L 265/2; Article 1(2), Euro-Mediterranean Agreement with Jordan [2002] OJ L 129/3 with reference to balanced economic and social relations and improving living and employment conditions; Article 1(2), Euro-Mediterranean Agreement with Lebanon [2006] OJ L 143/2 with reference to the prosperity of Lebanon and its people; Article 1(2), Euro-Mediterranean Agreement with Israel [2000] OJ L 147/3 and improvement of living and employment conditions; Article 1(2), Euro-Mediterranean Agreement with Egypt [2004] OJ L 304/39 on balanced economic and social relations.

to migrant workers.[63] This was due to the fact that these were the main countries of the region that supplied migrant labour to the EU.[64] Much like the previous Cooperation Agreements, the Euro-Mediterranean Agreements maintained the provisions on non-discrimination for all migrant workers as regards working conditions, remuneration and dismissal, and the equal treatment for them and their families in the field of social security.[65] Further, the Agreements stated that their provisions would only cover lawfully residing TCN workers, and they must not apply to migrants working illegally in the territories of the host countries.[66] Hence, illegality of residence was included explicitly as a condition which stripped an individual of rights.[67] Furthermore, under a Joint Declaration to the Agreements, the parties declared that they would examine issues related to access to the labour market for the spouse and children of migrant workers.[68] In the same Declaration they stated that equal treatment ought not to be invoked to obtain a renewal of a residence permit.[69] This Declaration must have been made to dissociate any potential extension of the interpretation of *El Yassini* to the new Agreements of cooperation with the Mediterranean countries.

The Court has confirmed the direct effect of the equal treatment provisions of the new Agreements. In *Echouikh*, the Court held that Article 65 of the Euro-Mediterranean Agreement with Morocco should be interpreted in the same way as Article 41(1) of the Association Agreement that predated it.[70] The Court also held that this Article was a specific expression of the principle of non-discrimination under Article

[63] The Euro-Mediterranean Agreement with Jordan did not contain provisions on equal treatment of migrant workers but rather a declaration of the Parties that they are willing to set up such rights in case Jordan so wished. Similar wording was inserted in Article 62 in the Euro-Mediterranean Agreement with Egypt. No such clauses were included in the Euro-Mediterranean Agreement with Lebanon. The Euro-Mediterranean Agreement with Israel mentions arrangements on social security issues but no equal treatment provisions.

[64] Demographic information in Commission, Information DG, The countries of the Greater Arab and Maghreb and the European Community. DE68, 1991.

[65] Articles 64, 65, Euro-Mediterranean Agreement with Morocco and Tunisia; Articles 67, 68, E Euro-Mediterranean Agreement with Algeria.

[66] Article 66, Euro-Mediterranean Agreement with Morocco and Tunisia; Article 69, Euro-Mediterranean Agreement with Algeria.

[67] This was the case also in the EEC–Turkey as interpreted in Case C-285/95, *Kol*, ECLI:EU:C:1997:280. See, however, Case C-311/13, *Tümer*, ECLI:EU:C:2014:2337.

[68] Joint Declaration relating to Article 64 of the Agreement.

[69] Ibid, para 2.

[70] Case C-336/05, *Echouikh*, ECLI:EU:C:2006:394.

12 of the EC Treaty.[71] As to the Declaration, it was invoked in the case of *Gattoussi*, which concerned the rights of Tunisian nationals under the Euro-Mediterranean Agreement.[72] Despite its invocation, the analysis of *El Yassini* was fully confirmed by the Court, which maintained that the effective application of non-discrimination could not leave Member State discretion on migration unaffected. The Court found that, in principle, Member States were not prohibited from taking measures against the right to remain of TCN workers whom they had authorized to enter their territory for the purpose of employment.[73] After all, immigration policy comes with a wide margin of discretion. But, as AG Ruiz-Jarabo Colomer suggested, this margin is limited by obligations of the Member States under Community law, as they cannot use migration measures as a justification for infringement of the free movement of workers framework or of international obligations of the Community.[74]

The Member States' obligation to guarantee the effectiveness of non-discrimination demands the protection of legitimate expectations of the worker and, relatedly, legal certainty.[75] This is why in cases where a Member State has granted migrant workers specific rights in relation to employment that are more extensive than the rights of residence conferred on them by that State, it cannot then reopen the question of that worker's situation on grounds unrelated to the protection of a legitimate national interest such as public policy, public security, or public health.[76] Overall, what we see in the Euro-Mediterranean Agreements is a more careful drafting and limitation of rights granted to migrant workers to avoid the potential extension thereof by rulings of the Court.[77]

In parallel to these evolutions, the cooperation with the ACP evolved by the transition from Lomé IV to Cotonou. Article 13 of the Cotonou Agreement referred more broadly to migration cooperation between the parties. Under Article 13(3), equal treatment was granted to legally employed migrant workers from ACP countries as regards working

[71] Ibid, para 63.

[72] C-97/05, *Gattoussi*, para 33.

[73] Ibid, para 36 with reference to C-416/96, *El-Yassini*, paras 58–62.

[74] Opinion of AG Ruiz-Jarabo Colomer in C-97/05, *Gattoussi*, para 58 with reference to Case 104/81, *Kupferberg & Cie.*, ECLI:EU:C:1982:362, paras 11–14, where it was held that the effects of the provisions of agreements must not be diminished by national measures.

[75] C-97/05, *Gattoussi*, paras 39–41.

[76] Ibid, para 40.

[77] The main fear of the Member States was that the extensive interpretations of the EEC–Turkey Agreement would find analogous application in this case; Thym (n 58) 35.

conditions, remuneration, and dismissal. There is no longer reference to equal treatment of migrant workers and their families as regards social security, which was previously found in the Declarations attached to Lomé. What is more, respect for human rights and the elimination of discrimination was reaffirmed under Article 13(1) based on existing obligations of international law. Finally, Article 13(2) of the Cotonou Agreement mentioned fair treatment of TCNs who are legally resident in EU Member States, and the objective of granting them rights and obligations comparable to citizens by integration policy; enhancement of non-discrimination in economic, social, and cultural life; and the development of measures against racism and xenophobia.[78] Even if at first glance this provision seems more extensive, it can be argued that this is not the case. First of all, the fair treatment mentioned in Article 13(2) of the Cotonou Agreement is not equal treatment. Second, as regards the objectives of granting extra rights to migrants, these are framed more like guidelines in the cooperation between the parties, rather than clauses that could be directly invoked by individuals under EU Law.

7.2.2 *Structuring Europe Agreements to Avoid Extensive Interpretations by the Court*

Shortly after the fall of the Iron Curtain, and with the expressed will of the post-Soviet states to accede to the EU, the latter progressively entered into Association Agreements with most of the CEECs.[79] These Agreements, which were called Europe Agreements to mark their political importance in reuniting Europe, were prepared so as to assist the economic reform of CEECs and to create closer political relations with the Community.[80] The Agreements sought to establish a free trade area

[78] These are the provisions relevant to labour migration. There are also paragraphs which deal with other categories of migration, like para 4 on the aim of reducing poverty and improving living conditions with a view to creating employment opportunities at home and hence 'normalizing' migration flows, and para 5 on illegal migration, return, and readmission.

[79] Europe Agreement with Poland [1993] OJ L 348/2; Europe Agreement with Hungary [1993] OJ L 347/2; Europe Agreement with the Czech Republic [1994] OJ L360/2; Europe Agreement with Slovakia [1994] OJ L 359/2; Europe Agreement with Romania [1994] OJ L 357/2; Europe Agreement with Bulgaria [1994] OJ L 358/3; Europe Agreement with Latvia [1998] OJ L 26/2; Europe Agreement establishing with Lithuania [1998] OJ L 51/2; Europe Agreement with Slovenia [1999] OJ L 51/3. Estonia was the only country with which a Europe Agreement was not concluded.

[80] Communication, Association Agreements with the Countries of Central and Eastern Europe, A General Outline, COM(90)398 final, Annex Association Agreements 2–3.

between the Community and the associated states, and were adopted in order to prepare the latter for their eventual accession to the Community.[81] A ten-year transitional period split into two five-year stages was envisaged in most of the Agreements.[82] The central focus of the Agreements was to assist the CEECs in their transition to market economy.[83] Free movement of workers was not provided for in these Agreements. The liberalization of free movement would only be considered after the social and economic conditions of the acceding Member States was brought in line with those of the Community.[84] Rather, certain minimum measures were put in place to improve the situation of migrant workers legally resident in the Member States.[85] Specifically, the Agreements provided for the application of equal treatment regarding working conditions, remuneration, or dismissal.[86] The Agreements did not impose an obligation to grant residence rights to family members of workers, and the right of family members to access the labour market was explicitly limited to the spouse and children of the worker during the worker's stay.[87] These limited rights of family members excluded seasonal workers or workers covered by bilateral agreements.[88]

[81] While this was not the initial purpose of the agreements as expressed ibid, the preambles of all the Europe Agreements mentioned the eventual aim of accession to the EU.

[82] One year in case of Latvia and Lithuania and six years divided in periods of four and two for Slovenia.

[83] Avis du Comité économique et social sur l'élargissement futur de la Communauté [1992] OJ C 313/40, point 3.1; Communication de la Commission au Conseil au-delà des Accords européens: Préparation des pays d'Europe centrale et orientale à l'adhésion COM(94)320 final 5.

[84] Association Agreements with the Countries of Central and Eastern Europe, A General Outline, COM(90)398 final, Annex Association Agreements 2–3.

[85] For a detailed analysis of the rights of migrant workers under the EA Agreements, see Iris Goldner Lang, *From Association to Accession: How Free Is the Free Movement of Persons in the EU* (Eleven 2011) 70–92.

[86] Article 37, EA with Poland, EA with Hungary, EA with Latvia, EA with Lithuania; Article 38, EA with the Czech Republic, EA with Slovakia, EA with Slovenia, EA with Romania, EA with Bulgaria. See also Case C-162/00, *Pokrzeptowicz-Meyer*, ECLI:EU:C:2002:57; Case C-438/00, *Deutscher Handballbund*, ECLI:EU:C:2003:255; Elspeth Guild, 'Workers' in Andrea Ott and Kirstyn Inglis (eds), *Handbook on European Enlargement: A Commentary on the Enlargement Process* (TMC Asser Press 2002).

[87] Declarations by the European Community 1, Chapter I of Title IV, included in all the EAs but the ones concluded in the late 1990s with Bulgaria, Latvia, and Slovenia; Article 37, EA with Poland, EA with Hungary, EA with Latvia, EA with Lithuania; Article 38, EA with the Czech Republic, EA with Slovakia, EA with Slovenia, EA with Romania, EA with Bulgaria.

[88] Ibid.

The Agreements also left a great deal of discretion to Member States to take into account their labour market situation in the context of progressive attribution of rights to labour migrants from associated countries. Specifically, the only obligation for Member States was to preserve access to employment accorded under bilateral agreements for already legally resident workers.[89] Potential improvements of the treatment of such workers or attribution of more rights could be considered by the Member States 'if possible'.[90] The Association Council had discretion to examine the granting of improvements, taking into account both the national labour market situation and the Community one.[91] Finally, following the end of the foreseen transitional period, the Association Council would examine other ways to improve the movement of workers in light of the social and economic conditions in the associated countries and the employment situation in the Community. These agreements, together with the identical provisions of the Stabilisation and Association Pact in the case of Croatia, set the basis for cooperation between the candidate countries and the EU until the conclusion of the enlargement, which is examined in Chapter 8.[92]

Similar protection for migrants is afforded by the Partnership and Cooperation Agreements concluded with Russia and several states from Southern Caucasus and Central Asia. These Agreements provide a basis for economic, social, financial, and cultural cooperation. They all provide for equal treatment as regards working conditions, remuneration, or dismissal of TCN workers originating from these states.[93] However, they do not grant any rights of access to the labour market for the workers' family, nor do they foresee a potential progressive attribution of more

[89] Article 41(1), EA with Poland, EA with Hungary, EA with Latvia, EA with Lithuania; Article 42(1), EA with the Czech Republic, EA with Slovakia, EA with Slovenia, EA with Romania, EA with Bulgaria.

[90] Ibid.

[91] Article 41(2), EA with Poland, EA with Hungary, EA with Latvia, EA with Lithuania; Article 42(2), EA with the Czech Republic, EA with Slovakia, EA with Slovenia, EA with Romania, EA with Bulgaria.

[92] Stabilisation and Association Agreement with Croatia [2005] OJ L 26/3, Chapter I Movement of workers.

[93] Article 17(1), Partnership and Cooperation Agreement with Tajikistan [2009] OJ L 350/3; Article 23, Partnership and Cooperation Agreement with Russia [1997] OJ L 327/3; Article 19(1), Partnership and Cooperation Agreement with Uzbekistan [1999] OJ L 229/3; Article 20(1), Partnership and Cooperation Agreement with Azerbaijan [1999] OJ L 246/3; Article 19(1), Partnership and Cooperation Agreement with the Kyrgyz Republic [1999] OJ L 196/48.

rights to migrant workers.[94] Unsurprisingly, the similarly worded provision of the Cooperation Agreement with Russia granting equal treatment as regards working conditions has been held by the Court to be directly effective.[95]

In this we see that the cost of ensuring an extensive protection for migrants' rights, as provided by the Court, limited the scope of application of non-discrimination only to the specific field of working conditions, remuneration, and dismissal. Short-term considerations related to risks of migration flows that could be caused by the underdevelopment of the CEECs at times when Member States did not have unlimited labour demands led to the limitation of the non-discrimination clauses in International Agreements concluded during this period. This has far-reaching implications in limiting the rights of migrants. However, as we shall see in Chapter 9, these implications can be contained in light of the incremental shaping of secondary law on the rights of migrants legally resident in the Member States. Before concluding this chapter, however, Section 7.3 will turn to the cooperation of the EU with economically developed European states. The analysis will point to the extensive attribution of rights to nationals coming from countries with higher development levels and thus less prone to migrating for economic reasons.

7.3 The Non-issue of Extending Free Movement Rights to Nationals of Developed European States

In the European Economic Area (EEA) Agreement, we see how the economic and social development of all countries involved and their long-standing economic cooperation and interdependence shaped the basis for a privileged partnership, which granted labour migrants from the European Free Trade Association (EFTA) countries rights that are equally extensive to the rights enjoyed by EU migrants.[96]

[94] Unlike the SAAs which create an obligation for Member States to preserve access to employment accorded under Bilateral Agreements for already legally resident workers and to examine the possibility of improving it.

[95] C-265/03, *Simutenkov*, ECLI:EU:C:2005:213.

[96] Agreement on the European Economic Area [1994] OJ L 1/3. The Agreement initially involved Switzerland, Austria, Finland, and Sweden. Switzerland did not ratify the Agreement, whereas Austria, Finland, and Sweden eventually joined the EU. See Resolution A3-0306/92 on economic and trade relations between the EEC and the EFTA countries in the European Economic Area [1992] OJ C 305/564, points A–C.

EFTA was created in the 1960s to promote free trade and economic integration of its Member States. The relation of the EU and EFTA dates back to the 1970s, when the EFTA states concluded bilateral free trade agreements with the EEC that did not include any right to free movement of workers.[97] The completion of the single market created new impetus in the relation of EFTA states with the Community and led to the signature of the EEA Agreement in 1992.[98] The original Agreement included Switzerland, Austria, Finland, Sweden, Iceland, Lichtenstein, and Norway. Eventually Switzerland did not ratify the agreement, whereas Austria, Finland, and Sweden became EU Member States during that period. As it currently stands, the Agreement applies to EU Member States on the one hand and Iceland, Lichtenstein, and Norway on the other.

The aim of the Agreement under Article 1(1) was to promote a continuous and balanced strengthening of the economic relations of the parties in light of creating a European Economic Area. The parties included both economic and social objectives in the preamble in a framing that is very similar to the objectives of the Community as expressed in the Maastricht Treaty, which had recently been adopted at that time.[99] In light of the alignment of objectives and of the similar development level of the EFTA and the EU Member States, it should not come as a surprise that the Agreement provided for extension of free movement of workers to EFTA nationals under Article 28. The article, which is framed similarly to the provision of Article 45 TFEU, grants nationals of the parties the right to accept offers of employment made to them, to move freely within the territory of the EEA states in search of employment, to reside in those states for the purpose of employment, as well as the right to remain there after being employed. Similarly to the

[97] Agreement between the EEC and Portugal [1972] OJ L 301/165; Agreement between the EEC and Sweden [1972] OJ L300/9; Agreement between the EEC and Austria [1972] OJ L 300/2; Agreement between the EEC and the Switzerland [1972] OJ L 300/189; Agreement between the EEC and Norway [1973] OJ L 171/2. In these Agreements, the Commission thought it was not necessary to include free movement of workers; see Communication, Contenu possible d'accords éventuels avec les États de l'AELE non candidats à l'adhésion, COM(71)701 45. The Communication in 45–48 mentioned the problems of discriminatory treatment of Community workers in Switzerland and, to a more limited extent, in Sweden and Finland due to the preferential treatment of workers in the Nordic Labour market. See also Declaration concerning workers, Agreement between the EEC and Switzerland [1972] OJ L 300/189.

[98] Address by Jacques Delors to the European Parliament on 17 January 1989, Bulletin of the European Communities (1989) Supplement 1/89.

[99] Recital 6 and 11 of the EEA Agreement; Cf Article 2, TEU Maastricht Treaty.

EU framework, Article 28(2) EEA Agreement provides for the application of non-discrimination as regards employment, remuneration, and working conditions for nationals working in EEA states. While the Agreement did not provide for rights of family members, Annex V thereto referred to the EU secondary law, which is applicable in the case of free movement of workers between the parties.[100] For this reason, protection of family life for EFTA workers is guaranteed at levels equal to those guaranteed for EU workers.

The Agreement did not provide for safeguard measures specific to risks created from movement of workers, but rather had a general safeguard clause under Article 112, similar to those existing under the EU framework, which allowed the parties to unilaterally resort to the measures deemed necessary in case of economic, social, or environmental difficulties of sectorial or regional nature.[101] Iceland attached a declaration to specify its understanding of Article 112 EEA Agreement to mean that safeguard measures may be applied to address serious disturbances on the labour market caused by large-scale labour movements due to the Agreement in specific geographical areas, types of jobs, or industrial branches.[102] Iceland justified this declaration on the basis of the 'one-sided nature of its economy and the fact that its territory is sparsely populated'.[103] It can be assumed that the inclusion of this declaration by Iceland could mean that free movement of workers between EEA states was not thought of as having the potential to cause risks for Community states in general.

Switzerland signed the EEA Agreement, but it did not eventually ratify it. It rather proceeded in the signature of a bilateral Agreement, which guarantees free movement of persons between that country and the EU.[104] The Agreement regulates movement of both economic and non-economic actors, as well as the right of establishment and the provision of services. On workers, the Agreement guarantees general rights of entry

100 See Annex V to the EEA Agreement, Free movement of workers.

101 See Article 223, Treaty of Rome, but also Article 135, Treaty of Accession of Denmark, Ireland, and the United Kingdom [1972] OJ L 73.

102 Declaration by the Government of Iceland on the use of safeguard measures under the EEA Agreement.

103 Similar in Declaration by the Government of Switzerland on safeguard measures, EEA Agreement.

104 Agreement between the European Community and its Member States, of the one part, and the Swiss Confederation, of the other, on the free movement of persons [2002] OJ L 114/6.

and residence, to access employment, as well as a general non-discrimination right.[105] What is more, the Agreement provides for family reunification rights and the right of family members to take up economic activity.[106] Further, the children of migrant workers enjoy access to education under equal treatment.[107] Article 10(1) of the Agreement provided for a transitional regime, which allowed Switzerland to maintain quantitative limits for a period of maximum six years as regards access to economic activity for workers who wished to enter and reside for a period of longer than four months.[108] Moreover, for two years after the entry into force of the Agreement, the parties were allowed to maintain controls on the priority of workers integrated in the regular labour market and wage and working conditions.[109] The Agreement also included a standstill clause to prevent the introduction of more restrictive measures towards the nationals of the parties.

In light of the objective circumstances of the Agreement and the fact that it regulated movement between a single highly developed country and all the EU Member States, the risks posed by migration could only materialize for the Swiss economy. It then appears understandable that there is not only an extensive attribution of rights equating EU workers and Swiss workers, but also a series of guarantees incorporated in the Agreement to protect the Swiss economy from the sudden influx of EU migrants.

The EEA and the Swiss Bilateral Agreement have not been subject to much contestation before the Court as regards the rights of migrant workers covered thereby. As to the former, the EFTA Court established under the Agreement to ensure its judicial control and interpretation in the EFTA states has produced case-law on the rights of labour migrants under the EEA agreement in the EFTA states. The Court of Justice of the EU has not been called to interpret any provision regarding worker's rights.[110] As regards the Swiss Agreement, limited case-law has addressed

[105] Ibid, Articles 2–4.

[106] Ibid, Article 3 and Annex I.

[107] Ibid, Article 3(6).

[108] Ibid, Article 10(2) on a quota system to ensure that in the first five years, certain residence permits will be guaranteed for EU workers and the self-employed, and Article 10(4) on unilateral measures to limit migration from EU Member States to a specific number in case of increased migration from the EU in the period of five to twelve years after entry into force of the Agreement.

[109] Ibid.

[110] See, however, Case C-897/19 PPU, *Ruska Federacija*, ECLI:EU:C:2020:262 on the extension of the Case C-182/15, *Petruhhin*, ECLI:EU:C:2016:630 to a naturalized Icelander (who was previously a Russian asylum seeker).

the application of the principle of non-discrimination as regards taxation, family benefits, and contributions to social security.[111]

In two cases concerning the coordination of social security systems between EU and EEA and Switzerland, the Court had the opportunity to clarify the reason behind the extensive rights attributed to EEA and Swiss nationals.[112] The UK, supported by Ireland, went against the Council, requesting the annulment of two Decisions adopted on the coordination of social security systems under these Agreements.[113] They claimed that Article 48 TFEU, which was mentioned as the substantive legal basis of the Decisions, was not appropriate, as it referred to the competence of the EU to adopt measures regarding EU workers. Instead, they argued that the relevant Decisions should have been adopted under Article 79(2)b TFEU, which referred to the competence of the EU to adopt measures as regards the rights of TCNs.

The Court confirmed Article 48 TFEU as the appropriate legal basis for the adoption of Decisions, justifying the finding with reference to the objectives of the two Agreements. Specifically, the Court repeated that the EEA Agreement had the objective of the fullest possible realization of free movement within the whole EEA, with the purpose of extending the EU internal market to the EFTA states.[114] Similarly, the Bilateral Agreement with Switzerland was concluded with the aim of bringing free movement of persons on the basis of the rules applicable at Community level.[115] The objectives pursued by the Agreements in question were emphasized by the Court as the reason behind the extensive attribution of rights. There is nothing novel in this. The objective and context of an Agreement as elements to be taken into account in its

[111] Case C-241/14, *Bukovansky*, ECLI:EU:C:2015:766; Case C-478/15, *Radgen*, ECLI:EU:C:2016:705; Case C-216/12 and C-217/12, Judgment of 19 September 2013, *Hliddal and Bornand*, ECLI:EU:C:2013:568; C-2/17, Judgment of 28 June 2018, *Crespo Rey*, ECLI:EU:C:2018:511.

[112] Case C-431/11, *United Kingdom/Council*, ECLI:EU:C:2013:589; Case C-656/11, *United Kingdom/Council*, ECLI:EU:C:2014:97.

[113] Council Decision 2011/407/EU of 6 June 2011 on the position to be taken by the EU within the EEA Joint Committee concerning an amendment to Annex VI (Social Security) and Protocol 37 to the EEA Agreement [2011] OJ 2011 L182/12; Council Decision 2011/863/EU of 16 December 2011 on the position to be taken by the EU in the Joint Committee established under the Agreement between the European Community and its Member States, of the one part, and the Swiss Confederation, of the other, on the free movement of persons as regards the replacement of Annex II to that Agreement on the coordination of social security schemes [2011] OJ L 341/1.

[114] C-431/11, *United Kingdom/Council*, para 50.

[115] Ibid, para 55. See also Case C-247/09, *Xhymshiti*, ECLI:EU:C:2010:698 para 31.

interpretation are provided for by Article 31 VCLT, and this rule of interpretation has been applied by the Court in the interpretation of International Agreements in general.[116]

Similarly to the EEA Agreement, the accession of Austria, Sweden, and Finland, which were EFTA states, did not involve discussions on the risk of migration. The candidate countries were equally developed; they were EFTA members and parties to the EEA Agreement signed in 1992, whose provisions had already provided for the extension of the free movement of workers regime between them and the Member States.[117] Austria was the only candidate that already had a large amount of labour migration from Southern and Eastern Europe.[118] For this reason, mirroring the first accession, Austria attached a Declaration which recognized its right to address the EU institutions in case of difficulties arising from free movement of workers, in order to find potential solutions.[119] The general safeguard clause was also included, but provided for a shorter period of two years in case of eventual need for protective measures.[120]

The analysis in this chapter highlights that the absence of migration-related risks in the context of cooperation of the EU with third states, and relatedly the possibility of maintaining economic growth and social progress for all the parties involved at similar levels, led to full attribution of rights of migrants from specific third states. Essentially, the economic development of the host countries, their similar demographic patterns, and the lack of massive migratory movements therefrom to the EU are the reason behind such an extensive protection in the framework created by the Agreements. Similar considerations existed in the accession of Finland, Sweden, and Austria, with immediate attribution of free movement rights and incorporation of the general safeguard clause. The lack of economic risks dictates the full attribution of rights. At the same time, for the system to be sustainable, that is, to be able to address economic

[116] See Case 270/80, *Polydor and others*, ECLI:EU:C:1982:43.

[117] Austria and Sweden were founding members of EFTA, while Finland joined in 1986. On free movement of workers, see Article 28, EEA Agreement.

[118] The Challenge of Enlargement, Commission Opinion on Austria's application for membership, Document drawn up on the basis of SEC(91)1590 final, Bulletin of the European Communities, Supplement 4/92.

[119] Joint Declaration on the free movement of workers by Austria, Act concerning the conditions of accession of Austria, Finland, and Sweden (1994 Accession Treaty) [1994] OJ C 241.

[120] Article 152, 1994 Accession Treaty.

and social objectives in the long-term, safeguard clauses were incorporated, which allowed derogations if need appeared.

Overall, this second period of development of EU migration law started with the aspiration to transform the EU legal order, to breathe political elements into it, and to grant rights to all migrants resident in EU territory. The parallel pursuit of economic and social objectives guiding the development of EU law limited these aspirations. For EU migrants, the aspiration of engaging them in a political project could not lead to the granting of unlimited social rights. A full extension of social rights without economic limitations would undermine the pursuit of economic objectives and would thus be economically unsustainable. For TCN migrants, on the other hand, granting them rights was acceptable, but it was impossible to reach a consensus on admission due to the short-term approach of the Council to the economic objectives served by migration. Despite the interests of different institutions, the strong basis of equal treatment rights in relation to working conditions was not contested, as such rights acted as the minimum guarantee to ensure an economically and socially sustainable EU. The EU labour market could not effectively function without this as the outcome would be unfair competition and social dumping. National societies would also be characterized by grave injustice and exclusion, were it not for these minimum rights, and would also be socially unsustainable. The real challenge, which existed for both EU and TCN migrants and affected them equally, was access to social security rights. While granting full equal treatment on social security rights would be in line with the social objectives of the EU, it would simultaneously have the potential of disrupting the redistribution system of different Member States and it could undermine the economic objectives. Searching for economic and social sustainability behind the regulation of social rights of migrants was a challenging endeavour that would continue to tantalize the EU institutions in the next period.

PART III

Realization and Paradoxes from the Failed Constitutional Treaty to Lisbon and Beyond

Following the aligned approach to the regulation of migration in the early years of the Community and the differentiation triggered by the political momentum of the 1990s, the period reviewed in this part can be characterized as one of realization and paradoxes. This final period primarily engages with valid law. Secondary law on migrants' rights was amended for EU migrants and adopted for TCN migrants during this time. The analysis first identifies the ultimate balancing of economic and social objectives behind the limitation of rights of EU migrants as a manifestation of a sustainable migration framework. Second, the investigation reveals the central role of economic considerations in the regulation of migration from third countries. It also suggests that national contestation and the lack of long-term considerations in the Council are among the reasons why the regulation of migration for TCNs cannot serve economic and social sustainability. Finally, concluding the historical analysis of the regulation of migration which started in Part I, this part reveals the paradoxes and tensions that arise from the way in which economic and social objectives are pursued through EU migration law. In so doing, it paves the way for the concluding remarks that will be made in Chapter 10 on the limits and potentials of an EU sustainable migration.

The period under review began with the failure of the Constitutional Treaty signed in 2004, which left unfulfilled the political promises of transformation of the EU into a fully fledged polity. The Lisbon Treaty subsequently incorporated most of the changes suggested in the text of the Constitutional Treaty and gave binding force to the Charter. During the same period, the EU was up against many challenges, both internal – like the unprecedented enlargement of the new millennium, the economic crisis that hit the Member States shortly after the Monetary Union was put in place and Brexit – and external – political unrest and displacement in the European neighbourhood, the COVID-19 pandemic, climate deterioration, and, most recently, a war on the EU's borders.

These challenges have brought to the forefront the question of if and how the EU can maintain its aspiration for growth by relying on the human potential available in the best possible way. At times of economic and social tensions, this led to questioning the extensive protection of EU migrants' rights. How could unlimited social rights be sustainable in a system of diverse interdependent economies which are under stress? At the same time, the ageing EU population is a stark reality, pointing to the inability of the current and projected demographics to support economic growth in the long run. Admitting a TCN workforce into the EU and enabling its mobility have, thus, become necessary. However, diverse political challenges, also linked to national unemployment, have strengthened populist dynamics on the ground, precluding the easy acceptance of admission of TCNs by national electorates. Moreover, criticism is prevalent in the scholarly output of this period.[1] Different reasons drive these criticisms: primary law is no longer used by the Court to support extensive interpretations of individual rights; integration through law has reached its limits, and scholars call for more room for political debate of EU policies; and spaces of liminal legality are created in areas where EU law does not – willingly or unwillingly – reach.[2]

In response to these concerns, the part develops as follows. Chapter 8 begins with an investigation of the 2004 enlargement and, subsequently, it examines the way in which the tension between economic and social objectives was resolved regarding the rights of EU migrants. In the relevant analysis, it is argued that the economic considerations conditioning EU migrants' rights and their balancing against extensive social rights frame the free movement framework as a sustainable migration framework. Following, Chapter 9 analyses the framework regulating migration from third countries and reveals the extensive attribution of rights to those TCN migrants who are considered crucial for the EU development project. Next to the legislative framework, the examination of the case-law highlights the consolidation of social objectives by an

[1] 'Editorial Comments: The Critical Turn in EU Legal Studies' (2015) 52 CMLRev 881.

[2] See Alezini Loxa and Vladislava Stoyanova, 'Migration as a Constitutional Crisis for the European Union' in Stijn Smet and Vladislava Stoyanova (eds), *Migrants' Rights, Populism and Legal Resilience in Europe* (Cambridge University Press 2022); Evangelia (Lilian) Tsourdi and Cathryn Costello, 'The Evolution of EU Law on Refugees and Asylum' in Paul Craig and Gráinne de Búrca (eds), *The Evolution of EU Law* (Oxford University Press 2021); Iris Goldner Lang, 'Towards "Judicial Passivism" in European Union Migration and Asylum Law?' in Tamara Ćapeta, Iris Goldner Lang, and Tamara Perišin (eds), *The Changing European Union: A Critical View on the Role of Law and the Courts* (Hart 2022).

emphasis on Charter rights. The investigation further shows the complete elimination of migrants' rights from Agreements concluded by the EU with third countries and the emphasis on operational cooperation to deflect migration, often without the use of any binding instruments, which has been extensively criticized in legal scholarship.[3] At the same time, though, having a system in place which guarantees rights for all legally resident TCNs means that no migrant is excluded from protection – or at least not those who physically make it to the EU.

[3] Violeta Moreno-Lax, 'The Informalisation of the External Dimension of EU Asylum Policy: The Hard Implications of Soft Law' in Evangelia (Lilian) Tsourdi and Philippe De Bruycker (eds), *Research Handbook on EU Migration and Asylum Law* (Edward Elgar 2022); See also contributions in Sergio Carrera, Juan Santos Vara, and Tineke Strik (eds), *Constitutionalising the External Dimensions of EU Migration Policies in Times of Crisis: Legality, Rule of Law and Fundamental Rights Reconsidered* (Edward Elgar 2019).

8

Economic and Social Sustainability behind the Rights of EU Migrants

8.1 Enlargement Limiting the Reach of Law in Order to Safeguard the EU

This chapter demonstrates that the current free movement framework is a manifestation of sustainable migration, where economic and social sustainability considerations dictate the attribution, limitation, or extension of rights of EU migrants. To show this, the analysis begins with an investigation of the 2004 enlargement, one of the most complicated enlargement processes which involved the accession of various states with diverse economies. The differentiation of clauses and transitional periods, compared to previous Accession Treaties, brings to the forefront the way economic considerations dictate the attribution of rights to soon-to-be EU migrants. The relevant section draws attention to the limitation of rights for nationals of the Central and Eastern European Countries (CEECs) in contrast to the full attribution of rights to nationals of acceding states who were not thought of as posing risks to the economic sustainability of the EU. And so, it highlights the legal tools devised to ensure sustainability of migration in the framework of accession. Following, Section 8.2 presents the current framework regulating free movement and suggests that its legal design should be understood as the most contemporary and elaborate manifestation of sustainable migration in law.

The massive enlargement of the EU during the new millennium had been progressively prepared since the 1990s to ensure that acceding states would not pose challenges to the EU project of growth. Eventually, accession took place via the Accession Treaties signed with the Czech Republic, Estonia, Latvia, Lithuania, Hungary, Poland, Slovenia, Slovakia, Malta, and Cyprus in 2003; Romania and Bulgaria in 2005; and Croatia in 2012. While the enlargement had the political significance of reuniting Europe, the drastic increase of EU population due to this accession was perceived as a risk, because the EU was struggling with internal unemployment, restrained growth, and an ageing society.[1] The most complicated transitional regime was thus put in place to avert risks. At the same time, the accession process put a lot of focus not only on growth aspects (unlike the previous enlargements), but also on the social advancement demanded from the candidate states and their obligation to equally support the European social model put in place by that stage.[2]

Overall, the process of enlargement stretched over more than a decade, beginning with the Europe Agreements reviewed in Chapter 7 for the CEECs, and the Stabilisation and Association Pact in the case of Croatia. The negotiations emphasized the economic and social considerations behind the regulation of labour migration from the candidate countries in different ways.[3] First, there was a fear of migration flows due to the difference in development levels between the candidate countries and the EU.[4] This was linked to the effects of migration for social and economic development more broadly, and the potential of adverse effects to the EU labour market.[5] Anticipated migration flows were discussed in comparison with the south enlargement, where similar fears of uncontrolled migration existed – but these in fact never materialized.[6] During the time of negotiation, many academic studies were examined by the

[1] Communication, Agenda 2000 Pour une Union plus forte et plus large, Vol I, COM(97) 2000 final 7.

[2] HAEU, GJLA-180, Union européenne, Le Conseil, Rapport du Groupe 'Élargissement' en date du 2 Octobre 1997 au COREPER, Objet: Élargissement, Examen des avis de la Commission sur les demandes d'adhésion à l'Union présentées par les pays associés d'Europe centrale et orientale, 11125/97 LIMITE ELARG 18.

[3] Michael Dougan, 'A Spectre Is Haunting Europe . . . Free Movement of Persons and the Eastern Enlargement' in Christophe Hillion (ed), *EU Enlargement: A Legal Approach* (Bloomsbury 2004).

[4] Commission Opinion on Romania, COM(97)2003 final 48, 88; Commission Opinion on the Czech Republic, COM(97)2009 final 23, 46; Commission Opinion on Poland, COM (97)2002 final 30, 49; Commission Opinion on Bulgaria, COM(97)2008 25, 44; Commission Opinion on Hungary, COM(97)2001 final 28, 48; Commission Opinion on Slovenia, COM(97)2010 final 27, 47; Commission Opinion on Slovakia, COM(97)2004 final 42, 75; Commission Opinion on Latvia, COM(97)2005 final 45; Commission Opinion on Croatia, COM (2004)257 final 98.

[5] HAEU, GJLA-206, European Commission, Secretary General, The free movement of persons for the pursuit of economic activity in the context of Enlargement, Information note by M Verheugen addressed to the Members of the Commission, Directors Generals and Heads of service, 12 April 2000, O/139/2000 SEC(2000)663/3.

[6] HAEU, DORIE-204, Annexe 2 à l'avis de la section des relations extérieures, de la politique commerciale et du développement du Comiteé économique et social sur 'L'élargissement de l'Union européenne' 24 Oct 1997: Rapporteur M Masucci CES 856/ 97 fin annexe 2 I-RD/CH/ic point 5.3.

Commission in order to explore the migration potential of these enlargements, but there were no conclusive indicators on anticipated migration.[7] The anticipation of migration flows was expressed as a pressing concern due to high levels of unemployment in the Member States.[8] In this context, a potential collapse of national employment markets could arise as (a) migrants from acceding states, who were more skilled, could take up employment, and no jobs would be left for the unskilled workers in Member States, and (b) migrants from the acceding states could take up work for lower wages and with more flexible arrangements, disrupting the potential of national workers to find work.[9]

Second, candidate countries and their labour force were considered to pose risks for the EU due to their social model.[10] Following the fall of communism and with the fast-track transition to market economy, the candidate countries had not managed to put in place a framework that could ensure social protection at work at levels similar to those offered by the EU, where social policy covered a broad range of subjects from living and working conditions, health and safety at work, equal opportunities, dialogue between social partners and social protection, among others.[11] This meant that the costs of the industrial sector, were they to use labour force from the candidate countries, would be extremely low, which could

[7] HAEU, GJLA-204, Commission Information note by M Verheugen, The free movement of persons for the pursuit of economic activity in the context of Enlargement, 12 April 2000, SEC (2000) 663/3, Section 3; Commission, Information note on the Free Movement of Workers in the context of Enlargement, 6 March 2001, Annex 1–3; Answers given by Mr Verheugen on behalf of the Commission on 28 February 2003 to Written Question E-0113/03 by Mogens Camre (UEN) to the Commission (28 January 2003) with the subject: Migrant workers from the new Member States [2004] OJ CE 88/587.

[8] Agenda 2000, Vol I, COM(97)2000 final 7; HAEU, DORIE-205 Rapport sur la communication de la Commission 'Agenda 2000 – Pour une Union plus forte et plus large' (COM (97)2000 – C4-0371/97) A4-0368/97/PARTIE C, Avis des commissions parlementaires et lettres des délégations du Parlement européen aux commissions parlementaires mixtes PE 224.339/Partie C/def, Avis (article 147 du règlement) à l'intention de la commission des affaires étrangères, de la sécurité et de la politique de défense, Rapporteurs: M. Oostlander et M Baron Crespo, Commission de l'emploi et des affaire sociales, Rapporteur pour avis: M Harald Ettl, point 24 and B.

[9] Agenda 2000, Vol II, COM(97)2000 final 20, 36; HAEU, DORIE-204, annexe 2 (n 6) point 5.4; HAEU, GJLA-206, European Commission, Secretary General, Corrigendum to the Information note by M Verheugen addressed to the Members of the Commission, Directors Generals and Heads of service, 14 April 2000, O/139/2000 SEC(2000)663/3 following the meeting of the heads of cabinet of 13 April 2000.

[10] Agenda 2000, Vol II, COM(97) 2000 final, Section 6.1.

[11] Ibid.

lead to distortion of competition and social dumping.[12] For this reason, for the first time in accession negotiations, we see an emphasis by the Commission on the full incorporation of the European social model in the candidate states, a model which, according to the Commission, is characterized by a balance between social justice and economic efficiency.[13]

Finally, the need for sustainable development of the acceding countries was also set in light of their emigration patterns.[14] There was a constant pressure on the candidate countries to accelerate their development both economically and in terms of social standards to ensure that they keep their nationals in their territories.[15] This emphasis had a double face: one related to eliminating push factors for migration, and a second one related to making use of human resources needed to restructure their economies, which would eventually become part of the EU economy.[16] The issue of antagonism between the labour of migrants from the acceding states, and the TCN migrant labour and the potential effects for the EU external relations also appeared in marginal ways.[17]

[12] Ibid, Section 7.2; HAEU, DORIE-204, annexe 2 (n 6) point 5.4; Parlement européen, Résolution sur la communication de la Commission intitulé 'Agenda 2000-Pour une Union plus forte et plus large' première partie, chapitre II, 'Cohésion économique et sociale' (COM (97) 2000 – C4-0523/97), A4-0210/98, 1998-06-18, PE 270.314/15 point M.

[13] Agenda 2000, Vol II, COM(97) 2000 final, Section 6.1. Commission Opinion on Romania, COM(97)2003 final 90; Commission Opinion on the Czech Republic COM (97)2009 final 85; Commission Opinion on Poland COM(97)2002 final 97; Commission Opinion on Bulgaria, COM(97)2008 80, 48; Commission Opinion on Estonia COM(97) 2006 final 44; Commission Opinion on Hungary, COM(97)2001 final 89; Commission Opinion on Lithuania, COM(97)2007 43; Commission Opinion on Latvia, COM(97)2005 final 83; Commission Opinion on Slovenia, COM(97)2010 final 49.

[14] HAEU, DORIE-207, Rapport sur la communication de la Commission "Agenda 2000" – Première partie. Chapitre Π, COM(97)2000 C4-0371/97, A4-0210/98, PE 225.091/def, Avis (Article 147 du règlement) à l'intention de la commission de la politique régionale, commission de l' emploi et des affaires sociales, Rapporteur pour avis: M Hans Lindqvist, Point 9 et Avis (Article 147 du règlement) à l'intention de la commission de la politique régionale, commission de la pèche, Rapporteur pour avis: M Pat the Cope Gallagher.

[15] Agenda 2000, Vol II, COM(97) 2000 final 41.

[16] HAEU, DORIE-205 (n 8) point 1.3.

[17] Agenda 2000, Vol II, COM(97) 2000 final, Section 6; HAEU-GJLA 246, Commission, DG External Relations, Director General Note for the attention of MM Prat, Cadieux, Abbott, Avery, Benavides, Nuttall, Coher, Rhein, DG I, Burghardt, Secr Gen, Brussels, 05.03.1992, 003389.

In this regard, transitional measures had to be put in place with due account of the different risks.[18] The Central and Eastern European enlargement had the potential to restore security in Europe, providing the basis for making the EU a global actor and enriching the internal market by, *inter alia*, human capital.[19] An immediate accession without specific safeguards could not guarantee the integration capacity of the EU or support its project of growth and progress. As a result, following the consideration of different options that could ensure a smooth transition, free movement of workers was regulated in the relevant Accession Treaties as follows.[20]

Labour migration in the first two years following accession would take place subject to national measures or bilateral agreements. Member States would be allowed to extend this two-year period by three more years.[21] In case of serious disturbance to the labour market, Member States could maintain national measures for a total of seven years.[22] Nationals of the acceding states already employed at the date of accession for more than twelve months or accepted to a national labour market following accession for a period longer than twelve months would enjoy

[18] Agenda 2000, Vol II, COM(97) 2000 final 20, 36; HAEU, DORIE-205 (n 8) point 24; Parlement européen, Résolution du 3 avril 1998 sur les effets de l'élargissement de l'Union européenne sur la coopération dans le domaine de la justice et des affaires intérieures, A4-0107/98 [1998] OJ C 138/214, point 17; Résolution du Parlement européen sur le rapport global de suivi sur le degré de préparation à l'adhésion à l'UE de la République tchèque, de l'Estonie, de Chypre, de la Lettonie, de la Lituanie, de la Hongrie, de Malte, de la Pologne, de la Slovénie et de la Slovaquie A5-0111/2004 [2004] OJ C 102E/829, point 15.

[19] Agenda 2000, Vol II, COM(97) 2000 final 4; HAEU, EN-2228, Study group on enlargement formed within Directorate F of the Commission and produced a report called 'A strategy for enlargement', November 1991, 4.

[20] For an overview, see Georg Ziegler, 'The Accession Negotiations on Free Movement of Workers' in Andrea Ott and Kirstyn Inglis (eds), *Handbook on European Enlargement: A Commentary on the Enlargement Process* (TMC Asser Press 2002).

[21] Act concerning the conditions of the 2003 Accession (2003 Accession Treaty) [2003] OJ L 236, Article 24, Annexes V, VI, VIII, IX, X, XII, XIII, and XIV, Paragraph 2; Protocol concerning the accession of Bulgaria and Romania to the European Union (2005 Accession Treaty) [2005] OJ L 157, Article 20, Annexes VI, VII, Paragraph 2; Act concerning the conditions of accession of the Republic of Croatia and the adjustments to the Treaty on European Union, the Treaty on the Functioning of the European Union and to the Treaty establishing the European Atomic Energy Community (2012 Accession Treaty) [2012] OJ L 112, Article 18, Annex V, Paragraph 2.

[22] 2003 Accession Treaty, Article 24, Annexes V, VI, VIII, IX, X, XII, XIII, and XIV, Paragraph 4; 2005 Accession Treaty, Article 20, Annexes VI, VII, Paragraph 4; 2012 Accession Treaty, Article 18, Annex V, Paragraph 4.

access to the labour market of that state.[23] What is more, labour migrants employed at the Member States during the transitional period would benefit from non-discrimination, as the application of Article 7 of Regulation 1612/68 was not subject to the transitional arrangements. At the same time, the transitional arrangements required that nationals of the acceding countries and their families should not be treated more restrictively than those of third countries working in that Member State.[24]

The Accession Treaties also provided for the possibility to review the transitional provisions within two years following accession.[25] Considerable discretion was left to Member States as to how they would unilaterally regulate labour migration from the acceding states in the transitional period. Specifically, they were allowed to individually open their labour markets to the nationals of the acceding states two years after accession.[26] At the same time, such Member States would be allowed to go back to restrictions within the first seven years if they underwent or foresaw disturbances on their labour market which could threaten the living standards or employment levels in a particular region or occupation.[27] In such a case, the Commission would review the Member State's request and decide on the extent to which the application of the relevant EU law provisions could be wholly or partially suspended. This type of resort to domestic law could 'in urgent and exceptional cases' take place by *ex post* notification.[28] What is more, where old Member States decided to suspend the application of free movement provisions, the acceding Member States were also protected insofar as they could restrict the application of free movement for migrant workers from all the other

[23] 2003 Accession Treaty, Article 24, Annexes V, VI, VIII, IX, X, XII, XIII, and XIV, Paragraph 2; 2005 Accession Treaty, Article 20, Annexes VI, VII, Paragraph 2; 2012 Accession Treaty, Article 18, Annex V, Paragraph 2.

[24] 2003 Accession Treaty, Article 24, Annexes V, VI, VIII, IX, X, XII, XIII, and XIV, Paragraph 14; 2005 Accession Treaty, Article 20, Annexes VI, VII, Paragraph 14; 2012 Accession Treaty, Article 18, Annex V, Paragraph 14.

[25] 2003 Accession Treaty, Article 24, Annexes V, VI, VIII, IX, X, XII, XIII, and XIV, Paragraph 3; 2005 Accession Treaty accession, Article 20, Annexes VI, VII, Paragraph 3; 2012 Accession Treaty, Article 18, Annex V, Paragraph 3.

[26] 2003 Accession Treaty, Article 24, Annexes V, VI, VIII, IX, X, XII, XIII, and XIV, Paragraph 1, Paragraph 12.

[27] 2003 Accession Treaty, Article 24, Annexes V, VI, VIII, IX, X, XII, XIII, and XIV, Paragraph 7; 2005 Accession Treaty, Article 20, Annexes VI, VII, Paragraph 7; 2012 Accession Treaty, Article 18, Annex V, Paragraph 7.

[28] Ibid.

acceding Member States, to seal themselves from disturbances in their developing labour markets.[29]

Rights of family members were regulated as follows. For migrants from acceding Member States who had already been employed in EU Member States for longer than twelve months, family members residing with them at the date of accession would have immediate access to the labour market of the specific state.[30] Family members who resided with the worker following accession and during the application of the transitional regime would have access to the Member State labour market after residence there for at least eighteen months, or from the third year following the date of accession.[31]

Finally, Member States also addressed the issue of posted workers. Germany and Austria were allowed to limit the application of EU law and thereby the movement of posted workers to their national labour markets to address serious existing and threatened disturbances in specific service sectors.[32] These services or sectors were mentioned in detail for each of these countries. By a declaration, Germany and Austria expressed their understanding of the phrase 'certain regions' to potentially comprise of the entire national territory.[33] In general, during the period of transitional arrangements, Member States were required to ensure that no new restrictions to the rights of migrant workers would be introduced (standstill clause) and that they gave preference to workers from the acceding Member States over those who are nationals of third countries as regards access to the labour market.[34]

[29] 2003 Accession Treaty, Article 24, Annexes V, VI, VIII, IX, X, XII, XIII, and XIV, Paragraph 11; 2005 Accession Treaty, Article 20, Annexes VI, VII, Paragraph 11; 2012 Accession Treaty, Article 18, Annex V, Paragraph 11.

[30] 2003 Accession Treaty, Article 24, Annexes V, VI, VIII, IX, X, XII, XIII, and XIV, Paragraph 8; 2005 Accession Treaty, Article 20, Annexes VI, VII, Paragraph 8; 2012 Accession Treaty, Article 18, Annex V, Paragraph 8.

[31] Ibid.

[32] 2003 Accession Treaty, Article 24, Annexes V, VI, VIII, IX, X, XII, XIII, and XIV, Paragraph 13; 2005 Accession Treaty, Article 20, Annexes VI, VII, Paragraph 13; 2012 Accession Treaty, Article 18, Annex V, Paragraph 13.

[33] Declaration no 19, Joint Declaration by the Federal Republic of Germany and the Republic of Austria on the free movement of workers: Czech Republic, Estonia, Hungary, Latvia, Lithuania, Poland, Slovenia and Slovakia, Treaty of Accession of the Czech Republic, Estonia, Cyprus, Latvia, Lithuania, Hungary, Malta, Poland, Slovenia and Slovakia [2003] OJ L 236.

[34] 2003 Accession Treaty, Article 24, Annexes V, VI, VIII, IX, X, XII, XIII, and XIV, Paragraph 14; 2005 Accession Treaty, Article 20, Annexes VI, VII, Paragraph 14; 2012 Accession Treaty, Article 18, Annex V, Paragraph 14.

Malta and Cyprus were not covered by these detailed arrangements. Instead, they joined immediately the free movement *acquis*. The higher economic and social development of these countries compared to the CEECs was the reason behind the immediate application of the free movement framework.[35] The stance of the Commission, as expressed in archival documents, is that Malta and Cyprus stood out from the rest of the candidate countries for three reasons: they did not share common borders with any Member States; the difference of wage levels between them and the Member States was not as marked; and the relevant research did not identify them as posing migration-related risks to the EU Member States most affected at the time (Germany and Austria).[36] For the same reasons, Malta was even allowed to unilaterally resort to procedures restricting the movement of EU workers to its territory for a period of seven years if it underwent or foresaw labour market disturbances that could seriously threaten the living standards or employment in a specific region or occupation.[37] A similar derogation on the application of free movement provisions was not envisaged for the EU Member States with respect to Maltese nationals. Likewise, the transitional arrangements on Cyprus provided for no restriction on the free movement of workers *acquis*.[38]

Similarly to all the previous Accession Treaties, a general safeguard clause was incorporated allowing for the potential adoption of protective measures for three years after accession in case of difficulties related to the economic situation of the old and new Member States.[39] In addition to this, another clause was added which provided for similar measures where new Member States failed to enforce the commitments undertaken

[35] Commission Opinion on Malta, COM(1993)312; Commission Opinion on Cyprus, COM (1993)313; Rapport de mise à jour de l'avis de la Commission sur la demande d'adhésion de Malte, COM(1999)69 final, Section 3.5, 25.

[36] HAEU, GJLA-204, European Commission, DG Enlargement, Argumentaire on the Transitional Arrangement for the free movement of persons, For use in the candidate countries, Brussels, 31 May 2001, ELARG/FC D(2001); HAEU, GJLA-206, Final version of Communication from Mr Verhaugen in Agreement with Mrs Diamantopoulou, Essential elements for the draft Common Positions concerning 'Freedom of movement of persons', version of 6 April 2001 sent to the Secretary General for the college on 18.04.01.

[37] 2003 Accession Treaty, Annex XIV Malta, Paragraph 2.

[38] 2003 Accession Treaty, Annex VII.

[39] 2003 Accession Treaty, Article 37; 2005 Accession Treaty, Article 36; 2012 Accession Treaty, Article 37.

during the accession negotiations, thereby causing a serious breach or an imminent risk of such breach to the functioning of the internal market.[40]

In the Accession Treaties of 2003 and 2005, Member States attached Declarations in recognition of the elements of 'differentiation and flexibility that applied to the free movement of workers regime'.[41] They acknowledged their intention to grant increased access to the acceding states' nationals under domestic law and to improve the employment opportunities in Member States upon accession. Finally, they declared their intention to 'move as quickly as possible to the full application of the acquis in the area of free movement of workers'.[42] The overview of the main provisions of the Accession Treaties points to the extremely detailed temporal limitation of the rights of migrant workers and the more flexible review process on the transitional arrangements not only by the EU institutions but also by the Member States, which could unilaterally decide how to address labour migration from acceding states based on their national needs.

A feature of past accession processes was that workers-nationals of the acceding states, who had been already legally employed in the territory of the Member States, would immediately enjoy their rights as EU workers. This was because of the recognition that such migrants were already actively contributing to EU growth and could not cause disruptions to national labour markets. This feature was also differentiated in the Central and Eastern European enlargement. No longer was prior lawful economic activity enough: migrants employed in Member States prior to accession were required to show a more concrete tie to the labour market. They had to have already been connected to the EU market for a period of longer than a year to be able to enjoy a broader set of rights. This incrementality in the attribution of rights for already employed migrants from acceding states was established precisely to avoid economic risks at times of more limited labour demand, and thereby to ensure that the accession would not take place in a way that would make it unsustainable for the economic development of the EU.

[40] 2003 Accession Treaty, Article 38; 2005 Accession Treaty Accession, Articles 37 and 39; 2012 Accession Treaty [2012] OJ L 112, Article 38.

[41] Declarations no 6, 7, 10, 11, 13, 14, 15, 16, 18, 2003 Accession Treaty; Joint Declaration on the free movement of workers 1 and 2, 2005 Accession Treaty.

[42] Ibid.

8.2 The Free Movement Framework as a Sustainable Migration Framework

Chapter 5 presented the political aspirations of generalizing free movement rights for EU citizens and their reflection in the case-law, which broadened the protection of EU migrants in light of the primary law provisions. For some time, political scientists and legal scholars alike investigated primary law and its invocation in the case-law as a basis for the construction of a direct link between EU migrants *qua* citizens and the EU legal order.[43] In parallel, the Treaty provided that free movement rights of all citizens were to be exercised in accordance with the conditions and limitations of secondary law. The Commission thus issued a proposal for a Directive which would regulate the exercise of these rights in light of the legal and political environment created by the citizenship of the Union.[44]

The proposal of the Commission suggested the extension of residence rights without any conditions for up to six months, the removal of conditions of differential treatment between EU migrants and Member State nationals after four years of residence, and the limitation of restrictions to family reunification.[45] These aspirations were watered down by the Council.[46] A closer investigation of the final text of Directive 2004/38, which now regulates these rights, as well as of the case-law of the Court, show that economic objectives dictate both the conditions and the limitations of the right to reside, the social rights enjoyed by EU

[43] See Sandra Mantu and others (eds), *EU Citizenship and Free Movement Rights: Taking Supranational Citizenship Seriously* (Brill Nijhoff 2020); Willem Maas, 'The Genesis of European Rights' (2005) 43 JCMS 1009; Dora Kostakopoulou, 'The Evolution of European Union Citizenship' (2008) 7 European Political Science 285; Dora Kostakopoulou, Sergio Carrera, and Moritz Jesse, 'Doing and Deserving: Competing Frames of Integration in the EU' in Elspeth Guild, Kees Groenendijk, and Sergio Carrera (eds), *Illiberal Liberal States: Immigration, Citizenship, and Integration in the EU* (Ashgate 2009).

[44] Proposal for a Directive on the right of citizens of the Union and their family members to move and reside freely within the territory of the Member States, COM(2001)0257 [2001] OJ C 270E/150, Section 1.3.

[45] Ibid.

[46] On the main changes by the Council, see Communication pursuant to the second subparagraph of Article 251(2) EC Treaty concerning the common position of the Council on the adoption of a Directive on the right of citizens of the Union and their family members to move and reside freely within the territory of the Member States, SEC (2003)1293 final – COD 2001/0111.

migrants, as well as family reunification rights.[47] After reviewing how such objectives are reflected in secondary law in Section 8.2.1, Section 8.2.2 turns to the evolution of case-law, which, rather than ensuring more extensive protection via primary law, now accepts the balancing of economic and social objectives decided by the legislature. In Section 8.2.3 the more extensive protection of EU migrant workers as reflected in law and case-law is identified. Finally, Section 8.2.4 examines family reunification provisions and the way in which economic and social considerations affect their interpretation. The analysis reveals the centrality of economic and social considerations for the rights of EU migrants, showcasing the free movement framework as the perfect example of sustainable migration whereby migrants are attributed extensive social rights if they have an economic function, and these rights are limited precisely to ensure the economic sustainability of their movement.

8.2.1 Economic Preconditions of Legal Residence

An analysis of the provisions of Directive 2004/38 shows how economic objectives condition free movement rights. The Directive provides detailed conditions under which the right of free movement and residence should be exercised by EU migrants and their family members, their rights to permanent residence, and the limitations of such rights for public policy, public security, and public health reasons.

First, all EU migrants enjoy a right of residence for up to three months under Article 6 Directive 2004/38. This right is generally thought of as unlimited, owing to the special status of EU citizenship. Even this limited right to enter and reside in a Member State free from any administrative requirement is dependent on a negative condition, namely that EU migrants should not become an unreasonable burden on the social assistance system of the host state under Article 14(1) Directive 2004/38. Subsequently, if EU migrants wish to reside in a Member State for a period longer than three months, they need to comply with the conditions of Article 7 Directive 2004/38. Recital 9 of the Directive suggests that Member States may allow more favourable treatment to jobseekers;

[47] Directive 2004/38/EC on the right of citizens of the Union and their family members to move and reside freely within the territory of the Member States amending Regulation 1612/68 and repealing Directives 64/221/EEC, 68/360/EEC, 72/194/EEC, 73/148/EEC, 75/34/EEC, 75/35/EEC, 90/364/EEC, 90/365/EEC and 93/96/EEC [2004] OJ L 158/77.

however, there are no more specific provisions on this in the text of the Directive.

A closer look at Article 7 Directive 2004/38 points to the economic considerations conditioning the security of residence of EU migrants in a Member State. Specifically, residence over three months is guaranteed only for EU migrants who cannot pose a risk to the economy of Member States. Residence is guaranteed for workers, self-employed persons, and their family members. Where EU migrants are not engaged in economic activity, their security of residence is dependent on them having sufficient resources and comprehensive health insurance.[48] Economic activity, or, at the very least, self-sufficiency, functions as a guarantee that they will positively contribute or, at least, that they will not negatively affect the economies of the Member States. The primary law guarantee of movement and residence derived from the EU citizen status is conditioned by the EU legislature to align free movement under the Directive with the Treaty objectives of growth and progress.

Directive 2004/38 allows some leeway for economic inactivity, but this is clearly delimited. Under Article 7(3), EU migrants can retain the status of worker or self-employed, and hence security of residence, if they are temporarily unable to work due to illness or accident, and if they are in duly recorded involuntary unemployment after having been employed for more than one year and have registered as jobseekers.[49] In case of involuntary unemployment after less than a year of employment they must have registered as jobseekers. In this case, EU migrants maintain the status of worker for no less than six months if they pursue vocational training. However, the retention of the worker status presupposes that the training is related to their previous employment, unless they have become voluntarily unemployed.

The intimate connection of security of residence to economic considerations appears under Article 14 Directive 2004/38 on the retention of the right of residence. According to it, EU migrants and their family members can retain the right to reside as long as they do not become an unreasonable burden on the social assistance system of the host state. Incorporating the considerations of the case-law, Article 14(3) provides that expulsion should not come as an automatic consequence of recourse

[48] Article 7(1) (b) and (c), Directive 2004/38.

[49] Case C-507/12, *Saint Prix*, ECLI:EU:C:2014:2007; Case C-442/16, *Gusa*, ECLI:EU:C:2017:1004; Case C-544/18, *Dakneviciute*, ECLI:EU:C:2019:761.

to social assistance.[50] This means that Member States can remove EU migrants if they consider that such migrants negatively affect their economies, but to do so, they need to comply with the principle of proportionality and to take into account various considerations.[51]

Security of residence becomes decoupled from economic considerations after five years of residence in a host state. That is when EU migrants can access permanent residence under Article 16 Directive 2004/38.[52] Under Recital 17, this right is attributed with a view to contributing to the social objectives of the EU by strengthening social cohesion. Finally, Article 24, which provides for equal treatment of EU migrants and their family members, allows for derogation. Article 24(2) provides that Member States have no obligation to grant equal access to social assistance during the first three months of residence or to migrants who entered as jobseekers. The same provision allows Member States to restrict equal treatment regarding maintenance aid for studies to economically active migrants and their families and to only allow such aid to economically inactive migrants after the acquisition of a right of permanent residence.

Despite these safeguards, which were put in place to avert the potential economic repercussions of unlimited free movement rights, Member States have time and again voiced their concerns on how the provisions of the Directive set the scene for 'benefit tourism'.[53] The Commission has communicated to Member States that the limitations in place ensure the proper functioning of the system, stressing that economically inactive citizens and people who enter as jobseekers are excluded from social assistance to begin with.[54] Social assistance is granted to people whose

[50] Case C-184/99, *Grzelczyk*, ECLI:EU:C:2001:458; Case C-456/02, *Trojani*, ECLI:EU:C:2004:488.

[51] Recital 16 inserted by the Council during the negotiations, Council Document ST 13263 2003 ADD 1 – Projet d'exposé des Motifs du Conseil 10/11/2003, Position commune arrêtée par le Conseil en vue de l'adoption d'une directive du Parlement européen et du Conseil relative au droit des citoyens de l'Union et des membres de leurs familles de circuler et de séjourner librement sur le territoire des États membres, modifiant le règlement (CEE) n° 1612/68 et abrogeant les directives 64/221/ CEE, 68/360/CEE, 72/194/CEE, 73/148/CEE, 75/34/CEE, 75/35/CEE, 90/364/CEE, 90/365/CEE and 93/96/CEE Orientations Communes Délai de consultation:14.11.20.

[52] Article 18, Directive 2004/38 for family members.

[53] The concerns escalated in the Member States' intention to limit equal treatment also for workers. Cf Nic Shuibhne, 'Reconnecting Free Movement of Workers and Equal Treatment in an Unequal Europe' (2018) 43 ELR 477.

[54] Communication, Free movement of EU citizens and their families: Five actions to make a difference, COM(2013)0837 final, Section 2.2.

income falls below a specific threshold, and they require support by states to meet a life in dignity. EU migrants who enjoy a right to reside in Member States do so under the condition of sufficient resources (either via employment or through proof of self-sufficiency) anyway, which would mean that their income must be higher than that under which social assistance is granted. Thus, they cannot pose a risk to public finances.

Overall, Directive 2004/38 operationalizes free movement rights for EU migrants under specific limitations and conditions as provided by Article 21(1) TFEU. The rights granted to EU migrants and the limitations thereto to protect national economies express a balancing between economic and social objectives so as to guarantee that migration is sustainable in the long-term, and that public finances are not affected by unlimited EU migration. The limitations regarding economically inactive and not self-sufficient EU migrants condition both the right to reside and access to social rights. This is not a surprise. Secondary law has always imposed such conditions on the rights of EU migrants. Nevertheless, equal treatment is provided not only under the Directive, but also under primary law, which was extensively used by the Court to extend both social and residence rights beyond the limits of secondary law during the 1990s and early 2000s, as discussed in Chapter 5. Section 8.2.2 examines the case-law and shows how the tension between primary law and the limitations set by secondary law under Directive 2004/38 were dealt by the Court during this period.

8.2.2 *Legal Residence under EU Law as a Condition of Social Rights*

Section 8.2.1 has shown how economic considerations underlie the rights of EU migrants in two ways. First, they appear behind the conditions of access to residence rights for a period longer than three months, and, second, they exist as a limitation behind the attribution of equal treatment rights for those not fulfilling the conditions of Article 7 Directive 2004/38. In this section I investigate how the Court has engaged with the balancing, opted for by the EU legislator, behind the need to promote EU citizen status, and the limitation of the rights of EU migrants so that they do not adversely affect the EU project of growth.

One of the first cases issued under the new framework was *Brey*, which concerned the residence rights of a German pensioner who claimed a compensatory supplement provided for under Austrian legislation to supplement his German pension.[55] The Court followed the wording and purpose of the Directive 2004/38 and confirmed that lawful residence was dependent on the self-sufficiency of an EU migrant. It emphasized that freedom of movement was the rule, and the conditions set for it under the Directive should be interpreted strictly and in line with proportionality, in order to assess whether the grant of social security benefits to an individual might burden the social assistance system of the Member State as a whole.[56] In that case the Court suggested that the proportionality assessment should take place with reference to the personal circumstances of the applicant and on a case-by-case basis. Jesse and Carter call this the 'swansong' of the Court's qualitative approach, examined in Chapter 5.[57]

Subsequently, *Dano*, where the Court religiously followed the conditions prescribed by Directive 2004/38, came out with a bang.[58] In this case, the Court held that access to social benefits under equal treatment presupposed not lawful residence of any kind, but lawful residence in accordance with the conditions of the Directive.[59] By setting these conditions, the EU legislature aimed at preventing the movement of people who could pose risks to the social assistance system of the Member States.[60] According to the Court, if EU migrants do not comply with the conditions of the Directive on residence rights, they may not claim equal treatment under EU primary law, as this would run contrary to the objective of secondary law, 'namely preventing Union citizens who are nationals of other Member States from becoming an unreasonable burden on the social assistance system of the host Member State'.[61] The Court also suggested that by setting these conditions, Article 7(1)

[55] Case C-140/12, *Brey*, ECLI:EU:C:2013:565.

[56] C-140/12, *Brey*, paras 70–72.

[57] Moritz Jesse and Daniel Carter, 'Life after the "Dano-Trilogy": Legal Certainty, Choices and Limitations in EU Citizenship Case Law' in Nathan Cambien, Dimitry Kochenov, and Elise Muir (eds), *European Citizenship under Stress, Social Justice, Brexit and Other Challenges*, vol 16 (Brill Nijhoff 2020) 144.

[58] Catherine Barnard, 'The Day the Clock Stopped: EU Citizenship and the Single Market' in Panos Koutrakos and Jukka Snell (eds), *Research Handbook on the Law of the EU's Internal Market* (Edward Elgar 2017); Julio Baquero Cruz, 'Partial Eclipse of Union Citizenship: From Grzelczyk to Dano' in *What's Left of the Law of Integration?* (Oxford University Press 2018); Niamh Nic Shuibhne, 'What I Tell You Three Times Is True: Lawful Residence and Equal Treatment after Dano' (2016) 23 Maastricht Journal of European and Comparative Law 908.

[59] Case C-333/13, *Dano*, ECLI:EU:C:2014:2358, para 70.

[60] Ibid, para 70 and Directive 2004/38, Recital 10.

[61] Ibid, para 74.

(b) Directive 2004/38 sought to prevent economically inactive EU migrants from using the host states' welfare system as means to fund their subsistence.[62]

This approach was confirmed in *Alimanovic* and later in *García-Nieto*, which concerned access to benefits during the first three-month period of unconditional residence.[63] The Court confirmed that only residence that complied with the conditions set by the Directive qualified for equal treatment, and not any kind of lawful residence. As put by AG Wathelet in *García-Nieto*, such an interpretation is consistent with the objective of the Directive to maintain the 'financial equilibrium of the social security system of the Member States' and to decide otherwise 'could result in relocation en masse liable to create an unreasonable burden on national social security systems'.[64]

The economic conditioning of a right to reside as a basis of equal treatment was confirmed more clearly in *Commission v the UK*.[65] The case concerned a UK law which required the existence of EU residence rights as a condition to access child benefit. The UK would essentially screen applicants who claimed this benefit and then expel them if they did not meet the conditions of Directive 2004/38 regarding residence in the UK. The Court confirmed its finding in *Brey* and *Dano* and linked these to *Bidar* and *Grzelczyk*. While acknowledging that the requirement of legal residence under EU law constituted indirect discrimination, the Court found this justified.[66] Specifically, it held that such limitations were in line with EU law and could achieve the legitimate objective of protecting public finances.[67]

One could suggest that the system in place is remedied in light of the guarantees of equal treatment after five years of residence, which prove integration and extend the rights of EU migrants in the host state in light of social considerations. Nevertheless, a look at the case-law of the Court on permanent residence creates room for more problematization.

[62] Ibid, para 76.

[63] Case C-67/14, *Alimanovic*, ECLI:EU:C:2015:597; Case C-299/14, *García-Nieto and others*, ECLI:EU:C:2016:114.

[64] Opinion of AG Wathelet in Case C-299/14, *García-Nieto and others*, ECLI:EU:C:2015:366, paras 70–71.

[65] Case C-308/14, *Commission/United Kingdom*, ECLI:EU:C:2016:436.

[66] C-308/14, *Commission/United Kingdom*, para 77. For a critique, see Charlotte O'Brien, 'The ECJ Sacrifices EU Citizenship in Vain: *Commission v. United Kingdom*' (2017) 54 CMLRev 209.

[67] C-308/14, *Commission/United Kingdom*, para 80.

In *Ziolkowski & Szeja*, the Court engaged with the right to permanent residence of Polish nationals during the transitional period of the Accession Treaties.[68] The Polish nationals in that case had legal residence in Germany on the basis of humanitarian grounds. The Court held that the applicants could indeed access permanent residence under Directive 2004/38, since there were no transitional arrangements regarding this. However, it also held that, to qualify for permanent residence under the Directive, one had to have legal residence that satisfied the conditions of the Directive.[69] This means that an EU migrant needs to be self-sufficient and to not pose a burden to the welfare system of the Member State, if they are to qualify for permanent residence under EU law. The length of residence is not the only qualifying factor, and social ties in a Member State are not a sufficient factor either. Economic conditions of having proven worthy, or not having adversely impacted the economy of the host state, are also attached to this status. As the applicants enjoyed legal residence on humanitarian grounds, this did not presuppose their self-sufficiency and, hence, they were excluded from the scope of the Directive.

Muir has referred to this case-law development as 'deconstitutionalization'.[70] By looking at the Treaty provisions on citizen's rights, Muir suggested that Article 21 TFEU functioned both as a benchmark against which the activities of EU and national authorities could be reviewed and as a legal basis for the adoption of further legislation.[71] Indeed as she showed, this double function is not uncommon in EU law and in the field of citizen's rights where 'the process by which political institutions have thought to circumscribe EU intervention may be reviewed against the very primary right that the legislation is intended to shape'.[72] Muir has rightly pointed out that the Court's view on primary law 'more ostensibly competes with those expressed by political authorities'.[73] Having these in mind, Muir looked at how the Court shifted its attention from the rights enshrined in primary law to the rights provided in secondary law, and

[68] Joined Cases C-424/10 and C-425/10, *Ziolkowski and Szeja*, ECLI:EU:C:2011:866.
[69] Ibid, para 51.
[70] Elise Muir, 'EU Citizenship, Access to "Social Benefits" and Third-Country National Family Members: Reflecting on the Relationship between Primary and Secondary Rights in Times of Brexit' (2019) 2018 European Papers – A Journal on Law and Integration 1353.
[71] Ibid, 1357.
[72] Ibid, 1358.
[73] Ibid.

suggested that this ‘deconstitutionalization’ allowed more space for political dialogue.[74] Thym has also referred to the evolution presented in this section as a stark reminder of the limits of integration through law.[75]

Looking at these evolutions in light of the demand for economic and social sustainability driving the development of EU law, the following could be added. Before the adoption of secondary law implementing the free movement rights of EU citizens, the Court emphasized the primary law objective of creating an ever-closer Union of the peoples of Europe. It used this political aspiration as a means to review secondary law in place, and to disconnect the economic limitations of the secondary law adopted in the 1990s from the social and political considerations of EU citizenship status inserted in the Maastricht Treaty. After the legislator balanced the different economic and social objectives and gave them concrete expression in Directive 2004/38, the Court refrained from using the broader framing of primary law as means to review secondary law. Rather, it restricted its interpretation by confirming the balancing between economic and social considerations chosen by the EU legislature. Taking a different approach would have made the system of free movement unsustainable. As Nic Shuibhne has also suggested, the aspiration of the greatest possible freedom might be legitimate, but it does not allow for sustainability of free movement rights under the current framework.[76] Having presented the evolution of judicial interpretation, Section 8.3.3 explores how the current framework still privileges the social rights of EU migrant workers, as they are the ones contributing to the project, and differentiates their treatment from that of economically inactive EU citizens.

8.2.3 *The Differentiated Status of Workers and Jobseekers*

Despite the aim of the Directive 2004/38 to harmonize the conditions of residence for all EU citizens, the treatment of economically active EU migrants is differentiated both by exceptions applicable to them in the Directive and through the parallel existence of other instruments granting them rights.

[74] Ibid, 1360, 1376.

[75] Daniel Thym, ‘When Union Citizens Turn into Illegal Migrants: The Dano Case’ (2015) 40 ELR 249, 260.

[76] Niamh Nic Shuibhne, ‘Reconnecting Free Movement of Workers and Equal Treatment in an Unequal Europe’ (2018) 43 ELR 477, 509.

First, in the Directive, there are exceptions that allow more privileged access to permanent residence to workers, self-employed persons, and their family members under Article 17. Under Recital 19 Directive 2004/38, the differentiated rights of economically active migrants are based on Regulation 1251/70 and Directive 75/34 and have been maintained as acquired rights.[77] What is more, workers, self-employed, and the members of their families enjoy full equal treatment rights and do not fall under the derogation of Article 24(2) Directive 2004/38. Further, under Article 14(4) Directive 2004/38, workers, first time jobseekers, and members of their families can in no case be expelled for economic reasons. Specifically, this Article provides that expulsion may in no case be adopted against economically active migrants, or EU migrants who entered the territory to seek employment. Such an expulsion would go against the long-standing right of EU migrants to move to take up work. Article 14(4)(b) provides, however, that the individuals need to be able to prove that they are indeed seeking employment, and that they have a genuine chance of being employed. In short, the claim of job-seeking is not sufficient of its own.

The differentiation in this, and the broader attribution of rights under Directive 2004/38, lies in the presumption that workers, by virtue of their status, cannot become a burden, but will rather be net contributors to the system. What is more, even if workers are entitled to equal treatment under Article 24, the chances are that they will never overburden national welfare systems, as they could be excluded from it for other reasons. Specifically, social assistance is usually aimed at supporting persons through mechanisms of solidarity so that they can have a decent livelihood. Workers and self-employed individuals would most probably be excluded on the basis of their finances, as they would have sufficient resources to ensure their livelihood without the need of state support.

In parallel to this, the Commission codified Regulation 1612/68 in line of the amendments it had undergone. Without creating new rights compared to the 1968 framework, free movement of workers is now regulated under Regulation 492/2011, which provides for a broader application of equal treatment under Article 7 in line with the broad

[77] Regulation 1251/70 on the right of workers to remain in the territory of a Member State after having been employed in that State [1970] OJ L 142/24; Directive 75/34/EEC concerning the right of nationals of a Member State to remain in the territory of another Member State after having pursued therein an activity in a self-employed capacity [1975] OJ L 14/10.

interpretation of the concept of social and tax advantages in the Court's case-law.[78] Family reunification rights of workers are no longer regulated by this instrument, but rather fall under Directive 2004/38. Nevertheless, in Article 10, the Regulation maintains the rights of children of workers and former workers to access education or vocational training under equal conditions to Member States nationals. Even after moving the conditions of family reunification to Directive 2004/38, the Regulation still provides for differentiated treatment not only to workers themselves but also, most importantly, to former workers and their family members.

The Court had already acknowledged the complicated link between the rights of residence of family members of workers and the rights of residence of former workers via their family members. Early on, the Court held that children of workers derived a right of residence from Article 12 Regulation 1612/68 to be able to access education in the host state.[79] This derived right of residence becomes autonomous when the parent loses the status of worker, in order to ensure that the child can continue their education.[80] The reasoning is that a worker who wants to move should not be exposed to the risk that if they lose their worker status, this would lead to the disruption of their children's education. A need to promote mobility, and thereby growth, is thus tied to an extended consideration of the importance of the protection of workers' children and their access to education.

In *Baumbast*, analysed in Chapter 5, the Court held that where a child enjoys a residence right to access education under Regulation 1612/68, this right can create residence rights for their primary carer.[81] Essentially, the loss of the status of worker by an EU migrant parent has no effect on the right of residence of their children. In subsequent case-law, the residence of the children of former workers created the basis for residence of their EU migrant parent. In *Ibrahim*, the Court confirmed *Baumbast*. Most importantly, it stated that EU migrants who are parents of children who had a residence right based on Regulation 492/2011 could enjoy a derived right of residence from their children without the need to satisfy the conditions of Directive 2004/38, that is, without the

[78] See Chapter 2. Articles 7–9, Regulation (EU) No 492/2011 on freedom of movement for workers within the Union [2011] OJ L 141/1, which also include equality in trade union membership and rights, and equality as regards access to housing.

[79] See Section 2.2.3.

[80] Case C-413/99, *Baumbast and R*, ECLI:EU:C:2002:493.

[81] Ibid; Case C-480/08, *Teixeira*, ECLI:EU:C:2010:83.

need to have sufficient resources and health insurance.[82] The existence of a worker status in the family at some point in time trumps the need to prove self-sufficiency to enjoy residence rights. The differentiation is based on a different function served by free movement of workers and free movement of citizens. Free movement of workers develops by extensive interpretations to promote mobility and, thereby, growth. The rights enjoyed by workers are based on the objective of creating the best possible condition for the integration of family members of people on the move.[83] Free movement of citizens develops with clearly construed limitations in secondary law to minimize the negative impacts of movement on national economies. The limitation of rights under the relevant Directive is based on the objective of maintaining the financial equilibrium of the Member States.[84]

This extensive protection of residence rights lies behind the more extensive application of equal treatment in access to social assistance for former workers. In *JD*, the Court held that parents of children who enjoyed a right of residence under Regulation 492/2011 should have access to social assistance under the more favourable conditions of Article 7(2) of Regulation 492/2011 and should not be covered by the derogation of Article 24(2) Directive 2004/38.[85] JD was a worker in Germany, where his daughters were attending school by virtue of Regulation 492/2011. Due to disruptions in his work, JD received social protection benefits for a period of nine months (subsidiary unemployment benefits and subsistence benefits for daughters), which were discontinued. Due to the length of the period during which JD was unemployed, the German authorities deemed that he could no longer retain the status of a worker, but he was rather considered a jobseeker. His right of residence at that stage was derived from the fact that his daughters were attending school by virtue of Regulation 492/2011. So, the national court wondered how the derogations from equal treatment, which were meant to apply to jobseekers under Directive 2004/38, should apply to persons who had the right of residence under Article 10 Regulation 492/2011, and who could no longer be considered workers.

[82] Case C-310/08, *Ibrahim and Secretary of State for the Home Department*, EU:C:2010:80, para 59.

[83] See also Case C-181/19, *Jobcenter Krefeld v JD*, ECLI:EU:C:2020:794, para 51.

[84] Ibid, para 66.

[85] Ibid.

As AG Pitruzzella mentioned in his Opinion, this case demanded that the Court clarify the limits of social solidarity.[86] And it did so by reference to the different objectives of free movement of workers and free movement of persons. In light of the objective of Directive 2004/38, the limitation to equal treatment is established as a means to minimize the negative economic impact of attribution of rights to migrants. In the case at hand, the Court held that there was an 'appreciable distinction' to be made between a EU migrant who worked in a Member State and had children in school there and then became unemployed (residence under Article 10 Regulation 492/2011), an EU migrant who resided in a Member State for less than three months (residence under Article 6(1) Directive 2004/38),[87] and an EU migrant who resided in a Member State as a first-time jobseeker (residence under Article 14(4) Directive 2004/38).[88] The latter two categories were those excluded from equal treatment in social assistance under Article 24(2) of the Directive 2004/38. The appreciable distinction which the Court mentioned essentially refers to the fact that an EU migrant has worked and contributed to growth in the first scenario. Due to this, their subsequent unemployment, together with the fact of having children in the host Member State, means that their claim to equal treatment should be accepted, as it would not adversely affect the economy of Member States.

What is more, in *Chief Appeals Officer and Others*, the Court drew a clear line between the permissible limitations to free movement of persons and free movement of workers.[89] In this case, which concerned social assistance for family members of EU migrant workers, the Court clarified that the unreasonable burden argument can justify limitations in the context of free movement of persons, but not in the context of free movement of workers. To justify this, the Court reminded that EU migrant workers personally contribute to the financing of the social policies followed by Member States by paying taxes and, due to this, they should be able to profit for social rights under the same conditions that national workers do.[90]

The analysis herein shows that both secondary law and case-law acknowledge a clear link between the economic contribution of an EU

[86] Opinion of AG Pitruzzella delivered Case C-181/19, *Jobcenter Krefeld v JD*, ECLI:EU:C:2020:377, para 1.
[87] C-299/14, *García-Nieto and others*, scenario.
[88] C-181/19, *JD*, para 67.
[89] Case C-488/21, *Chief Appeals Officer and Others*, ECLI:EU:C:2022:737.
[90] Ibid, para 71.

migrant and the more extensive social rights they are entitled to. The economic function of the migrant is once more the source of more extensive social rights, as has been the case from the early years of Community law. The connection between economic objectives served by migrant labour and the social safeguards that should guide the economic development reflects the way economic and social sustainability shapes EU migrants' rights. Section 8.2.4 will investigate how this connection appears in the regulation of family reunification for EU migrants.

8.2.4 The Case of Family Reunification: Social Objectives Furthering the Reach of EU Law within Defined Limits

Directive 2004/38 regulates family reunification for EU migrants. Family members mentioned in Article 2 are entitled to accompany or join the EU migrant in the host state and have a right to work there under Article 23. The Directive protects the rights of family members not in light of a functionalist narrative, but rather in connection to an aspiration to preserve family unity under the Charter.[91] Article 3 also mentions a wider group of family members whose reunification should be facilitated by Member States. The scope of family members falling under the Directive and the conditions of family reunification are considerably more extensive than the family reunification rights of legally resident TCNs under the Family Reunification Directive. However, this does not mean that the framework in place is completely stripped of economic considerations acting as a limit to migrants' rights.

First, the way family reunification rights are enjoyed by EU migrants is differentiated based on their economic function. EU workers or self-employed persons are not subject to conditions on income or housing as a precondition for reunification. This is not the case for students, pensioners, and self-sufficient EU migrants, who need to prove they have sufficient resources and comprehensive insurance. When it comes to family reunification for students, the circle of family members that can claim a right to family reunification is more limited.[92] In addition, as in the case of workers, permanent residence can be acquired under more favourable conditions for family members of EU migrants who

[91] Proposal on Citizen's Rights Directive, COM(2001)0257 final, Section 2.4.
[92] Article 7(4), Directive 2004/38.

contribute as workers or self-employed.[93] Aside from the legal regulation of the matter, the Court has engaged with the rights of EU migrants to family reunification in a significant amount of case-law which highlights the way economic and social objectives persist behind the attribution of rights. Section 8.2.4.1 examines the persistence of economic movement as a precondition for the rights of circular migrants, while Section 8.2.4.2 investigates the social orientation of the case-law behind the protection of the rights of EU children.

8.2.4.1 The Impossibility of Disconnecting Economic Considerations from the Rights of Circular Migrants

Economic objectives served by family reunification rights were apparent in the historical development of the EU legal framework analysed in Chapter 2. Social objectives are achieved by the extensive reach of EU law. The importance of attributing family reunification rights to EU migrants lies not so much in them being accompanied by their family members in a host state, but rather in the fact that they can claim such rights upon return to their state of origin. The link between an EU migrant and EU law, created by virtue of the migrant's contribution to growth, is strong enough to break the restrictions imposed by national law to its own nationals.

The case-law of the Court safeguarded the rights of EU migrants to be joined or accompanied by their family members in light of the need to guarantee that workers moved in liberty and dignity, and could thus be integrated in the host state.[94] The Court saw family life as a necessary precondition for promoting the living standards and social cohesion within Member States. Having established such rights in secondary law and having fortified them in the case-law, the Court used the functional imperative of free movement to promote the rights of EU migrants in their home state. In *Singh*, the Court held that the extension of the reach of EU law to trump national restrictions was necessary in order to remove obstacles to the free movement of workers.[95] The formula is classic. An EU migrant would be deterred from leaving their country of origin and pursue economic activity if they knew that, upon return, their family members could not join them under conditions at least equivalent

[93] Article 17(3), Directive 2004/38.

[94] See C-413/99, *Baumbast*, para 50; Case C-308/89, *Di Leo*, ECLI:EU:C:1990:400, para 13.

[95] Case C-370/90, *The Queen/Immigration Appeal Tribunal and Surinder Singh*, ECLI:EU:C:1992:296.

to those which they would normally enjoy in the host state.[96] The privileged treatment of returning EU migrants was linked with the abolition of obstacles to free movement, which was necessary for the promotion of the objectives of the Treaty.[97] Against this backdrop, EU law demanded the application of secondary law on family reunification rights when EU migrants returned to their home state. In *Eind*, the Court further held that there was no need for the migrant to continue the pursuit of economic activities upon return to their home state.[98] Such a requirement would run counter to the objectives of EU law to ensure that nationals of Member States took up work abroad. What is more, the personal motivation of the migrant to move to another Member State is irrelevant. The extended protection of EU law is not dependent on whether EU migrants moved to take up work or to circumvent national migration law, as long as they genuinely engaged in economic activity abroad.[99]

Following the adoption of Directive 2004/38, the reasoning of the Court shifted. It no longer emphasized the need to guarantee the specific free movement of economic actors, but rather focused on the aim of strengthening the rights of free movement and residence of all EU migrants regardless of whether they were net contributors.[100] In this context the Court mentioned the need to abolish obstacles to free movement of all persons under Article 3(1)(c) EC Treaty rather than on the specific functional imperatives of the free movement provisions.[101] The Court further stated that free movement for EU citizens implies the right to leave one's Member State of nationality and to become established in another Member State under the same conditions.[102]

But does this imply the elimination of economic considerations from the mix? A literal reading of the Court's case-law would require an unconditional right for EU migrants to establish themselves across the EU, and it would demand the elimination of economic objectives served by such move. It would further demand the more extensive protection of EU law applicable to all EU migrants, regardless of whether their move

96 C-370/90, *Singh*, para 19. See also Case C-459/99, *MRAX*, ECLI:EU:C:2002:461, para 53; Case C-60/00, *Carpenter*, ECLI:EU:C:2002:434 on services, para 38.
97 Case C-291/05, *Eind*, ECLI:EU:C:2007:771, para 32.
98 C-291/05, *Eind*, para 44.
99 C-370/90, *Singh*, para 23; Case C-109/01, *Akrich*, ECLI:EU:C:2003:491, para 55.
100 Case C-127/08, *Metock and others*, ECLI:EU:C:2008:449, para 59.
101 Ibid, para 68.
102 Ibid. The case overturned C-109/01, *Akrich*.

served economic ends or not. This, however, is not the case. The Court has held that if EU migrants wanted to claim the privileged treatment of Directive 2004/38 against their home country upon return, their movement would need to be in line with the conditions of Article 7 of the Directive.[103] Only if they have established themselves under conditions of self-sufficiency or economic contribution can they enjoy such rights and circumvent national limitations. As discussed earlier, this would require a type of movement that, even without contributing to growth, at the very least does not hinder it. This means that as a minimum, EU migrants would have to be self-sufficient in the host state. Scholars have discussed how this is not a condition that can be met by all EU migrants, leading to exclusion from protection for those who could pose risk to the growth project.[104] This implication is actually the consequence of shaping migrants' rights with due regard to economic and social sustainability.

8.2.4.2 The Social Orientation behind the Extensive Rights of Union Children

The emphasis on the safeguarding Member States' economies is not reproduced with the same force in the case-law on family reunification rights for EU children. In a series of cases concerning residence rights for TCN parents of minor children with EU nationality, the Court has used the citizenship provisions as a basis of extending the rights of their migrant parents. This is, perhaps, the only type of case-law where social considerations regarding the protection of children are capable of significantly extending the rights of TCNs. Even in this socially oriented case-law, economy enters the mix through the requirement that the TCN parent needs to be able to provide sufficient resources to enjoy residence rights.

The residence rights of TCN parents of EU children are judicially constructed by reference to primary law, as they fall outside the scope of Directive 2004/38. Directive 2004/38 provides for family reunification of dependent relatives in the ascending line. In the cases examined by the Court on this matter, it was not the TCN parents who were dependent on the EU children, but vice versa. This did not stop the Court from

[103] Case C-456/12, *O.*, ECLI:EU:C:2014:135; Case C-457/12, *S. and G.*, ECLI:EU:C:2014:136, which recognized that similar rights can be derived from Article 45, TFEU for frontier workers.

[104] Eleanor Spaventa, 'Family Rights for Circular Migrants and Frontier Workers: *O and B, and S and G*' (2015) 52 CMLRev 753.

establishing residence rights by reference to Union citizenship and the need of genuine enjoyment of the substance of rights conferred by Article 20 TFEU.[105] The genuine enjoyment of Union citizenship rights is linked to respect for family life under Article 7 CFR and the obligation to take into account the best interests of the child under Article 24(2) CFR. This emphasis on rights is not sufficient to take away any economic guarantees underlying the residence rights of EU children and their TCN parents. Rather, the legality of residence of the child is based on a combination of Article 21 TFEU and Directive 2004/38, which has been interpreted to mean that the sufficiency of resources is considered by reference to the resources of the TCN parent.[106] The ultimate limit to residence under a combination of Article 21 and Directive 2004/38 is that the TCN parent must be able to fulfil the conditions of Article 7 of Directive 2004/38 in all cases.[107] If this is not possible because the parent cannot prove sufficient resources and comprehensive sickness insurance, then in extreme cases a right to reside could be based on Article 20 TFEU, but that would only be the case if the Union child had to leave the territory of the EU altogether because of the impossibility of granting a residence right to their TCN parent.[108]

A case which highlighted the tension of economic and social considerations behind the attribution of rights to TCN parents of Union children was *Bajratari*.[109] In that case, the children's sufficiency of resources was based on income obtained from unlawful employment, as the parents had lost their residence permit. The Court had to engage with how to achieve the balance between the social and economic objectives pursued by Directive 2004/38 – more specifically, the objective of strengthening the rights of Union citizens to move and reside freely in the Member States and promoting social cohesion on the one hand, while protecting the public finances of the Member State on the other.[110] In his Opinion,

105 Case C-200/02, *Zhu and Chen*, ECLI:EU:C:2004:639; Case C-34/09, *Ruiz Zambrano*, ECLI:EU:C:2011:124; Case C-165/14, *Rendón Marín*, ECLI:EU:C:2016:675 in purely internal situations. Case C-304/14, *CS*, ECLI:EU:C:2016:674; Case C-133/15, *Chavez-Vilchez and others*, ECLI:EU:C:2017:354; Case C-82/16, *KA and Others*, ECLI:EU:C:2018:308.

106 C-86/12, *Alokpa and Moudoulou*, ECLI:EU:C:2013:645.

107 C-86/12, *Alokpa and Moudoulou*, para 31.

108 Ibid, para 32; Case C-87/12, *Ymeraga and Ymeraga-Tafarshiku*, ECLI:EU:C:2013:291, para 36.

109 Case C-93/18, *Bajratari*, ECLI:EU:C:2019:809.

110 Opinion of AG Szpunar in C-93/18, *Bajratari*, ECLI:EU:C:2019:512, paras 36–47.

AG Szpunar elaborated on the reason why the sufficiency of resources was evaluated with regard to the parent rather than the child in line with the case-law in *Chen* and *Zambrano* and noted that 'if they were adults, such children would have not only Union citizenship, which is destined to be the fundamental status of nationals of the Member States, but also the status of worker'.[111] In this Opinion, issued in 2019, nearly thirty years after the establishment of EU citizenship, this excerpt is a stark reminder of what links EU migrants to the EU legal order. It could be argued that reference to the worker status is made in support of the fact that as an adult, an EU national would have the opportunity to exercise their rights by fulfilling the conditions of Article 7 Directive 2004/38. But this is certainly not the case, as those conditions could be fulfilled by an adult as a worker, a self-employed, a student, or a self-sufficient person. What the aforementioned quote emphasizes is that the rupture of the link between the EU migrant and their state of origin, and, relatedly, the basis of claims made against that host state is to a large extent due to financial solidarity owed by Member States to EU migrants based on their economic contribution.

The Court followed the AG Opinion and explained the way the balancing took place by implying that such an evaluation was the lesser of two evils. Specifically, the Court recalled that the resources available to EU children would always be evaluated with reference to the income of their parents. However, when the parent is in a precarious situation due to unlawful residence, the risk of losing the sufficient resources required and of the Union child becoming a burden on the social assistance system would be greater.[112] While on first reading, the exclusion of income from unlawful employment could achieve the objective of protecting public finances, this objective is already ensured by the safeguards provided in Article 14 Directive 2004/38, which allows Member States to check if the conditions of the Directive are fulfilled throughout the period of residence.[113] In light of this, introducing a condition regarding the lawfulness of income of the parent was found to constitute a disproportionate interference, which went beyond what is necessary to achieve the objective pursued.[114]

[111] Ibid, para 83, reference omitted.
[112] C-93/18, *Bajratari*, para 37.
[113] Ibid, paras 38–41.
[114] Ibid, para 42.

The more protective approach of the Court regarding children has been linked in scholarship with the fortification of the status of EU citizenship or with a recognition of children as actors in their own right and not as appendices to economic actors.[115] I would argue that while the latter might be true, the derivative rights of parents of EU children should not be understood as transforming the basis of free movement rights and disentangling them from effective market contribution. Similar arguments have failed with regard to the claims of EU nationals who have never left their state of origin and their partners. Already since *McCarthy* and *Dereci*, the Court insisted on the necessity of movement meeting the conditions of Directive 2004/38 to be able to claim family reunification rights under EU law.[116] Arguments on the dependency of adult EU nationals to a TCN as a basis for claiming the more protective treatment of EU law have not succeeded. Instead, the Court has insisted that a relationship of dependency – one that would be so strong to create a right of residence under Article 20 TFEU and the effective enjoyment of rights test – would be conceivable only in exceptional cases where there could be no form of separation imaginable between the EU national and the member of their family on which they were dependent.[117] Emotional ties would not be enough. The differentiation should thus be understood in line with the greater vulnerability of children whose interests fall to be protected by societies at large in line with the need to promote the social objectives of the EU. The consistent invocation of Article 24 CFR in the relevant case-law would support that.

8.2.5 *Consolidation of Balancing and No More Attempts to Tip the Scale*

Different scholars have commented with great disappointment the different judicial evolutions of this period which point to the continued economic basis of the rights EU migrants enjoy from EU law.[118]

[115] Clare McGlynn, *Families and the European Union Law, Politics and Pluralism* (Cambridge University Press 2006).

[116] Case C-434/09, *McCarthy*, ECLI:EU:C:2011:277; Case C-256/11, *Dereci and others*, ECLI:EU:C:2011:734.

[117] Case C-836/18, *Subdelegación del Gobierno en Ciudad Real v RH*, ECLI:EU:C:2020:119, para 56; C 82/16, *K.A. and Others*, EU:C:2018:308, para 65.

[118] Moritz Jesse and Daniel Carter, 'The "Market Insider": Market-Citizenship and Economic Exclusion in the EU' in Moritz Jesse (ed), *European Societies, Migration, and the Law: The 'Others' amongst 'Us'* (Cambridge University Press 2020); Dimitry

Ultimately, the economic limitations set to the exercise of EU migrants' rights under secondary law, and the hesitation of the Court to review them for compliance with primary law proves the strong economic basis of EU free movement rights. At the same time, if we look at this evolution having in mind both how the EU legal order created rights for migrants and that economic and social objectives sit at the core of this legal order, a more nuanced explanation could arise. This explanation would have as a starting point the impossibility of maintaining economic growth and social progress, by the creation of unlimited residence rights and corresponding social rights for all EU migrants. If the EU legal order is to deliver on the parallel pursuit of economic and social objectives, then the balance could not be tipped in favour of unlimited social rights for EU migrants. In other words, sustainability under EU law demands the economic and social sustainability of EU migrants' rights.

During this period, the legislative evolution by the adoption of Directive 2004/38 showed the intention to create residence rights for all EU migrants in light of the ever-closer Union of peoples. However, such rights meet an ultimate limit of self-sufficiency. It is accepted that EU migrants should be able to enjoy rights, even if they are not net contributors to the host state. Nevertheless, this does not mean that rights could be created for those that negatively impact the public finances of the Member States. In parallel, social cohesion within the Member States is promoted by the creation of a permanent status that disconnects the attribution of social rights from economic considerations. Next to this broader scope of migrants enjoying EU law rights, those who actively contribute by their economic activity are still privileged in the rights granted by EU law. In this set-up, the due consideration of a parallel pursuit of economic and social objectives, as well as the related attribution and limitation of social rights to EU migrants, frame the free movement framework as a sustainable migration framework.

Kochenov, 'The Oxymoron of "Market Citizenship" and the Future of the Union' in Dimitry Kochenov and others (eds), *The Internal Market and the Future of European Integration: Essays in Honour of Laurence W. Gormley* (Cambridge University Press 2019); Niamh Nic Shuibhne, 'The Resilience of EU Market Citizenship' (2010) 47 CMLRev 1597; Síofra O'Leary and Sara Iglesias Sánchez, 'Free Movement of Persons and Services' in Paul Craig and Gráinne de Búrca (eds), *The Evolution of EU Law* (Oxford University Press 2021); Sybe Alexander de Vries and others (eds), *EU Citizens' Economic Rights in Action: Re-thinking Legal and Factual Barriers in the Internal Market* (Edward Elgar 2018).

Regarding the case-law, during this period, the Court deferred to the legislature. It acknowledged the balancing of economic and social objectives as they were transposed in secondary law, and no longer invoked primary law to alter this balancing. The Court continues to emphasize the special citizen status when it comes to cases related to Union children, recognizing a particular vulnerability. But it does so when the attribution of rights does not come with extra costs for the host state. To do otherwise under the current consolidation of balancing behind secondary law would be unsustainable. Having concluded the historical investigation of EU migrants' rights, Chapter 9 will look at how economic and social considerations eventually shaped the regulation of migration from third countries.

9

Economic Objectives and Social Demands behind an Incoherent System of Regulation for TCNs

9.1 The Failure of the System of Admission to Promote Economic Objectives

Following the Tampere Council and the unfulfilled promise of regulating migration for TCNs, The Hague Programme set the political guidelines at the beginning of the period under review.[1] Acknowledging the importance of legal migration for the economic development of the EU, the Council invited the Commission to develop a framework on the regulation of legal migration with due regard to demands for migrant labour by 2005, while noting that the determination of volumes of admission was a competence of Member States.[2] In response, the Commission issued a plan on the legislative initiatives that could be adopted to meet the competitiveness goals of the Lisbon strategy.[3] In this policy plan, the Commission pointed to the advantages of a horizontal admission framework for the last time.

Without support by the Member States and after the failed efforts to regulate migration presented in Chapter 6, the Commission suggested the adoption of one horizontal instrument and different sectoral Directives in order to grant labour migrants a minimum set of rights, while at the same time attracting specific categories of migrant workers crucial for the development of the EU economy.[4] The sectoral approach in the regulation of admission was the only viable option to overcome Member States' reservations and align migration law with the economic objectives of the EU.[5] The analysis in this section highlights how economic objectives lie behind the differentiation of rights TCNs enjoy

[1] Council of the European Union, The Hague Programme: strengthening freedom, security and justice in the European Union [2005] OJ C 53/1.

[2] Ibid, Section 1.4.

[3] Communication, Policy Plan on Legal Migration, COM(2005)0669 final, Section 1.2.

[4] Ibid, Section 2.

[5] Communication, Towards a Common Immigration Policy, COM(2007)0780 final 4, 7–8.

under the instruments, before engaging with how economic fears significantly dilute social rights and the effectiveness of these instruments in Section 9.2. Section 9.3 demonstrates the way in which the rights of TCN migrants are reconstructed in the case-law through a strong emphasis of the Court on the Charter. Finally, Section 9.4 points out to the incoherence of the system of fundamental rights protection for EU and TCN migrants.

During this period, the regulation of migration took shape in the following way. Admission takes shape under a sectoral regime which provides entry and residence to specific categories of TCNs: researchers and students, intra-corporate transferees, highly skilled workers, and seasonal workers.[6] These sectoral instruments provide for specific rights attached to each category of migrants. The admission of researchers was first regulated in a Directive adopted in 2005, which was recast.[7] Currently the admission of researchers and students is regulated in a single instrument, the Researchers and Students Directive. This recasting and unification did not alter the economic and social considerations behind their admission. Further, the admission of highly skilled workers is regulated in the Blue Card Directive adopted in 2009, which was amended in 2021. In the analysis that follows, all these instruments – that is, both the 2005 and the 2016 Directives on researchers and the two Blue Card Directives – are taken into account. The changes they introduced and potential shifts in the way economic and social considerations appear therein are commented when necessary.

[6] Directive (EU) 2016/801 on the conditions of entry and residence of third-country nationals for the purposes of research, studies, training, voluntary service, pupil exchange schemes or educational projects, and au pairing (recast) [2016] OJ L 132/21; Directive 2014/66/EU on the conditions of entry and residence of third-country nationals in the framework of an intra-corporate transfer [2014] OJ L 157/1; Directive 2009/50/EC on the conditions of entry and residence of third-country nationals for the purposes of highly qualified employment [2009] OJ L 155/ 17 (Blue Card Directive 2009) and Directive (EU) 2021/1883 on the conditions of entry and residence of third-country nationals for the purpose of highly qualified employment, and repealing Directive 2009/50/EC [2021] OJ L 382/1 (Blue Card Directive 2021); Directive 2014/36/EU on the conditions of entry and stay of third-country nationals for the purpose of employment as seasonal workers [2014] OJ L 94/375.

[7] Before Directive 2016/801, the admission of researchers was regulated under Directive 2005/71/EC on a specific procedure for admitting third-country nationals for the purposes of scientific research [2005] OJ L 289/15 and of students under Directive 2004/114/EC on the conditions of admission of third-country nationals for the purposes of studies, pupil exchange, unremunerated training or voluntary service [2004] OJ L 375/12.

In parallel, the Single Permit Directive and the Family Reunification Directive regulate horizontally the rights of all migrants legally resident in the EU regardless of whether they enjoy residence rights under national or EU law.[8] It should be noted that the Single Permit Directive underwent a revision in March 2024.[9] The analysis below refers to the currently applicable Single Permit Directive and explicit note is made for changes introduced for the first time in the 2024 recast version.

Finally, the Long-term Residents Directive extends the protection and the rights afforded to migrants due to their long presence and integration in the Member States.[10] Through a horizontal examination of the conditions for entry and the rights the instruments establish, the economic and social objectives behind the current form of regulation of migration from third countries becomes clear.

All the sectoral Directives that regulate admission have been put in place to contribute to the economic objectives of the EU. The harmonization of admission aimed at ensuring that the necessary human capital would be available to drive the desired growth.[11] This becomes clear if we look at the recitals of the different Directives, all of which are aligned with the economic targets set by EU during the years they were adopted.[12] At the same time, national contestation and fear about the effects of the attribution of rights to national economies have limited both the extent of rights TCNs are entitled to under the different

[8] Directive 2011/98/EU on a single application procedure for a single permit for third-country nationals to reside and work in the territory of a Member State and on a common set of rights for third-country workers legally residing in a Member State [2011] OJ L 343/1 and Directive 2003/86/EC of 22 September 2003 on the right to family reunification [2003] OJ L 251/12.

[9] Final Compromise text, Directive (EU) 2024/ . . . of the European Parliament and of the Council of . . . on a single application procedure for a single permit for third-country nationals to reside and work in the territory of a Member State and on a common set of rights for third-country workers legally residing in a Member State (recast), A9-0140/117.

[10] Directive 2003/109/EC of 25 November 2003 concerning the status of third-country nationals who are long-term residents [2003] OJ L 16/ 44.

[11] European Council, The Stockholm programme, An Open and Secure Europe Serving and Protecting Citizens [2010] OJ C 115/1. See Researchers and Students Directive, Recital 3; Intra-Corporate Transfers Directive, Recital 4; Blue Card Directive 2021, Recital 1; Seasonal Workers Directive, Recital 6.

[12] Researchers Directive, Recital 2; Blue Card Directive 2009, Recital 3 mentioning the Lisbon European Council objective of making the Community the most competitive and dynamic knowledge-based economy in the world by 2010; Seasonal Workers Directive, Recital 4 and Researchers and Students Directive, Recital 3; Intra-Corporate Transfers Directive, Recital 3; Blue Card Directive 2021, Recital 1 on the Europe 2020 strategy for Smart, sustainable and inclusive growth.

instruments and the instruments' contribution to achieving the economic objectives of the EU.[13]

In any case, considering this shared objective, the instruments present crucial similarities. As a rule, admission is based on the fulfilment of certain conditions and the absence of grounds for limitation of admission (negative conditions).[14] Provided that an applicant meets the conditions of admission, migrants are entitled to a residence permit for a period of time, the minimum and maximum duration of which are defined in the relevant Directives as per Table 9.1.

Looking more closely into the Directives, we find many similarities on the substantive conditions that need to be met for entry to the EU to ensure the admission of individuals who will actively contribute to EU growth, while minimizing the potential economic risks, thus aligning migration to economic sustainability. Such similarities are framed differently in the relevant texts, due to their sectoral nature.[15] Despite the different framing, all the Directives require sufficient resources on the part of the TCN who applies for admission and an appropriate health insurance. At the same time, the legislative texts emphasize the need to ensure that in all cases the migrant does not become a burden on the social security system of Member States.[16] In the case of highly skilled workers, sufficient resources are proven by the contract the applicants need to provide and by the requirement that their employment meets a certain salary threshold.[17] When it comes to researchers, the Directives specify that the applicants need to have sufficient means of subsistence.[18]

[13] Cf Kees Groenendijk, 'Equal Treatment of Workers from Third Countries: The Added Value of the Single Permit Directive' (2015) 16 ERA Forum 547; Jean-Baptiste Farcy, 'Labour Immigration Policy in the European Union: How to Overcome the Tension between Further Europeanisation and the Protection of National Interests?' (2020) 22 European Journal of Migration and Law 198.

[14] Case C-544/15, *Fahimian*, ECLI:EU:C:2017:255.

[15] Commission Staff Working Document, Executive Summary of the Fitness Check on EU Legislation on legal migration SWD(2019)1055 PART 2/2, Annex 5, 52.

[16] Ibid.

[17] Proposal for a Directive on the conditions of entry and residence of third-country nationals for the purposes of highly qualified employment, COM(2007)0637 final, Explanatory Memorandum, Article 5; Proposal for a Directive on the conditions of entry and residence of third-country nationals for the purposes of highly skilled employment, COM(2016)0378 final, Explanatory Memorandum, Article 5.

[18] Explicit requirement on sufficient means in Researchers Directive 6(2)(b) and Researchers and Students Directive 7(1)(e) which can be provided either in the form of employment by the research institution or through any other grant, while for students this entails proving sufficiency of resources, Seasonal Workers Directive 5(3) and 6(3).

Table 9.1 *Security of residence*

	Length of permit	Potential renewal
Researchers Directive	Minimum one year unless the research project is planned for less	Renewable under conditions
Researchers and Students Directive	Minimum one year unless the research project is planned for less Minimum two years for researchers covered by EU or multilateral programmes, including mobility measures Maximum one year for au pairs Maximum six months for trainees unless the duration of the agreement is longer	Renewable under conditions for researchers and trainees Renewable for maximum six months at justified request for au pairs
2009 Blue Card Directive	Minimum one and maximum four years. If the contract is for less than one year, then for the duration of the contract plus three months	Renewable under conditions
2021 Blue Card Directive	Minimum two years; if the contract is for less, then for that period plus three months	Renewable under the conditions
Seasonal Workers Directive	Five to nine months in any twelve-month period	Extension for a maximum period of nine months in total Facilitation of re-entry for seasonal workers admitted at least once in the past five years and who have respected the conditions of the Directive

As for seasonal workers, the work agreement required for admission has to specify remuneration. The need to do so in this case also serves social objectives in parallel to the economic ends served by the seasonal workers' admission. The specification of remuneration was deemed vital to avoid unfair advantages for the employer and, relatedly, exploitation of workers.[19] All the Directives also require a proof of address. However, when admission relates to migrant groups that are considered more vulnerable to exploitation, the requirement of proof of address turns into a requirement of adequate accommodation that meets specific characteristics, as is the case for seasonal workers, au pairs, and trainees.[20] Behind the requirement of adequate accommodation lies the consideration that these migrant groups are more vulnerable to exploitation, and the requirement indirectly enshrines social objectives in the regulation of admission. As can be seen in Table 9.2, admission conditions are essentially framed so as to ensure that migrant admission will not pose the slightest risk to economic growth, and that relatedly migration will be economically sustainable.

The grounds for refusal, withdrawal, and non-renewal of permits are also to a large extent unified as Table 9.3 shows. In all the Directives, the central ground for rejection or non-renewal is repeated as almost self-evident – that is, the failure to fulfil the criteria of admission. In addition, we find grounds that exist as negative conditions for admission: the inexistence of fraud in the application process, and the requirement that the applicant should not be a threat to public policy, public security, and public health. The Directives also contain limitations linked to the fight against irregular migration. Such limitations appear either related to the nature of the employer (to what extent economic activity effectively takes place or whether an employer is set up for the purpose of facilitating entry) or to the risk of overstaying one's initial permit (found in the Seasonal Workers Directive). Essentially, most of the grounds of refusal, withdrawal, or non-renewal are connected to public order considerations.

However, social objectives also condition certain of these grounds for rejection or non-renewal, to ensure that migration will be aligned with some minimum social guarantees for the migrants. Specifically, all the relevant Directives contain clauses allowing rejection or non-renewal due to failure of the employer to meet their labour law obligations.[21] Social considerations in relation to the external world also appear in the Blue

[19] Proposal for a Directive on the conditions of entry and residence of third-country nationals for the purposes of seasonal employment, COM(2010)379, Explanatory Memorandum, Article 5.

[20] Fitness Check (n 15), Annex 5, 52; Seasonal Workers Directive, Recital 41.

[21] These clauses were not included in the initial Researchers Directive and Blue Card Directive 2009, but after revision they now appear in all the relevant texts.

Table 9.2 *Admission conditions*

	Employment	Sufficient resources not to have recourse to social assistance	Sickness insurance	Accommodation
Researchers Directive	Hosting agreement by research institution	Condition for signing the hosting agreement	✓	
Researchers and Students Directive	Hosting agreement by research institution, trainee agreement or agreement with the host family for au pairs	Possibility to request that the host entity takes responsibility for subsistence for researchers, students, and trainees, and possibility to set a minimum sum of pocket money to be paid for au pairs	✓	Possibility to request that the host entity take responsibility for accommodation
2009 Blue Card Directive	Contract/offer of at least one year	Specific salary threshold	✓	Possibility to require address
2021 Blue Card Directive	Contract/offer for at least six months	Specific salary threshold	✓	Possibility to require address
Seasonal Workers Directive	Contract/offer	✓	✓	Requirement of adequate accommodation

Table 9.3 *Grounds for refusal, withdrawal, and non-renewal*

	Fraud	Public policy	Employer obligations	Illegal migration	Volumes of admission	Union preference
Researchers Directive	✓	✓				
Researchers and Students Directive	✓	✓	✓	✓	✓	✓
2009 Blue Card Directive	✓	✓		✓	✓	✓
2021 Blue Card Directive	✓	✓	✓	✓	✓	✓
Seasonal Workers Directive	✓	✓	✓	✓	✓	✓

Card Directives, both of which include a clause on ethical recruitment. Under this clause, Member States have the possibility to reject an application for Blue Card where professionals come from developing countries in sectors suffering from a lack of personnel and they stem from the EU commitment to tackle – or at least to not contribute to – the shortage of healthcare workers and the education sector in developing countries.[22] While similar considerations were mentioned in the recitals of the Directives on researchers, they were not incorporated in the legal provisions.[23] Additionally, only the Blue Card Directive includes provisions related to the right of Member States to withdrawal or non-renewal of a permit where the worker has no resources, and needs recourse to the social assistance system for subsistence. This is connected to the fact that Blue Card holders are the only migrants entitled to unemployment benefit during their stay. This more privileged treatment is related to the greater demand for highly skilled workers. As will be discussed later in relation to the differentiated rights enjoyed by TCN migrants, in the current system of regulation, the demand for migrants (rather than their contribution) becomes the reason for attribution of more extensive rights.

The Directives further contain provisions which allow withdrawal or non-renewal of a residence permit where the TCN was admitted for purposes other than those for which their admission was authorized. Looking at the legislative history of the Researchers and Students Directive, we see that the Council insisted on the introduction of this clause. This was, in turn, subject to reservation by both the Commission and the Parliament. In the end, the clause was inserted in the Directive, and was accompanied by a common statement of the Commission and the Parliament, in which these institutions tried to qualify the provision and emphasized that it should not constitute a precedent for the future legal migration instruments.[24] The timing of the revision seems too close to the *Ben Alaya* case to be coincidental.[25] *Ben Alaya* concerned the admission of students under the Students Directive. The German

[22] Blue Card Directive 2009, Recital 22; Blue Card Directive 2021, Recital 41.

[23] Researchers Directive, Recital 6; Researchers and Students Directive, Recital 13.

[24] Communication from the Commission to the Parliament pursuant to Article 294(6) TFEU concerning the Position of the Council on the adoption of a Directive on the conditions of entry and residence of third-country nationals for the purposes of research, studies, training, voluntary service, pupil exchange schemes or educational projects and au pairing, COM(2016)0184 final.

[25] Case C-491/13, *Ben Alaya*, ECLI:EU:C:2014:2187.

government rejected the applicant's application for admission because it entertained doubts as to whether he was truly motivated to study in Germany. Upon referral of the case to the Court, it held that Member States were not allowed to introduce more conditions than those stated in the Directive, as such action would be contrary to its objective to promote mobility of TCNs.[26] Contrary to the suggestion of AG Mengozzi, who made reference to the possibility of rejecting an application for entry if there was precise and specific evidence that pointed to abuse or misuse of the Directive, the Court affirmed the right to entry created in the relevant Directive.[27] In light of this case, which affirmed that the Students Directive created a right of residence for TCNs, it is not hard to imagine the motivation of the Council to incorporate clauses which would allow broader discretion for the Member States.

Economic considerations also appear as a blanket ground to limit entry. In general, the right to entry of TCN migrants is without prejudice to the right of Member States to regulate the volumes of admission of TCNs under Article 79(5) TFEU. This right was given expression via specific clauses in all the relevant Directives. Essentially, Member States can refuse admission, even if a migrant meets all requirements, to protect their labour markets. The legal fitness check on secondary law on migration, conducted by the Commission in 2019, questioned the open framing of the provisions transposing Article 79(5) TFEU in the Directives and enquired whether admission quotas could be fixed at zero level and, thus, undermine the *effet utile* of the *acquis*.[28] What is more, the relevant framework is shaped under the umbrella principle of Union preference. This principle formed part of the previous attempts of the Commission to horizontally regulate entry and residence of TCNs and was articulated in a 1994 Council Resolution.[29] This principle suggests that TCNs may enter the EU labour market provided that a post cannot be filled by a worker who is already part of the labour market. This so-called labour market test, guided by the Union preference principle, means that Member States maintain discretion to reject admission where a vacancy can be filled by an EU national, a TCN legally resident in a Member State and already part of its labour market, or a long-term

[26] Ibid, para 27.

[27] Opinion of AG Mengozzi in C-491/13, *Ben Alaya*, ECLI:EU:C:2014:1933.

[28] Fitness Check (n 15), Annex 5.

[29] Council Resolution of 20 June 1994 on limitation on admission of third-country nationals to the territory of the Member States for employment [1996] OJ C 274/31.

resident in any Member State. In the 2001 Proposal, the Commission suggested a system to operationalize it and prove the fulfilment of the labour market test by Member States.[30] In the current framework, even though the test is included as a reason to reject an application for admission, there is no procedure to be followed for it.

It is important to note here that the labour market test was not included in the first Researchers Directive. This can be explained by the economic need for researchers at the time when the Directive was proposed and adopted. Specifically, in the 2004 proposal, there was particular emphasis on the number of researchers needed by the EU to reach the Barcelona growth target in research activities.[31] Acknowledging that it was impossible to meet this target without external recruitment of TCNs, the Commission emphasized that researcher admission could not be subject to the discretion of Member States to control numbers of admission.[32] However, the possibility of subjecting the recruitment to Union preference came back in the recast Directive, adopted in 2016. The proposal for the recast does not elaborate on why these new grounds were added. Instead, the explanatory memorandum mentions that these were standard conditions under the existing migration Directives.[33] This, connected to the fact that the current Directive includes this test as a ground for non-renewal but excludes researchers from its ambit, must mean that the alignment came on a technical level, but the differentiation as to the treatment of researchers should persist.

Overall, looking at the criteria for admission, the following observations can be made. The Commission's ambition to put in place a harmonized system of admission was clearly tied to the need to promote the economic objectives of the EU and to align the regulation of migration

30 Proposal for a Directive on the conditions of entry and residence of third-country nationals for the purpose of paid employment and self-employed economic activities, COM(2001)0386 final [2001] OJ C 332E/248.

31 Proposal for a Directive and two Proposals for Recommendations on the admission of third-country nationals to carry out scientific research in the European Community, COM(2004)0178, Section 1.3.

32 Ibid, Explanatory Memorandum, Section 1.5. See also Council Recommendation of 12 October 2005 to facilitate the admission of third-country nationals to carry out scientific research in the European Community [2005] OJ L 289/26, point 1.b. calling on Member States to refrain from using quotas for this type of admission.

33 Proposal for a Directive on the conditions of entry and residence of third-country nationals for the purposes of research, studies, pupil exchange, remunerated and unremunerated training, voluntary service and au pairing [recast], COM(2013)0151 final, Explanatory Memorandum, Articles 18–20.

with economic sustainability. At the same time, the way national fears on the economic repercussions of migration appear in both primary and secondary law set the system up for failure. Specifically, some of the conditions of admission included in the Directives can significantly limit the right to entry created in secondary law.[34] Such limitations can prove detrimental to the very objective served by the regulation of migration, which is to ensure the economic sustainability of the EU. Among the different conditions that appear in the Directives, the discretion of Member States under their right to regulate the volumes of admission is the most problematic. The inclusion of this requirement in primary law shows the limits of Member States' understanding of the role of migration for the EU collective project. But next to that, the fact that the Directives do not introduce a system of review by the EU institutions means that Member States can apply this right in very diverse ways and limit the effectiveness of EU law. Having explained how economic objectives, economic fears, and certain social demands are reflected in secondary law, Section 9.2 examines the differentiated protection introduced by the Directives for migrant workers depending on how essential they are deemed to be for the EU project of growth.

9.2 Differentiated Rights and Privileged Statuses

Under EU migration law as it stands today, TCNs enjoy different rights depending on how much their contribution is needed to the EU development project. On a basic level, the Single Permit Directive lays down a minimum core of rights for all migrants, resident in EU territory, regardless of from where they draw their right to reside, whether national or EU law.[35] The Single Permit Directive is primarily aligned with the social objectives of the EU, as it aims to guarantee fair treatment to all migrants at EU level. Of course, as has been emphasized throughout this historical investigation, the social objectives of the EU are closely connected with the economic ones, and, relatedly, the economic and social pillars of sustainability expressed in the primary objectives are pursued in parallel in the regulation of migration. In this regard, a closer look at the history and the recitals of the Single Permit Directive reveals that the attribution of rights is also related to economic objectives connected both to the

[34] C-491/13, *Ben Alaya*; Case C-578/08, *Chakroun*, ECLI:EU:C:2010:117. See also Opinion of AG Szpunar in C-544/15, *Fahimian*, ECLI:EU:C:2016:908, para 42.

[35] Article 3(2), Single Permit Directive on those excluded from its scope.

economic contribution of TCNs but also to the avoidance of social dumping.[36]

In general, in the attribution of rights to TCN migrants, we see the reproduction of the considerations of the EU institutions and the Court behind the rights of EU migrants at the initial stages of the Community project. The first such consideration is that TCNs equally contribute through their work to the EU and, therefore, they should enjoy a set of rights. Secondly, granting equal rights throughout EU territory ensures that there is no unfair competition between the Member States, but also between TCN and EU migrants, thus avoiding social dumping and migrant exploitation.[37] In reproducing such considerations, the Single Permit Directive constitutes yet another attempt to align migration with the economic and social objectives of the EU, as well as with economic and social sustainability.[38] In parallel, each sectoral Directive includes more specific provisions and grants rights of different kind and extent to TCN workers.

The analysis in Sections 9.2.1–9.2.3 maps the rights TCN workers enjoy under all these instruments. Section 9.2.1 engages with the extension of rights for categories of migrants deemed crucial for the EU economy. Subsequently, Section 9.2.2 shows the dilution of equal treatment in secondary law through the introduction of fragmented provisions and various limitations. Finally, Section 9.2.3 investigates how equal treatment was erased from the cooperation of the EU with third countries during this period. The examination reveals the problematic way in which economic objectives served by specific types of migrant admission shape the differentiation of migrants' rights.

9.2.1 Attribution of Rights in Order to Maximize Economic Benefits

The rights of TCN migrants are defined horizontally in the Single Permit Directive and are differentiated based on the function of different

[36] Single Permit Directive, Recital 19.

[37] See Proposal for a Directive on a single application procedure for a single permit for third-country nationals to reside and work in the territory of a Member State and on a common set of rights for third-country workers legally residing in a Member State, COM (2007)638 final 3 and 7; Case C-302/19, *INPS*, ECLI:EU:C:2020:957, para 34.

[38] The recast is further aligned with the social objectives; see European Parliament legislative resolution of 13 March 2024 on the proposal for a Recast Single Permit Directive (COM(2022)0655 – C9-0163/2022 – 2022/0131(COD)), points 2, 6.

categories of migrants for the EU economy. Specifically, all migrants enjoy the right to enter, stay, and move within the territory of the host state, and to exercise the activity for which their stay was authorized under the Single Permit Directive. Researchers are also allowed to teach next to their scientific work, while highly skilled workers are the only category of people who enjoy access to any type of employment after some time of legal residence. On the other side of the rights spectrum, seasonal workers are restricted to the exercise of a specific activity. However, to protect them from exploitation, the Directive recognizes their right to change employer within the specific field of activity in line with social considerations. The recast Single Permit Directive also creates a right to change employer under specific conditions, thereby enhancing the rights of all migrants legally resident in the Member States.[39]

Section 9.1 showed that security of residence is dependent upon the Directive from which TCN migrants draw residence rights. In most cases, security of residence is attached to a job contract and can be provided for a period of minimum and maximum time provided in the Directives. Until the recent revision of the Single Permit Directive, only highly skilled workers had a right to reside to find work. Specifically, student and researchers can enjoy residence as jobseekers for a limited period, and the reason behind this was to allow Member States to tap into the employment potential of the already trained and qualified workforce.[40] A similar right to reside beyond the specific employment exists for highly skilled workers, who have the possibility of being unemployed for a period of time without risking the validity of their residence permit. After the revision of the Single Permit Directive, all legally resident migrants should enjoy such a right for a different time period dependent on the duration of their permit.[41]

All TCNs legally resident in any Member State are also allowed to move within the EU territory for up to 90 days in any 180-day period. This movement refers to short-term mobility; it is based on Schengen, and it does not relate to the exercise of economic activity.[42] Free movement for the purpose of economic activity is provided only to specific categories of migrants. Specifically, the Researchers and Students

[39] Article 11(2), 2024 Single Permit Directive.

[40] Students and Researchers Directive, Recital 53.

[41] Article 11(4), 2024 Single Permit Directive.

[42] Regulation 2016/399 on a Union Code on the rules governing the movement of persons across borders (Schengen Borders Code) [2016] OJ L 77/1.

Directive provides for temporary mobility to allow migrants to carry out their work in another Member State. Further, the Blue Card Directives and the Student and Researchers Directive allow for long-term mobility – that is, the possibility to move permanently to another Member State and take up work there.[43] It is purely economic objectives that dictate the free movement rights of highly skilled workers and researchers based on the necessity of making the EU internationally competitive for such migrants and improving labour market efficiency.[44] The mobility of researchers and highly skilled workers also creates free movement rights for their family members. Specifically, for migrants falling under the scope of the Researchers and Students Directive, the Blue Card Directive and the Long-term Residents Directive, family members enjoy intra-EU mobility rights in order to be able to follow their sponsor in case of move.

Notably, economic needs served by the admission of researchers and highly skilled workers are the reason behind the introduction of derogations from the Family Reunification Directive. Specifically, the Blue Card Directives and Researchers and Students Directive include more favourable provisions on family reunification for the categories of migrants falling within their scope. These more favourable provisions, which cover not only the conditions of family reunification but also the rights enjoyed by family members, are linked to the need to make the EU more attractive as a destination to these particular migrants.[45] Indicatively, access to employment is easier for family members of highly skilled workers and researchers. The analysis in Section 6.2.1 showed that access of family members to employment can be limited to ensure that their migration does not become an economic liability for Member States in times of recession.[46] This limitation does not apply to Blue Card holders and researchers. The Blue Card Directive includes a derogation from such limitation and demands the direct access of family members to

[43] This is of course aside from long-term residents, whose mobility rights were discussed in Section 6.2.2.

[44] Proposal for Researchers Directive, COM(2004)178 final, Explanatory Memorandum, Article 13. See also Blue Card Directive 2021, Recital 53; Blue Card Directive 2009, Recital 15.

[45] See Researchers Directive, Recital 18; Council Recommendation of 12 October 2005 [2005] OJ L 289/26, Recital 9 and point 3; Researchers and Students Directive, Recital 11; Blue Card Directive 2009, Recital 23; Blue Card Directive 2021, Recital 50; Intra-Corporate Transfers Directive, Recital 40.

[46] See Article 14, Family Reunification Directive.

employment.[47] The Researchers and Students Directive on the other hand provides that access of family members to employment should not be limited, unless exceptional circumstances exist, such as particularly high levels of unemployment.[48] Overall, in derogating from the minimum standards of the Family Reunification Directive and introducing more relaxed conditions for reunification and more extensive rights for the specific groups of migrants, the objective is no longer ensuring migration in dignity for the worker. Rather, family reunification is used instrumentally as a means to attract migration of specific kind.

In addition to this, the Blue Card Directive is the only instrument that derogates from the Long-term Residents Directive by granting preferential conditions for access to the long-term resident status. Specifically, the 2009 Directive provided that the Blue Card holder and their family members could accumulate periods of residence in different Member States in order to fulfil the five-year duration requirement.[49] It also provided that the long-term resident status would not be lost in case of absence of the highly skilled worker from EU territory for a period of twelve to eighteen months, which could be extended to twenty-four months if Member States preferred.[50] Economic considerations behind this differentiated access of Blue Card holders to the long-term resident status appear in the following way. The EU needs highly qualified personnel to maintain growth, so it is shaping a framework where such highly qualified personnel get easier access to a set of rights, in order to make the EU an attractive destination for these workers.[51] This is fully understandable in terms of marketing the EU as an attractive destination for specific migrants; however, it is highly questionable from the perspective of non-discrimination in the adoption and implementation of EU law. Despite the Commission's recent suggestion to allow all migrants to accumulate periods of residence in different Member States in order to acquire the long-term residence status, the Council's position was that such accumulation could only extend to all highly skilled workers in general.[52]

[47] Article 15(6), Blue Card Directive 2009; Article 17(6), Blue Card Directive 2021.

[48] Article 26(6), Researchers and Students Directive.

[49] Article 16(2), Blue Card Directive 2009; Article 18, Blue Card Directive 2021.

[50] Article 16(4), Blue Card Directive 2009.

[51] Proposal for a Blue Card Directive, COM(2007)0637 final; Blue Card Directive 2009, Recital 20; Blue Card Directive, Recitals 51 and 52.

[52] See Proposal for a Directive concerning the status of third-country nationals who are long-term residents (recast), COM(2022)650 final, Explanatory Memorandum, Article 4.

In this sense, it becomes clear that the legal system put in place attributes more rights to those who are seen as crucial for the development of the EU project. In parallel, the economic fears of Member States, their short-term approach to migration, and the possibility to attract such individuals by parallel national schemes has led to the introduction of so many conditions for the exercise of mobility rights that the economic objectives pursued fail to be achieved in practice. The requirements for cross-border movement under both the Blue Card Directive and the Researchers and Students Directive are very close to requirements for entry, thereby hampering the objectives of the instruments, which is to abolish obstacles to mobility as a means to promote growth and relatedly to align the regulation of migration to the economic sustainability of the EU. Similar problems appear in relation to the pursuit of social objectives in the instruments. As Section 9.2.2 will discuss, the instruments regulating the rights of TCN migrants offer a diluted version of equal treatment in EU law.

9.2.2 *The Dilution of Equal Treatment in Secondary Law*

Equal treatment between TCN migrants and nationals of the Member States is guaranteed in all the relevant Directives. However, unlike the broad clauses inserted in Association Agreements concluded in the 1970s and 1980s, the framework in place now provides detailed enumeration of the areas where equal treatment must be granted, as well as the acceptable limitations to these areas.[53] The force of general equal treatment clauses in EU law has shaped very extensive protection for individuals.[54] In view of this, and of the extensive interpretations of the Court on equal treatment of migrants, it should not come as a surprise that Member States tried to restrict the formulation of equal treatment in the relevant Directives. Table 9.4 shows the areas where the Directives provide for equal treatment rights, as well as the potential limitations that can be introduced to equal treatment.

Cf with Council Document, Proposal for a Directive concerning the status of third-country nationals who are long-term residents (recast) – Mandate for negotiations with the Parliament ST 16000 2023 INIT, 28 November 2023.

[53] Cf Ana Beduschi, 'An Empty Shell? The Protection of Social Rights of Third-Country Workers in the EU after the Single Permit Directive' (2015) 17 European Journal of Migration and Law 210.

[54] Elise Muir, *EU Equality Law: The First Fundamental Rights Policy of the EU* (Oxford University Press 2018).

Table 9.4 *Equal treatment*

	Single Permit Directive	Researchers Directive	Researchers and Students Directive	2009 Blue Card Directive	2021 Blue Card Directive	Seasonal Workers Directive
Working Conditions	✓	✓	✓	✓	✓	✓
Education and Vocational Training	Limitations possible	Limitations possible	Limitations possible	Limitations possible	Limitations possible	Limitations possible
Recognition of Professional Qualifications	✓	✓	✓	✓	✓	✓
Tax Benefits	Limitations possible	✓	Limitations possible			Limitations possible
Social Security	Limitations possible	✓	Limitations possible	✓	✓	Limitations possible
Access to Goods and Services	Limitations possible	✓	Limitations possible	Limitations possible	Limitations possible	✓
Freedom of Association	✓		✓	✓	✓	✓
Employment Advice Services	✓	✓	✓	✓	✓	✓

First of all, unlimited equal treatment is guaranteed regarding working conditions; however, there is a lack of coherence in the way this is framed in the relevant Directives.[55] Despite the different framing, it is safe to assume that the right applies to all legally resident migrants without differentiation, as it constitutes an expression of Article 13 CFR.[56] Equal treatment as regards recognition of professional qualifications is also provided in all the Directives.[57] In addition, all the Directives provide equal treatment as regards access to advice services afforded by employment offices.[58] This should not come as a surprise in light of the continuous emphasis in different Commission documents on training the existing workforce to correspond to new needs and on ensuring that labour needs are covered by TCNs already resident and active in the internal market.[59] Finally, all the Directives also provide for freedom of association and affiliation. The Seasonal Workers Directive makes explicit reference to the right to strike and take industrial action, including the right to negotiate and conclude collective agreements. In any case, the relevant right is a specific expression of Article 12 CFR, and as a result, it should not be differentiated between different categories of TCNs, as the right is guaranteed to everyone regardless of their nationality.[60]

As to the rest of the areas where equal treatment is required, they appear with different limitations and variations. Some can be explained due to other rights enjoyed by TCNs (whether they enjoy mobility rights or not, and what is the status under which they entered), while others are firmly based on economic considerations of averting risks from migration. Specifically, in the area of education, limitations appear in all the instruments, allowing Member States to exclude study grants from equal access to migrants.[61] What is more, Member States are given the

[55] Some Directives (Researchers and Students Directive, Blue Card Directive, Single Permit Directive) include health and safety in the workplace, whereas both versions of the Blue Card Directive also include the minimum working age, working hours, leave and holidays in the relevant provisions.

[56] Fitness Check (n 15), Annex 5, Section 2.5.

[57] Ibid, Section 1.5 suggesting the extension of the right to applicants who have not yet been authorized to enter the EU.

[58] This was not the case in Researchers Directive and Blue Card Directive 2009, but now they are all recast.

[59] Communication, European Skills Agenda for Sustainable Competitiveness, Social Fairness and Resilience, COM(2020)274 final.

[60] Fitness Check (n 15), Annex 5, Section 2.5.

[61] In the Proposal for a Blue Card Directive, COM(2007)0637 final, Explanatory Memorandum, Article 15, the Commission stated that the reason for limitation of access

possibility to set conditions of access to university and higher education.[62] In the Single Permit Directive, the text mentions appropriate language proficiency, payment of fees, or specific educational prerequisites as possible conditions, and Member States can also limit access to education if it is not linked to the specific employment activity of the TCN.[63] A similar possibility on limiting equal treatment regarding access to education or training directly linked to the employment activity also exists in the Seasonal Workers Directive.[64] Finally, the Single Permit Directive provides for the possibility to limit the application of equal access to education to TCNs who are employed, or are registered as unemployed, and to exclude students.[65] In the area of education, the Fitness Check conducted in 2019 by the Commission suggested:

> While some [restrictions] appear 'logical', such as the restriction in the SPD [Single Permit Directive] that the right can be limited to those who are in employment or are registered as unemployed, the reason why others have been introduced in one or more Directives (but not in others) cannot be easily explained, such as the restrictions related to language proficiency and the fulfilment of specific educational prerequisites.[66]

Arguably, even such limitations are not really justified if we take into account the social aims pursued by the Directives. Apart from aligning migration with the economic objectives of the EU, the relevant instruments seek to secure fair treatment for migrants and to achieve some kind of social progress in the form of rights attributed to migrants. The emphasis put on education as part of the integration policies pursued at EU level to ensure social cohesion necessitates full equal treatment as regards access to education.[67] That is, of course, since the aim of regulating migration is not only meeting the economic sustainability objectives but also the social ones.

Another area of tension is access to social security, social assistance, and social protection, which are differentiated between the categories of

to study grants was that the TCN workers would not normally be entitled to them on the basis of their contribution as workers.

62 Article 14(2), Blue Card Directive 2009; Article 16(2), Blue Card Directive 2021; Article 12(2), Single Permit Directive; Article 11(3), Long-term Residents Directive.

63 Article 12(2)(a)(iv), Single Permit Directive.

64 Article 23(2)(ii), Seasonal Workers Directive.

65 Article 12(2)(a)(i) and (ii), Single Permit Directive.

66 Fitness Check (n 15), Annex 5.

67 Communication, Action plan on Integration and Inclusion 2021–2027, COM(2020)758 final and in the European Skills Agenda, COM(2020)274 final.

TCNs. The Legal Fitness Check suggested that the limitation of access to social security in employment-related Directives is justified, as this is linked to the condition that migrants have sufficient resources to not become a burden.[68] Equal treatment applies to social security as a recognition that workers contribute by their work and tax payments to public finances, and to serve as a safeguard against unfair competition that may result from exploitation.[69] Social assistance, in contrast, was deliberately excluded from the relevant Directives because incoming migrants should have sufficient resources not to require financial support.[70] Social assistance and social protection is secured only for long-term residents, but even in their case, it can be limited to core benefits. This was not what the Commission aimed for in the original proposals. As regards the Directives that also provide rights to free movement in the EU, limitations can be introduced, and equal treatment can be limited to the Member State where the migrants have their registered place of residence.[71]

It should be noted that all these Directives operate within the context of Article 20 CFR, which provides for general non-discrimination rights within the scope of EU law. Unequal treatment is thereby allowed to the extent it can be justified. Relatedly, the Legal Fitness Check suggested that EU migration law, in the way it is formed through the relevant Directives, could be described as a 'fine-tuning of legitimate differentiated treatment'.[72] Looking at the way equal treatment is dissected and diluted in the relevant provisions, it is clear that limitations are inserted in order to avoid repercussions of granting rights to public finances. In cases where equal treatment comes with no cost for national economies, there is no reason to discriminate. However, in light of the parallel pursuit of economic and social sustainability as manifested in primary law objectives, the question that remains open is to what extent social cohesion can be guaranteed and when equal treatment is intentionally limited to

[68] Fitness Check (n 15), Annex 5.

[69] Proposal Seasonal Workers Directive, COM(2010)379, Explanatory Memorandum, Article 15.

[70] Proposal for a Blue Card Directive, COM(2007)0637 final, Explanatory Memorandum, Article 15; Proposal for Researchers Directive, COM(2004)178 final, Article 12.

[71] Such limitations appear in the Blue Card Directive 2009 and the Long-term Residents Directive but not in the Blue Card Directive 2021 and the Researchers and Students Directive.

[72] Fitness Check (n 15), Annex 5, 66.

deprive migrants from EU law protection.[73] This limitation of social rights of TCN migrants does not align well with social sustainability objectives. This is especially because all these TCN migrants come within the scope of EU law because they are admitted as workers and thereby contribute to the project of growth.

9.2.3 Erasure of Equal Treatment and Informalization of the Relation of EU with Third Countries

In parallel to the framework of admission and rights shaped for all legally resident migrants discussed in Section 9.2.2, in this period we witness the erasure of equal treatment clauses in the Agreements concluded by the EU with third countries, and the further informalization of cooperation with third countries in the area of migration.

The Stabilisation and Association Agreements (SAAs) concluded with many Western Balkan countries were the only agreements that set up some minimum rules on equal treatment for workers legally employed in the Member States with regard to working conditions, remuneration, or dismissal.[74] These Agreements did not include equal treatment on social security and did not provide for any kind of right to entry or access to the labour market. This is so even though such Agreements were signed as pre-accession instruments. What is more, the wording of the relevant provisions is different from those of the Euro-Mediterranean Agreements, as they stipulate that equal treatment must be granted subject to the conditions and modalities applicable in each Member State. This could be understood as an attempt to limit the direct effect of the relevant provisions. The identical wording was used in Europe Agreements, and was found by the Court to have direct effect.[75] Even though there is no case-law on SAAs, there is no reason to assume that

[73] Cf Martin Ruhs, *The Price of Rights: Regulating International Labor Migration* (Princeton University Press 2013).

[74] Article 44, SAA with the former Yugoslav Republic of Macedonia [2004] OJ L 084/13; Article 46, SAA with Albania [2009] OJ L 107/166; Article 49, SAA with Montenegro [2010] OJ L 108/3; Article 49, SAA with Serbia [2013] OJ L 278/16; Article 47, SAA with Bosnia and Herzegovina [2015] OJ L 164/2. See, however, similar Article 86(2), SAA with Kosovo [2016] OJ L 71/3, which recognizes the rights of Kosovo people under the EU *acquis* with no differentiation from TCNs and no special rights attributed to migrant workers.

[75] Case C-162/00, *Pokrzeptowicz-Meyer*, ECLI:EU:C:2002:57, paras 23–25 on EA with Poland, and Case C-438/00, *Deutscher Handballbund*, ECLI:EU:C:2003:255, paras 27–29 on EA with Slovakia.

the Court would follow a different approach. In addition, the SAAs grant rights of access to the labour market to the worker's spouse and children who are legally residing with them during the worker's authorized stay of employment.

Aside from these Agreements, which were signed as pre-accession instruments, the approach of the EU to labour migration from third countries has undergone a massive shift. With a general system of admission in place for different categories of TCN workers, development cooperation during this period focused on preventing the entry of all those who attempt to join the EU irregularly. The tensions in the Mediterranean region are perceived as a crisis to be addressed by flexible non-binding arrangements.[76] The objective of cooperation has not changed in so far as its declared focus is still on protection of legal migrants, the development potential of migration for the host state, and combatting illegal migration.[77] However, these objectives demand different legal means of cooperation in light of the evolution of EU law. Relatedly, the EU no longer negotiates any binding instrument that can create channels of admission or rights for nationals from specific third countries. Rather, it emphasizes addressing the root causes of migration and creating better living conditions in the region.[78]

During the relevant period, and in parallel to the shaping of an autonomous EU migration framework, the EU was also dealing with the effects of the 2008 economic crisis with diverse repercussions for national economies. In this regard, it would be hardly imaginable for Member States to support binding instruments that created cooperation on admission and rights for workers from third countries. Instead, what they wanted to promote was smart planning that would allow the EU to admit labour migration when needed, while maintaining cooperation with the Mediterranean countries with a view to assisting their development. The means chosen to do this was to informalize cooperation based on a differentiated dialogue with each Mediterranean country.[79] In so doing, Migration Partnerships which are soft-law instruments are now

[76] Communication, A dialogue for migration, mobility and security with the southern Mediterranean countries, COM(2011)292 final 3.

[77] See Council of the European Union, First Euro-Med Ministerial Meeting on Migration, Algarve 18, 19 November 2007, Conclusions 15805/07.

[78] A dialogue for migration, mobility and security with the southern Mediterranean countries, COM(2011)292 final 6.

[79] Ibid, 8.

preferred so as to guarantee the EU can maintain regular migration channels so that it can have the manpower it needs, while at the same time maximizing the impact of migration for development.[80] Mobility Partnerships are signed in the form of political declarations that set the goals for migration cooperation between the EU and third countries. The EU has signed Mobility Partnerships with Morocco, Tunisia, and Jordan in the Euro-Mediterranean region.[81] These declarations do not affect the obligations of the parties under the Euro-Mediterranean Agreements.

In conclusion, the evolution of the framework of cooperation with third countries on migration has undergone a major shift which is based on changing geopolitical circumstances and labour needs in the EU. The more intense labour needs were, the more rights were attributed to migrant workers under Association Agreements. At the same time, we need to remember that, even though in first reading it might look like the rights of such migrants are excluded from EU law, this is not the case; rather, the basis of protection has changed. This means that migrant workers legally resident in the EU and coming from countries in the Euro-Mediterranean no longer enjoy rights on the basis of Association Agreements, but rather on the basis of EU secondary law. Hence, despite the reconfiguration of cooperation, there is a constant understanding on the part of the EU that the rights of migrant workers located in EU territory are non-negotiable due to their active contribution to the EU development project. Rather, what remains negotiable is the regulation of entry or, perhaps, the emphasis on avoiding entry to ensure that no more will come than the EU is able to make use of. The functional role of the migrants, which set the basis for their rights, is now showing its ugly face, by ensuring the exclusion not of those who cannot contribute, but of those whose contribution is no longer needed. Following the examination of the legislative evolutions of this period, Section 9.3 will turn to the consolidation of social rights in the case-law of the Court.

[80] Ibid.

[81] Joint Declaration establishing a Mobility Partnership between the Kingdom of Morocco and the European Union and its Member States of 7 June 2013; Joint Declaration establishing a Mobility Partnership between Tunisia and the European Union and its Member States of 3 March 2014; Joint Declaration establishing a Mobility Partnership between the Hashemite Kingdom of Jordan and the European Union and its participating Member States of 9 October 2014. The EU has signed Mobility Partnerships with Moldova in 2008, Georgia in 2009, Armenia 2011, Azerbaijan 2013, and Belarus 2016.

9.3 The Consolidation of Social Rights in the Case-Law

Contrary to the legislative intention to differentiate social rights between different categories of migrants and to dilute equal treatment by allowing for derogations to avoid presumed economic repercussions, the Court has followed a consistent approach and has guaranteed the rights of migrants by reviewing different national limitations in light of the Charter. While economic considerations are not absent from its reasoning, the Court consistently emphasizes the protection afforded by the Charter to consolidate the rights of TCN migrants.

In the following sections, a broad-range of case-law related to rights of TCN migrants in social security, family reunification, and security of residence under both secondary law and the EEC–Turkey Agreement is examined. The analysis in Sections 9.3.1–9.3.4 showcases the Court's perception on the interplay of social and economic objectives behind migrant protection. Subsequently, in Section 9.3.5, I explain how the approach of the Court not only consolidates the social objectives of the EU project, and relatedly the social pillar of sustainability, but also the constitutional architecture of the EU legal system. The interpretations of the Court follow its meta-teleological technique of adjudication, that is, the interpretation of secondary law as means to fill the normative gaps of the EU constitutional order in the making.[82]

9.3.1 The Judicial Reconstruction of Social Rights of Migrant Workers

Against the incoherent economic obsession with conditioning the rights of migrants in secondary law so that they do not pose risks for the economy, the Court has put forward a positive vision related to the rights all migrants should enjoy under EU law. This concerns not only migrants covered under secondary law but also those whose residence status in Member States is irregular. Specifically, in *Tümer*, the Court had to interpret the scope of application of Directive 80/987/EEC on the

[82] Cf Miguel Poiares Maduro, 'Interpreting European Law: Judicial Adjudication in a Context of Constitutional Pluralism' (2008) 1 European Journal of Legal Studies 137 and Elise Muir, 'The Court of Justice: A Fundamental Rights Institution among Others' in Bruno de Witte, Elise Muir, and Mark Dawson (eds), *Judicial Activism at the European Court of Justice* (Edward Elgar 2013).

protection of employees in the event of insolvency of their employer.[83] Tümer, a Turkish national living in the Netherlands, had worked for a company that was declared insolvent. His application for insolvency benefit was rejected on the ground that he was not legally resident in the Netherlands. In that case, the Netherlands argued that since the Directive was based on Article 137 EC, which provided the Union with competence to adopt Directives with a view to achieving social objectives related to the improvement of working conditions, it could not apply to TCNs, even regularly resident ones.[84] If regularly resident aliens were to be protected, the state argued that the concept of employee could be construed under national law to exclude irregularly resident TCNs.

AG Bot suggested that excluding TCN workers from protective measures adopted for employees would not be compatible with the purpose of the EU social policy, as it would encourage the recruitment of foreign labour in order to reduce wage costs.[85] Additionally, with reference to *Germany and others v Commission*, he emphasized that the Court had already acknowledged the relation of the Union's social policy to the policy that applied to workers from third countries.[86] The AG proceeded to suggest that the crucial factor triggering obligations under the relevant Directive was the employment relationship of a person to an insolvent employer.[87] Importing a condition of nationality in the scope of the Directive would go against its objective to guarantee all employees in the EU a minimum level of protection.[88] He then went on to examine whether there was discretion on the part of Member States to exclude irregularly resident migrants. In this examination, he suggested that since the employee status was the crucial status, making it conditional to legal residence would go against non-discrimination.[89] The AG suggested that irregularly resident TCNs who had worked and paid contributions were in a comparable situation to other employees, and there was nothing to justify a differentiated treatment.[90]

[83] Case C-311/13, *Tümer*, ECLI:EU:C:2014:2337. Directive 80/987/EEC of 20 October 1980 on the approximation of the laws of the Member States relating to the protection of employees in the event of the insolvency of their employer [1980] 283/23.
[84] Opinion of AG Bot in C-311/13, *Tümer*, ECLI:EU:C:2014:1997, para 34.
[85] Ibid, para 52.
[86] Ibid.
[87] Ibid, para 54.
[88] Ibid.
[89] Ibid, para 60.
[90] Ibid, para 89.

The Court confirmed the AG's approach and noted that EU social policy was concerned with promoting the living and working conditions of both nationals of the EU Member States and TCNs.[91] It held that Member States could not define the term 'employee' in such a way as to undermine the social objective of the Directive.[92] As a result, the Directive was found to preclude national laws, such as the Dutch one, which strip irregularly resident TCNs of protection. As long as somebody is in employment, the social rights they derive therefrom should not be undermined because their residence is not legal. This case is significant in showing the application of EU social policy for all migrants engaged in the EU development project. What is more, it is crucial for understanding how the economic contribution made by migrants' work is at the heart of the protection afforded by EU law.

Next to this case, the Court has also handed down rulings reconstructing equal treatment and limiting the effects of secondary law for the rights of migrants. The line of reasoning that underlies the relevant case-law was set in *Kamberaj*, which concerned discriminatory conditions for access to a housing benefit by a long-term resident. In that case, the Court held that while the provisions of the Long-term Residence Directive provided for equal treatment in access to social security, social assistance, and social protection as defined in national law, these concepts could not be defined unilaterally by Member States without the risk of undermining the effectiveness of the Directive.[93] The interpretation of what constitutes social security, social assistance, and social protection under national law needs to comply with the Charter. Article 34 CFR guarantees equal treatment regarding access to specific social benefits in order to guarantee decent living to all those who lack sufficient resources.

In light of this, the Court held that national courts should interpret the relevant concept of social assistance in the Long-term Residents Directive in light of the Charter in order to assess whether benefits of different kinds fell under the categories of benefits where equal treatment should be provided.[94] The Court further stated that the derogation allowed under Article 11(4) of the Directive should be interpreted strictly in light of the social purpose of integration.[95] It also clarified that the provision of

[91] C-311/13, *Tümer*, para 32.

[92] Ibid, paras 42, 45.

[93] Case C-571/10, *Kamberaj*, ECLI:EU:C:2012:233, para 78.

[94] Ibid, para 81.

[95] Ibid, para 86.

the Directive which allowed the limitation of equal treatment only to core benefits could not be invoked on a case-by-case basis. Rather, such a derogation needs to be expressed clearly at the time of implementation of the Directive in national law.[96] It further suggested that the meaning and scope of core benefits for the purposes of equal treatment should be construed with reference to the purpose of integration as the objective for long-term residents.[97] It thus held that core benefits are benefits that enable individuals to meet their basic needs such as food, accommodation, and health, and should be aligned with the minimum benefits covered by the Charter.[98]

A similar reasoning was followed by the Court in relation to rights under the Single Permit Directive in *Martinez Silva*.[99] In that case, a migrant worker was excluded from a grant that was provided to households with at least three minor children and income below a minimum amount. The Single Permit Directive provides for equal treatment not in line with national law, but with reference to social security as defined in Regulation 883/2004 and, more specifically, the family benefits covered under Article 3(1)(j) thereof.[100] The Court found that the benefit at issue fell under Article 3(1)(j) of Regulation 883/2004, with reference to previous case-law where it had held that family benefits covered all kinds of benefits which are automatically granted to families on the basis of objective criteria without discretionary assessment of personal needs, and which are intended to meet family expenses, as a public contribution to the family's budget to alleviate the burdens involved in the maintenance of children.[101] Once more, the Court pointed to the possibility to derogate from equal treatment provided in the Directive, but it held that such a possibility existed only if the Member State explicitly chose so at the transposition of the Directive.[102]

The line of case-law developed in *Kamberaj* for long-term residents, and applied in *Martinez Silva* under the Single Permit Directive, has been since confirmed regarding different types of benefits claimed by

[96] Ibid, para 87.
[97] Ibid, para 90.
[98] Ibid, paras 91–92.
[99] Case C-449/16, *Martinez Silva*, ECLI:EU:C:2017:485.
[100] Regulation 883/2004 on the coordination of social security systems in the EU [2004] OJ L 166/1.
[101] Ibid, paras 22–23.
[102] Ibid, para 29.

TCNs.[103] The Court has followed a clear line of reasoning in promoting fair treatment for this group. When it comes to core benefits, to determine if they need to be granted under equal treatment conditions, Member States need to comply with the Charter. If a benefit serves the purpose set out in Article 34 CFR, then TCNs can in no case be excluded therefrom. The central evaluation then seems to concern the purpose of the benefit: does it aim at making life liveable and ensuring a decent existence for all? If so, it needs to be granted to long-term residents in light of the objective of integration, and to all migrants covered under the Single Permit Directive in light of the objective of ensuring fair treatment. Then as regards non-core benefits, Member States must explicitly exclude migrants therefrom by derogating from equal treatment when they transpose the relevant Directives. It is only in such cases that the Court considers that the relevant discriminatory attribution falls within national law and the measures cannot be reviewed for compliance with the Charter.

In this case-law, we see that the Court puts forward the social objectives served by secondary law (integration of long-term residents and fair treatment) not as a by-product of the economic contribution of the migrants, but rather under a positive vision of social justice in line with the social sustainability objectives of primary law. In doing so, the Court connects the protection of migrants under EU law with the evolution of the legal order and the incorporation of human rights guarantees under the Charter. By correlating the derogations allowed under secondary law to the provisions of the Charter, it dictates minimum safeguards of fundamental rights protection, thereby limiting the space for derogation by Member States and the EU legislator.[104]

9.3.2 *Social Rights Compensating for the Lack of a Right to Remain for Turkish Workers*

A similar extension of social rights has taken place in relation to social security rights of Turkish workers. In the relevant case-law, it is not the

[103] See Case C-302/19, *INPS*, ECLI:EU:C:2020:957. For holders of long-term residence permit in Case C-303/19, *INPS*, ECLI:EU:C:2020:958; Case C-350/20, *INPS*, ECLI:EU:C:2021:659; Case C-462/20, *ASGI and others*, ECLI:EU:C:2021:894; Case C-94/20, *Land Oberösterreich*, ECLI:EU:C:2021:477.

[104] Cf Proposal for a Directive, On a single application procedure for a single permit for third-country nationals to reside and work in the territory of a Member State and on a common set of rights for third-country workers legally residing in a Member State (recast), COM(2022)655 final, Explanatory Memorandum, Article 12, on raising the standards of protection in line with the case-law.

Charter that directed the extensive interpretation of the Court, but rather an understanding of rights as compensatory for the work somebody has carried in the EU, in cases where EU law does not grant a right to remain and enjoy such rights in EU territory.

This was the case in *Akdas*, where the Court found that non-discrimination should lead to exportability of benefits for Turkish workers, where the same does not apply to EU workers.[105] Akdas, a Turkish worker in the Netherlands, became incapacitated to work and obtained a supplementary benefit to ensure a minimum income level. He returned to Turkey, where he retained the benefit under Article 39(4) of the Additional Protocol to the Agreement. Dutch law was eventually amended, leading to a progressive withdrawal and termination of the benefit for all workers who had no residence in the Netherlands. The question addressed to the Court was whether such withdrawal for recipients who resided outside the Member State went against Article 6(1) of Decision 3/80.

The Court acknowledged that the wording of the Decision did not tie residence in the host state to continuation of benefits of such kind.[106] At the same time, EU secondary law on social security for EU migrants had been amended and had introduced an exception to the exportability of benefits like the one in question.[107] This meant that EU migrants who found themselves in circumstances like those of Akdas would have the benefit withdrawn if they moved outside the Netherlands. The Court held that such a difference in treatment would not be incompatible with Article 59 of the Additional Protocol to the Agreement, which required that Turkish workers were not treated more favourably than EU ones.[108] In order to justify this, the Court invoked the limited residence rights of Turkish nationals. It pointed out that Turkish migrants, unlike EU ones, had no right to remain in the host state if they could no longer contribute

105 Case C-485/07, *Akdas and others*, ECLI:EU:C:2011:346.

106 Ibid, paras 80–82.

107 Ibid, paras 85–87. Regulation 1247/92 amending Regulation 1408/71 on the application of social security schemes to employed persons, to self-employed persons and to members of their families moving within the Community [1992] OJ L 136/1 inserted into Regulation 1408/71 on the application of social security schemes to employed persons and their families moving within the Community [1971] OJ L 149/2 a new Article 10a, which introduced an exception to the requirement of exportability laid down in Article 10(1).

108 C-485/07, *Akdas and others*, para 88.

to the labour force.[109] For them, there is no option to maintain residence and, thereby, the benefit. According to the Court, the fact that they have no right to stay because they can no longer contribute with their labour power should not be construed as a voluntary conduct that leads to loss of their rights.[110]

What happens where the Turkish worker is not forced to leave the territory of the host state? This situation was addressed by the Court in *Demirci*, where a Turkish worker requesting the continuation of exportability of the benefit had acquired Dutch citizenship next to the Turkish one.[111] In this case, as AG Wahl explained, the objective of Article 6 of Decision 1/80 is to compensate workers for the 'the misfortunes they have suffered in the host Member State', an objective which is reasonable precisely due to the contribution the migrant workers have made in the host state.[112] Following the AG, the Court held that such compensation is no longer needed where the worker manages to acquire the nationality of the host state.[113] An opposite conclusion would mean that Turkish workers who acquire the nationality of the Member State would be treated more favourably both compared to Turkish workers who no longer belong to the labour force and have no right to reside, and to nationals of Member States, who would have to maintain their residence in the Netherlands to receive the benefit.[114]The Court has also ruled on cases where the acquisition of nationality of the host state by a worker did not imply the loss of rights derived from the Turkish worker status. This was the case in *Khaveci and Inan*, which concerned family reunification rights for Turkish workers naturalized in the host state.[115] The Court based the differentiation between *Demirci* and *Khaveci and Inan* on the fact that the workers in question had the possibility to enjoy the benefit, if they maintained residence in the Netherlands, and on the social purpose

[109] Ibid, paras 93–95.
[110] C-485/07, *Akdas and others*, para 94. See also Katharina Eisele and Anne Pieter van der Mei, 'Portability of Social Benefits and Reverse Discrimination of EU Citizens vis-à-vis Turkish Nationals: Comment on Akdas' (2012) 37 ELR 204.
[111] Case C-171/13, *Demirci and others*, ECLI:EU:C:2015:8.
[112] Opinion of AG Wahl in C-171/13, *Demirci and others*, ECLI:EU:C:2014:2073, paras 54–55.
[113] C-171/13, *Demirci and others*, para 54.
[114] Ibid, para 59. See also Case C-258/18, *Solak*, ECLI:EU:C:2020:98. See, however, Case C-677/17, *Çoban*, ECLI:EU:C:2019:408, para 32.
[115] Joined Cases C-7/10 and C-9/10, *Kahveci and Inan*, ECLI:EU:C:2012:180.

of Decision 1/80, which created rights for family members and not for the workers themselves.[116]

The significance of this case-law and, relatedly, its financial repercussions for Member States led to a revision of Decision 3/80 in order to limit this extensive protection.[117] Despite the revision, some observations are to be drawn from the consistently extensive application of social security rights in the case-law. There is an implicit understanding by the Court that Turkish workers who can no longer contribute their work and are thus forced to leave the host state, not being able to claim any residence right from EU law, need to be compensated and extensively protected. The basis of such protection is none other than non-discrimination. The extension of social security rights to compensate for a lack of a right to remain should be seen in light of the parallel pursuit of economic and social objectives by EU law. Migrants contribute to economic development by their labour and are granted rights as a compensation for such labour in a legal order constantly guided by the pursuit of economic and social sustainability.

9.3.3 *Social Objectives and Economic Risks behind Family Reunification*

Another instrument which highlights the intimate connection of the economic and social pillars of sustainability pursued in the regulation of migration is the Family Reunification Directive. Section 6.2.1 outlined the social objectives served by its adoption. However, the Directive does not only regulate the conditions under which family reunification should take place; more importantly, it creates a right to family reunification for

[116] C-171/13, *Demirci and others*, paras 67–71.

[117] Council Decision of 6 December 2012 on the position to be taken on behalf of the European Union within the Association Council set up by the Agreement establishing an association between the European Economic Community and Turkey, with regard to the adoption of provisions on the coordination of social security systems 2012/776/ [2012] OJ L 340/19. For an analysis of the relevant case-law and its implication and amendments, see Paul Minderhoud, 'Decision No 3/80 of the EEC–Turkey Association Council: Significance and Developments' in Daniel Thym and Margarite Zoeteweij-Turhan (eds), *Rights of Third-Country Nationals under EU Association Agreements: Degrees of Free Movement and Citizenship* (Brill Nijhoff 2015); Paul Minderhoud, 'Social Security Rights under Decision No 3/80 of the EEC–Turkey Association Council: Developments in the EU and in the Netherlands' (2016) 18 European Journal of Social Security 268. See also Judgment of 18 December 2014, *United Kingdom/ Council*, C-81/13, ECLI:EU:C:2014:2449.

all TCNs who fall within its scope.[118] This was acknowledged by the Court in its case-law during the period under review.

In *Parliament v Council*, the Court held that the Family Reunification Directive goes further than international human rights instruments on the protection of family life for migrants.[119] Specifically, looking at international human rights law, the Court confirmed that, as a rule, there is no right for aliens to be allowed to enter the territory of a Member State for the purpose of family reunification and the corresponding protection of family life. Contrary to international human rights law and going beyond it, the Directive creates positive obligations for Member States to authorize family reunification if the conditions stated therein are fulfilled.[120] Relatedly, the Court has held that any limitations to the rights conferred by the Directive should be interpreted strictly and has used the Charter as a basis of review of restrictive national practices. In the respective case-law the balancing of economic and social objectives conditioning the rights attributed under the Directive is clear.

Specifically, the Family Reunification Directive provides that Member States may require evidence that the sponsor has accommodation regarded as normal for a comparable family, health insurance, and stable and regular resources to maintain themselves and their family, so they do not become a burden to the social assistance system of the Member States.[121] In *Chakroun*, the Court elaborated on how stable and sufficient resources should be perceived and if this requirement should exclude migrants who may be eligible for certain types of social assistance.[122] Taking the right to entry created for family members under the Directive as a starting point, the Court held that family reunification was the general rule. As a result, the conditions provided for it should be interpreted strictly.[123] The Court further pointed out that the margin of appreciation of Member States should not be exercised in such a way as to undermine the objective of the Directive, namely to promote family reunification, and its effectiveness.[124] This strict interpretation in line with the objective of the Directive also needs to be aligned with the protection of fundamental rights, and specifically respect for family life,

[118] See, however, Case C-706/18, *Belgische Staat*, ECLI:EU:C:2019:993.
[119] Case C-540/03, *Parliament/Council*, ECLI:EU:C:2006:429.
[120] Ibid, para 60.
[121] Article 7, Family Reunification Directive.
[122] Case C-578/08, *Chakroun*.
[123] Ibid, paras 41–43 with reference to *Parliament/Council*, C-540/03, para 60.
[124] Ibid, para 47.

as protected by the Charter and the ECHR.[125] In this context, the Court interpreted the requirements of Article 7(1)(c) of the Family Reunification Directive as meaning that the concept of social assistance referred to assistance which compensated for lack of stable, regular, and sufficient resources and could not cover assistance that enabled exceptional or unforeseen needs to be addressed.[126] This was confirmed by the Court in *O and S*, this time mentioning the need to align the interpretation of the Directive not only with Article 7 CFR but also with Article 24 on the rights of the child.[127]

Subsequently, in *Khachab*, the Court had the opportunity to clarify the meaning of regular and stable resources.[128] Following the line of reasoning established in *Chakroun*, the Court emphasized that this requirement should be interpreted in light of Article 7 CFR and with a view to promoting family life.[129] The presence of stable and regular resources implies the existence of a degree of permanence and continuity, allowing the Member State to assess whether the sponsor has the prospect of maintaining the resources for a period after the submission of the application. This prospective assessment was thought to be in line with the system of the Directive, which allows for refusal of renewal where the sufficient resources criterion is no longer satisfied.[130] What is more, this interpretation was aligned by the Court with the objective of Article 7(1) of the Family Reunification Directive – that the sponsor or his family should not become a burden on the social assistance system of the Member States during their stay.[131] The assessment, however, should take place in line with the principle of proportionality, and on a case-by-case basis in accordance with the requirement of Article 17 of the Directive.[132]

As with the case law on EU migrants, the Court acknowledged the limits set by the legislator on the rights of TCN migrants in light of the economic objectives of the EU project. Nevertheless, it firmly grounded the review of such limitations in the changed architecture of the EU legal order, and it emphasized the need to guarantee the rights of individuals

[125] Ibid, para 44.
[126] Ibid, para 49.
[127] Joined Cases C-356/11 and C-357/11, *O. and S.*, ECLI:EU:C:2012:776, paras 76–77.
[128] Case C-558/14, *Khachab*, ECLI:EU:C:2016:285.
[129] Ibid, para 28.
[130] Ibid, para 37.
[131] Ibid, para 39.
[132] Ibid, paras 42–43.

under EU law in light of the Charter. The use of the Charter in these cases has a double function. First, it consolidates the constitutional architecture of EU law. Second, it appears as a particular manifestation of the social objectives of EU law, and relatedly of how the social pillar of sustainability is pursued by a strong grounding on human rights considerations.

9.3.4 *Security of Residence Promoting the Social Objectives of the EU*

The Court has followed a similar approach also in relation to interpretation of the provisions of the Long-term Residents Directive. The long-term resident status is attributed to all migrants residing in a Member State for a period of five years under Article 4(1) of the Directive. However, not all types of legal residence count towards the fulfilment of the five-year duration criterion. Specifically, the Directive excludes certain categories of legal residence based on the presumption that the migrant in question has no intention to stay in the Member State for an extended period of time.[133]

The Court has had the opportunity to define what is meant by stay on temporary grounds and, thus, what types of permits are excluded from the calculation of the residence duration.[134] In light of the purpose of integration served by the Directive, the Court held that the permits excluded are based on the consideration that their holders do not seem to have prima facie any intention to settle in the EU for the long term.[135] In other words, their legal status objectively represents an intention to exist in the host Member State for a limited period of time. When it comes to national residence permits that are limited (for example, in terms of access to a specific occupation), but do not prevent the long-term residence of the migrant, these cannot be excluded from the calculation of the period necessary for the long-term resident status.[136] If they were excluded, this would allow much leeway to Member States, in consequence depriving the Directive of its effectiveness.

While the duration of residence is the main criterion for access to the status, the Directive also provides for the following

[133] Article 3(2), 4(2) Long-term Residents Directive.

[134] Cases C-502/10, *Singh*, ECLI:EU:C:2012:636 and C-624/20, *Staatssecretaris van Justitie en Veiligheid*, ECLI:EU:C:2022:639.

[135] C-502/10, *Singh*, para 47.

[136] Ibid, para 51.

conditions.[137] Applicants for long-term residence permit need to prove that they have stable and regular resources, and health insurance, and may also be required to comply with integration conditions. In these requirements, we see that the social aim of furnishing security of residence to migrants who have stayed for long in the EU is tied to guarantees that they will not become a burden on the host state. The Court has also engaged with the criterion of stable and regular resources. In the relevant case-law, it emphasized duration of residence as the central criterion of the Directive, which shows that the TCN has managed to put down roots in the host state.[138] Consequently, it held that while the concept of resources may be interpreted by analogy to the relevant concept in Directive 2004/38, it should have a different scope.[139] This is because first, the acquisition of the long-term resident status is definitive, so the interpretation of the resources condition should be in line with the purpose of preserving the social assistance system of the Member States.[140] Second, the text of the relevant provision mentions that resources should be stable and regular, compared to Directive 2004/38 which only mentions stable. In addition to these reasons of differentiation, AG Saugmandsgaard Øe added another one, on which the Court stayed silent.[141] That is the paradoxical formulation of the relevant instruments in a way that allows Member States to withdraw the residence permit of a EU migrant who no longer has sufficient resources if they do not have permanent residence status, while such withdrawal is not foreseen for long-term residents.[142] In view of this, the more exacting economic conditions for access to protection are based on the fact that the social protection enjoyed by long-term residents cannot be taken away when they become economically redundant. In this regard, the Court suggested that the relevant requirement meant that Member States could evaluate the resources on the basis of their nature and regularity, and this would imply an assessment of sufficiency and sustainability of resources, rather than an assessment of their origin.[143]

[137] Article 5, Long-term Residents Directive.
[138] Case C-302/18, *X v Belgische Staat*, ECLI:EU:C:2019:830, para 30.
[139] Ibid, para 34.
[140] Ibid, para 35.
[141] Opinion of AG Saugmandsgaard Øe delivered in C-302/18, *X v Belgische Staat*, ECLI:EU:C:2019:469, para 64.
[142] Ibid, paras 64–66. See also C-308/14 *Commission/United Kingdom*, and Article 28(2), Directive 2004/38.
[143] C-302/18, *X v Belgische Staat*, paras 40–41.

The Court has also ruled on the conditions of loss of the relevant status. Article 9 of the Long-term Residents Directive provides that the status may be lost due to absence from the EU territory for a period of longer than twelve consecutive months. The Court has held that since the Directive creates a right to a status whose nature is permanent, the rules leading to the loss of such status should be interpreted strictly and that the physical presence of a migrant in EU territory is sufficient to interrupt their absence from the territory.[144] This interpretation was also supported both by the purpose of the Directive to bring the rights of long-term residents as close as possible to those of EU nationals and by the need to achieve legal certainty for the migrants concerned.[145]

The social purpose of this Directive as a reason for more extensive protection has also been identified by the Court. In *Commission v Netherlands*, the Commission took action against the Dutch legislature, which imposed excessively high charges for the acquisition of long-term resident status.[146] AG Bot suggested that the margin of manoeuvre of Member States should be limited by the purpose and effectiveness of the Directive, and by respect for fundamental rights.[147] Relatedly, he pointed out the double purpose served by migrant integration under EU law: to promote social and economic cohesion by granting them rights, and to contribute to the attainment of the internal market by granting them mobility rights.[148] To the AG, the charges imposed by the Dutch legislation constituted an indirect means of limiting the exercise of the rights conferred by the Directive, and could lead to discrimination against migrants who did not have sufficient financial resources.[149] He also emphasized the comparability of long-term residents to EU migrants, and failed to see how such a difference in treatment would be justified on the basis of objective reasons.[150]

[144] Case, C-432/20, *Landeshauptmann von Wien*, ECLI:EU:C:2022:39, paras 33–36.

[145] Ibid, para 38. See Proposal for a Directive concerning the status of third-country nationals who are long-term residents (recast), COM(2022)650 final which suggested the extension of permissible absence to twenty-four months and Council Document, Proposal for a Directive concerning the status of third-country nationals who are long-term residents (recast) – Mandate for negotiations with the Parliament ST 16000 2023 INIT, 28 November 2023 which proposes eighteen months instead.

[146] Case C-508/10, *Commission/Netherlands*, ECLI:EU:C:2012:243/.

[147] Opinion of AG Bot in C-508/10, *Commission/Netherlands*, paras 54, 67.

[148] Ibid, paras 55–57.

[149] Ibid, paras 63, 69.

[150] Ibid, para 66.

In light of the arguments put forward by the Netherlands, the AG also had the possibility to elaborate on the rights created by primary and secondary law for EU and TCN migrants. Specifically, the Dutch government argued that a residence permit granted under secondary law created rights for the migrants, whereas a residence permit granted to EU migrants was merely declaratory.[151] The AG suggested that such a differentiation could no longer hold in line with the development of EU law.[152] While it is true that for EU migrants a residence permit has declaratory effect, the same is true for TCN migrants, in the sense that secondary law directly confers rights on them.[153] The Court emphasized the purpose of the Directive appearing in Recitals 4, 6, and 12, which is to contribute to the integration of migrants and to the effective attainment of the internal market as an area of free movement of people.[154] In line with the AG, it confirmed that the fulfilment of the conditions of the Directive created a right for migrants to obtain the long-term resident status. Member States cannot impose charges which are so high as to have the object or the effect of creating an obstacle for TCNs who are entitled to obtain that status, otherwise the objective and spirit of the Directive would be undermined.[155]

Overall, the extensive interpretations of the Court on this instrument had two consequences: it ensured the social protection of long-term residents in the Member States, and it shaped the Commission proposal for revision of secondary law with closer attention to fundamental rights considerations.[156]

9.3.5 Social Rights for Migrant as an Indirect Way of Promoting the Constitutional Elements of EU Law

Primary law on the regulation of migration does not create obligations on the substantive conditions that should inform migrants' rights. The

[151] Ibid, para 71.
[152] Ibid, para 73.
[153] Ibid, para 74 with reference to case-law on Decision 1/80 of the EEC–Turkey Association Agreement and on the Family Reunification Directive.
[154] Ibid, para 66.
[155] Ibid, para 73. See also Case C-309/14, *CGIL and INCA*, ECLI:EU:C:2015:523.
[156] Proposal for a Directive concerning the status of third-country nationals who are long-term residents (recast), COM(2022)650 final, Explanatory Memorandum, Article 5 on resources and integration conditions and Article 12 on removing the permissible limitation of equal treatment to core benefits.

shared competence of the EU on migration is defined in the Treaties by reference to the areas where the EU can adopt legislation. At the same time, the Lisbon Treaty refers to fair treatment and solidarity as principles that should guide the adoption of such legislation. The Court has not referred to the relevant Treaty provisions when reviewing secondary legislation. Rather in the case-law analysed in the previous sections, the Court consolidated the rights of TCN migrants by reference to the Charter. Specifically, the Court consistently held that secondary law creates EU law rights for migrants, the limitations of which should be interpreted strictly and reviewed for compliance with the Charter.

At this stage, it should be noted that the Court has dealt with very few cases regarding the right of first admission of a migrant. In such cases it has been reserved. Despite recognizing the creation of a right to entry in accordance with the conditions of the relevant Directive, the Court does not normally push for review of state discretion. However, when it comes to migrants who are already in EU territory, the Court acknowledges the importance of fundamental rights protection for all individuals who fall within the scope of EU law. Such rights are extended in light of the Charter, which completed the constitutional architecture of the EU. In the relevant case-law, it can be argued that it is not only the social objectives of EU law that are promoted by the Court's interpretation and emphasis on the Charter, but also the integration of the EU legal order.

By this, I mean that in the first years of the Community project, the Court used primary law with an emphasis on economic freedom as a means to promote the integration of Member States and to fortify the Community legal order in light of a constitutional end that was absent from the Treaty text.[157] With the political ambition of the EU project under stress, the failed Constitutional Treaty, and the reformed architecture of the EU legal system with the adoption of the Charter, the Court turned to another instrument that could advance integration, namely the Charter. It has consistently made use of the provisions of the Charter to review secondary law on migration and limit state discretion in an area of shared competence. The Court's interpretation on the relevant secondary law is framing the space of fundamental rights policy exercised by the EU legislature. Both the revision of the Single Permit Directive and the proposed revision of the Long-term Residents Directive were presented

[157] See Chapter 2. Cf G Federico Mancini, 'The Making of a Constitution for Europe' (1989) 26 CMLRev 595.

by the Commission with stronger emphasis on fundamental rights protection for migrants in line with the case-law.[158]

This approach of the Court stands in stark contrast to the interpretations followed on EU migrants' rights, where it has accepted a consolidation of balancing of economic and social objectives by the EU legislature as expressed in Directive 2004/38. The differentiation could also be connected to the maturity of the legal framework on EU migrants, which has been constantly transforming since the 1960s. Secondary law on migration, on the other hand, is very recent. As shown throughout this historical investigation, it has developed in an 'environment in which national jealousies and priorities are never far from the surface'.[159] In cases related to TCN migrants, the Court consistently reviews national law in light of a more positive vision of what individual rights should look like in a legal system whose constitutional architecture is completed by the adoption of the Charter.

This differentiated approach, however, has led to paradoxical interpretations in cases where the Court had to relate the rights of EU and TCN migrants. Maintaining the focus on case-law, Section 9.4 showcases the paradoxes that derive from the emphasis on the different status of EU and TCN migrants and the parallel acknowledgement that safeguarding the economy demands the limitation of rights for both categories.

9.4 Migrants, Citizens, Differentiation, and Incoherence

The analysis in this part revealed the different approach of the Court in its case-law on EU and TCN migrants during this period. Specifically, while the Court has accepted the balancing of economic and social objectives decided by the EU legislature regarding EU migrants, it has extensively interpreted the rights of TCN migrants in view of the constitutional architecture of the EU. In parallel, the analysis carried out

[158] See Proposal for a Directive, on a single application procedure for a single permit for third-country nationals to reside and work in the territory of a Member State and on a common set of rights for third-country workers legally residing in a Member State (recast), COM(2022)655 final, Explanatory Memorandum, Article 12 with reference to C-302/19, *INPS*; Proposal for a Directive concerning the status of third-country nationals who are long-term residents (recast), COM(2022)650 final, Explanatory Memorandum, Articles 5, 12.

[159] Neil Walker, 'In Search of the Area of Freedom, Security and Justice: A Constitutional Odyssey' in Neil Walker (ed), *Europe's Area of Freedom, Security, and Justice* (Oxford University Press 2004).

throughout the book has shown that economic and social objectives condition the rights of both categories of migrants. While EU citizenship provisions have shown their teeth when it comes to rights claimed by migrants against their host state, the movement of EU migrants is very much conditioned by economic considerations, and so are the social rights they can claim. Similarly, the rights TCN migrants draw from secondary law are granted precisely in order to achieve the economic objectives of EU law.

The case-law of the Court has developed through the emphasis on the Union citizenship status as the normative foundation of the rights of EU migrants. Even in cases where such status cannot guarantee rights to economically inactive migrants, the Court still emphasizes its primary nature. At the same time, the Court implicitly, and its AGs explicitly, emphasizes that the rights of EU and TCN migrants are different in their nature.[160] While it is true that the rights of EU and TCN migrants are created under different legal bases and have a different normative outlook, this does not preclude cases where the rights attributed to both groups are of a similar extent and serve the same objectives. This is the case for family reunification rights of EU and TCN migrants, for example. In such cases, the emphasis on the fundamental status of EU citizenship and the different treatment for TCN migrants creates paradoxical outcomes which complicate our understanding of the EU fundamental rights protection system.[161]

Exemplary in this regard is the decision of the Court in *X v État belge*, which demonstrates that the insistence on a differentiation of rights between EU and TCN migrants that is not reflected in secondary law, can adversely affects the potentials of EU citizenship, while at the same time it implicitly encourages Member States to undermine the rights of TCNs.[162] The case concerned the right to an autonomous residence

[160] Opinion of AG Szpunar in C-544/15, *Fahimian*, and in C-579/13, *P and S*, ECLI:EU:C:2015:39; Opinion of AG Mengozzi in C-257/17, *C and A*, ECLI:EU:C:2018:503 and in C-138/13, *Dogan*, ECLI:EU:C:2014:287. In the context of cases exclusively dealing with EU migrants, Advocates General have made very grand statements; indicative is the Opinion of AG Jacobs in C-168/91, *Konstantinidis*, ECLI:EU:C:1992:504 and the famous dictum 'civis europeus sum'.

[161] Cf Sara Iglesias Sánchez, 'The Constitutional Status of Foreigners and European Union Citizens: Loopholes and Interactions in the Scope of Application of Fundamental Rights' in Daniel Thym (ed), *Questioning EU Citizenship: Judges and the Limits of Free Movement and Solidarity in the EU* (Hart 2017).

[162] Case C-930/19, *Belgian State*, ECLI:EU:C:2021:657.

permit for family members of EU citizens, when such family members are victims of domestic violence. Article 13 of Directive 2004/38 requires that the family members are either economically active or have sufficient resources and health insurance, while Article 15 of the Family Reunification Directive provides that the conditions for granting such an autonomous residence permit are provided by national law. The referring court suggested that the only thing that differentiates the conditions under which an autonomous residence right should be granted to a TCN victim of domestic violence is whether their spouse is an EU migrant or not. Due to this, it asked whether the relevant article of Directive 2004/38 should be invalidated as constituting a case of unequal treatment. The Court acknowledged that the two provisions established different conditions even though they shared the same objective – protecting family members who are victims of violence.[163] It then went on to examine all the elements of the relevant framework and to evaluate whether the autonomous rights of family members of EU and TCN migrants could be comparable. The Court found that, even though the specific provisions have the same objective, they exist in Directives that relate to different fields, principles, subject matters, and objectives. It emphasized the difference between the two categories of migrants, suggesting that beneficiaries of rights under Directive 2004/38 'enjoy a different status and rights of a different kind'.[164] However, it did not review secondary law on EU migrants for compliance with the Charter. Instead, it suggested that the paradoxical outcome which leads to the stronger protection for family members of TCN migrants is the result of Belgian law, which did not impose equally strict conditions for family members of TCN migrants, even though it had the discretion to.[165]

This case is exemplary of the analysis of the Court in that it highlights the tensions inherent in EU law and case-law and the way it qualifies the rights of migrants. Instead of reviewing Directive 2004/38 for compliance with the Charter, the Court accepts the economic balancing that results in limitation of the rights of EU migrants and their family members. At the same time, it defers to national law to lower the standard of protection for TCN migrants and to ensure the more favourable treatment of EU migrants. And in general, it puts forward the Charter as a basis of review of national law on TCN migrants, when it consistently

[163] Ibid, para 70.
[164] Ibid, para 89.
[165] Ibid, para 88.

fails to invoke the Charter in relation to EU migrants.[166] Indeed, as Nic Shuibhne suggested in a different context, the Court's case-law is characterized by a 'hegemonic attribution of supremacy to secondary law, which fails to engage the constitutional protocols epitomising the Union legal order more generally'.[167] In the specific case analysed, the Court accepted as legitimate the standards of Directive 2004/38 without further examination of the relevance of the economic conditioning for victims of domestic violence. The minimum standards of protection are ultimately the ones dictated by the economic and social balance as it has taken place for EU migrants.[168]

Essentially, in this period the dust settled. The EU project had been continuously on the road to transformation, as ingrained in the language of the Treaties, but it had also come a long way. Different actors came to different realizations, which affected legislation and case-law on migrants' rights in the following way. The Council realized that it could no longer block admission and rights of TCN migrants because EU growth would be impossible to maintain without their labour. The Commission realized that the Council could not go as far as accepting the shaping of a supranational community whereby EU and TCN migrants alike would enjoy rights directly from the EU legal order. The Court also realized that integration could not only be promoted via law but also needed to find support in democratic processes, and for this reason deferred to the political balancing behind different instruments as legitimate balancing for the purposes of EU law. This does not mean that any effort for integration through law was blocked. During this period the Court proceeded in review of national legislation in light of the Charter in the same way that it employed economic freedoms provisions during the first period reviewed in Part I. With the coming of age of the EU legal order, fundamental rights provisions become a powerful integration technique.[169] This chapter thus concludes the historical overview of EU migration law from the establishment of the European Coal and

[166] See Section 8.2; Cf Niamh Nic Shuibhne, 'Integrating Union Citizenship and the Charter of Fundamental Rights' in Daniel Thym (ed), *Questioning EU Citizenship: Judges and the Limits of Free Movement and Solidarity in the EU* (Hart 2017).

[167] Niamh Nic Shuibhne, 'Limits Rising, Duties Ascending: The Changing Legal Shape of Union Citizenship' (2015) 52 CMLRev 889, 891.

[168] See also Vladislava Stoyanova, 'On the Bride's Side? Victims of Domestic Violence and Their Residence Rights under EU and Council of Europe Law' (2019) 37 Netherlands Quarterly of Human Rights 311.

[169] Cf Muir (n 82) 92.

Steel Community to the present. The persistence of the economic and social pillar of sustainability in the regulation of migration, as they were manifested in the language of economic and social objectives of EU primary law has been revealed throughout the historical investigation. The task of the remaining chapter, therefore, is to draw on the findings of this historical investigation so as to link the balancing of economic and social objectives behind the regulation of EU migration to the contemporary demand of sustainable migration and to conclude by discussing the potentials and limitations of an EU sustainable migration.

10

Conclusion

10.1 Economic and Social Sustainability in the Past of EU Migration Law

The task of looking back at the history of EU law in search for answers is a challenging one due to 'the remorseless pace of development' of the EU legal framework.[1] Positioning the time of doctrinal consolidation in the present, the analysis proceeded in a necessary critical reconstruction of the history of EU migration law. This concluding chapter will first summarize the findings of the historical investigation in this section and suggest that the problem behind the new objective of sustainable migration lies not so much in the effort to align migration with economic and social demands. This has after all been a constant feature of EU law as distilled from the historical investigation. Rather the problem lies in the way the economic and social objectives of the EU are perceived by different actors. Section 10.2 analyses the limitations that exist in the way EU law has historically aligned migrants' rights to the economic and social objectives of primary law and reflects on what an EU sustainable migration can and cannot mean for the rights of migrants. Essentially this section highlights that structural features of the EU legal order set very clear limits in attempts to envision an EU sustainable migration law. Finally, Section 10.3 presents a vision of what an EU sustainable migration law could mean if the way economic and social objectives are considered was redirected and grounded on the current *acquis*.

On the findings of the historical investigation, already in the first period of Community law – reviewed in Part I – the existence of the economic pillar of sustainability was emphasized behind the attribution of rights to migrants, manifested in the language of economic objectives served by migration. This period was characterized by the reconstruction

[1] Neil Walker, 'Legal and Constitutional Theory of the European Union' in Paul Craig and Gráinne de Búrca (eds), *The Evolution of EU Law* (Oxford University Press 2021) 91.

of Western economies. Free movement of factors of production, among which was labour, was necessary to spearhead the post-war growth of the founding Member States in the 1950s and 1960s. Next to Community migrants, guest workers and workers from former colonies supported the growth of Western economies until the oil crisis of the 1970s. At the time, Community workers and TCNs employed in European industries were attributed extensive rights pursuant to a clear acknowledgement that they were all equally contributing and participating in this project of growth. Equal treatment and raising the standard of living for all people who pursued a life in the EU – and who contributed with their work towards the achievement of social progress – was a non-issue.

The changing economic circumstances after the 1970s and the repeated enlargements of the EU and its continuous legal transformation nuanced the way economic considerations served as the basis of rights and promotion of social standards. Member States became more diverse: they were differently affected by the oil crisis, and they had different economic development levels and labour needs. In these circumstances, faced with the need to seal themselves off from the effects of transnational markets and with national unemployment on the rise, they attempted to close their borders and limit the rights of migrants so as to become unattractive destinations. The plan of the Commission, as expressed in legislative proposals published at the time, continued unhindered, with the hope that the effects of the crisis would be eventually overcome. During this period, positive action to promote the social objectives of the legal order was not really considered. The reason for this was a perception that economic growth would raise living standards for the population of Member States automatically. The attribution of social rights was considered in a superficial way, being mostly focused on equal working conditions to counter the economic effects of social dumping. Overall, during this first period, the economic objectives served by migration dictated the aligned treatment of all migrants due to a demand for equal treatment for all those who contributed to the development of the Community.

In the second period, reviewed in Part II, the appearance of economic and social objectives was more ambiguous. While the economic and social pillar of sustainability continued to determine the rights attributed to migrants, elements of differentiation between EU and TCN migrants were put in place in line with the ambition to create a political community. During that time, the promise of EU growth and the changing political landscape after the fall of the Berlin Wall created the impetus for closer integration and more consistent protection of the individual behind the factor of production. The aspiration of reuniting Europe put emphasis on turning the project of growth into a project of prosperity for the people of Europe. At the same time, economic worries of Member States blocked any attempt by the Commission to shape a framework that could regulate the rights of migrants in light of long-term economic needs and fluctuations. Member States via the Council deflected the issue of TCNs' rights so as to maintain a semblance of control in case of fluctuations in national economies.

Regarding EU migrants, the political aspirations of the time led to the establishment of EU citizenship in primary law. However, economic concerns precluded the creation of a framework that would shape residence rights for EU migrants based on their importance for the EU polity in the making. This political aspiration was, nevertheless, considered by the Court. By insisting on the new fundamental status established in primary law, the Court significantly restricted the limitations set by secondary law regarding the rights of EU migrants. Taking the objectives of the EU project at face value, the Court also consolidated the protection of migrant workers regardless of their nationality, thereby promoting the social objectives of the EU. To do so, it maintained the approach developed in the case-law on Community migrants and extended it to TCN migrants as well, suggesting that equal contribution to the EU project required equal rights. This protective case-law was a cause of concern for Member States, who feared repercussions for their national economies. For this reason, their economic concerns appeared behind the limitation of migrants' rights in the Association Agreements, concluded or revised at the time.

Next to the political aspirations for EU citizenship, the transformation of the EU project also demanded a closer pursuit of social progress, and relatedly more emphasis on the social pillar of sustainability. Even though legislation could not be adopted to extend the rights of EU migrants in light of their citizen status, legislation attributing rights to TCN migrants resident in the EU succeeded. The results of this legislation were not as far reaching as the Commission had hoped. Despite this, it managed to convince the Member States of the need to attribute at least a minimum set of rights to those who would not pose risks to EU growth, and to the extent that they would not pose such risks. This was the case with the Students Directive, the Family Reunification Directive, and the Long-term Residents Directive adopted at that time, which created EU law rights for migrants, even if such rights could be significantly limited by considerations related to economic reasons.

Finally, in the third period, reviewed in Part III, the transformation of the EU project was completed, and the way in which the economic and social pillars of sustainability appear behind the regulation of migration was consolidated. From a small Community of states, based on largely similar and interdependent economies, the EU developed into a political and economic Union comprised of Member States with different systems of social protection and different levels of economic performance. The enlargement of the EU in the new millennium consolidated a diverse mix of economic needs and ideals of social progress. In parallel, the labour needs of industries began to revive, and these were matched by demographic predictions of an ageing EU population that could not sustain growth. The failure to adopt the Constitutional Treaty put an end to aspirations of making something more of the movement of individuals, and the economic crisis of 2008 consolidated the need to always balance the rights of EU migrants against potential economic risks, even if such migrants were now called EU citizens.

During this period, sustainable migration became perfected in the rights enjoyed by EU migrants. Specifically, the balancing of economic and social considerations behind the rights of EU migrants meant that they could not enjoy unlimited residence rights by virtue of their status. Rather, when they migrate, their rights should be limited based on economic considerations. If they do not contribute to the EU project, they should at least not negatively affect the economies of host states. This consideration was consolidated in Directive 2004/38, and the balancing of individual rights against economic considerations was confirmed by the Court. At the same time, economic demands and demographic projections created the need for labour migration. Despite the Member States' reluctance to harmonize migration law, it became clear that human labour was necessary not to spearhead growth, but rather to maintain it. As the Member States were very unequally affected by migration and not equally in need of migrant workers, a system of entry was created for those workers who were most needed: highly skilled workers (including researchers) and low-skilled workers. In this framework, social considerations demanded the incorporation of labour law standards in the employment of such migrants, and these are more extensive when it comes to migrants considered more vulnerable to exploitation. Fair treatment for TCNs translated into differentiated treatment to attract the migrants the EU project most needs, notably researchers and highly skilled workers. At the same time, the rights include very strict safeguards to avoid settlement migration for those that are only temporarily needed. What we witness in this period is also the emphasis of the Court on social rights for migrants in light of the Charter. While in the case of EU migrants, the Court has accepted the balancing of economic and social objectives carried by the EU legislature and does not invoke primary law or Charter rights as a basis for review, this is not the case for TCN migrants. In the relevant case-law, the Court has consistently invoked the Charter to extend the protection of the rights of migrants against attempts by Member States to curtail them.

The investigation identified the constant pursuit of the economic and social pillars of sustainability via the regulation of migration. The language of sustainability was not part of EU migration law until very recently. However, the economic and social pillars of sustainability have always found expression in the attempts of shaping an autonomous EU migration law as a legal system with specific characteristics. These characteristics are the attribution of rights to migrants because of their contribution to growth, the limitation of rights due to perceived risks to growth (regardless of whether such risks are evidence based or not), an emphasis on work-related rights as means to social progress without a broader conception of the individual behind the economic actor, and the incorporation of clauses to guarantee that there is always a safety valve to stop migration in case of threats to the economy. A more detailed explanation of how economic and social considerations manifested themselves in law-making and adjudication in Sections 10.1.1 and 10.1.2 will further reveal the centrality of sustainability in the development and interpretation of EU migration law.

10.1.1 Economic and Social Considerations in EU Law-Making

A preliminary point to be raised is that EU law does not channel 'a prior general political authority and its integrated sense of the public good'.[2] Rather it is a means to stabilize the commitments of Member States to achieve 'various complex public goods under a new transnational political authority'.[3] For this reason, the way economic and social

[2] Neil Walker, 'The Theoretical Foundations of EU Law' in Claire Kilpatrick and Joanne Scott (eds), *Contemporary Challenges to EU Legality* (Oxford University Press 2021) 38.

[3] Ibid.

considerations are taken into account and are channelled into laws varies for different institutional actors.

The Commission is the only actor insistent on achieving long-term economic and social development for the EU. It has consistently shown a proactive stance on the attribution of rights to migrants with the aim of shaping EU instruments that can align migration with the objectives of growth and progress, thus implicitly promoting an EU sustainable migration during all the years of its legislative activity. In the regulation of entry for TCN migrants, the Commission has emphasized the need to guarantee the more efficient allocation of resources and the proper functioning of the EU economy. Each proposal the Commission issued included safeguards that could guarantee the functioning of such system, including in cases of recession. In addition, the attribution of social rights to migrants has also been constantly suggested. While originally this attribution of rights was based on the contribution of the migrant to the economy and had the purpose of minimizing unfair competition in the labour market, after the 1990s the Commission has focused on the necessity of attribution of rights to promote social cohesion across EU territory and to thus allow for more socially sustainable societies. In parallel, the Commission put a lot of emphasis on long-term approach to the regulation of migration. Despite this, in the final period examined, the Commission has become more realistic, in the sense that it suggests proposals which can secure some minimum support of the Council, rather than proposals that are actually geared towards achieving economic and social sustainability by the regulation of migration. This was the case with the regulation of admission, where even though the Commission consistently acknowledged the horizontal regulation of admission as the ideal system, it continued to pursue sectoral regulation of the matter, as it became clear that it cannot gather support for horizontal measures.[4]

In contrast to the Commission's approach, the Council takes into account economic considerations related to the specific circumstances at national level. In doing so, it does not differentiate between EU and TCN migrants, but rather relates migration as such to the economy of the Member States. Relating migrant rights to the achievements of economic objectives was emphasized only during the years prior to the oil crisis. Thereafter the Member States have repeatedly acknowledged the need to

[4] See Attracting skills and talent to the EU, COM(2022)657 final; Fitness Check on EU Legislation on legal migration SWD(2019)1055.

commit to the common project of growth in political declarations, but when it comes to the negotiation of specific legal instruments, the focus turns to ensuring economic and social growth in the short-term and within each national setting. This largely explains the struggle behind the adoption of a framework regulating migration from third countries. In a sense, this dissonance between the Council and the Commission also points to the limits of solidarity between Member States when the EU project does not deliver unhindered growth for all the members of the club.

The problem is aggravated by the fact that economic considerations in the Council are shaped by the immediate economic circumstances on the ground, with no thought to how to align migration with future needs of national economies. In contrast to the long-term planning demanded by sustainability, the Council has been particularly short-sighted when addressing migration. Furthermore, even though the Council is supposed to reflect the collective political interests of Member States in the common EU project, national considerations predominate. Especially regarding TCN migrants, when Member States are up against national unemployment or recession, it is impossible for them to agree on any migration-related measure that could lead to the attribution rights. This is, of course, also connected to the shared competence on migration and the fact that even if Member States can foresee the demand for workers, they know that they can fulfil this demand through national migration law measures. In this context, the creation of EU rights for migrants can only cause tension in national politics. In addition to the issue of shared competence, the approach of the Council, as attested in the analysis, is tied to what Neyer has identified as institutional deficiencies of the European political order, according to which the political discourse in the Council does not identify with the integration process and is rather catered to domestic interests.[5]

Hence, even though there has been no evidence to support the negative effects of the different Commission proposals on national economies (as was the case in the context of enlargement, in the case of social rights of EU workers in the new millennium, and in the case of mobility rights for TCNs), the Council cannot reach an agreement. As to the social objectives, once again, the focus is rather on the national level. It is at the

[5] Jürgen Neyer, 'Saving Liberal Europe: Lessons from History' in Antonina Bakardjieva Engelbrekt and Xavier Groussot (eds), *The Future of Europe: Political and Legal Integration beyond Brexit* (Hart 2019) 24.

national level that the Council considers how to promote social cohesion or how to fight national unemployment, covering labour demands with little to no concern as to how to align national approaches with the transnational aspirations of collective economic growth and social progress.

Finally, the Parliament, especially in the second period, but also throughout the examination, has put forward a rights-based approach as a means to promote the social conditions across EU territory. It also seeks to advance political ideals of including all residents in the Member States in the project of peace and prosperity. This does not seem to deliver much when it comes to the legislative proposals, which are all eventually restricted by the Council. Having seen how economic and social considerations are expressed by different EU actors and channelled into EU law-making, Section 10.1.2 turns to how these considerations are reflected in the case-law and reveals the particular use of economic and social objectives by the Court to progress integration. Looking at these two sections together identifies the centrality of economic and social considerations for all institutional actors and shows the pursuit of sustainable migration as an objective even before the explicit appearance of the term in EU policy discourse.

10.1.2 Economic and Social Considerations in the Case-Law

The analysis carried out in this book fits well with earlier scholarly examination of the Court as a political actor and claims related to judicial activism. Such claims rest on two contrasting positions described by Dawson.[6] There is a liberal position which suggests that the role of the Court in promoting EU integration is politically empowering for the individual.[7] By empowering individuals to enforce their rights under EU law, the Court is providing individuals with access to the law, and thereby opens new political pathways.[8] At the same time, there is a second, republican view on the social role of the law.[9] This view entails

[6] Mark Dawson, 'The Political Face of Judicial Activism: Europe's Law-Politics Imbalance' in Bruno de Witte, Elise Muir, and Mark Dawson (eds), *Judicial Activism at the European Court of Justice* (Edward Elgar 2013).

[7] Ibid 11 with reference to Federico Mancini and David Keeling, 'Democracy and the European Court of Justice' (1994) 57 The Modern Law Review 175.

[8] Dawson (n 6) 11.

[9] Ibid with reference to Richard Bellamy, *Political Constitutionalism: A Republican Defence of the Constitutionality of Democracy* (Cambridge University Press 2007); Fritz Scharpf,

that courts should express and carry forward the views of a political community as mediated in the legislation, rather than protect and empower individuals. As Dawson suggests, what is considered the proper judicial function in the liberal position becomes an 'usurpation of power' in the republican position, where individual rights and legal entitlements are utilized to overturn the settled preferences of a political community.[10] It is under this reading that the Court can be understood as a political actor, and it is in this context that the Court has been seen as 'activist' in judicially settling questions that should be balanced and decided in political arenas.[11]

The liberal position on the role of the Court has been supported by members of the Court. Former Judge and Advocate General Mancini has proudly suggested that the case-law of the Court in the early years of Community law coincides with the making of a constitution for Europe.[12] Acknowledging that the Treaty framework could not be seen as a constitutive act, Mancini described the endeavour of the Court to constitutionalize the Treaty as being 'to fashion a constitutional framework for a federal-type structure in Europe'.[13] Mancini himself admits a degree of activism on behalf of the Court in using law to foster the integration of Europe.[14] This acknowledgement fits squarely with the scholarly analysis of the central role of the Court for the construction of the EU legal order as an integrated constitutional order.[15] Looking at the role of the Court in the process of legal integration, Burley and Mattli suggested in the 1990s that its action fits a neofunctionalist model of integration where judicial actors can advance a political agenda.[16] By political agenda, Burley and Mattli meant a pro-European agenda, and they argued that the Court had promoted the role of individuals by giving them a stake in the implementation of Community law only in

'Legitimacy in the Multilevel European Polity' (2009) 1 European Political Science Review 173; Bruce Ackerman and James Fishkin, *Deliberation Day* (Yale Univ Press 2004).

[10] Dawson (n 6) 12.

[11] Ibid.

[12] Federico Mancini, 'The Making of a Constitution for Europe' (1989) 26 CMLRev 595, 595.

[13] Ibid 596.

[14] Ibid 612.

[15] Neil Walker, 'Opening or Closure? The Constitutional Intimations of the ECJ' in Loïc Azoulai and Miguel Poiares Maduro (eds), *The Past and Future of EU Law: The Classics of EU Law Revisited on the 50th Anniversary of the Rome Treaty* (Hart 2010) 41.

[16] Anne-Marie Burley and Walter Mattli, 'Europe before the Court: A Political Theory of Legal Integration' (1993) 47 International Organization 41, 57.

such ways as would promote Community goals.[17] In their work, they tie the political and activist stance of the Court to promoting the visibility, effectiveness, and scope of EU law, as well as the power of the Court, while at the same time 'presenting itself as the champion of individual rights and the protector of the prerogatives of lower national courts'.[18] This analysis, as well as the literature examining the Court as a political actor, fits well with the findings of the present investigation and reveals that the Court has used economic and social objectives at different points in time as a means to progress integration.

Specifically, in the early years of the Community project, economic objectives dominated the reasoning of the Court. The extensive creation of rights for Community and TCN migrants was based on the contribution of the individual to the project of growth, as shown in Part I. Even in cases where such contribution was minor, the Court emphasized how the economic objectives of the project can be served by the attribution or extension of rights of migrants. The political aspirations of the EU affected the case-law during the second period, as demonstrated in Part II. At the time, there was an emphasis on the 'ever-closer Union of peoples' goal in order to extend rights beyond the economic function of EU migrants under their new citizen status. During the third period examined in Part III, there is a consistent reliance on the Charter in cases concerning TCN migrants, not driven by an economic logic, but with the aim of promoting social objectives in a legal system that recognizes the need to attribute rights to all individuals who come within its scope. At the same time, the political aspirations for a Union of peoples appear in a confusing way. While the Court acknowledges the limitation of rights of EU migrants in light of the balancing of economic and social objectives undertaken by the legislator in Directive 2004/38, it has used the political aspirations to establish a differentiation between EU and TCNs on a discourse level. Even in cases where Directive 2004/38 sets less favourable conditions for the rights of EU migrants compared to the rights of TCN migrants on family reunification, the Court emphasized the political goals of the EU for its nationals, and did not examine

[17] Ibid 60. The authors discuss the extensive construction of the scope of EU law in preliminary references, comparing it to the restrictive criteria for individual standing in actions for annulment; Fabien Terpan and Sabine Saurugger, 'The Politics of the Court of Justice of the European Union' in Paul James Cardwell and Marie-Pierre Granger (eds), *Research Handbook on the Politics of EU Law* (Edward Elgar 2020) 33, who refer to 'biased' Court.

[18] Burley and Mattli (n 16) 64.

whether secondary law can stand review under the Charter.[19] It also emphasizes the rights of EU migrants *qua* citizens, but it no longer invokes primary law to extend their access to social rights. Rather, the Court defers to the balancing carried out by the legislature, and does not try to trump the limitations of Directive 2004/38 with a broader interpretation of either primary provisions on citizenship or the Charter.[20]

Looking at the evolution of the case-law, we need to bear in mind that the more progressive rulings of the Court presented in Part II took place at a time when Treaty provisions demanded non-economic free movement rights for EU citizens, while secondary law giving effect thereto was adopted prior to the relevant Treaty amendments. Directive 2004/38 came into effect after the Treaty provisions established such rights, and hence expressed the clear will of the legislature to set limits on the social rights of EU migrants *qua* citizens. This limitation by the legislature, which has led to what Muir called a deconstitutionalization process, brings to mind another comment made by scholars emphasizing the political role of the Court.[21]

According to Burley and Mattli, to enhance and preserve the power of the Court, 'they [judges] must preserve and earn anew the presumed legitimacy of law by remaining roughly faithful to its canons'.[22] This means that the Court needs to stay within the boundaries of existing law. Mancini similarly suggested that as democracy advanced and politics (meaning EU politics) asserted its claims, judges should take a step back, otherwise they risked becoming 'so embroiled in the passions' that they could harm their independence.[23] Related to this, Terpan and Saurugger have suggested that since the 1990s, the Court has been exercising self-restraint in its adjudication, also hinting that in the relevant period there

[19] Case C-930/19, *Belgian State*, ECLI:EU:C:2021:657.

[20] Moritz Jesse and Daniel Carter, 'Life after the "Dano-Trilogy": Legal Certainty, Choices and Limitations in EU Citizenship Case Law' in Nathan Cambien, Dimitry Kochenov, and Elise Muir (eds), *European Citizenship under Stress, Social Justice, Brexit and Other Challenges*, vol 16 (Brill Nijhoff 2020); Niamh Nic Shuibhne, 'What I Tell You Three Times Is True: Lawful Residence and Equal Treatment after Dano' (2016) 23 Maastricht Journal of European and Comparative Law 908.

[21] Elise Muir, 'EU Citizenship, Access to "Social Benefits" and Third-Country National Family Members: Reflecting on the Relationship between Primary and Secondary Rights in Times of Brexit' (2019) 2018 European Papers – A Journal on Law and Integration 1353.

[22] Burley and Mattli (n 16) 73.

[23] Mancini (n 12) 613.

was no longer a permissive consensus on the part of the Member States.[24] Keeping this in mind, what should we make of the much more consistent approach of the Court on using the Charter as the benchmark of review in cases concerning TCN migrants? In these cases, I argue that we can see the Court being political by using the cases on TCN migration to promote the power and strength of the Charter and, thereby, to constitutionally perfect an integrated legal order. As Mancini has suggested, self-restraint does not mean strict constructionism in the interpretation of EU law.[25]

In this intricate mix of self-restraint and striving to achieve further integration, we see that just as the Court is deconstitutionalizing the rights of EU migrants *qua* citizens, it is constitutionalizing the rights of TCN migrants. When it comes to TCN migrants (either as family members of EU migrants or as individuals coming within the scope of EU law), the Court never misses a chance to use the Charter as a means to strengthen the protection afforded by the secondary legislation in place and, relatedly, to consolidate the position of the Charter in the constitutional architecture of the EU law. As Muir has suggested, the review of compliance of legislation with fundamental rights appears as a powerful integration technique.[26] This is because, as she argues, 'by merging the content of legislation and autonomous concepts having primary law value, the Court circumscribes the possibility for EU political institutions to define the format and limits of EU fundamental rights policy through legislation'.[27] Muir's point was made in relation to other areas of EU law, but finds equal application in the case-law regarding rights of TCN migrants examined in Section 9.3, where the interpretation of the Court with an emphasis on the Charter is now channelled in proposals for revision of secondary legislation.[28]

24 Terpan and Saurugger (n 17) 34.

25 Ibid.

26 Elise Muir, 'The Court of Justice: A Fundamental Rights Institution among Others' in Bruno de Witte, Elise Muir, and Mark Dawson (eds), *Judicial Activism at the European Court of Justice* (Edward Elgar 2013) 92.

27 Ibid 92–93.

28 Proposal for a Directive on a single application procedure for a single permit for third-country nationals to reside and work in the territory of a Member State and on a common set of rights for third-country workers legally residing in a Member State (recast), COM (2022)655 final, Explanatory Memorandum, Article 12 with reference to Case C-302/19, *INPS*, ECLI:EU:C:2020:957. See also 2024 Single Permit Directive.

Overall, the analysis carried out in this book has shown how in the first period of aligned paths, economic aspirations drove legislative openness on migrants' rights. In the second period of political aspirations, the slow resurgence of growth matched with an anticipated enlargement of the EU (and the addition of working population) pointed to legislative closure and differentiation between EU and TCN migrants. In the third period of realization, failed political aspirations marked the economic conditioning of the rights of EU migrants and the set-up of an incoherent framework on the rights of TCN migrants. Throughout all these periods, the Commission has been proactive, while the Council has been reactive, or even destructive. This is so especially if we consider the way in which it has downgraded protection in all relevant secondary law on the rights of both EU and TCN migrants, and renegotiated International Agreements to limit the effects of EU law as construed by the Court. The Court, on the other hand, has been consistently reconstructing the rights of migrants. This reconstruction of migrants' rights takes place not in light of what the EU should become, but rather in light of what it currently is under the Treaty framework, complemented with a binding Charter, which provides sufficient basis to consolidate the constitutional architecture of EU law. The approach of all these institutions, as it derives from the past seventy years of EU migration law, is not without gaps and paradoxes. Potential ways of addressing these and framing an EU sustainable migration law are discussed in Section 10.3. Before going into that, Section 10.2 engages with the limitations that appear in the current system.

10.2 The Inherent Limits of an EU Sustainable Migration

The critical historical study conducted in this book showed that EU migration law was never meant to be inclusive, in the sense of linking migrants to a transnational legal order and creating a civic post-national membership.[29] Many authors have argued that EU migration law has been shaped on the exclusion of different people for different reasons.[30]

[29] Cf Yasemin Nuhoğlu Soysal, *Limits of Citizenship: Migrants and Postnational Membership in Europe* (University of Chicago 1994).

[30] Although different authors have pointed to different reasons. See Étienne Balibar, *Nous, citoyens d'Europe?* (La Découverte 2001); Peo Hansen, 'Making Sense of a Neoliberal Fortress?: EU Migration Policy in the Nexus of Economy, Security and Rights' (Nordisk Samarbejdsråd for Kriminologi 2011); Steve Peers, 'Building Fortress Europe: The Development of EU Migration Law' (1998) 35 CMLRev; Thomas Spijkerboer,

This book contributes to the relevant literature by suggesting that another reason for exclusion is the economic function of the migrant for the EU development project. The EU legal order is shaped around the constant pursuit of growth and progress. In this regard, an EU sustainable migration is doomed to have little room for those who cannot contribute to the project of growth.

In Section 1.3.2, I suggested that the minimum core features of sustainability are its economic, social, and environmental pillars; a long-term approach; and inter- and intra-generational justice demands. Questions on justice and its relation to the EU have been picked up by scholarship and this contribution does not aim to examine them in depth.[31] Various scholars have engaged with the possibilities and limitations of imagining distributive justice in a transnational setting.[32] Among them, Williams has suggested that, while the EU discourse includes occasional references to solidarity, economic cohesion, and social justice, there is no political or constitutional obligation for the EU to coordinate any process of redistribution of resources within or outside its borders.[33] Drawing on different theoretical contributions, this section shows how questions of justice and social and economic sustainability appear in the current form of EU migration law by identifying three limitations related to the EU's pursuit of growth, the way EU law attributes rights to migrants, and the position of migration law in the EU legal architecture.

'Bifurcation of People, Bifurcation of Law: Externalization of Migration Policy before the EU Court of Justice' (2018) 31 Journal of Refugee Studies 216; Daniel Carter, 'Inclusion and Exclusion of Migrant Workers in the EU' and Moritz Jesse and Daniel Carter, 'The "Market Insider": Market-Citizenship and Economic Exclusion in the EU' both in Moritz Jesse (ed), *European Societies, Migration, and the Law: The 'Others' amongst 'Us'* (Cambridge University Press 2020).

31 Dimitry Kochenov, Andrew T Williams, and Gráinne de Búrca (eds), *Europe's Justice Deficit?* (Hart 2015).

32 Daniel Augenstein, 'We the People: EU Justice as Politics' in Dimitry Kochenov, Andrew T Williams, and Gráinne de Búrca (eds), *Europe's Justice Deficit?* (Hart 2015) with reference to Damian Chalmers, 'Damian Chalmers: Kinship, Markets, and Justice in Europe' in Grainne de Burca, Dimitry Kochenov, and Andrew Trevor Williams (eds), *Debating Europe's Justice Deficit: The EU, Swabian Housewives, Rawls, and Ryanair* (2013); Richard Bellamy, 'Political Justice for an Ever Closer Union of European Peoples' in Grainne de Burca, Dimitry Kochenov, and Andrew Trevor Williams (eds), *Debating Europe's Justice Deficit: The EU, Swabian Housewives, Rawls, and Ryanair* (2013); John Rawls, *Political Liberalism* (Columbia University Press 1993); Philip Pettit, 'A Republican Law of Peoples' (2010) 9 European Journal of Political Theory 70.

33 Andrew T Williams, 'The Problem(s) of Justice in the European Union' in Dimitry Kochenov, Andrew T Williams, and Gráinne de Búrca (eds), *Europe's Justice Deficit?* (Hart 2015) 39.

To put it simply, this section highlights how sustainable migration might be an accurate term to describe parts of EU migration law, but it has not ensured that the legal framework is a just one.

On the first limitation, the historical study highlighted the close connection between the extent to which rights have been attributed to migrants by the EU and the existence of growth. This emphasis of the EU on growth has been identified by Somek as having the implication of shifting the discussion away from the political control of the economy.[34] The claim to inclusion through rights, he argues, does not extend to political concerns over the basic distributive structures; it rather takes them for granted.[35] Similarly to Somek, Wilkinson has transposed Streek's dilemma between market justice (in the form of inclusion via equal opportunities) and social justice (in the form of redistribution) to the EU, suggesting that after the golden age of post-war growth, the 'equilibrium between capitalism and democracy has become more difficult to maintain'.[36] In this book, we have seen how the only years in which the Commission could, in one way or another, make the case for a harmonized migration system that would provide for equal treatment of EU and TCN migrants was before the 1970s oil crisis. The economic circumstances from the oil crisis to this day, and the extension of the EU to cover very diverse economies, make the slightest consideration of ever returning to the post-war growth years impossible. Wilkinson's suggestion was put forward to support the contention that questions of justice in the EU should be resolved by adding political justice to the debate; this would allow democratic space to question the preference for market justice embedded in the EU system.[37] In addition to his suggestion, which is supported by other scholars, I would also add that we should reconsider whether the EU project can deliver growth to begin

[34] Alexander Somek, 'From Workers to Migrants, from Distributive Justice to Inclusion: Exploring the Changing Social Democratic Imagination' (2012) 18 ELJ 711, 720.

[35] Alexander Somek, 'The Preoccupation with Rights and the Embrace of Inclusion: A Critique' in Dimitry Kochenov, Andrew T Williams, and Gráinne de Búrca (eds), *Europe's Justice Deficit?* (Hart 2015) 308.

[36] Michael A Wilkinson, 'Politicising Europe's Justice Deficit: Some Preliminaries' in Dimitry Kochenov, Andrew T Williams, and Gráinne de Búrca (eds), *Europe's Justice Deficit?* (Hart 2015) 121, reference omitted; Wolfgang Streeck, *Buying Time: The Delayed Crisis of Democratic Capitalism* (Patrick Camiller and David Fernbach trans, 2nd ed., Verso 2017).

[37] Wilkinson (n 36) 133–136.

with.[38] The limited potential of considering the attribution of rights to migrants at times when there is no growth and the limited potential of reconsidering growth as the ultimate EU law objective point to the inherent limitations of EU migration law.[39] With the current emphasis on growth, it is hardly imaginable that EU migration law has any potential to change.

The second limitation of EU migration law relates to the conception of individual rights under EU law.[40] The analysis highlighted the intimate link behind the attribution of rights to migrants and the effects of such rights on growth. Linking rights to broader questions of justice, Somek has suggested that in a transnational market setting, the distribution of resources becomes irrelevant, and the relative treatment of individuals and equal opportunities are afforded central place.[41] Looking at the market to correct inequalities, the concern is not on redistribution, but rather on equal access to opportunities.[42] In the EU context, questions of justice become questions of rights, with an emphasis specifically on non-discrimination.[43] In such a set-up, human rights do not need to be followed by strong legislative measures and can be promoted judicially by courts. The emphasis on inclusion in the form of rights attribution, as suggested by Somek, is apparent in the development of EU migration law. This development has been based on the attribution of mobility and equal treatment rights to people as a means to achieve social progress. Given this, the maximum level of inclusion of migrants under EU law can be achieved by attributing rights to those who do not negatively

[38] See Augenstein (n 32); Agustín José Menéndez, 'Whose Justice? Which Europe?' in Dimitry Kochenov, Andrew T Williams, and Gráinne de Búrca (eds), *Europe's Justice Deficit?* (Hart 2015); Floris de Witte, 'Emancipation through Law?' in Loïc Azoulai, Ségolène Barbou des Places, and Etienne Pataut (eds), *Constructing the Person in EU Law: Rights, Roles, Identities* (Hart 2016). The emphasis on growth is an inherent part of sustainable development. Cf Julian Reid, 'Interrogating the Neoliberal Biopolitics of the Sustainable Development-Resilience Nexus' (2013) 7 International Political Sociology 353; For critique and alternative conceptions of sustainability see Ashish Kothari and others (eds), *Pluriverse: A Post-Development Dictionary* (Tulika Books 2019).

[39] Gareth Davies, 'Social Legitimacy and Purposive Power: The End, the Means and the Consent of the People' in Dimitry Kochenov, Andrew T Williams, and Gráinne de Búrca (eds), *Europe's Justice Deficit?* (Hart 2015) 259 discusses how the very choice is 'constitutionally denied'.

[40] See also Augenstein (n 32) 164.

[41] Somek (n 34) 724.

[42] Ibid.

[43] See also Williams (n 33) 33 who suggests that reliance on human rights cannot resolve substantive justice issues; Somek (n 34) 720; Somek (n 35) 297.

impact growth (by being self-sufficient and not having recourse to the social assistance system of Member States), but making the case, legal or political, for demanding inclusion (in the form of residence rights and corresponding social rights) for TCN migrants would be challenging. As Somek suggested, migrant workers' geographic movement attests 'the inclusive growth of capitalism'.[44] At the same time, people who would like to move to be part of this inclusive growth are faced with what Somek calls the most elementary obstacle, namely lack of access to a society to begin with.[45] In the current form of EU migration law, it would be extremely challenging to make the case for a right to entry or residence of economically inactive TCN migrants. Such a case could only be made in relation to migrants who have already contributed to the project of growth (like long-term residents and former workers). It is important to understand that whatever EU migration law will look like, it will always exclude those who cannot contribute – that is, unless the core parts of this legal system are amended.

A final limitation of an EU sustainable migration comes from the institutional structure of the EU and the conferral of powers. The analysis showed that only during the first period did economic and social objectives drive a positive development of the EU legal system. The similar development levels of the Member States and their common need for migration led to a common approach on how to best achieve economic and social objectives. After that period, unequal development levels and repeated economic challenges have turned Member States to considering how to best achieve economic and social objectives in closed national communities. The issue here is not (or is not mainly) the balancing of economic and social objectives, but rather the Member States' understanding of how their national objectives relate to the EU ones.[46] The problem behind achieving an EU sustainable migration lies not so much in the efforts for reform, as in the inability of Member States to perceive migration as an area of collective concern. The Commission has time and again brought consistent proposals on the negotiation table that would allow the regulation of migration to serve the economic and social

[44] Somek (n 34) 725.

[45] Ibid 722.

[46] See Niamh Nic Shuibhne, 'Editorial: Is It Time to Worry Yet?' (2009) 34 ELR 521. Cf Paul Craig, 'Institutions, Power, and Institutional Balance' in Paul Craig and Gráinne de Búrca (eds), *The Evolution of EU Law* (Oxford University Press 2021) 85 on institutional failure in the migration crisis.

objectives of the EU legal order in view of long-term needs of national economies.[47] The inability to garner support for such proposals is connected both to the shared competence of the EU in the area of migration and to the lack of social legitimacy of the EU in the eyes of national electorates.[48]

The shared competence of the EU on migration means that Member States can eventually admit the labour they need to keep their economies running via national migration schemes. This allows them to individually cover labour demands and to achieve the needed growth without regard to growth on the collective level. The existence of such national frameworks, which do not guarantee sufficient rights to migrants, creates barriers to the development at EU level. Where a position could be filled internally by the movement of a resident TCN from one Member State to another, this is now subject to barriers and delays that make it no different from entering the EU for the first time. At the same time, the pursuit of growth at state level is not always matched with considerations of promoting the social rights of migrants under national laws.

Regarding social legitimacy, the balancing of economic growth and social objectives has led to a situation where EU migrants have no claim to residence or social protection if they do not contribute to the EU economy. In addition to this, EU nationals who have not left their Member State can be subject to reverse discrimination and they are excluded from the scope of EU law. These situations are the outcome of a very specific balancing of economic and social objectives that lie behind the pursuit of sustainable migration applicable in the free movement framework. If this free movement framework was indeed discussed and understood as a sustainable migration framework, it would not lead to lack of social legitimacy. However, this framework is linked to and part of a completely different institutional discourse and aspiration of creating a political Union for the people of Europe.

Somek has suggested that the European support of freedom of choice (in the form of economic rights) was accompanied by 'a vague Durkheimian hope' that it would create solidarity on the basis of market

[47] Cf Proposal for a Council Act establishing the Convention on rules for the admission of third-country nationals to the Member States, COM(1997)387 final; Proposal for a Directive on the conditions of entry and residence of third-country nationals for the purpose of paid employment and self-employed economic activities, COM(2001)0386 final [2001] OJ C 332E/248.

[48] See Davies (n 39).

transactions.[49] The lived experience of those excluded from EU law has revealed the failure to create such transnational solidarity; it has fractured the social legitimacy of the EU and shaped space for Eurosceptic tendencies.[50] Like Somek, Neyer has also pointed out that the legal and institutional set-up of the EU is made for supporting liberalization rather than social integration.[51] This set-up, paired with the fragmentation of political authority of the EU and the disempowerment of political competence at national level, means, according to Neyer, that EU politics are usually driven by national concerns of Member States, rather than addressing pan-European problems.[52]

In sum, we see the specific limits to how migration law could be sustainable for the EU. These limits stem from the emphasis on growth as the driving force of rights (and the limitation of rights when they can no longer be instrumental to sustaining growth), the emphasis on rights geared towards achieving growth (versus broader concerns with social justice), and the structure of the EU legal and political system. Nor are these limits peculiar to migration: they relate to the political, economic, and institutional set-up of the EU. The question that naturally arises is whether there is a possibility to overcome some of these limitations – at least partially – by considering how the rights of TCN migrants might develop with closer consideration of the economic and social sustainability objectives of EU law.

10.3 The Realistic Potential of an EU Sustainable Migration

Section 10.2 discussed three specific limitations of EU migration law and of the broader EU architecture. Despite these limitations, there is still some room for evolution in the EU's pursuit of a sustainable migration. To go further than demonstrating the historical embeddedness of social and economic sustainability in EU migration law, an embeddedness which is also reflected in Article 3(3) TEU, and to apply the system-

[49] Alexander Somek, 'Alienation, Despair and Social Freedom' in Loïc Azoulai, Ségolène Barbou des Places, and Etienne Pataut (eds), *Constructing the Person in EU Law: Rights, Roles, Identities* (Hart 2016) 53.

[50] See Niamh Nic Shuibhne, 'Editorial: What Is "Europe" and Who Is It For?' (2012) 37 ELR 673; Charlotte O'Brien, 'Civis Capitalist Sum: Class as the New Guiding Principle of EU Free Movement Rights' (2016) 53 CMLRev 937; Davies (n 39) who attributes this to the characteristics of technical law-making which pre-empts contestation.

[51] Neyer (n 5) 26.

[52] Ibid 31.

theoretical understanding of sustainability in the framing of an EU sustainable migration, would entail three requirements that are at present absent. First, that migration law should respect the function of the EU legal system in delivering the promised objectives of growth and social progress. Second, that migration law should be shaped with a view to long-term considerations (both in relation to the fluctuations of the economy and to the position of migrants in a society) to be able to address external stress caused to the system. And finally, that migration law should be able to respect the structure of the legal system in terms of horizontal and vertical division of competences.

Connected to the system-theoretical understanding of sustainability, a substantive question arises related to the place of justice as part of sustainability. Drawing on the work of Douglas-Scott and her proposal on employing human rights and Critical Legal Justice as a legal toolbox that can offer mechanisms to the EU to avoid injustice, without however offering an ideal, transcendental theory of justice,[53] there are ways in which migrants' rights could be extended and consolidated in a way that is better aligned to the pursuit of sustainability.

The first necessary action would be to amend secondary law so that it can better serve both economic and social objectives under long-term considerations. Account should be taken of the long-term economic fluctuations in the Member States and, relatedly, the fluctuations in labour demand that need to be effectively addressed by migration, as well as the place of migrants in future EU societies. The most far-reaching change would be the horizontal regulation of admission for all categories of migrants and the recasting of the sectoral regulation currently in place. The current legislative initiatives of the Commission paired with the failure of similar attempts in the past make such a scenario unlikely.[54]

Removing this proposal for change from the table, other more limited changes could have far-reaching results. One of these would be to demand more favourable conditions for the mobility of migrants. In general, effective mobility rights for all legally resident migrants make

[53] Sionaidh Douglas-Scott, 'Justice, Injustice and the Rule of Law in the EU' in Dimitry Kochenov, Andrew T Williams, and Gráinne de Búrca (eds), *Europe's Justice Deficit?* (Hart 2015). Douglas-Scott's Critical Legal Justice is close to Neyer's account of procedural justice in supranational systems. See Jürgen Neyer, *The Justification of Europe: A Political Theory of Supranational Integration* (Oxford University Press 2012).

[54] See proposals in Section 6.1.2; Attracting skills and talent to the EU, COM(2022)657 final and Fitness Check on EU Legislation on legal migration SWD(2019)1055.

sense in terms of aligning migration to the economic objectives of the EU, and such an amendment would not go further than primary law provisions.[55] It is aligned with the provision of Article 79(1) TFEU as it would lead to more efficient management of flows, while it would also give substance to Article 45(2) CFR. Such a change would also be aligned with solidarity demanded under Article 80 TFEU. In 1961, when the first framework of free movement was introduced, with significant clauses limiting the rights of EU migrants, Lionello Levi Sandri suggested that the rights attributed to EU migrants derived from the 'new spirit of European solidarity'.[56] It was presented as a concession made by the Member States with a view to creating a labour market which would ensure the best use of the Community's human potential.[57] It is easy to see how true and effective mobility rights for TCN migrants resident in the EU could fit with interstate solidarity based on the promotion of the economic objectives of this legal order. This time the EU's human potential would extend to cover not only EU migrants but also TCN migrants resident in the Member States. The suggested revision of the Long-term Residents Directive could have been a first step in that direction; however, the emphasis of the Member States on maintaining economic limitations to the exercise of mobility rights through the labour market test will limit any significant transformation of the *status quo*.

Moreover, the framework of protection of rights of TCNs and the differentiation it introduces based on how much a migrant is needed should also be revisited. It can hardly be imagined that fair treatment as demanded by Article 79(1) TFEU implies differentiated attribution of rights based on how crucial a migrant is for the EU economy. The attribution of more rights to migrants who are urgently needed is both arbitrary and out of line with a long-term planning around migration law. We might know what type of migrants the EU economy needs today, but we cannot predict what type of migrants will be most needed in the future. In this context, the revision of the Single Permit Directive is

[55] Cf Moritz Jesse, 'The "Integration" of Economic Immigrants: Lessons to Be Learnt from Free Movement of Persons on the EU's Internal Market' (2023) 37 Journal of Immigration, Asylum and National Law 31. See, however, Jean-Baptiste Farcy, 'Labour Immigration Policy in the European Union: How to Overcome the Tension between Further Europeanisation and the Protection of National Interests?' (2020) 22 European Journal of Migration and Law 198.

[56] Lionello Levi Sandri, The free movement of workers in the countries of the European Economic Community, Bulletin of the European Economic Community (1961) 66.

[57] Ibid.

welcome, but more work needs to be done to reach the extensive scope of equal treatment, family reunification rights, and access to long-term resident status enjoyed by highly skilled migrants.

Arguing for the extension of social rights of TCNs, however, is more challenging. If we look at EU migrants, the Court has acknowledged that financial solidarity among Member States dictates the attribution of social rights to them.[58] By engaging in a common project of growth, Member States have accepted that they may have to incur the costs for an EU migrant because of the economic benefits they collectively derive from the EU project. After all, a host state's citizen can migrate to another Member State, too, and will enjoy benefits there. This case for financial solidarity, no matter how strong, has not gone very far since the 2004 enlargement of the EU. If anything, the diverse nature of Member States' economies set the basis for limiting social rights of EU migrants to ensure that the strong welfare states of the West and North would not have to carry the burden for the migrants from the South and East. Regardless of whether this claim had any factual basis, this narrative redefined the degree to which EU states are ready to recognize a full extension of social rights even to the nationals of Member States who are already part of the collective project of growth.[59] It is in this limitation of social rights due to economic considerations that we can see a model of sustainable migration perfected in the free movement framework through Directive 2004/38.

The attribution of social rights to TCN migrants can be based on their contribution to the project of growth. However, an extension of social rights in a way comparable to those of EU migrants is definitely harder to

[58] It was exemplified in the extensive attribution of rights in Case C-184/99, *Grzelczyk*, ECLI:EU:C:2001:458 but such a reason behind the attribution of rights existed already in Case 15/69, *Ugliola*, ECLI:EU:C:1969:46.

[59] Daniel Thym (ed), *Questioning EU Citizenship: Judges and the Limits of Free Movement and Solidarity in the EU* (Hart 2017); Stamatia Devetzi, 'EU Citizens, Residence Rights and Solidarity in the Post-Dano/Alimanovic Era in Germany' (2019) 21 European Journal of Migration and Law 338; Elspeth Guild, 'Does European Citizenship Blur the Borders of Solidarity?' in Elspeth Guild, Cristina Gortázar Rotaeche, and Dora Kostakopoulou (eds), *The Reconceptualization of European Union Citizenship* (Brill Nijhoff 2014); Paul Minderhoud, 'Back to the Roots? No Access to Social Assistance for Union Citizens Who Are Economically Inactive' in Daniel Thym (ed), *Questioning EU Citizenship: Judges and the Limits of Free Movement and Solidarity in the EU* (Hart 2017); Sandra Mantu and Paul Minderhoud, 'Exploring the Links between Residence and Social Rights for Economically Inactive EU Citizens' (2019) 21 European Journal of Migration and Law 313.

justify. That is because the states of origin of TCN migrants are not directly involved in the EU project of growth. In Chapter 4, I analysed the extension of social rights to migrants originating from states associated with the EU and engaged in trade or economic cooperation. The interdependence of their economies created the basis for attribution of rights. However, after the setting in place of an autonomous EU migration policy that attributes rights to TCNs based on their residence, such clauses have disappeared. One might also say that they are no longer needed. How would such an inclusion be justified? In this case, it could only take place by a commitment to advancing the social objectives of the EU project in line with the approach followed by the Court, and with a stronger emphasis on human rights as a tool not only for progress but also for integration of the migrant in the national community under a long-term view of the place migrants will occupy in future EU societies.

In any case, shaping migration law that is sustainable for the EU legal system is bound to meet resistance, due the different development levels of the Member States, their different needs in migrant labour for economic gains, and the different ideological approaches to migration highlighted by populist trends in the past decade. In this context, the problem-solving capacity of positive integration at EU level could be stymied by non-negotiable conflicts between national and supranational actors.[60] The Court has the potential to reconstruct and consolidate the rights of migrants. The direction of its rulings during the period reviewed in Part III point to this conclusion. However, more clarity and coherence would be required when doing so, to also advance legal certainty and to thereby promote justice as suggested by Douglas-Scott. This reconstruction would continue on the path of rights as equal opportunities presented earlier with the corresponding limitations for broader social justice demands. It might not be the ideal option, but it is the only realistic one, considering how the EU legal system is shaped.

10.4 Conclusion

Overall, the book set out to investigate how the economic and social pillars of sustainability, as historically conveyed in the economic and social objectives of the EU legal order, have shaped migrants' rights in EU law. Starting from the inconclusive appearance of sustainable

[60] By analogy, Fritz Scharpf, *Governing in Europe: Effective and Democratic?* (Oxford University Press 1999) 11–13.

migration as a new objective for EU migration law and by conducting a critical legal historical study, I have demonstrated how the economic and social pillars of sustainability are embedded in the establishment and evolution of EU migration law. In addition, my analysis showed the inherent limitations of the pursuit of an EU sustainable migration for migrants' rights under EU law.

I hope that the investigation concluded in this book will inspire a closer interrogation of the concept of sustainability and its interplay with different EU legal norms. Instead of unquestionably following EU institutional discourse and integrating new policy concepts into legal writing, there is value in focusing intellectual inquiries on the extant legal framework and questioning whether there is anything new under the sun. At the same time, the close examination of the economic and social pillars of sustainability and their relation to migration can prove crucial for the extension of migrants' rights. Maintaining the focus on migration for economic growth can only get us so far. It is particularly important to extend the social and mobility rights of TCN migrants if we are to achieve socially sustainable societies.

BIBLIOGRAPHY

Books

Ackerman BA and Fishkin JS, *Deliberation Day* (Yale University Press 2004)

Alter KJ, *Establishing the Supremacy of European Law: The Making of an International Rule of Law in Europe* (Oxford University Press 2003)

Arter D, *The Politics of European Integration in the Twentieth Century* (Dartmouth 1993)

Augenstein D (ed), *'Integration through Law' Revisited: The Making of the European Polity* (Ashgate 2012)

Azoulai L and Maduro MP (eds), *The Past and Future of EU Law: The Classics of EU Law Revisited on the 50th Anniversary of the Rome Treaty* (Hart 2010)

Balibar É, *Nous, citoyens d'Europe?* (La Découverte 2001)

Barbier J-C, Rogowski R and Colomb F (eds), *The Sustainability of the European Social Model: EU Governance, Social Protection and Employment Policies in Europe* (Edward Elgar 2015)

Behrman S and Kent A (eds), *Climate Refugees: Global, Local and Critical Approaches* (Cambridge University Press 2022)

Bellamy R, *Political Constitutionalism: A Republican Defence of the Constitutionality of Democracy* (Cambridge University Press 2007)

Bengoetxea J, *The Legal Reasoning of the European Court of Justice: Towards a European Jurisprudence* (Clarendon Press 1993)

Böhning WR, *The Migration of Workers in the United Kingdom and the European Community* (Oxford University Press for the Institute of Race Relations 1972)

Böhning WR and Werquin J, *Some Economic, Social and Human Rights Considerations Concerning the Future Status of Third-Country Nationals in the Single European Market* (International Labour Office 1990)

Bosselmann K, *The Principle of Sustainability: Transforming Law and Governance* (2nd ed, Routledge 2017)

Boyle AE and Freestone D (eds), *International Law and Sustainable Development: Past Achievements and Future Challenges* (Oxford University Press 1999)

Brightman M and Lewis J (eds), *The Anthropology of Sustainability: Beyond Development and Progress* (Palgrave Macmillan 2017)

Brownlie I, *Principles of Public International Law* (7th ed, Oxford University Press 2008)

Butler G and Wessel RA (eds), *EU External Relations Law: The Cases in Context* (Hart 2022)

Campbell A, *Common Market Law* (Supplement 2/71, Longmans 1971)

Ćapeta T, Goldner Lang I and Perišin T (eds), *The Changing European Union: A Critical View on the Role of Law and the Courts* (Hart 2022)

Carrera S, Santos Vara J and Strik T (eds), *Constitutionalising the External Dimensions of EU Migration Policies in Times of Crisis: Legality, Rule of Law and Fundamental Rights Reconsidered* (Edward Elgar 2019)

Costello C, *The Human Rights of Migrants and Refugees in European Law* (Oxford University Press 2016)

Craig P and de Búrca G, *EU Law: Text, Cases, and Materials* (7th ed, Oxford University Press 2020)

The Evolution of EU Law (3rd ed, Oxford University Press 2021)

D'Alisa G, Demaria F and Kallis G (eds), *Degrowth: A Vocabulary for a New Era* (Routledge 2015)

de Sadeleer N, *Environmental Principles: From Political Slogans to Legal Rules* (Oxford University Press 2002)

de Vries SA et al. (eds), *EU Citizens' Economic Rights in Action: Re-Thinking Legal and Factual Barriers in the Internal Market* (Edward Elgar 2018)

de Witte B, Muir E and Dawson M (eds), *Judicial Activism at the European Court of Justice* (Edward Elgar 2013)

Dillard J, Dujon V and King MC (eds), *Understanding the Social Dimension of Sustainability* (1st ed, Routledge 2008)

Dobson A, *Justice and the Environment: Conceptions of Environmental Sustainability and Theories of Distributive Justice* (Oxford University Press 1998)

(ed), *Fairness and Futurity: Essays on Environmental Sustainability and Social Justice* (Oxford University Press 1999)

Dougan M, Nic Shuibhne N and Spaventa E (eds), *Empowerment and Disempowerment of the European Citizen* (Hart 2012)

Dryzek JS, *The Politics of the Earth: Environmental Discourses* (3rd ed, Oxford University Press 2012)

Eisele K, *The External Dimension of the EU's Migration Policy: Different Legal Positions of Third-Country Nationals in the EU: A Comparative Perspective* (Brill Nijhoff 2014)

Ekardt F, *Sustainability: Transformation, Governance, Ethics, Law* (Springer International Publishing 2020)

Faist T, Fauser M and Kivisto P (eds), *Migration-Development Nexus: A Transnational Perspective* (Migration, Diasporas and Citizenship Series) (Palgrave Macmillan 2011)

Fauri F (ed), *The History of Migration in Europe: Perspectives from Economics, Politics and Sociology* (Routledge 2015)

Goedings SAW, *Labor Migration in an Integrating Europe: National Migration Policies and the Free Movement of Workers; 1950–1968* (Sdu Uitgevers 2005)

Goldner Lang I, *From Association to Accession: How Free Is the Free Movement of Persons in the EU* (Eleven International Publishing 2011)

Guild E, *European Community Law from a Migrant's Perspective* (Katholieke Universiteit Nijmegen 2000)

Immigration Law in the European Community (Brill Nijhoff 2001)

The Legal Elements of European Identity: EU Citizenship and Migration Law (Kluwer Law International 2004)

Guild E, Rotaeche CG and Kostakopoulou D (eds), *The Reconceptualization of European Union Citizenship* (Brill Nijhoff 2014)

Hailbronner K, *Immigration and Asylum Law and Policy of the European Union* (Kluwer Law International 2000)

Hollifield JF, *Immigrants, Markets, and States: The Political Economy of Postwar Europe* (Harvard University Press 1992)

Holmes S, Middelschulte D and Snoep M, *Competition Law, Climate Change & Environmental Sustainability* (Institute of Competition Law 2021)

Humphreys M, *Sustainable Development in the European Union: A General Principle* (Routledge 2017)

International Union for Conservation of Nature United Nations Environment Programme World Wide Fund For Nature, *Caring for the Earth: A Strategy for Sustainable Living* (1991) https://portals.iucn.org/library/efiles/documents/cfe-003.pdf

Isiksel T, *Europe's Functional Constitution: A Theory of Constitutionalism beyond the State* (Oxford University Press 2016)

Joerges C and Ghaleigh NS (eds), *Darker Legacies of Law in Europe: The Shadow of National Socialism and Fascism over Europe and Its Legal Traditions* (Hart 2003)

Karageorgiou E, 'Rethinking Solidarity in European Asylum Law: A Critical Reading of the Key Concept in Contemporary Refugee Policy' (PhD Dissertation, Lund University, Media Tryck 2018)

Kochenov D, *EU Citizenship and Federalism: The Role of Rights* (Cambridge University Press 2017)

Kochenov D, Cambien N and Muir E (eds), *European Citizenship under Stress: Social Justice, Brexit and Other Challenges* (Brill Nijhoff 2020)

Kochenov D, Williams AT and de Búrca G (eds), *Europe's Justice Deficit?* (Hart 2015)

Kothari A et al. (eds), *Pluriverse: A Post-Development Dictionary* (Tulika Books 2019)

Lafferty WM and Meadowcroft J (eds), *Implementing Sustainable Development: Strategies and Initiatives in High Consumption Societies* (Oxford University Press 2000)

Lecourt R, *L'Europe des juges* (Bruylant 1976)

Leino-Sandberg P, Hillebrandt MZ and Koivisto I (eds), *(In)Visible European Government: Critical Approaches to Transparency as an Ideal and a Practice* (Routledge 2023)

Lowe V, *International Law* (Oxford University Press 2007)

Maas W (ed), *Democratic Citizenship and the Free Movement of People* (Martinus Nijhoff 2013)

Macrory R, Havercroft I and Purdy R (eds), *Principles of European Environmental Law, Proceedings of the Avosetta Group of European Environmental Lawyers* (Europa Law Publishing 2004)

Mantu S et al. (eds), *EU Citizenship and Free Movement Rights: Taking Supranational Citizenship Seriously* (Brill Nijhoff 2020)

McGlynn C, *Families and the European Union Law, Politics and Pluralism* (Cambridge University Press 2006)

Muir E, *EU Equality Law: The First Fundamental Rights Policy of the EU* (1st ed, Oxford University Press 2018)

Neyer J, *The Justification of Europe: A Political Theory of Supranational Integration* (Oxford University Press 2012)

Nic Shuibhne N, *The Coherence of EU Free Movement Law: Constitutional Responsibility and the Court of Justice* (Oxford University Press 2013)

Nicola F and Davies B (eds), *EU Law Stories: Contextual and Critical Histories of European Jurisprudence* (1st ed, Cambridge University Press 2017)

O'Brien C, *Unity in Adversity: EU Citizenship, Social Justice and the Cautionary Tale of the UK* (Hart 2017)

Ott A and Inglis K, *Handbook on European Enlargement: A Commentary on the Enlargement Process* (TMC Asser Press 2002)

Peers S, *EU Justice and Home Affairs Law* (4th ed, Oxford University Press 2016)

Phelan W, *Great Judgments of the European Court of Justice: Rethinking the Landmark Decisions of the Foundational Period* (Cambridge University Press 2019)

Pieraccini M and Novitz T (eds), *Legal Perspectives on Sustainability* (Bristol University Press 2020)

Pollack MA, *The Engines of European Integration: Delegation, Agency, and Agenda Setting in the EU* (Oxford University Press 2003)

Rawls J, *Political Liberalism* (Columbia University Press 1993)

Robertson M, *Sustainability Principles and Practice* (3rd ed, Routledge 2021)

Ruhs M, *The Price of Rights: Regulating International Labor Migration* (Princeton University Press 2013)

Scharpf F, *Governing in Europe: Effective and Democratic?* (Oxford University Press 1999)

Scott M, *Climate Change, Disasters, and the Refugee Convention* (Cambridge University Press 2020)

Sen A, *The Idea of Justice* (Penguin 2010)

Soysal YN, *Limits of Citizenship: Migrants and Postnational Membership in Europe* (University of Chicago 1994)

Streeck W, *Buying Time: The Delayed Crisis of Democratic Capitalism* (Patrick Camiller and David Fernbach trans, 2nd ed, Verso 2017)

Teixeira PG, *The Legal History of the European Banking Union: How European Law Led to the Supranational Integration of the Single Financial Market* (Hart 2020)

Thym D (ed), *Questioning EU Citizenship: Judges and the Limits of Free Movement and Solidarity in the EU* (Hart 2017)

European Migration Law (Oxford University Press 2023)

Van Elsuwege P and Chamon M, *The Meaning of 'Association' under EU Law: A Study on the Law and Practices of EU Association Agreements* (Publications Office of the European Union 2019)

van Middelaar L, *The Passage to Europe: How a Continent Became a Union* (Liz Waters trans, Yale University Press 2013)

Voigt C and Bugge HC (eds), *Sustainable Development in National and International Law, What Did the Brundtland Report Do to Legal Thinking and Legal Development, and Where Can We Go from Here?* (Europa Law Publishing 2008)

von Carlowitz HC, *Sylvicultura Oeconomica, Oder Haußwirthliche Nachricht Und Naturmäßige Anweisung Zur Wilden Baum Zucht* (Leipzig 1713)

Walker N, Shaw J and Tierney S, *Europe's Constitutional Mosaic* (Hart 2011)

Weatherill S, *The Internal Market as a Legal Concept* (Oxford University Press 2017)

Wiesbrock A, *Legal Migration to the European Union* (Brill Nijhoff 2010)

World Commission on Environment and Development, *Our Common Future* (Oxford University Press 1987)

Book Chapters

Arnull A, 'The Many Ages of the Court of Justice of the European Union' in Claire Kilpatrick and Joanne Scott (eds), *New Legal Approaches to Studying the Court of Justice: Revisiting Law in Context* (Oxford University Press 2020)

Augenstein D, 'We the People: EU Justice as Politics' in Dimitry Kochenov, Andrew T Williams and Gráinne de Búrca (eds), *Europe's Justice Deficit?* (Hart 2015)

Baker S et al. (eds), 'Introduction: The Theory and Practice of Sustainable Development in EU Perspective' in Susan Baker, Maria Kousis, Dick Richardson and Stephen Young (eds), *The Politics of Sustainable Development: Theory, Policy and Practice within the European Union* (Routledge 1997)

Baquero Cruz J, 'Partial Eclipse of Union Citizenship: From Grzelczyk to Dano' in Julio Baquero Cruz (ed), *What's Left of the Law of Integration?* (Oxford University Press 2018)

Barnard C, 'The Day the Clock Stopped: EU Citizenship and the Single Market' in Panos Koutrakos and Jukka Snell (eds), *Research Handbook on the Law of the EU's Internal Market* (Edward Elgar 2017)

Blanco Sío-López C and Tedeschi P, 'Migrants and European Institutions: A Study on the Attempts to Address the Economic and Social Challenges of Immigration in EU Member States' in Francesca Fauri (ed), *The History of Migration in Europe: Perspectives from Economics, Politics and Sociology* (Routledge 2015)

Butler G and Wessel RA, 'EU External Relations Law and Navigating the Case Law of the Court of Justice of the European Union' in Graham Butler and Ramses A Wessel (eds), *EU External Relations Law: The Cases in Context* (Hart 2022)

Carrera S, 'The External Dimensions of EU Migration and Asylum Policies in Times of Crisis' in Sergio Carrera, Juan Santos Vara and Tineke Strik, *Constitutionalising the External Dimensions of EU Migration Policies in Times of Crisis* (Edward Elgar 2019)

Carter D, 'Inclusion and Exclusion of Migrant Workers in the EU' in Moritz Jesse (ed), *European Societies, Migration, and the Law: The 'Others' amongst 'Us'* (Cambridge University Press 2020)

Choudhry S, 'Citizenship and Federations: Some Preliminary Reflections' in Kalypso Nicolaidis and Robert Howse (eds), *The Federal Vision: Legitimacy and Levels of Governance in the United States and the European Union* (Oxford University Press 2001)

Craig P, 'Institutions, Power, and Institutional Balance' in Paul Craig and Gráinne de Búrca (eds), *The Evolution of EU Law* (Oxford University Press 2021)

Davies G, 'Social Legitimacy and Purposive Power: The End, the Means and the Consent of the People' in Dimitry Kochenov, Andrew T Williams and Gráinne de Búrca (eds), *Europe's Justice Deficit?* (Hart 2015)

Dawson M, 'The Political Face of Judicial Activism: Europe's Law-Politics Imbalance' in Bruno de Witte, Elise Muir and Mark Dawson (eds), *Judicial Activism at the European Court of Justice* (Edward Elgar 2013)

De Capitani E, 'Progress and Failure in the Area of Freedom, Security and Justice' in Francesca Bignami (ed), *EU Law in Populist Times: Crises and Prospects* (Cambridge University Press 2020) de Sadeleer N, 'Environmental Principles, Modern and Post Modern Law' in Richard Macrory, Ian Havercroft and Ray Purdy (eds), *Principles of European Environmental Law, Proceedings of the Avosetta Group of European Environmental lawyers* (Europa Law Publishing 2004)

de Vries K, 'The Integration Exception: A New Limit to Social Rights of Third-Country Nationals in European Union Law?' in Daniel Thym (ed), *Questioning EU Citizenship: Judges and the Limits of Free Movement and Solidarity in the EU* (Hart 2017)

de Witte B, 'Direct Effect, Primacy, and the Nature of the Legal Order' in Paul Craig and Gráinne de Búrca (eds), *The Evolution of EU Law* (Oxford University Press 2021)

de Witte F, 'Emancipation Through Law?' in Loïc Azoulai, Ségolène Barbou des Places and Etienne Pataut (eds), *Constructing the Person in EU Law: Rights, Roles, Identities* (Hart 2016)

Deakin S and Rogowski R, 'Reflexive Labour Law, Capabilities and the Future of Social Europe' in Ralf Rogowski (ed), *Transforming European Employment Policy: Labour Market Transitions and the Promotion of Capability* (Edward Elgar 2011)

Dougan M, 'A Spectre Is Haunting Europe . . . Free Movement of Persons and the Eastern Enlargement' in Christophe Hillion (ed), *EU Enlargement: A Legal Approach* (Bloomsbury 2004)

Douglas-Scott S, 'Justice, Injustice and the Rule of Law in the EU' in Dimitry Kochenov, Andrew T Williams and Gráinne de Búrca (eds), *Europe's Justice Deficit?* (Hart 2015)

Everson M, 'The Legacy of the Market Citizen' in Jo Shaw and Gillian More (eds), *New Legal Dynamics of European Union* (Clarendon Press 1995)

'A Very Cosmopolitan Citizenship: But Who Pays the Price? In Michael Dougan, Niamh Nic Shuibhne and Eleanor Spaventa (eds), *Empowerment and Disempowerment of the European Citizen* (Hart 2012)

Faist T and Fauser M, 'The Migration–Development Nexus: Toward a Transnational Perspective' in Thomas Faist, Margit Fauser and Peter Kivisto (eds), *The Migration-Development Nexus* (Palgrave Macmillan 2011)

Foucault M, 'La philosophie analytique de la politique' in Daniel Defert, François Ewald and Jacques Lagrange (eds), *Dits et écrits, 1954–1988* (vol 3, Gallimard 1994)

Goldner Lang I, 'Towards "Judicial Passivism" in European Union Migration and Asylum Law?' in Tamara Ćapeta, Iris Goldner Lang and Tamara Perišin (eds), *The Changing European Union: A Critical View on the Role of Law and the Courts* (Hart 2022)

Groenendijk K, 'Categorizing Human Beings in EU Migration Law' in Dirk Jacobs, Andrea Rea and Saskia Bonjour (eds), *The Others in Europe* (Editions de l'Université de Bruxelles 2011)

Groussot X and Petursson GT, 'The EU Charter of Fundamental Rights Five Years On: The Emergence of a New Constitutional Framework?' in Ulf Bernitz, Sybe de Vries and Stephen Weatherill (eds), *The EU Charter of Fundamental Rights as a Binding Instrument: Five Years Old and Growing* (Hart 2015)

Groussot X and Zemskova A, 'The Resilience of Rights and European Integration' in Antonina Bakardjieva Engelbrekt and Xavier Groussot (eds) *The Future of Europe: Political and Legal Integration beyond Brexit* (Hart 2019)

Guild E, 'Does European Citizenship Blur the Borders of Solidarity?' in Elspeth Guild, Cristina Gortázar Rotaeche and Dora Kostakopoulou (eds), *The Reconceptualization of European Union Citizenship* (Brill Nijhoff 2014)

'Workers' in Andrea Ott and Kirstyn Inglis (eds), *Handbook on European Enlargement: A Commentary on the Enlargement Process* (TMC Asser Press 2002)

Guild E and Wieland R, 'The UN Global Compact for Safe, Orderly and Regular Migration: What Does It Mean in International Law?' in Giuliana Ziccardi Capaldo (ed), *The Global Community Yearbook of International Law and Jurisprudence 2019* (Oxford University Press 2020)

Handler P, 'Legal History' in Dawn Watkins and Mandy Burton (eds), *Research Methods in Law* (Routledge 2013)

Hervey T, 'Migrant Workers and Their Families in the European Union: The Pervasive Market Ideology of Community Law' in Jo Shaw and Gillian More (eds), *New Legal Dynamics of European Union* (Clarendon Press 1995)

Holder J, 'An Idea of Ecological Justice in the EU' in Dimitry Kochenov, Andrew T Williams and Gráinne de Búrca (eds), *Europe's Justice Deficit?* (Hart 2015)

Idriz N, 'Hierarchies of Privilege: Juxtaposing Family Reunification Rights, Integration Requirements, and Nationality in EU Law' in Moritz Jesse (ed), *European Societies, Migration, and the Law: The 'Others' amongst 'Us'* (Cambridge University Press 2020)

Iglesias Sánchez S, 'Free Movement as a Precondition for Integration of Third-Country Nationals in the EU' in Elspeth Guild, Kees Groenendijk and Sergio Carrera (eds), *Illiberal Liberal States: Immigration, Citizenship, and Integration in the EU* (Ashgate 2009)

'The Constitutional Status of Foreigners and European Union Citizens: Loopholes and Interactions in the Scope of Application of Fundamental Rights' in Daniel Thym (ed), *Questioning EU Citizenship: Judges and the Limits of Free Movement and Solidarity in the EU* (Hart 2017)

Jacobs M, 'Sustainable Development as a Contested Concept' in Andrew Dobson (ed), *Fairness and Futurity: Essays on Environmental Sustainability and Social Justice* (Oxford University Press 1999)

Jesse M and Carter D, 'The "Market Insider": Market-Citizenship and Economic Exclusion in the EU' in Moritz Jesse (ed), *European Societies, Migration, and the Law: The 'Others' amongst 'Us'* (Cambridge University Press 2020)

Jesse M and Carter DW, 'Life after the "Dano-Trilogy": Legal Certainty, Choices and Limitations in EU Citizenship Case Law' in Nathan Cambien, Dimitry Kochenov and Elise Muir (eds), *European Citizenship under Stress: Social Justice, Brexit and Other Challenges* (vol 16, Brill Nijhoff 2020)

Kelemen RD, 'The EU Rights Revolution: Adversarial Legalism and European Integration' in Tanja A Börzel and Rachel A Cichowski (eds), *The State of the European Union, 6: Law, Politics, and Society* (Oxford University Press 2004)

Kochenov D, 'The Oxymoron of "Market Citizenship" and the Future of the Union' in Dimitry Kochenov et al. (eds), *The Internal Market and the Future of European Integration: Essays in Honour of Laurence W. Gormley* (Cambridge University Press 2019)

Kostakopoulou D, 'The Area of Freedom, Security and Justice and the Political Morality of Migration and Integration' in Hans Lindahl (ed), *A Right to Inclusion and Exclusion?: Normative Fault Lines of the EU's Area of Freedom, Security and Justice* (Hart 2009)

Kostakopoulou D, Carrera S and Jesse M, 'Doing and Deserving: Competing Frames of Integration in the EU' in Elspeth Guild, Kees Groenendijk and Sergio Carrera (eds), *Illiberal Liberal States: Immigration, Citizenship, and Integration in the EU* (Ashgate 2009)

Kramer L, 'Sustainable Development in EC Law' in Christina Voigt and Hans Christian Bugge (eds), *Sustainable Development in National and International Law, What Did the Brundtland Report Do to Legal Thinking and Legal Development, and Where Can We Go from Here?* (Europa Law Publishing 2008)

Kumm M, 'The Moral Point of Constitutional Pluralism, Defining the Domain of Legitimate Institutional Civil Disobedience and Conscientious Objection' in Julie Dickson and Pavlos Eleftheriadis (eds), *Philosophical Foundations of European Union Law* (Oxford University Press 2012)

Kyriakidis A, 'Sustainability and Eurozone 2.0: Still Impossible?' in Beate Sjåfjell, Charlotte Villiers and Georgina Tsagas (eds), *Sustainable Value Creation in the European Union: Towards Pathways to a Sustainable Future through Crises* (Cambridge University Press 2022)

Larsen G, 'An Inquiry into the Theoretical Basis of Sustainability, Ten Propositions' in Jesse Dillard, Veronica Dujon and Mary C King (eds), *Understanding the Social Dimension of Sustainability* (1st ed, Routledge 2008)

Lowe V, 'Sustainable Development and Unsustainable Arguments' in Alan E Boyle and David Freestone (eds), *International Law and Sustainable Development: Past Achievements and Future Challenges* (Oxford University Press 1999)

Loxa A and Stoyanova V, 'Migration as a Constitutional Crisis for the European Union' in Stijn Smet and Vladislava Stoyanova (eds), *Migrants' Rights, Populism and Legal Resilience in Europe* (Cambridge University Press 2022)

Magis K and Shinn C, 'Emergent Principles of Social Sustainability' in Jesse F Dillard, Veronica Dujon and Mary C King (eds), *Understanding the Social Dimension of Sustainability* (Routledge 2009)

Matera C, 'An External Dimension of the AFSJ? Some Reflections on the Nature and Scope of the Externalisation of the AFSJ Domains' in Ester Herlin-Karnell, Maria Fletcher and Claudio Matera (eds), *The European Union as an Area of Freedom, Security and Justice* (Routledge 2019)

Menéndez AJ, 'Whose Justice? Which Europe?' in Dimitry Kochenov, Andrew T Williams and Gráinne de Búrca (eds), *Europe's Justice Deficit?* (Hart 2015)

'European Citizenship after Martínez Sala and Baumbast: Has European Law Become More Human but Less Social?' in Loïc Azoulai and Miguel Poiares Maduro (eds), *The Past and Future of EU Law: The Classics of EU Law Revisited on the Fiftieth Anniversary of the Rome Treaty* (Hart 2010)

Menz G, 'Employers and Migrant Legality: Liberalization of Service Provision, Transnational Posting, and the Bifurcation of the European Labour Market' in Cathryn Costello and Mark Freedland (eds), *Migrants at Work: Immigration and Vulnerability in Labour Law* (Oxford University Press 2014)

Minderhoud P, 'Decision No 3/80 of the EEC-Turkey Association Council: Significance and Developments' in Daniel Thym and Margarite Zoeteweij-Turhan (eds), *Rights of Third-Country Nationals under EU Association Agreements: Degrees of Free Movement and Citizenship* (Brill Nijhoff 2015)

'Back to the Roots? No Access to Social Assistance for Union Citizens Who Are Economically Inactive' in Daniel Thym (ed), *Questioning EU Citizenship: Judges and the Limits of Free Movement and Solidarity in the EU* (Hart 2017)

Moraru M, 'EU Return Directive: A Cause for Shame or an Unexpectedly Protective Framework?' in Evangelia Tsourdi and Philippe De Bruycker (eds), *Research Handbook on EU Migration and Asylum Law* (Edward Elgar 2022)

Moreno-Lax V, 'The Informalisation of the External Dimension of EU Asylum Policy: The Hard Implications of Soft Law' in Evangelia (Lilian) Tsourdi and Philippe De Buycker (eds), *Research Handbook on EU Migration and Asylum Law* (Edward Elgar 2022)

Muir E, 'The Court of Justice: A Fundamental Rights Institution among Others' in Bruno de Witte, Elise Muir and Mark Dawson (eds), *Judicial Activism at the European Court of Justice* (Edward Elgar 2013)

Nic Shuibhne N, 'Integrating Union Citizenship and the Charter of Fundamental Rights' in Daniel Thym (ed), *Questioning EU Citizenship: Judges and the Limits of Free Movement and Solidarity in the EU* (Hart 2017)

Nicola FG, 'Waiting for the Barbarians: Inside the Archives of the European Court of Justice' in Claire Kilpatrick and Joanne Scott (eds), *New Legal Approaches to Studying the Court of Justice: Revisiting Law in Context* (Oxford University Press 2020)

Noll G, 'Viciously Circular: Will Ageing Lock the European Union into Immigrant Exclusion?' in Stijn Smet and Vladislava Stoyanova (eds), *Migrants' Rights, Populism and Legal Resilience in Europe* (Cambridge University Press 2022)

Novitz T and Pieraccini M, 'Agenda 2030 and the Sustainable Development Goals: "Responsive, Inclusive, Participatory and Representative Decision-Making"?' in Margherita Pieraccini and Tonia Novitz (eds), *Legal Perspectives on Sustainability* (Bristol University Press 2020)

'Sustainability and Law: A Historical and Theoretical Overview' in Margherita Pieraccini and Tonia Novitz (eds), *Legal Perspectives on Sustainability* (Bristol University Press 2020)

Novitz T, 'Social Sustainability, Labour and Trade: Forging Connections' in Margherita Pieraccini and Tonia Novitz (eds), *Legal Perspectives on Sustainability* (Bristol University Press 2020)

'Addressing Social Dumping and Unfair Competition – An Analysis of EU Pillar Initiatives from a Sustainability Perspective' in Ann-Christine Hartzén, Andrea Iossa and Eleni Karageorgiou (eds), *Law, Solidarity and the Limits of Social Europe* (Edward Elgar 2022)

O'Leary S and Iglesias Sánchez S, 'Free Movement of Persons and Services' in Paul Craig and Gráinne de Búrca (eds), *The Evolution of EU Law* (Oxford University Press 2021)

Pastore F, 'Visas, Borders, Immigration: Formation, Structure, and Current Evolution of the EU Entry Control System' in Neil Walker (ed), *Europe's Area of Freedom, Security, and Justice* (Oxford University Press 2004)

Peers S, 'Family Reunion and Community Law' in Neil Walker (ed), *Europe's Area of Freedom, Security, and Justice* (Oxford University Press 2004)

Pescatore P, 'Les Objectifs de la Communauté européenne comme principe d'interprétation dans la jurisprudence de la Cour de Justice', *Miscellanea W.J. Ganshof van der Meersc* (Bruylant 1972)

Plender R, 'An Incipient Form of European Citizenship' in Francis Geoffrey Jacobs and University of London (eds), *European Law and the Individual* (Elsevier/North-Holland 1976)

Poiares Maduro M, 'Europe's Social Self: "The Sickness Unto Death"' in Jo Shaw (ed), *Social Law and Policy in an Evolving European Union* (Hart 2000)

Rasmussen M, 'From Costa v. ENEL to the Treaties of Rome: A Brief History of a Legal Revolution' in Loïc Azoulai and Miguel Poiares Maduro (eds), *The Past and Future of EU Law: The Classics of EU Law Revisited on the 50th Anniversary of the Rome Treaty* (Hart 2010)

Reslow N, 'Transformation or Continuity? EU External Migration Policy in the Aftermath of the Migration Crisis' in Sergio Carrera, Juan Santos Vara and Tineke Strik, *Constitutionalising the External Dimensions of EU Migration Policies in Times of Crisis* (Edward Elgar 2019)

Richardson D, 'The Politics of Sustainable Development' in Susan Baker et al. (eds), *The Politics of Sustainable Development: Theory, Policy and Practice within the European Union* (Routledge 1997)

Rodin S and Perišin T, 'Transformation or Reconstitution of Europe: The European Critical Legal Studies Perspective' in Siniša Rodin and Tamara Perišin (eds), *The Transformation or Reconstitution of Europe: The Critical Legal Studies Perspective on the Role of the Courts in the European Union* (Hart 2018)

Santos Vara J, 'Soft International Agreements on Migration Cooperation with Third Countries: A Challenge to Democratic and Judicial Controls in the EU' in Sergio Carrera, Juan Santos Vara and Tineke Strik, *Constitutionalising the External Dimensions of EU Migration Policies in Times of Crisis* (Edward Elgar 2019)

Shaw J, 'View of the Citizenship Classics: Martínez Sala and Subsequent Cases on Citizenship of the Union' in Loïc Azoulai and Miguel Poiares Maduro (eds), *The Past and Future of EU Law: The Classics of EU Law Revisited on the Fiftieth Anniversary of the Rome Treaty* (Hart 2010)

'Towards a Political Europe?: Citizens, Elections and the European Parliament' in Dimitry Kochenov et al. (eds), *The Internal Market and the Future of European Integration: Essays in Honour of Laurence W. Gormley* (Cambridge University Press 2019)

Somek A, 'The Preoccupation with Rights and the Embrace of Inclusion: A Critique' in Dimitry Kochenov, Andrew T Williams and Gráinne de Búrca (eds), *Europe's Justice Deficit?* (Hart 2015)

'Alienation, Despair and Social Freedom' in Loïc Azoulai, Ségolène Barbou des Places and Etienne Pataut (eds), *Constructing the Person in EU Law: Rights, Roles, Identities* (Hart 2016)

'Pragmatism, Innovation and Prophecy: Conjectures Concerning the Grounds of Belief in an Inventive Court' in Tamara Ćapeta, Iris Goldner Lang and Tamara Perišin (eds), *The Changing European Union: A Critical View on the Role of Law and the Courts* (Hart 2022)

Spijkerboer T, 'Coloniality and Recent European Migration Case Law' in Stijn Smet and Vladislava Stoyanova (eds), *Migrants' Rights, Populism and Legal Resilience in Europe* (Cambridge University Press 2022)

Terpan F and Saurugger S, 'The Politics of the Court of Justice of the European Union' in Paul James Cardwell and Marie-Pierre Granger (eds), *Research Handbook on the Politics of EU Law* (Edward Elgar 2020)

Thym D, 'Constitutional Foundations of the Judgments on the EEC-Turkey Association Agreement' in Daniel Thym and Margarite Zoeteweij-Turhan (eds), *Rights of Third-Country Nationals under EU Association Agreements: Degrees of Free Movement and Citizenship* (Brill Nijhoff 2015)

'Ambiguities of Personhood, Citizenship, Migration and Fundamental Rights in EU Law' in Loïc Azoulai, Ségolène Barbou des Places and Etienne Pataut (eds), *Constructing the Person in EU Law: Rights, Roles, Identities* (Hart 2016)

'The Evolution of Citizen's Rights in Light of the European Union's Constitutional Development' in Daniel Thym (ed), *Questioning EU Citizenship: Judges and the Limits of Free Movement and Solidarity in the EU* (Hart 2017)

'Institutional and Constitutional Framework' in Evangelia Tsourdi and Philippe De Bruycker (eds), *Research Handbook on EU Migration and Asylum Law* (Edward Elgar 2022)

Timmermans C, 'Martínez Sala and Baumbast Revisited' in Loïc Azoulai and Miguel Poiares Maduro (eds), *The Past and Future of EU Law: The Classics of EU Law Revisited on the Fiftieth Anniversary of the Rome Treaty* (Hart 2010)

Tridimas T, 'Foreword' in Beate Sjåfjell, Georgina Tsagas and Charlotte Villiers (eds), *Sustainable Value Creation in the European Union: Towards Pathways to a Sustainable Future through Crises* (Cambridge University Press 2022)

Tsourdi E (Lilian) and Costello C, 'The Evolution of EU Law on Refugees and Asylum' in Paul Craig and Gráinne de Búrca (eds), *The Evolution of EU Law* (Oxford University Press 2021)

Vitiello D, 'Legal Narratives of the EU External Action in the Field of Migration and Asylum: From the EU-Turkey Statement to the Migration Partnership Framework and Beyond' in Valsamis Mitsilegas, Violeta Moreno-Lax and Niovi Vavoula (eds), *Securitising Asylum Flows* (Brill Nijhoff 2020)

Voigt C, 'Article 11 TFEU in the Light of the Principle of Sustainable Development in International Law' in Beate Sjåfjell and Anja Wiesbrock (eds), *The Greening of European Business under EU Law: Taking Article 11 TFEU Seriously* (Routledge 2015)

Walker N, 'In Search of the Area of Freedom, Security and Justice: A Constitutional Odyssey' in Neil Walker (ed), *Europe's Area of Freedom, Security, and Justice* (Oxford University Press 2004)

'Opening or Closure? The Constitutional Intimations of the ECJ' in Loïc Azoulai and Miguel Poiares Maduro (eds), *The Past and Future of EU Law: The Classics of EU Law Revisited on the Fiftieth Anniversary of the Rome Treaty* (Hart 2010)

'Legal and Constitutional Theory of the European Union' in Paul Craig and Gráinne de Búrca (eds), *The Evolution of EU Law* (Oxford University Press 2021)

'The Theoretical Foundations of EU Law' in Claire Kilpatrick and Joanne Scott (eds), *Contemporary Challenges to EU Legality* (Oxford University Press 2021)

Weatherill, 'The Beauty and the Beast: Is European Union Internal Market Law "Over-Constitutionalised"?' in Tamara Ćapeta, Iris Goldner Lang and

Tamara Perišin (eds), *The Changing European Union: A Critical View on the Role of Law and the Courts* (Hart 2022)

Weiler JHH, 'Ideals and Idolatry in the European Construct' in Bill McSweeney (ed), *Moral Issues in International Affairs: Problems of European Integration* (Macmillan 1998)

'Deciphering the Political and Legal DNA of European Integration, An Exploratory Essay' in Julie Dickson and Pavlos Eleftheriadis, *Philosophical Foundations of European Union Law* (Oxford University Press 2012)

'Federalism without Constitutionalism: Europe's Sonderweg' in Kalypso Nicolaidis and Robert Howse (eds), *The Federal Vision: Legitimacy and Levels of Governance in the United States and the European Union* (Oxford University Press 2001)

Werner H, 'Migration and Free Movement of Workers in Western Europe' in Philippe J. Bernard (ed), *Les travailleurs étrangers en Europe occidentale* (Publication de l'Institut d'études et de recherches interethniques et interculturelles 1976) 22

Wilkinson MA, 'Politicising Europe's Justice Deficit: Some Preliminaries' in Dimitry Kochenov, Andrew T Williams and Gráinne de Búrca (eds), *Europe's Justice Deficit?* (Hart 2015)

Williams AT, 'The Problem(s) of Justice in the European Union' in Dimitry Kochenov, Andrew T Williams and Gráinne de Búrca (eds), *Europe's Justice Deficit?* (Hart 2015)

Winter G, 'Fundament and Two Pillars; The Concept of Sustainable Development 20 Years after the Brundtland Report' in Christina Voigt and Hans Christian Bugge (eds), *Sustainable Development in National and International Law, What Did the Brundtland Report Do to Legal Thinking and Legal Development, and Where Can We Go from Here?* (Europa Law Publishing 2008)

Ziegler G, 'The Accession Negotiations on Free Movement of Workers' in Andrea Ott and Kirstyn Inglis (eds), *Handbook on European Enlargement: A Commentary on the Enlargement Process* (TMC Asser Press 2002)

Articles

Åhman H, 'Social Sustainability – Society at the Intersection of Development and Maintenance' (2013) 18 Local Environment 1153

Al-Husban M and Adams C, 'Sustainable Refugee Migration: A Rethink towards a Positive Capability Approach' (2016) 8 Sustainability 451

Alexander W, 'Free Movement of Non-EC Nationals: A Review of the Case-Law of the Court of Justice' (1992) 3 European Journal of International Law 53

Alexandris Polomarkakis K, 'The European Pillar of Social Rights and the Quest for EU Social Sustainability' (2020) 29 Social & Legal Studies 183

Andrade PG, 'EU External Competences in the Field of Migration: How to Act Externally When Thinking Internally' (2018) 55 Common Market Law Review 15

Andriychuk O, 'The Concept of Sustainability in EU Competition Law: A Legal Realist Perspective' (2021) 23 Yearbook of Antitrust and Regulatory Studies 11

Baker S, 'Sustainable Development as Symbolic Commitment: Declaratory Politics and the Seductive Appeal of Ecological Modernisation in the European Union' (2007) 16 Environmental Politics 297

Bañkowski Z and Christodoulidis E, 'The European Union as an Essentially Contested Project' (1998) 4 European Law Journal 341

Barnard C and Leinarte E, 'The Creation of European Citizenship: Constitutional Miracle or Myopia?' (2022) 24 Cambridge Yearbook of European Legal Studies 24

Bauböck R, 'The Three Levels of Citizenship within the European Union' (2014) 15 German Law Journal 751

Beduschi A, 'An Empty Shell? The Protection of Social Rights of Third-Country Workers in the EU after the Single Permit Directive' (2015) 17 European Journal of Migration and Law 210

Briant Carant J, 'Unheard Voices: A Critical Discourse Analysis of the Millennium Development Goals' Evolution into the Sustainable Development Goals' (2017) 38 Third World Quarterly 16

Brown ED, 'Regent Developments in the Social Policy of the European Economic Community' (1966) 3 Common Market Law Review 184

Burley A-M and Mattli W, 'Europe before the Court: A Political Theory of Legal Integration' (1993) 47 International Organization 41

Burrows N, 'The Promotion of Women's Rights by the European Economic Community' (1980) 17 Common Market Law Review 191

Callovi G, 'Regulation of Immigration in 1993: Pieces of the European Community Jig-Saw Puzzle' (1992) 26 The International Migration Review 353

Christian DE, 'Resistance to International Worker Mobility: A Barrier to European Unity' (1955) 8 Industrial and Labor Relations Review 379

Closa C, 'The Concept of Citizenship in the Treaty on European Union' (1992) 29 Common Market Law Review 1137

Costanza R and Mageau M, 'What Is a Healthy Ecosystem?' (1999) 33 Aquatic Ecology 105

Cremona M, 'Citizens of Third Countries: Movement and Employment of Migrant Workers within the European Union' (1995) 22 Legal Issues of Economic Integration 87

Davies B, 'Why EU Legal History Matters – A Historian's Response' (2013) 28 American University International Law Review 1337

de Boer T and Zieck M, 'The Legal Abyss of Discretion in the Resettlement of Refugees: Cherry-Picking and the Lack of Due Process in the EU' (2020) 32 International Journal of Refugee Law 54

de Búrca G, 'The Road Not Taken: The European Union as a Global Human Rights Actor' (2011) 105 The American Journal of International Law 649

de Lange T, 'A New Narrative for European Migration Policy: Sustainability and the Blue Card Recast' (2020) 26 European Law Journal 274

de Lange T and Vankova Z, 'The Recast EU Blue Card Directive: Towards a Level Playing Field to Attract Highly Qualified Migrant Talent to Work in the EU?' (2022) 24 European Journal of Migration and Law 489

de Sadeleer N, 'Sustainable Development in EU Law: Still a Long Way to Go' (2015) 6 Jindal Global Law Review 39

de Witte B, 'Legal Methods for the Study of EU Institutional Practice' [2022] European Constitutional Law Review 1

Demaria F and Kothari A, 'The Post-Development Dictionary Agenda: Paths to the Pluriverse' (2017) 38 Third World Quarterly 2588

den Heijer M, Riijpma J and Spijkerboer T, 'Coercion, Prohibition, and Great Expectations: The Continuing Failure of the Common European Asylum System' (2016) 53 Common Market Law Review 607

Desmond A, 'A New Dawn for the Human Rights of International Migrants? Protection of Migrants' Rights in Light of the UN's SDGs and Global Compact for Migration' (2020) 16 International Journal of Law in Context 222

Devetzi S, 'EU Citizens, Residence Rights and Solidarity in the Post-Dano/Alimanovic Era in Germany' (2019) 21 European Journal of Migration and Law 338

Duyssens D, 'Migrant Workers from Third Countries in the European Community' (1977) 14 Common Market Law Review

Edens DF and Patijn S, 'The Scope of the EEC System of Free Movement of Workers' (1972) 9 Common Market Law Review 322

'Editorial Comments: The Critical Turn in EU Legal Studies' (2015) 52 Common Market Law Review 881

Eeckhout P, 'The EU Charter of Fundamental Rights and the Federal Question' (2002) 39 Common Market Law Review 945

Eisele K and van der Mei AP, 'Portability of Social Benefits and Reverse Discrimination of EU Citizens vis-à-vis Turkish Nationals: Comment on Akdas' (2012) 37 European Law Review 204

Erpelding M, 'Juristes internationalistes, juristes mixtes, Euro-Lawyers: l'apport de l'expérience semi-coloniale à l'émergence d'un droit supranational' (2022) 22 Clio @ Themis

Everson M and Joerges C, 'Reconfiguring the Politics–Law Relationship in the Integration Project through Conflicts–Law Constitutionalism' (2012) 18 European Law Journal 644

Farcy J-B, 'Labour Immigration Policy in the European Union: How to Overcome the Tension between Further Europeanisation and the Protection of National Interests?' (2020) 22 European Journal of Migration and Law 198

Gallie WB, 'Essentially Contested Concepts' 56 (1955–1956) Proceedings of the Aristotelian Society, New Series 167

Greenwood C, 'Nationality and the Limits of the Free Movement of Persons in Community Law' (1987) 7 Yearbook of European Law 185

Groenendijk K, 'Legal Concepts of Integration in EU Migration Law' (2004) 6 European Journal of Migration and Law 111

'Equal Treatment of Workers from Third Countries: The Added Value of the Single Permit Directive' (2015) 16 ERA Forum 547

Guild E, 'The UN Global Compact for Safe, Orderly and Regular Migration: To What Extent Are Human Rights and Sustainable Development Mutually Compatible in the Field of Migration?' (2020) 16 International Journal of Law in Context 239

Hailbronner K, 'Perspectives of a Harmonization of the Law of Asylum after the Maastricht Summit' (1992) 29 Common Market Law Review 917

Hailbronner K and Polakiewicz J, 'Non-EC Nationals in the European Community: The Need for a Coordinated Approach' (1992) 3 Duke Journal of Comparative & International Law 49

Hilpold P, 'Opening up a New Chapter of Law-Making in International Law: The Global Compacts on Migration and for Refugees of 2018' (2020) 26 European Law Journal 226

Hollifield JF, 'Immigration-Related Problems and Issues Facing the EC on the Road to 1992' (1991) 14 In Defense of the Alien 73

Holmes S, 'Climate Change, Sustainability, and Competition Law' (2020) 8 Journal of Antitrust Enforcement 354

Hoogenboom T, 'Integration into Society and Free Movement of Non-EC Nationals' (1992) 3 European Journal of International Law 36

Iacovides MC and Vrettos C, 'Falling through the Cracks No More? Article 102 TFEU and Sustainability: The Relation between Dominance, Environmental Degradation, and Social Injustice' (2022) 10 Journal of Antitrust Enforcement 32

Iglesias Sánchez S, 'Constitutional Identity and Integration: EU Citizenship and the Emergence of a Supranational Alienage Law' (2017) 18 German Law Journal 1797

Ireland P, 'Facing the True Fortress Europe: Immigrant and Politics in the EC' (1991) 29 Journal of Common Market Studies 457

Jacobs, 'Social Europe in Delay' (1990) 6 International Journal of Comparative Labour Law and Industrial Relations 26

Janker J and Thieme S, 'Migration and Justice in the Era of Sustainable Development Goals: A Conceptual Framework' (2021) 16 Sustainability Science 1423

Jesse M, 'The Value of Integration in European Law: Implications of the Forster Case on Legal Assessment of Integration Conditions for Third-Country Nationals' (2011) 17 European Law Journal 172

'The "Integration" of Economic Immigrants: Lessons to Be Learnt from Free Movement of Persons on the EU's Internal Market, Journal of Immigration, Asylum and Nationality Law' (2023) 37 Journal of Immigration, Asylum and National Law 3

Joerges C and Neyer J, 'From Intergovernmental Bargaining to Deliberative Political Processes: The Constitutionalisation of Comitology' (1997) 3 European Law Journal 273

Kenig-Witkowska MM, 'The Concept of Sustainable Development in the European Union Policy and Law' (2017) 1 Journal of Comparative Urban Law and Policy 64

Klein Solomon M and Sheldon S, 'The Global Compact for Migration: From the Sustainable Development Goals to a Comprehensive Agreement on Safe, Orderly and Regular Migration' (2019) 30 International Journal of Refugee Law 584

Kochenov D, 'The Essence of EU Citizenship Emerging from the Last Ten Years of Academic Debate: Beyond the Cherry Blossoms and the Moon' (2013) 62 International and Comparative Law Quarterly 97

Kostakopoulou D, 'Ideas, Norms and European Citizenship: Explaining Institutional Change' (2005) 68 The Modern Law Review 233

'European Union Citizenship: Writing the Future' (2007) 13 European Law Journal 623

'The Evolution of European Union Citizenship' (2008) 7 European Political Science 285

Laske C, 'The Impact of the Single European Market on Social Protection for Migrant Workers' (1993) 30 Common Market Law Review 515

Lewin K, 'The Free Movement of Workers' (1965) 2 Common Market Law Review 300

Lichtenberg H, 'The Rights of Turkish Workers in Community Law: Case C-237/91 Kazim Kus v Landeshauptstadt Wiesbaden (1993) 2 Common Market Law Review 887

Littig B and Griessler E, 'Social Sustainability: A Catchword between Political Pragmatism and Social Theory' (2005) 8 International Journal of Sustainable Development 65

Loozen E, 'Strict Competition Enforcement and Welfare: A Constitutional Perspective Based on Article 101 TFEU and Sustainability' (2019) 56 Common Market Law Review 1265

Loxa A, 'Den Nya Migrations- Och Asylpakten Och Löftet Om En Hållbar EU-Migration' [2022] Europarättslig Tidskrift 175

'An EU Sustainable Migration: Institutional Discourse and Migration Politics' (2024) Journal of Common Market Studies (in press)

Maas W, 'The Genesis of European Rights' (2005) 43 Journal of Common Market Studies 1009

'Migrants, States, and EU Citizenship's Unfulfilled Promise' (2008) 12 Citizenship Studies 583

Mancini GF, 'The Making of a Constitution for Europe' (1989) 26 Common Market Law Review 595

Mancini GF and Keeling DT, 'Democracy and the European Court of Justice' (1994) 57 The Modern Law Review 175

Manners I, 'Normative Power Europe: A Contradiction in Terms?' (2002) 40 Journal of Common Market Studies 235

Mantu S and Minderhoud P, 'Exploring the Links between Residence and Social Rights for Economically Inactive EU Citizens' (2019) 21 European Journal of Migration and Law 313

McGlynn C, 'Families and the European Union Charter of Fundamental Rights: Progressive Change or Entrenching the Status Quo' (2001) 26 European Law Review 582

'Reclaiming a Feminist Vision: The Reconciliation of Paid Work and Family Life in European Union Law and Policy' (2001) 7(2) Columbia Journal of European Law 241

Menéndez AJ, 'Which Citizenship? Whose Europe? – The Many Paradoxes of European Citizenship' (2014) 15 German Law Journal 907

Minderhoud P, 'Social Security Rights under Decision No 3/80 of the EEC-Turkey Association Council: Developments in the EU and in the Netherlands' (2016) 18 European Journal of Social Security 268

Moebius I and Szyszczak E, 'Of Raising Pigs and Children' (1998) 18 Yearbook of European Law 125

Muir E, 'Of Ages in and Edges of EU Law' (2011) 48 Common Market Law Review 39

'EU Citizenship, Access to "Social Benefits" and Third-Country National Family Members: Reflecting on the Relationship between Primary and Secondary Rights in Times of Brexit' (2019) 2018 European Papers - A Journal on Law and Integration 1353

Müller-Graff P-C, 'The Legal Bases of the Third Pillar and Its Position in the Framework of the Union Treaty' (1994) 31 Common Market Law Review 493

Neunreither K, 'Transformation of a Political Role: Reconsidering the Case of the Commission of the European Communities' (1972) 10 Journal of Common Market Studies 233

Nic Shuibhne N, 'Editorial: Is It Time to Worry Yet?' (2009) 34 European Law Review 521

'Margins of Appreciation: National Values, Fundamental Rights and EC Free Movement Law' (2009) 34 European Law Review 230

'The Resilience of EU Market Citizenship' (2010) 47 Common Market Law Review 1597

'Editorial: What Is "Europe" and Who Is It For?' (2012) 37 European Law Review 673

'Limits Rising, Duties Ascending: The Changing Legal Shape of Union Citizenship' (2015) 52 Common Market Law Review 889

"What I Tell You Three Times Is True': Lawful Residence and Equal Treatment after Dano' (2016) 23 Maastricht Journal of European and Comparative Law 908

'Reconnecting Free Movement of Workers and Equal Treatment in an Unequal Europe' (2018) 43 European Law Review 477

'What Is the Autonomy of EU Law, and Why Does That Matter' (2019) 88 Nordic Journal of International Law 9

Nicola FG, 'Critical Legal Histories in EU Law' (2013) 28 American University International Law Review 1173

Niessen J, 'European Community Legislation and Intergovernmental Cooperation on Migration' (1992) 26 International Migration Review 676

Novitz T, 'The Paradigm of Sustainability in a European Social Context: Collective Participation in Protection of Future Interests?' (2015) 31 International Journal of Comparative Labour Law & Industrial Relations 243

O'Brien C, 'Social Blind Spots and Monocular Policy Making the ECJ's Migrant Worker Model' (2009) 46 Common Market Law Review 1107

'Civis Capitalist Sum: Class as the New Guiding Principle of EU Free Movement Rights' (2016) 53 Common Market Law Review 937

'The ECJ Sacrifices EU Citizenship in Vain: Commission v. United Kingdom' (2017) 54(1) Common Market Law Review 209

O'Keeffe D, 'Practical Difficulties in the Application of Article 48 of the EEC Treaty' (1982) 19 Common Market Law Review 35

'The Free Movement of Persons and the Single Market' (1992) 17 European Law Review 3

'Recasting the Third Pillar' (1995) 32(4) Common Market Law Review 893

O'Keeffe D and Johnson E, 'From Discrimination to Obstacles to Free Movement; Recent Developments Concerning the Free Movement of Workers 1989–1994' (1994) 31 Common Market Law Review 1313

O'Leary S, 'Nationality Law and Community Citizenship: A Tale of Two Uneasy Bedfellows' (1992) 12 Yearbook of European Law 353

Oliver P, 'Non-Community Nationals and the Treaty of Rome' (1985) 5 Yearbook of European Law 57

Orford A, 'In Praise of Description' (2012) 25 Leiden Journal of International Law 609

Peers S, 'Towards Equality: Actual and Potential Rights of Third-Country Nationals in the European Union' (1996) 33(1) Common Market Law Review 7

'Building Fortress Europe: The Development of EU Migration Law' (1998) 35 (6) Common Market Law Review 1235

Pettit P, 'A Republican Law of Peoples' (2010) 9 European Journal of Political Theory 70

Poiares Maduro M, 'Interpreting European Law: Judicial Adjudication in a Context of Constitutional Pluralism' (2008) 1 European Journal of Legal Studies 137

Rasmussen M, 'Towards a Legal History of European Law' (2021) 2021 6 European Papers - A Journal on Law and Integration 923

Reid J, 'Interrogating the Neoliberal Biopolitics of the Sustainable Development-Resilience Nexus' (2013) 7 International Political Sociology 353

Scharpf FW, 'Legitimacy in the Multilevel European Polity' (2009) 1 European Political Science Review 173

Schermers HG, 'Case C-192/89, S.Z. Sevince v. Staatssecretaris van Justitie, Preliminary Ruling of 20 September 1990 Requested by the Raad van State of the Netherlands on the Netherlands on the Interpretation of Certain Provisions of Decisions 2/76 and 1/80 of the Association Council Established by the Association Agreement between the EEC And Turkey' (1991) 28 Common Market Law Review

Schønberg S and Frick K, 'Finishing, Refining, Polishing: On the Use of Travaux Préparatoires as an Aid to the Interpretation of Community Legislation' (2003) 28 European Law Review 149

Schönberger C, 'European Citizenship as Federal Citizenship – Some Citizenship Lessons of Comparative Federalism' (2007) 19 European Public Law Organization's - EPLO Publications

Séché J-C, 'Free Movement of Workers under Community Law' (1977) 14 Common Market Law Review 384

Selanec NB and Petrić D, 'Migrating with Dignity: Conceptualising Human Dignity through EU Migration Law' (2021) 17 European Constitutional Law Review 498

Simmonds KR, 'The Concertation of Community Migration Policy; Joined Cases 281/85; 283; 284 and 285/85 and 287/85; Germany and Others v Commission; Judgment of 9 July 1987' (1988) 25 Common Market Law Review 177

'The Fourth Lomé Convention' (1991) 28(3) Common Market Law Review 521

Singer LH, 'Free Movement of Workers in the European Economic Community: The Public Policy Exception' (1977) 29 Stanford Law Review 1283

Somek A, 'From Workers to Migrants, from Distributive Justice to Inclusion: Exploring the Changing Social Democratic Imagination' (2012) 18 European Law Journal 711

Spaventa E, 'Family Rights for Circular Migrants and Frontier Workers: O and B, and S and G' (2015) 52 Common Market Law Review 753

Spijkerboer T, 'Bifurcation of People, Bifurcation of Law: Externalization of Migration Policy before the EU Court of Justice' (2018) 31 Journal of Refugee Studies 216

Steenbergen, 'All the King's Horses. . .: Probabilities and Possibilities for the Implementation of the New Title IV EC Treaty' (1999) 1 European Journal of Migration and Law 29

Stoyanova V, 'On the Bride's Side? Victims of Domestic Violence and Their Residence Rights under EU and Council of Europe Law' (2019) 37 Netherlands Quarterly of Human Rights 311

ter Heide H, 'The Free Movement of Workers in the Final Phase' (1969) 6 Common Market Law Review 466

Thym D, 'EU Migration Policy and Its Constitutional Rationale: A Cosmopolitan Outlook' (2013) 50 Common Market Law Review 709

'When Union Citizens Turn into Illegal Migrants: The Dano Case' (2015) 40 European Law Review 249

'"Citizens" and "Foreigners" in EU Law. Migration Law and Its Cosmopolitan Outlook' (2016) 22 European Law Journal 296

Van Hees SRW, 'Sustainable Development in the EU: Redefining and Operationalizing the Concept' (2014) 10 Utrecht Law Review 60

Verschueren H, 'EC Social Security Coordination Excluding Third Country Nationals: Still in Line with Fundamental Rights after the Gaygusuz Judgment?' (1997) 34(4) Common Market Law Review 991

Voigt C, 'From Climate Change to Sustainability: An Essay on Sustainable Development, Legal and Ethical Choices' (2005) 9 Worldviews 112

von Bogdandy A, 'Founding Principles of EU Law: A Theoretical and Doctrinal Sketch' (2010) 16 European Law Journal 95

'European Law beyond "Ever Closer Union" Repositioning the Concept, Its Thrust and the ECJ's Comparative Methodology' (2016) 22 European Law Journal 519

Weber A, 'Case C-18/90, Bahia Kziber v. Office National de l'Emploi (ONEM), Preliminary Ruling of 31 January 1991, Requested by the Cour Du Travail de Liège (5th Chamber) on the Interpretation of Certain Provisions of the Cooperation Agreement between the EEC and the Kingdom of Morocco, Not yet Reported' (1991) 28(4) Common Market Law Review 959

Weiler JHH, 'The Community System: The Dual Character of Supranationalism' (1981) 1 Yearbook of European Law 267

'Thou Shalt Not Oppress a Stranger: On the Judicial Protection of the Human Rights of Non-EC Nationals – A Critique' (1992) 3 European Journal of International Law 65

Williams AT, 'Taking Values Seriously: Towards a Philosophy of EU Law' (2009) 29 Oxford Journal of Legal Studies 549

Wyatt D, 'The Social Security Rights of Migrant Workers and Their Families' (1977) 14 Common Market Law Review 411

Working Papers

Bellamy R, 'Political Justice for an Ever Closer Union of European Peoples' in Gráinne de Búrca, Dimitry Kochenov and Andrew Trevor Williams (eds), *Debating Europe's Justice Deficit: The EU, Swabian Housewives, Rawls, and Ryanair* (EUI Working Papers 2013)

Bivand Erdal M et al., 'Defining Sustainable Migration' (PRIO Paper 2018) EMN Norway Occasional Papers

Carling J and Bivand Erdal M, 'Is "Sustainable Migration" a Valuable Concept?' (PRIO Policy Brief 2018)

Chalmers D, 'Damian Chalmers: Kinship, Markets, and Justice in Europe' in Grainne De Burca, Dimitry Kochenov and Andrew Trevor Williams (eds), *Debating Europe's Justice Deficit: The EU, Swabian Housewives, Rawls, and Ryanair* (EUI Working Papers 2013)

Dick E et al., 'Regional Migration Governance: Contributions to a Sustainable International Migration Architecture' (Briefing Paper 2018) Deutsches Institut für Entwicklungspolitik (DIE)

Giakouminaki O, 'The Administrative Acquis of EU Public Procurement Law: A Study on Administrative Law as a Tool of European Integration' (Thèse de doctorat, Paris 2 2021)

Hansen P, 'Making Sense of a Neoliberal Fortress? EU Migration Policy in the Nexus of Economy, Security and Rights' (Nordisk Samarbejdsråd for Kriminologi 2011)

Lélé SM, 'Sustainability: A Plural, Multi-Dimensional Approach' [1993] Working Paper, Pacific Institute for Studies in Development, Environment, and Security

Lenaerts K and Gutiérrez-Fons JA, 'To Say What the Law of the EU Is: Methods of Interpretation and the European Court of Justice' (Working Paper AEL 2013/9 2013)

Picard P and Worrall T, 'Sustainable Migration Policies' (Université catholique de Louvain, Center for Operations Research and Econometrics (CORE) 2011) 2011/40

Somek A 'Europe: From Emancipation to Empowerment' (The London School of Economics and Political Science 2013) LSE 'Europe in Question' Discussion Paper series 60

Others

Statewatch European Monitoring and Documentation Centre on Justice and Home Affairs in the European Union Compilation No 3, Maastricht Immigration Programme (1991) and Follow Up (1993), Supplement to: 'Key Texts on Justice and Home Affairs in the European Union, Volume 1 (1976–1993)'

INDEX

For EU product safety concerns, contact us at Calle de José Abascal, 56–1°, 28003 Madrid, Spain or eugpsr@cambridge.org.

www.ingramcontent.com/pod-product-compliance
Lightning Source LLC
LaVergne TN
LVHW011704200926
848484LV00004B/1071

* 9 7 8 1 0 0 9 5 7 3 1 4 6 *